Homer's Cosmic Fabrication

AMERICAN PHILOLOGICAL ASSOCIATION

AMERICAN CLASSICAL STUDIES

Volume 52

Series Editor

Kathryn J. Gutzwiller

Studies in Classical History and Society
Meyer Reinhold

Sextus Empiricus
The Transmission and Recovery of Pyrrhonism
Luciano Floridi

The Augustan Succession
An Historical Commentary on Cassius Dio's Roman History *Books 55–56 (9 B.C.–A.D. 14)*
Peter Michael Swan

Greek Mythography in the Roman World
Alan Cameron

Virgil Recomposed
The Mythological and Secular Centos in Antiquity
Scott McGill

Representing Agrippina
Constructions of Female Power in the Early Roman Empire
Judith Ginsburg

Figuring Genre in Roman Satire
Catherine Keane

Homer's Cosmic Fabrication
Choice and Design in the Iliad
Bruce Heiden

HOMER'S COSMIC FABRICATION

Choice and Design in the *Iliad*

Bruce Heiden

OXFORD
UNIVERSITY PRESS
2008

OXFORD
UNIVERSITY PRESS

Oxford University Press, Inc., publishes works that further
Oxford University's objective of excellence
in research, scholarship, and education.

Oxford New York

Auckland Cape Town Dar es Salaam Hong Kong Karachi
Kuala Lumpur Madrid Melbourne Mexico City Nairobi
New Delhi Shanghai Taipei Toronto

With offices in
Argentina Austria Brazil Chile Czech Republic France Greece
Guatemala Hungary Italy Japan Poland Portugal Singapore
South Korea Switzerland Thailand Turkey Ukraine Vietnam

Published by Oxford University Press, Inc.
198 Madison Avenue, New York, New York 10016

www.oup.com

Library of Congress Cataloging-in-Publication Data

Heiden, Bruce A.
Homer's cosmic fabrication: choice and design in the Iliad/
Bruce Heiden.
p. cm.
ISBN 978–0–19–534107–2
1. Homer. Iliad. 2. Epic poetry, Greek—History and
criticism. 3. Achilles (Greek mythology) in literature. 4. Trojan
War—Literature and the war. I. Title.
PA4037.H425 2008
883'.0109—dc22 2008023584

1 3 5 7 9 8 6 4 2

Printed in the United States of America
on acid-free paper

In the elder days of Art,
  Builders wrought with greatest care
Each minute and unseen part;
  For the Gods see everywhere.

Longfellow, “The Builders”

Preface

In the autumn of 1994 I was well into writing a book on the *Iliad* that would have been rather different from this one had I completed it. Instead I set it aside because of a discovery that promised (or threatened) to overshadow the work-in-progress and demanded immediate and thorough exploration. The important details and implications of this discovery are explained in the introduction to this book.

A great many colleagues and learned friends have assisted my work on this project through stimulating exchanges in person or via email, reactions to the journal publications and conference talks in which early results were disseminated, and careful reading of the manuscript in any of its various draft versions prior to this publication. During the early stages Mark Edwards was a steadfast source of both encouragement and astute criticism. At a late stage Pura Nieto-Hernandez read a draft of the entire manuscript with remarkable care, and her abundant expert comments suggested or stimulated many improvements. Kathryn Gutzwiller, the editor of the American Philological Association American Classical Studies series in which this volume appears, acted as a valued collaborator in the final stages of revision. The comments of the anonymous readers were also very helpful. My colleague Anthony Kaldellis read an earlier draft of the manuscript and offered many useful observations; but he also merits special thanks for the stimulus of his conversation about both the book and Greek literature generally. Margalit Finkelberg read a substantial portion of an earlier draft and improved the work with expert suggestions and criticism. Among the others who have helped in various ways I would be remiss not to mention Jenny Strauss Clay, David Konstan, Donald Lateiner, Françoise Létoublon, Bruce Louden, James Morrison, René Nünlist, Pietro Pucci, Robert Rabel, Jay Reed, Joseph Russo, Elizabeth Scharffenberger, Seth Schein, and John Van Sickle. Any scholar lucky enough to be read by such critics will always feel challenged to exceed himself.

David Hahm, the chair of the Department of Greek and Latin at the Ohio State University during most of the time the work was under way, assisted in many small but valuable ways that are warmly appreciated. David Lincove, the classics librarian at Ohio State during part of the time, and Donna Distel, assistant librarian, helped me identify, locate, or obtain elusive printed resources on many occasions.

Odysseus had Penelope; I have Karen Dennis, an equally good friend of Athena and at least as discriminating a lover of poetry. Unfortunately I'm not a good enough poet to give KD the lasting renown she deserves, but for what it's worth I dedicate this book about the *Iliad* to her.

Acknowledgments

Chapter 1 of this book first appeared in slightly different form in the journal *Arethusa* (Heiden 2002b). Part of chapter 2 first appeared in *Classica et Mediaevalia* (Heiden 2000b). Chapter 3 first appeared in slightly different form in the journal *Symbolae Osloenses* (Heiden 2000a). Part of chapter 4 first appeared in slightly different form in *Gaia* (Heiden 2003a). I am grateful to the editors and publishers of these journals for granting permission to reprint this material.

Contents

Abbreviations Frequently Used in the Figures

Ach	Achilles
Act	Action
Aft	Aftermath
Aga	Agamemnon
Aux	Auxiliary
D/A	Decision/Action
Dec	Decision
Gks	Greeks
H-A-P	Hera-Athena-Poseidon
Hek	Hektor
Pat	Patroklos
Prob	Problem
Res	Resolution

List of Figures

Homer's Cosmic Fabrication

Introduction

Reading, Choice, and Design

This study of the *Iliad* presents a series of experiments aimed at improving our grasp of the design of the *Iliad* and its significance for interpretation. Preliminary versions of these experiments have appeared in a series of articles published between 1996 and 2003. A brief review of the first of these (Heiden 1996) will introduce the objectives and methods of the project.

In the early 1990s two major studies of the *Iliad*, Oliver Taplin's *Homeric Soundings* (1992) and Keith Stanley's *Shield of Homer* (1993), each proposed that the *Iliad* was designed for performance in three parts, with intermissions positioned at fixed points in the text. Taplin proposed that planned intermissions came between *Iliad* 9.713 and 11.1[1] and 18.353 and 354, while Stanley proposed that they came between *Iliad* 7.482 and 8.1 and 17.761 and 18.1. While these speculations of course could not arrive at anything like historical certainty, each invited an intriguing view of the written *Iliad* from the perspective of its possible effects in performance. Taplin coordinated intermission placements with points in the narrative where action ceases because a day ends. Stanley coordinated them with passages that allegedly frame large sections of text. According to Stanley these large sections arrange material in ring-compositional shapes that focus attention upon passages in central positions.

These speculations, divergent in their rationales as well as their details, were symptomatic of a certain casualness Taplin and Stanley shared, not toward the *Iliad*, but toward intermissions. It was hardly self-evident that one rationale was preferable to the other, or that intermissions should correlate with points of either narrative stasis or (claimed) formal closure. I noted that the *Iliad* begins amid continuous action and ends similarly. A check of comparanda such as Greek tragedies confirmed my intuition that planned intermissions would often effect suspenseful "cliffhanger" interruptions of dramatic trajectories.

As Taplin and Stanley were not the first to speculate about fixed intermissions in performances of the *Iliad*, it seemed worthwhile to consider whether the question was amenable to a more systematic approach. After surveying the older intermission proposals along with the recent additions, I analyzed and critiqued

1. Taplin's *Iliad* omits book 10, which he deems spurious.

their premises in the article that began this project ("The Three Movements of the *Iliad*," 1996).[2] Suggesting that speculation about intermissions in the *Iliad* should include examination of specimen intermissions and general theorization of what intermissions contribute to performances, I noted that intermissions may function cognitively as points of emphasis that cue attention to important themes or dramatic crises. Since none of the proposed intermission placements even claimed to provide consistent orientation of that type, I suggested a different method of speculation. As an experiment, I would frame *hypotheses* about specific *functions* of intermissions, and then seek passages in the *Iliad* that might fulfill those functions, if intermissions occurred there. This experiment could not answer the historical question of whether the *Iliad* was actually performed with planned intermissions anywhere, but it might elicit textual material pertinent to the question of whether the *Iliad* could have had intermissions that served certain specific functions.

In contemplating the options for an initial hypothesis, I had conceptualized an intermission as a pause that demarcates the end of one performance segment (or "movement") and the beginning of another. From this I recognized that the experiment was actually seeking locations appropriate for beginnings and ends of performance segments, and that the locations sought were not all unknowns, since one beginning (that of the whole epic, or book 1) and one end (book 24) were already given. These passages, which had already fed my doubts about the intermissions proposed by Taplin and Stanley, seemed to offer a foothold: an initial hypothesis about the functional characteristics of "*Iliad* beginnings" might be framed in terms of characteristics of the one known *Iliad*-beginning, and a separate but corresponding hypothesis about the functional characteristics of "*Iliad*-ends" might be framed in terms of characteristics of the one known *Iliad*-end.

What characteristics would be functionally relevant? I decided that the optimal features should be (1) functional with respect to a *broad spectrum* of imaginable audience members, (2) easily *recognizable* to such audiences, and (3) presumptively *important* to those audiences. In the case of the *Iliad*, which tells a story, I thought that these features would be *consequential junctures in the epic's plot*. With that as a preliminary hypothesis I examined the specimens. I immediately realized that book 1 of the *Iliad* does narrate a highly consequential juncture in the plot, since it sets the whole story on course through Achilles' decision to withdraw from battle and obtain Zeus's agreement to punish the Greeks. Positing this as the salient functional characteristic of an *Iliad*-beginning, I found only two other books that qualified as similar, book 9, in which Achilles refuses the appeal of Agamemnon's envoys, and book 16, in which he permits Patroklos to replace him in the battle. Turning to book 24, I found that in it Zeus effects the close of the narrative by deciding, in

2. Other proposals discussed included Wade-Gery 1952, Davison 1965, and Schadewaldt 1975; for further bibliography see Heiden 1996: 7 n. 8 and 8 n. 10.

opposition to Hera, that Achilles should return Hektor's body, and by arranging its ransom through his messengers Iris, Thetis, and Hermes. Positing Zeus's decisive intervention as the salient functional characteristic of an *Iliad*-end, I found only two other books that qualified, book 8, in which Zeus forbids divine interference on the battlefield and unveils part of his plan to Hera, and book 15, in which he again forbids interference and reveals his plan to Hera in even more detail.

The procedure of extrapolation thus indicated two candidates for internal beginnings and two for internal ends. But in order for the experiment to have discovered qualifying *intermissions*, these candidates also had to satisfy additional criteria unrelated to the cognitive function that the candidate beginnings shared with book 1 and the candidate ends with book 24. Since the experiment stipulated that an intermission is a pause that comes right between a segment-end and a segment-beginning, the following constraints applied: (1) the candidate beginnings and ends had to be equal in number, and (2) each internal segment-end had to be so positioned in the transmitted sequence of the *Iliad* that a segment-beginning followed it immediately, and each internal segment-beginning had to be so positioned that a segment-end immediately preceded. I found of course that the two candidate beginnings were equal in number to the two candidate ends. More surprisingly, the four candidates also satisfied the second requirement, that of relative positioning: book 9 (beginning) immediately follows book 8 (end), and book 16 (beginning) immediately follows book 15 (end). The experiment had identified a set of intermission placements, between books 8 and 9 and between books 15 and 16, that would be satisfactory in the sense that these positions demonstrably fulfilled a set of reasonable criteria for planned intermissions. In fact, with respect to the posited criteria, these intermission placements would be uniquely satisfactory: any alternative placements I could imagine would be eliminated by one or several of the criteria. Therefore any rival proposal would have to argue that an alternative set of *criteria* was equally or more reasonable, and also show that when applied systematically the new criteria indicated alternative intermissions.

It so happens that the specific placements my experiment identified represented a new contribution to the scholarly discussion. But a comparison of my approach with its predecessors would note only a superficial distinction in the fact that, for example, my experiment places one intermission a little later in the *Iliad* than Stanley does and another a little earlier. In framing the issue of performance design in terms of the cognitive function of intermission placements, my experiment asked and answered a different and more important question than previous discussions had, so that even if the experiment had indicated placements identical to some previously suggested, this result would have revealed something new about their significance. The experiment was also able to contribute a novel proposal because its reconceptualization of the problem focused attention upon a category of evidence not previously considered in this connection, the plot of the story and the cognitive implications of its presentation. Moreover, the experiment had discovered something *about* the plot that had escaped general notice, to judge from commentators' casual references to one or several "turning points" in the epic: the *Iliad* actually has an array of "turning points," *half* of which focus upon decisions made by Achilles (the ones commentators were most likely to mention), and another half of which focus upon decisions made by *Zeus* (much less likely to have attracted comment).

Finally, the prior specification of functional criteria and their systematic application made it possible to distinguish among alternative proposals with an unprecedented degree of logical rigor. The experiment had sought only possible intermissions that satisfied a specific and intricate set of *independent* constraints: (1) similar cognitive functionality in terms of the epic's plot, (2) pertinence to the *given* beginning and end of the epic, (3) *separate* thematic criteria for selecting candidate beginnings and candidate ends, (4) qualifying beginnings and endings of *exactly* equal number, (5) mandatory positioning of qualifying ends and beginnings in *sequenced pairs*, and (6) *systematic and consistent* satisfaction of all these criteria. Other proposals that cite certain textual features and posit intermissions in accordance with those features are exposed to the obvious criticism that they define and project intermissions idiosyncratically to suit the selected data. The proposal that my experiment indicated is not susceptible to that criticism. It is very unlikely that any alternative proposal could satisfy either the same criteria adopted for the experiment, or alternative criteria of equal appropriateness, specificity and rigor. Thus, the experiment appeared to *disqualify* all possible planned intermission placements except the ones that it indicated as uniquely optimal.

Of course, the experiment proved nothing about historical performances of the *Iliad* (as the article explicitly acknowledged). But in the course of its methodical speculation about comprehending the *Iliad* in performance, the experiment did incidentally hit upon something pertinent to *reading* the *Iliad* in the transmitted *written* format. For many readers of the *Iliad* comprehension could be significantly enhanced, even without supplementary explication, simply by inserting "intermission" punctuation marks at the end of books 8 and 15 and thus setting off and emphasizing for attention all the sections that narrate the most critical junctures of the plot. Anybody who has ever taught the mega-epic to a class of first-time readers will recognize why this is a useful thing to know. Indeed, I myself have found that imagining the epic punctuated in the manner and places suggested greatly improved my ability to recall the contents of the *Iliad* and the location of specific passages. The indicated intermissions are not only cognitively superior to other proposed arrangements, they are also cognitively superior to the transmitted linear arrangement that lacks intermissions altogether.

This discovery intersected with another Homeric topic that was incidental to the experiment's original goal. Since the late nineteenth century, scholars had occasionally claimed that the *Iliad* arranged its content in such a way that "parallel" passages were repeated in similar positions in the epic (with similarity of position usually defined in terms of proximity to the beginning of the epic or the end). These analyses, of which Cedric Whitman's was the best known and the aforementioned Keith Stanley's the most ambitious and recent, always made a number of observations that gave one occasion to wonder whether the authors "might be on to something."[3] But the comprehensive schemas of "parallels" had generally met with cool reception from professional Homerists, for reasons both bad and good. The bad concerned the schemas' taint of association with the "Unitarian" resistance to Homeric "Analysis" and "oral poetics," which aroused determination to protect the gains of progressive research against any possible reemergence of the superstition it had banished, "The Poet." This reason was bad insofar as it granted received ideas an automatic exemption from challenge instead of judging the challenges on their merits. But skeptics had plenty of better reasons to hold "parallel" analyses like Stanley's and Whitman's at arm's length. They are full of contradictions and exceptions; they employ inconsistent criteria of comparison; and the supposedly parallel passages often seem either unimportant, or important only with respect to features other than those compared. The analyses themselves sometimes trivialize the alleged patterns by emphasizing their formal properties of "balance" and "symmetry," thus giving the impression that the poet of the *Iliad* labored obsessively just to produce neat figures that were, to speak frankly, aesthetically juvenile, and not really neat. Moreover, despite the fact that the authors trawled for "parallels" with an undiscriminating net, they somehow failed to catch analogies that should have been obvious. For example, while Whitman links book 9 and book 16, he associates neither with book 1.[4] No description of thematic patterning in the *Iliad* had ever even mentioned the relationship of books 8, 15, and 24, which my "Three Movements" article pointed out for the first time.

The coordination of beginning-books and end-books in my articulation was indeed broadly similar to analyses of "structure" like Stanley's and Whitman's, in that it linked distant passages according to shared properties. And one could say that it fulfilled their aspiration of demonstrating that the whole epic constituted a kind of unity, since its arrangement oriented attention to (1) what appeared to be a single plot trajectory that informs the whole epic, (2) the beginning and end of the whole epic, and (3) intermediate points approximately equidistant from the beginning and end. But other features of the three-movement design marked it as a radical departure. For one thing, it was very economical, linking only six passages, while other analyses of structure made many, many connections. The comparable modules were all of the same dimension, transmitted "books." The

3. Whitman 1958; Stanley 1993. Whitman's analysis had received sympathetic attention in Richardson's introduction to volume 6 of the *Cambridge Commentary on the Iliad* (Richardson 1993). For a good analytical bibliography of research on "ring composition" in Homer and other Greek authors, see Steinrück 1997b. For further bibliography on schematic proposals specific to the *Iliad*, see Heiden 2000a: 34–35 nn. 1–5. As of this writing the most recent new contribution is Louden 2006, which is explicitly based on Stanley's work.

4. Whitman 1958: 279–82.

pattern of linkages among the six books was very simple and absolutely consistent. The comparisons were based upon only a single criterion—the role of each passage in the overarching plot of the epic—which was consistently applied. Most important, this criterion pertained to the cognitive function of the passages, and the arrangement also performed a cognitive function, that of orientation, which complemented the cognitive function of the passages. The chief merit of this design was not its orderliness but its usefulness. Thus its coordination of beginnings and ends gave the analysis of patterns in the *Iliad* a new rationale, a new method, new evidence, and new possibilities.

To put it all another way: the experimental search for functional intermissions had discovered a specific and previously unnoticed convergence between the cognitive convenience of a reader of the *Iliad* and the poem's presentation of content. Obviously the convergence would have been closer and more conclusive in itself if the transmitted text already included the "movement" punctuators, or if the scholia recorded some knowledge of them. Still, the transmitted *Iliad* appears to provide readers with a certain plot that it conveys in a special arrangement that does substantial work toward orienting the reader's attention to the critical junctures, with only a bit of punctuation needed to augment the effect. Given the monumental scale of the *Iliad*, the substantial convergence between poem and reader indicates, though it does not prove, the implementation of a technical plan to assist comprehension by furnishing orientation. In that case the poem might well offer other useful cues as yet unnoticed. A way to find out would be to extend the experiment by positing more features of a reader's cognitive activity and applying them systematically to discover whether, where, and how the poem's indications converged with them. That, in short, is what this study does.

LITERARY INTELLIGIBILITY: TOWARD A HEURISTIC MODEL

Some users of this book may at this point feel like protesting that this study has sacrificed any claim to epistemological objectivity in projecting "a reader's cognitive activity"; while others may be waiting for me to base a claim of hermeneutical objectivity on a premise of psychological universalism.[5] But I do not think that either empiricism or idealism frames an object that is recognizable as "literature" to literary readers. A textual object independent of readers may describe a linguistic corpus, but when we call that corpus a "poem" we are viewing it phenomenologically rather than empirically. Nor does the literature of readers require, much less achieve, a very definite cognitive match between reader and poem, or between one reader and another. We readers of literature generally recognize that we enact personal choices in what we read and how we read it; literature *indulges* in choice. Nevertheless our freedom of choice does not usually entail radical subjectivism and

5. The following discussion of reading is loosely indebted to Iser 1978. The framing of the present project focuses upon the cognitive "repertoire" of reading rather than the experience of actual readers reading.

personal idiosyncrasy in reading, any more than it does in our other activities, because it includes the freedom to cooperate with others. We often choose to cooperate, and we can bring it off well enough to feel somewhat satisfied with the results, at least some of the time. Cooperation has many forms, some of them quite loose, and a minimal description of "cooperation" might be "some aspiration toward some convergence of goals among parties." The activity of reading itself, although often physically solitary, manifests a certain voluntary convergence between a reader and others, as the reader picks up a text and works at deriving benefit from the work that someone put into composing it. Readers collaborate with authors, and they also collaborate with other readers when they compare, criticize, and convergently adapt their readings as they see fit.

This collaboration is, in literary reading, much looser and more improvisatory than "the authority of interpretive communities" to which Stanley Fish referred in the subtitle of a famous book, and it rarely involves specific interpretive assumptions that by being "in force" render a certain structure of meanings "obvious and inescapable."[6] Perhaps the only "assumption" needed is that one potential collaborator assume that another possesses the cognitive *ability* to converge to an effect deemed satisfactory. In any given case, this cognitive ability can be imagined as an inchoate repertoire of cognitive functions that the potential collaborators might draw upon and improvisationally adapt, and toward which their efforts could converge. When readers of a literary work opt to regard its author as a collaborator, they in effect postulate an inchoate range of cognitive goals and activities upon which their efforts and the author's might converge. The impression of understanding a literary work, or any aspect of it, is the impression of such a convergence between reader and author. This impression is, strictly speaking, a *fiction* of the reader's, one similar to our routine impressions of other minds, and for the purpose of literary reading comparably reliable. The reader's fiction of an author is less a biographical proposition or an illusion than a sense of the type of collaboration the literary work promises.

Literary readers normally regard the author's text and its linguistic system (e.g., "French") as important indicators of the cognitive functions that a fruitful collaboration might deploy. But many of the author's signs are neither textual nor properly speaking linguistic; they are constructed *from* linguistic signs (just as lexemes are constructed from morphemes, and morphemes from phonemes). The continuity of a character, for example, is something a reader must work at constructing; the text does not normally repeat everything about the character each time the character is mentioned.[7] The text does not normally even repeat the character's name; proper names are frequently replaced by pronouns, and the antecedent of a pronoun is an "idea" the reader has (i.e., a provisional function for constructing the character), not the verbal sign of the character's proper name. The use of pronouns illustrates how the work of reading a story

6. Fish 1980: vii.

7. Emmott 1997 astutely analyzes many extralinguistic cognitive activities involved in comprehending narratives.

employs the text's verbal signs as *provisional* indicators from which it constructs *other* provisional indicators that are *extra*linguistic. The extralinguistic signs are as essential to reading as the linguistic signs, and more definitively literary.[8]

Given literary reading's intrinsic underdeterminacy, provisionality, and inchoate potential, efforts to frame "compelling" interpretations and arguments seem somewhat misguided. The interpretive conclusions of literary scholars, whatever their disciplinary authority, seldom prevail for long with readers; but this should not be surprising, because few readers of literature, including scholars, actually find the stability of authoritative conclusions to be of much use to their *reading*. What they do find useful is the loose, improvisational convergence of collaboration. The practical measure of a contribution to the literary dialogue is less the issues it supposedly resolves than its convergence with other practices in the collaboration. Accordingly, this study aims to serve potential collaborators by demonstrating a few cognitive tools I have found useful in reading the *Iliad*, so that others may adopt and adapt them as they see fit. The experimental procedure will posit certain cognitive functions and simulate their systematic application to the *Iliad*, just as my "Three Movements" article did in positing criteria for planned intermissions to see what they turned up. The repertoire of tested functions does not aim at completeness, and the selection is not meant to exclude other functions that users of this book may wish to simulate and explore themselves. The ones I have chosen are susceptible to convergence from many directions and readers; they are "commonsense" reading functions, although they are applied in a methodical and not a commonsense manner.[9]

THE *ILIAD* AS A STORY

As the initial provisional function of the simulation, I have selected *story*; that is, this experiment will adopt the stance of a reader who provisionally categorizes

8. This role of extralinguistic signs explains why it is not an outrageous falsity to refer to the Richmond Lattimore translation of the *Iliad* simply as "the *Iliad*": Lattimore's translation can be called "the *Iliad*" because a translation that is deemed reasonably accurate is thought to provide the reader with adequate indications of certain extralinguistic functions that closely approximate some of those a reader of the Greek text would also perform. Whether one reads the OCT Greek text or Lattimore in English, much of the characteristically literary work of reading concerns these extralinguistic functions.

9. Modern Homeric scholarship has often disdained cognitive practices associated with reading, on the grounds that they are anachronistic. The paradigm of a "Homeric" poetry unaffected by literacy has licensed a research enterprise focused on multiform diachronic "traditions" rather than stable poetic "works" such as the *Iliad* and *Odyssey* we read in written format. But the claim of anachronism is based on a facile identification of "reading" with physical "books." Reading is not just holding a book in one's hands, it is a repertoire of cognitive activities that are often performed *with* books. It is far from self-evident that all of these activities *require* books. Therefore, the claim of "oral poetics" to recover a set of cognitive practices *distinct* from those of reading is premature until it specifies exactly what practices it denies to "orality" and why books should be thought *indispensable* to those practices. Otherwise, the absence of books in a certain milieu might just as well indicate a form of low-tech "reading-before-books" as a uniquely "oral" mode of cognition. This study will be of indirect help to those working to elucidate the *Iliad* through "oral poetics" because it makes more visible reading practices that oral poetics excludes in clearing the ground for an alternative poetics that is uniquely "oral." It also makes convergences between the *Iliad* and these reading practices more visible. Oralist Homeric scholars may then justify excluding the reading practices, if they can. This study does not itself make or defend historical counterclaims, apart from a few *en passant* observations that the historical claims of others are insufficiently argued and convey an exaggerated sense of certainty.

the *Iliad* as a "story," and who deploys a repertoire of provisional and adaptable cognitive functions that are pertinent to the intelligibility of stories. The simulation will also assume that the reader uses a standard Greek text of the *Iliad*, and possesses very good knowledge of the Homeric Greek language system (i.e., its lexicon and syntax). The model will initially posit an inchoate repertoire of "story" functions consisting of two subsidiary repertoires: (1) *characters*, and (2) *actions* that the characters deliberate, perform, or undergo. It will also posit a goal-function, that of deriving some *edification* from the story. A preliminary deployment of the initial functions will help clarify what they are, what signs in the *Iliad* converge with them, and some ways the convergences might indicate further adaptation of the cognitive repertoire to achieve more convergence.

Characters, Actions, and Themes

Readers of the *Iliad* interested in characters and actions would immediately recognize the poem's convergence with their general goal. The epic begins by locating the story in the choices of named characters—the wrath of Achilles and the plan of Zeus—and the narrative never proceeds for long without focusing upon characters. In the first narrated scene, for example, the priest Chryses comes before the Achaians to ask the return of his daughter in exchange for ransom. Agamemnon refuses and explains why. Chryses calls upon Apollo to help him, and Apollo helps, sending a plague upon the Achaians. Disturbed by their suffering, Hera then inspires Achilles to call an assembly, where he asks the seer Kalchas to explain what the Achaians should do to avert the plague. The characters in this passage are recognizable as thinking persons: they strive, confront obstacles, deliberate how to overcome them, choose, and take action.[10]

In any specimen passage of the *Iliad* one finds the narrator focusing attention upon one character at a time, identifying a problem each character perceives, and describing his or her effort to address it. This effort in turn shifts the problem onto another character, who then becomes the focus of attention as he or she, too, articulates a problem and attempts to address it. The dilemma-situations are presented largely through direct speeches, while events other than speech are narrated quite concisely. Through their speeches the characters articulate the problems they want to address and what they propose to do about them. Moreover a speech may itself enact part of a projected solution, since the character addressed may be perceived as causing the problem and possessing some power to solve it. In the aforementioned passage from book 1 the function of articulating problems and solutions is borne entirely by the characters' speeches and the narrator's brief introductions, and no speech lacks a function in a narrated crisis.

The characters' actions, in other words, are functionally organized as representations of dilemma-situations. They therefore suggest a new provisional and

10. The dynamically interpersonal design of Homeric scenes was well brought out by Bassett 1938: 57–80. On the opening scenes see Clark 2001: 3. Also relevant is the discussion of dissent in the Achaian assembly by Barker 2004.

adaptable function, the "dilemma schema," which would be a repertoire of cognitive functions that organize the characters and actions intelligibly in their dynamic unfolding as a dramatic story. This repertoire is available to the reader as an aspect of story design so familiar that it can usually be deployed unconsciously. It also renders aspects of the *Iliad* intelligible, because it converges with the epic's own indications. This would not be the case if the reader deployed a blatantly idiosyncratic function.

Another point about the characters' actions: the characters in the crisis of book 1 act in roles. Agamemnon is the "lord of men," Apollo is "Silverbow, protector of Chryse, Killa and Tenedos," Chryses is Apollo's priest. When Agamemnon confronts the dilemma of Chryses' appeal, he confronts it not only as an individual, but as the occupant of a role, for without the role of "lord of men" he would be affected differently by the situation (he might not be the one holding Chryses' daughter) and he would have a different scope of choice (he might not have the power to dismiss and threaten the priest). Moreover, even the characters' private motivations are not unique to them: Chryses pleads both as a priest and as a father, and other fathers can well understand his pain; Agamemnon rejects the father's plea both as a king and as a man who covets Chryses' sexy daughter. In other words, the problems, choices, and actions in the story indicate certain presumed social relationships. These relationships are not unique to the *Iliad*: the narrator explains *who* the "lord of men" is, but he does not need to explain what a "lord of men" is, why Agamemnon would have wanted to keep a sexy concubine for his bed, or why Chryses would have been so upset at the abduction and rape of his daughter. The characters of the *Iliad*, therefore, are not just Agamemnon, Chryses, Apollo, and Achilles, that is, individuals facing certain particular problems and trying to solve them. They are also a king facing a king's problem and attempting a king's solution, a priest facing a priest's problem, a god facing a god's problem, and so forth. Readers who adapted their character-functions to converge with this dimension would find the story more intelligible, and derive more benefit from collaboration with the author's work.

Characters such as these converge with a reader's interest in *edification*, which was the goal-function initially posited above as pertinent to the "story" function. These characters indicate a thematic dimension to the story;[11] their problems and choices suggest the problems and choices of an abstract realm of social relationships to which the story gives concrete form. The characters and their dilemmas furnish vehicles for elaborate thematic developments. The speeches of the *Iliad* express themes that resonate beyond the immediate narrative context of delivery, and they are often more developed thematically than would be necessary merely in order to explain a character's choice in a particular crisis situation. In book 9, for example, Achilles could have stated and explained his rejection of Agamemnon's offer much more concisely than he did. The length of the speech is

11. Compare the analysis of character and plotting in novels in Phelan 1989.

in part a function of its explicit and developed evocation of themes. These features of Homeric speeches indicate an inchoate subsidiary repertoire of cognitive functions useful to eliciting the specific intelligibility of the speeches.

Many speeches in the *Iliad* also address dilemmas through paradigm narratives in which deliberating characters project in advance the consequences of a choice they are contemplating.[12] These special speeches indicate another cognitive function for the reader to adapt and deploy. Paradigm narratives condense the extension of time, so that a whole trajectory of events can be observed in a short span. The rhetorical use of paradigm stories assumes that dilemmas, like character roles, are not unique: problems implicitly belong to certain types that may arise repeatedly, solutions also belong to certain types, and events follow certain typical trajectories, so that the consequences of a choice in a past dilemma supposedly indicate the consequences to be expected if the same choice is made in a similar dilemma whose future outcome is still uncertain. Since paradigm narratives are intended to be edifying to the characters in the story, they also indicate and converge with a reader's interest in edification.

Paradigm narratives may be stories about characters, like Phoinix's story about Meleager, but they may also be omens or other sequences in which events follow a certain trajectory from which the course of a still-unfolding dilemma can be (putatively) inferred. Paradigm narratives therefore indicate two more subsidiary repertoires of cognitive functions, *trajectory* and *mapping*, the latter referring to the cognitive function of drawing multipoint relationships between two functions (which in this case would both be trajectories). Mapping a paradigm narrative onto a dilemma in the main narrative involves drawing at least two kinds of relationships: (1) the paradigm narrative and the problem situation in the main narrative must be apperceived as analogous, and (2) the events *within* each narrative respectively must be apperceived as participating in a trajectory. Relationships of the second type, event trajectories, are modeled on the physical effects of contiguous objects upon one another, as observed in the real world: for example, an eagle holds a snake, the snake bites the eagle, the eagle drops the snake, and the snake falls to the ground. These relationships of contact may be called *synaptic*. In contrast, the relationships of analogy generally do not involve physically contiguous entities (e.g., Achilles is at Troy, but Meleager is not), and the things compared are often more dissimilar than similar (e.g., humans in the main narrative might be compared to birds, weather phenomena, humans of the distant past, or fantastic personifications of human emotions). These comparisons involve a fairly high degree of arbitrariness, and require effort to see. They may be called *synairetic*, because one chooses to bring together for purposes of comparison and inference things that would otherwise remain apart.[13] Therefore, the paradigm narratives are themselves dilemmas for their addressees, who

12. See Alden 2000. I have published a brief review of this book; see Heiden 2003b. On bird omens as paradigm narratives, see Collins 2002: 17–41. Also see my brief comments in *Classical Review* (Heiden 2004).

13. *Synairesis* from Greek *sun* ("together") + *hairein* (middle voice *haireisthai*, "to choose").

must think them through (deliberate indicated choices) in order to glean insight into the probable trajectory of a certain choice. And handling the dilemma of the paradigm involves construing indicators furnished by its narrative design, that is, extralinguistic relationships supposedly deliberated by the speaker, indicated by the paradigm, and abstractable from it.

Orientation

As stories told purposefully by some characters to others in order to enhance cooperation toward shared goals, paradigm narratives indicate a teller-tale-audience collaboration that bears comparison to author-work-reader collaborations. The paradigm narratives afford a relatively simple approach to the dilemmas of a reader who seeks edification from a story. Yet even so, in the *Iliad* paradigm narratives are often occasions of disagreement. But the reader who seeks edification from the *Iliad* is likely to find it much more problematic than any paradigm story the *Iliad* embeds. For one thing, the paradigms embedded in the main narrative are always addressed by a particular character to another particular character (e.g., Phoinix to Achilles) and oriented toward a particular dilemma they face in the story. But the poet of the *Iliad* stands aside from his story in attributing it to an invisible, necessarily inscrutable goddess, and he identifies no particular addressee at all, making for an extremely underdetermined (i.e., indeterminate but repeatedly open to ad hoc redetermination) relationship between the poem and anyone who might read it.[14] The relationship between the epic-as-paradigm and whatever dilemmas a reader might apply it to is also therefore radically ungiven and open to redetermination.

The *Iliad* is also a very long paradigm narrative. One reason dilemmas are hard to resolve is just that events take time: choosing a good action involves foreseeing its future trajectory, which is hard; it may also be hard to remember the past, and hard to see how past and future relate to one another and to a still-current dilemma. Paradigm narratives embedded in the *Iliad* are always very short, in order to render visible a trajectory that characters cannot perceive within their own situation. Even despite its great length the *Iliad* conforms to this model, because the real-life dilemmas of its actual readers have much more extension in time than the length of a complete reading. Still, although the *Iliad* is short compared to the dramas of real life, as a narrated story it is very long, and thus it manifests to a very high degree the fundamental difficulty of constructing relationships among events that are spread out in time.

In other words, coordination between story-teller and story-reader involves a function of orientation that, in the case of a long story like the *Iliad*, may require indications that supplement the signs of the event trajectories and call for additional cognitive work. Accordingly, *orientation* should be added to the repertoire of cognitive functions for experimental simulation. In studying the

14. Scodel 2002: 173 observes that "[the Homeric epics] distance themselves from self-interested, contextually determined storytelling."

Iliad the problem of orientation presents two aspects: (1) Does the *Iliad* provide a satisfactory object of orientation, that is, something toward which a reader *could* be oriented? (2) If it does, and it provides orientation, what signs does it use to indicate the orientation? These questions had received partial answers in my article discussed earlier, "Three Movements," where the experiment indicated that the "plot" of the *Iliad* was a satisfactory object of orientation, and that the epic arranges the segments that narrate the plot's major junctures in such a way that the addition of a little segment punctuation achieved a very significant degree of orientation.

But the analysis of the plot of the *Iliad* in "Three Movements" was far from exhaustive. A few years later I published an article (Heiden 2002b) especially devoted to analysis of the "plot" of the *Iliad*. Entitled "Structures of Progression in the Plot of the *Iliad*," this article adapted Thomas Pavel's research on dramatic plots to develop a cognitive schema for describing dramatic actions in the *Iliad*. The article showed that when the schema was experimentally applied, it disclosed discernible event trajectories in the epic's narrative. While these trajectories are many and diverse, they all converge on a single agent: Zeus. This character's planning demarcates a central orientation of all the action in the *Iliad* and shapes the epic's overarching event trajectory. That research therefore provides a more developed answer to our first question about orientation, whether the *Iliad* furnishes a satisfactory object. In adapted form it now makes up chapter 1 of this book.

"Three Movements" also touched upon another aspect of orientation that merited further analysis. In saying that, in book 1, "all other events . . . provide a setting for Achilleus' withdrawal" (1996: 18) and in identifying "books" of the *Iliad* as narrative units appropriate for comparison, the hypothesis implicitly treated the "books" as units of orientation. In other words, it seemed that the *Iliad* converged with a reader's need for orientation not only in furnishing a coherent event trajectory that encompassed the whole epic, but also in furnishing orientation within shorter horizons, the narrative episodes known as "books." In the case of the "books" the textual tradition of the *Iliad* has already supplied segment-punctuation, and generations of readers have approved it by use. But many scholars have objected to the "book divisions" on the grounds that they were not part of the original composition. This claim, it may be noted, is purely speculative, since there is no reliable information about any aspect of the original composition of the *Iliad*, or about the origin of the "book divisions," whether as part of that composition or separate from it. But a more pertinent point to make about the claim is that it is entirely historical, and thus strictly speaking irrelevant to the question of how the transmitted "book divisions" function in the work of reading. Nevertheless, the claim that the "book divisions" are historically inauthentic has been seen as equivalent to a claim that they are an obstacle to comprehension.

Some scholars, in particular Taplin, have also attempted to show that the "book divisions" bear a faulty relationship to the narrative and actually mislead readers of the epic.[15] This approach at least has the merit of focusing attention upon the function of the "book divisions" rather than their supposed historical origin. But Taplin investigated only one aspect of the relationship of the "book divisions" to the narrative, their placement with respect to narration of continuous action. A thorough investigation would have to consider other aspects, some of them much more meaningful from the standpoint of comprehension. In my article "The Placement of 'Book Divisions' in the *Iliad*" (1998a) I published a tabular analysis of *scenes* that precede and follow "book-divisions" in the *Iliad*. Investigating the role of these scenes in the unfolding story, I found that scenes following markers (i.e., passages that begin transmitted "books") always initiate consequential developments in the story, while scenes that precede markers (i.e., scenes that conclude transmitted "books") never turn the action in a new direction. Thus the placement of "book divisions" in the *Iliad* follows a consistent rationale: each of the twenty-three transmitted "book divisions" occurs at the junction of a low-consequence and high-consequence scene, in that order. Moreover, no such junctures occur inside any of the transmitted "books," so the coincidence of marker placement and low consequence–high consequence junctures is completely systematic: it accounts for all of the transmitted marker placements, and disqualifies any others that might be imagined. In coinciding with these junctures, the "book divisions" offer consistent orientation to scenes that a reader cannot afford to miss.

I later extended this research by adapting the paradigm of event trajectories that I had used to analyze the overarching "plot" of the *Iliad* to analysis of the transmitted "books" and how their action proceeds from start to finish. This analysis of the event trajectories of the "books" makes up chapter 2 of this study. It finds that the transmitted articulation of the *Iliad* is in fact congruent with important narrative subtrajectories, and that the marked articulation cues attention to the subtrajectories.[16] Thus through its marked segmentation the poem assists a reader's work in seeking local orientation. The markings themselves, whatever their historical origin, are not an imposition upon the text, but a supplementation that cooperates with the text's *other* indications—the narrative trajectories—and enhances their efficiency for readers. For readers, the segment markings *might as well* be original.[17]

Having shown that the *Iliad* presents satisfactory objects of orientation in its overarching event trajectory and the event trajectories of its marked segments,

15. Taplin 1992: 285–93.

16. On the "paratext," see de Jong 1996: 20–35 (developing work by Gérard Genette); she suggests that Homer's "oral text" had verbal paratextual markers.

17. This is not a vague or evasive historical claim: it is not a historical claim at all. But anyone who does wish to make historical claims about the origin of the "book divisions" *in the Homeric epics*—for example by positing a terminus post quem for their appearance—should take careful account of their function in the poems. Otherwise their speculation concerns a scholarly chimera, "book divisions," but not those that mark the segmentation of the *Iliad* and *Odyssey*. In fact, conscientious speculation about the origin of the Homeric "book divisions" has little or nothing to work with except the transmitted placements. See chapter 2 for discussion of supposed evidence for the postcompositional insertion of the "book divisions."

this study then turns to the question of how the epic furnishes orientation toward the whole story. This was the specific topic of "Three Movements," whose methodology and results I summarized earlier. Chapter 3 incorporates the same analysis in slightly modified form. Observing that the centrality of Zeus's agency (interacting with Achilles' demands) is emphasized in only six out of twenty-four books (books 1, 8, 9, 15, 16, and 24), the analysis demonstrates that the six orienting books are so distributed that it is possible to arrange the *Iliad* in three series each of which begins and ends with one of the six orienting books (1–8, 9–15, 16–24). Since this arrangement indubitably clarifies the transmitted poem's internal arrangement of signs, facilitates a reader's work with the overarching event trajectory, and does not conflict with or obscure other legible signs in the *Iliad*, there is every reason for Homeric scholars to make use of it themselves, and to make it known to students and others whose comprehension and appreciation of the *Iliad* stands to benefit. Its adoption represents a legitimate collaboration with the presumed author of the *Iliad*, one neither more intrusive nor more speculative than the well-accepted practices of inscribing each hexameter verse on a separate line, or inserting marks of punctuation to ease comprehension of syntax.

Trajectories of Thematic Transformation

We have seen that the reader who experimentally adopts the three-movement design finds the poem converging through its orientation to the epic's overarching event trajectory. This convergence also suggests an efficient way the poem might provide readers with *thematic* orientation. In an epic as long as the *Iliad* thematic orientation can be even more elusive than orientation to the events, because themes are abstract, synairetic ("chosen together"), and inherently somewhat incompletely indicated. The poetry of the *Iliad* suggests synairetic relationships only in the margins of the narrative, for example in similes, or in speeches where the characters express their personal motivations somewhat more abstractly than necessary. In other words, the poet supplies cues, but they are considerably weaker than the cues to the synaptic path of events. Even in reading any single narrated dilemma, a reader would find more to cue which character faces what problem than to cue what the situation might imply thematically. And since themes are so weakly cued in the first place, a reader seeking orientation to thematic developments that span the whole epic faces a demanding task.[18]

"Three Movements" had already indicated that the three-movement design offers some thematic orientation, since the arrangement consistently aligns books that focus upon Achilles' reliance on Zeus (books 1, 9, and 16) and likewise

18. The *Iliad* sometimes repeats a theme a few times in a relatively brief span of verses, thus multiplying the chances a reader has to recognize its presence and importance; Segal 1971 pointed out that the "theme of the mutilation of the corpse" recurred with accelerating frequency in the last third of the epic. The discussion entitled "Fire and Other Elements" in Whitman 1958: 128–53 is the classic exposition of thematic repetition in the *Iliad*.

consistently aligns those focusing upon Zeus' plans (books 8, 15, and 24). I therefore hypothesized that the same three-movement design that cues orientation to the epic's event trajectory might also cue orientation to themes that develop throughout the epic, especially when their indications occur in books that stand far apart from one another in the sequence of reading. In an article entitled "Major Systems of Thematic Resonance in the *Iliad*" (2000a) I investigated this possibility. A preliminary step postulated and confirmed that most "books" of the *Iliad* have a certain comprehensive or nearly comprehensive *thematic* orientation (as distinct from the narrative orientation discussed in "Placement of 'Book Divisions'"). This supported the use of "books" as units of comparison in the "Three Movements" experiment, and indicated that the "books" offered units of thematic comparability.[19] But when the "three movements" were represented diagrammatically in parallel series, analysis showed that each position (as defined by relationship to the beginnings and ends of the movements) coincided with thematic analogies among the books of like position in the three movements. The analysis also showed thematic analogies among books within each movement. Although when explained verbally this multiplication of analogies sounds complex, diagrammatic representation shows that it is very simple, and that it effects orientation very efficiently, since the intramovement and transmovement analogous positions coincide. As I subsequently realized (and discussed, 2003a), the coordination of internal and external positions indicates that the orientational potential of the "three-movement" design is better realized if the movements are imagined as cycles rather than linear series. The three-cycle design offers the reader constant assistance in maintaining thematic orientation within the whole epic. It functions as an implicit map.

With the thematic map of the *Iliad* clearly in view, I next asked whether its orientation might extend beyond analogies among whole books to thematic convergences of scenes that the analogous books contain. Selecting a specimen pair of books, 3 and 6, which occupy analogous positions in cycle I, I closely compared them scene by scene. The survey disclosed numerous thematically analogous *situations* in the paired books. These thematically analogous passages are not aggregates of motifs or verbal formulas, but coherent narrated situations that indicate comparable abstract concepts. Moreover, the convergence between the two books is very systematic: virtually every scene in each book has a thematic counterpart in the other, and the comparable scenes even proceed in similar (though not identical) order. It would appear that the three-cycle design furnishes orientation *both* to themes that characterize books as narrative ensembles *and* to themes that characterize scenes within books.

However, the thematic orientation just described does not lead the reader's attention toward repetitive "parallels" in symmetrical balance. The abstract

19. The aggregates of short and in some cases formulaic motifs from which Stanley and others had attempted to demonstrate thematic "parallels" are much less cognitively significant and efficiently orientative than the "books," which are few in number, prominent in scale, unique, coherent, and meaningful.

analogies require active synairesis of passages that are both discontiguous and *different* in many respects. The intellectual force of synairesis, therefore, exerts itself against resistance and discontinuity within the very convergences that the design indicates as themes. Moreover the same orientation that cues attention to indicators of thematic convergence also cues attention to indications of thematic divergence.

If these divergences were unintelligible "noise," they might indicate the limit of the poem's orientation. But closer examination found that they did not seem random. Instead, the later passages (book 6) seemed to work transformations on the earlier (book 3). Therefore the experiment added *trajectory of thematic transformation* to the repertoire of cognitive functions, and deployed it experimentally in interpretations of the observed thematic variants among thematically analogous passages in books 3 and 6. The entire analysis of books 3 and 6 was originally published in an article entitled "Cyclic Design and Thematic Resonance in *Iliad* Books 3 and 6" (2003a). Its simulations are included in chapter 4 of this book, where they are augmented by additional simulations, here published for the first time, that systematically apply the same postulated functions to two other specimen pairs in cycle I, books 1 and 8, and books 2 and 7.

The interpretive simulation of chapter 4, which could be described as a "heuristic commentary," is then carried forward in the new investigations of chapters 5, 6, and 7. Chapter 5 systematically tests the thematic transformation function on books 1 and 9 (Achilles' decisions, the "head" segments of cycle I and cycle II respectively), and chapter 6 tests it on books 8 and 15 (Zeus's decisive interventions, the "tail" segments of the same cycles). Chapter 7 approaches book 24, which, coming as it does at the conclusion of the epic, evokes many cued themes from earlier books. In these chapters, preliminary surveys of analogously positioned books confirm that analogous positioning cues attention to thematically analogous situations within books, as it did in books 3 and 6. Each chapter then proceeds to analysis of the themes and their transformations.

These interpretations suggest that the *Iliad* indicates one theme above all: choice. It is not only that the epic's drama advances through choices, but that the particular dramatic choices imply conceptualizations of what choice is and what choices are possible. In the *Iliad* the theme of choice follows a trajectory in which the relationship between choices and the problem situations in which they are made displays increasing underdetermination and imaginative freedom as available options are transformed, combined, and reconstructed. It might be said that the characters—especially Zeus—approach their dilemmas with more and more fabricative creativity.

From this perspective, the design of the *Iliad*—that is, the productive convergence between the poem's signs and the heuristic model's cognitive functions—may be seen as more than a technical aid to comprehension, but as itself a bearer of significance. The concluding chapter of this study considers the thematic implications of poetic design with especial reference to the one great work of art described in the *Iliad*, the shield of Achilles. Then it briefly considers the mythic designs of Zeus, both within the *Iliad* and beyond it. The poetic fabrication of the *Iliad* indicates the work that remains for gods and mortals in transforming the natural environment into a hospitable cosmos. Here is yet another trajectory that the design of the *Iliad* indicates: the pragmatic trajectory in which readers imagine the deliberative problem-posing of the Muses and poets, and direct it into pondering contemplation of what the *Iliad* means for themselves.

PART I

Dramatic Legibility and Poetic Design

1

Persons, Problems, and Choices

The Progression of Events in the Iliad

According to Aristotle (*Poetics* 1451a) the *Iliad*, like the *Odyssey*, is constructed "around a single action" (*περὶ μίαν πρᾶξιν*). For Aristotle this was an important aspect of the epic's effectiveness, since good stories were supposed to enact a "complete and whole action" (*τελείας καὶ ὅλης πράξεως ... μίμησιν*, 1450b) that was easily taken in and remembered (*εὐμνημόνευτον*, 1451a). But during the past two centuries most professional Homeric scholars have followed the lead of F. A. Wolf, who dismissed Aristotle's description of the action of the *Iliad* as merely an anachronistic projection, and denied that the *Iliad* could in any way or degree narrate a single action.[1] However liberating it may feel to reject The Philosopher's once-sacrosanct authority, in this case it brings no gain in sophistication, since without some projection, that is, without the complementary work of a reader, no poem as such can be described at all. To reject Aristotle's description on good grounds we would have to determine that its work did not cooperate with the poem's indications. Our heuristic model permits this fresh approach. Aristotle's description can be reframed as a refinement of the "orientation" function discussed in the introduction. Postulating an additional "single action" reading function facilitates investigation of whether the *Iliad* supplies indications convergent with that function.

Some of the factors already discussed in the introduction indicate that Aristotle's description of a "whole" misses the mark as far as the action of the *Iliad* is concerned. Aristotle describes a whole as an unbroken sequence ("beginning, middle, and end") whose elements are a succession of necessary causes and effects. But the *Iliad* advances by narrating its characters' dilemmas and choices, and these neither arise as the necessary results of antecedent causes nor cause the dilemmas and choices that follow. Choices occur in underdetermined situations that could go a number of ways. Choices also do not proceed in linear temporal sequence; characters may choose to defer action, or retrospectively reframe dilemmas long after their initial onset. In short, characters may forge

1. Wolf 1985 (1795): 125 n. 91: "in these matters [sc. wholes in Greek poetry] Aristotle was too often diverted from historical method." Lord 1960: 148: "Had Homer been interested in Aristotelian ideas of unity, he would not have been Homer, nor would he have composed the *Iliad* and *Odyssey*." The survey of Latacz 1991a: 381–414 repeatedly notes how research into the "structure" of the *Iliad* has been obstructed or neglected.

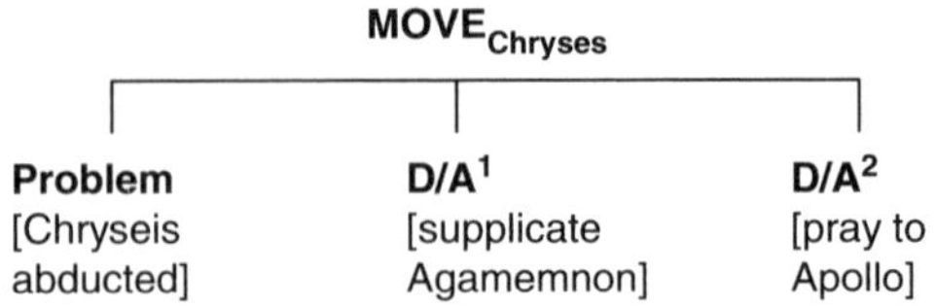

FIGURE 1.1. Move of Chryses.

optional relationships among story elements that stand great distances apart in either the sequence of narrated events or the sequence of the telling.

It would, however, be overly hasty to conclude that because the *Iliad* does not display the *kind* of unity that Aristotle described, its action has no unity of *any* kind. One would have to analyze the action in terms of choices. How would such an analysis be performed? Thomas Pavel has proposed an insightful and useful system for diagrammatic representation of dramatic plots in terms of the dilemmas and choices of characters.[2] To illustrate Pavel's system, let us say that the dramatic trajectory of a dilemma-situation in the *Iliad* involves a character who confronts a problem, makes a decision about how to deal with it, and acts to carry out the decision. The dramatic trajectory from a problem to an action can be called a Move (like a move in a board game). For example, as the story begins, the priest Chryses faces the Problem that the Greeks are holding his daughter Chryseis as their captive. Chryses' first Decision/Action is to approach the Greek assembly as a suppliant and ask for her to be returned in exchange for ransom. When this fails because Agamemnon rejects his appeal, the priest attempts a second Decision/Action: he seeks the help of Apollo. The relationship of events in this Move can be represented linearly in Pavel's system as follows: Problem + Decision/Action (1,2) = Move (Chryses). Figure 1.1 represents the same Move in diagram form.

The story advances as Chryses' Move in turn presents a Problem for Apollo: how should the god respond to the priest's prayer? Apollo's Decision/Action has two parts: (1) he sends a plague upon the Greeks, and (2) he reveals to his seer Kalchas the reason for the plague. In the linear format the embedding of one whole Move in another is rather cumbersome to express, but in a diagram it can be quite clear, as shown by figure 1.2, a representation of the advancement from Move (Chryses) to Move (Apollo).

When a Move in the *Iliad* ends it is seldom because a character's Decision/Action has achieved its goal and solved his or her Problem. Instead a condition that resolves, suspends, reframes, or obviates a character's Problem usually arrives indirectly from a different character's Move. For example, when Achilles withdraws from the battle, the Achaians face the Problem of holding off the Trojans without him. Their Move involves a number of strategies that fall

2. This discussion and the accompanying diagrams are adapted from the system developed in Pavel 1985, with some modifications of terminology. Pavel's work has previously been applied to the *Iliad* in Clark 2001 and Heiden 2002b (an earlier version of the material in this chapter). Pavel's system of diagrammatic analysis includes other features that are not explored in this book, although they are useful to studying the *Iliad* and suggest provisional functions that could be added to the model repertoire.

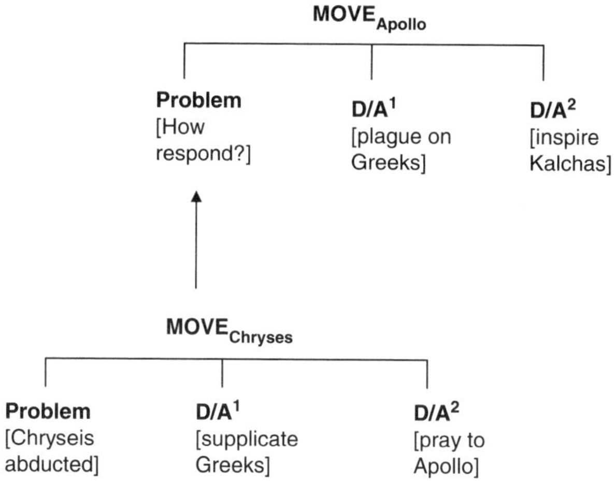

FIGURE 1.2. Embedded Move.

roughly into two classes: D/A¹: they improvise substitutes for Achilles, and D/A²: they try to persuade Achilles to return. The Problem disappears when Achilles returns; but Achilles returns because Patroklos has been killed, not because the Achaians asked him to. Thus it is Achilles' Move (= Problem [Patroklos killed] + (Decision/Action [take vengeance on Trojans]) that terminates the trajectory of the Achaians' Move. Figure 1.3 displays this relationship between the Achaians' Move and Achilles'.

Sometimes the agents who make a Move from a Problem to an Action make deliberate use of incidentally available characters or circumstances. For example, when Achilles faces the Problem that Agamemnon has confiscated Briseis, in order

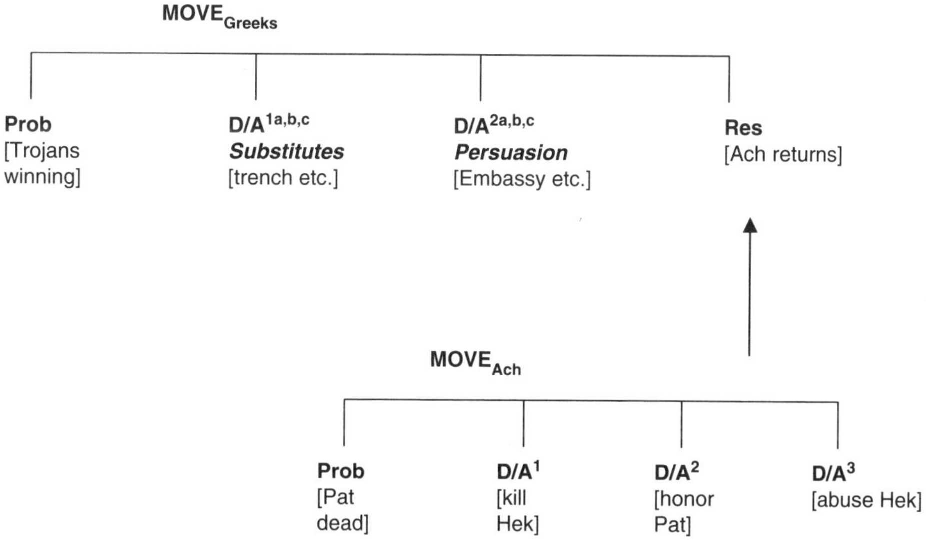

FIGURE 1.3. Relationship between the Achaians' Move and Achilles'.

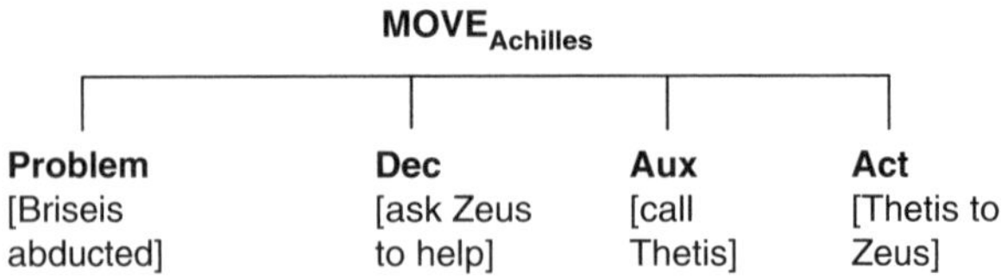

FIGURE 1.4. Move with Auxiliary.

to take the Action of getting Zeus to punish the Greeks until they restore his honor, Achilles calls upon Thetis to intercede. Pavel (1985: 18) calls this kind of intermediate step an Auxiliary. Not every Move includes Auxiliaries. When the linear expression of a Move includes the term "Auxiliary," Pavel puts the Auxiliary Action in parentheses to indicate its optional and subordinate nature relative to other Actions in the same Move. Figure 1.4 illustrates Achilles' Move with its Auxiliary.

Either a Problem, an Auxiliary, or a Decision/Action may consist of a series (Pavel 1985: 20). For example, Chryses attempts two Actions in response to the Problem of the abduction of his daughter, (1) appealing to Agamemnon, and (2) praying to Apollo. The schematic representation of an embedded series is illustrated by Figure 1.1 and Figure 1.2.

Pavel's system of representing dramatic plots reveals important relationships among story events like those of the *Iliad*. When characters take action to address problems, events have an intrinsic trajectory of movement furnished by a character's intention to move from a state in which he confronts a problem to a goal-state in which the problem has been resolved or obviated. But although the functional elements of the event trajectories are the same, the trajectories themselves may differ in many dimensions, one of which is length. In the *Iliad* a few Moves develop exceptionally long trajectories, either because they require many actions in pursuit of the goal or because they contribute to many new problems that must also be dealt with. Thus event trajectories may constitute hierarchies in which a number of very short trajectories participate in longer trajectories, and these in turn participate in a few very long trajectories. Our "orientation/single action" reading function should therefore include a "Move-hierarchy" function to investigate the hierarchical relationships among the Moves.

A Move-analysis of the events in the *Iliad* and their hierarchical relationships reveals that there is one central character whose decisions and actions dominate all the events of the epic. In this respect the trajectories of events do indeed approximate a "single action," and a single, rather simple Move diagram can concisely illustrate the hierarchical relationships among all the major decisions that advance the action of the *Iliad*.[3] These relationships should be deemed

3. While the Move-analysis corresponds to a feature of the *Iliad* that may loosely be called the epic's *plot*, from now on I shall refrain from using this word, because as a term in common usage by readers, playgoers, storytellers, and scholars, "plot" may quite legitimately refer to diverse aspects of a narrative's design, depending on the circumstances. This discussion does not aim to analyze the entire "plot" of the *Iliad*, and it should not be seen as inviting a debate,

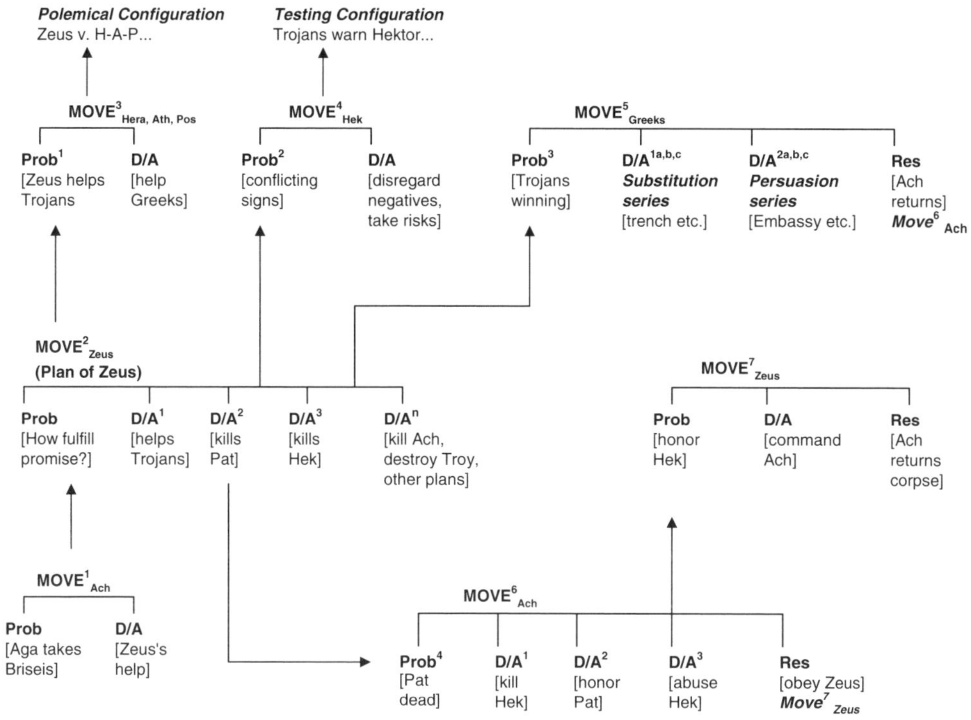

FIGURE 1.5. Major Moves in the Action of the *Iliad*.

indications of an overarching event trajectory that approximates Aristotle's "single action" formulation. They confirm that the "single action" reading function works in cooperation with the poem's author.[4]

Figure 1.5 schematizes the advancing action of the *Iliad* as the relationships of seven hierarchically superior Moves made by five major characters: Achilles,

fraught with risk of confusing equivocations, about exactly which aspect of the "plot" has been analyzed either well or badly. The point of the diagrammatic analysis is not to take the notion of "plot" as given and try to explain how it works, but rather to take as given the phenomenon of *dilemma-situations* (Moves, in Pavel's terminology), and see what it can explain about the progression of events in the *Iliad*. Most other recent discussions of the "plot" of the *Iliad* are not analyses of the "event trajectories" as here defined, and since they are fundamentally unlike the analysis here, their particular merits and deficiencies need not detain us now. These analyses include Mueller 1984: 28–76; Morrison 1992; Rabel 1997; Lowe 2000: 103–28; and Latacz 2000a: 151–57. Since Lowe makes much use of game theory, including the terminology of Moves, it is necessary to point out that his analysis centers on narrative rules that ultimately govern a concatenation of causes and effects. I would maintain, on the contrary, that the storyteller of the *Iliad* is careful to indicate at every juncture in the narrative that the course of events is underdetermined, even where customs of acknowledged currency or supposed physical laws are at issue, and that the direction of the action is therefore subject to the characters' choices. Note *Iliad* 18.239–41, where Hera compels the sun to set against its will (ἀέκοντα), and *Iliad* 19.407, where Hera gives Achilles' horse Xanthos the power to speak (αὐδήεντα δ' ἔθηκε) and the Erinyes then take the power away (19.418). On the so-called pivotal contrafactuals as indications of choice in the story see Morrison 1992:112–14; Louden 1993; and Heiden 1997: 225.

4. As I turn to the analysis, I reiterate that the experiment simulates the systematic application of a provisional reading function, and does so in order to elicit an aspect of the poem's potential. The analysis does not make a claim about any actual reading of the *Iliad* by any actual person (including myself). In practice, most readers of stories are satisfied with an inchoate impression of coherent progression, whose details they do not verify systematically; and most readers of this research, including scholars who have read the *Iliad* quite carefully but with different interests

Zeus, Hektor, the Achaian army as a group, and the group of pro-Achaian divinities consisting of Hera, Athena, and Poseidon.[5] In Move^1, Achilles faces the problem that Agamemnon has taken Briseis from him. His Decision/Action is to get Zeus on his side.[6] Move^1 (Achilles) then poses a new Problem, this one for Zeus, who now must decide how he will fulfill his promise to Thetis. His Decision/Action is a developing Plan with proliferating parts: he helps the Trojans in the battle (D/A^1), but in doing so he also brings about the death of Patroklos (D/A^2). He also plans the death of Hektor (D/A^3) and many other events; it is not clear where the planning of Zeus stops (D/A^n).[7]

Move^2 (Zeus) now poses four new Problems for four characters. It frustrates Hera, Athena, and Poseidon (counted as one group-character for the purposes of this analysis), who favor the Greeks (Problem^1). Their Decision/Action is to help the Greeks. Problem^1 + Decision/Action = Move^3 (Hera, Athena, Poseidon). This becomes the occasion for a series of Moves, summarized in the diagram (polemical configuration: Zeus v. H-A-P), in which Zeus acts to block their intervention, one or more of them act to circumvent him, and so on until Zeus finally prevails.[8] The second Problem it poses is for Hektor, who now mistakenly sees an opportunity to win great glory. His Decision/Action is to attack the Greek ships. Problem^2 + Decision/Action = Move^4 (Hektor). Hektor's attack in turn becomes the occasion for a series of Moves (testing configuration: Trojans and Zeus warn Hektor, fig. 1.5) in which Hektor repeatedly ignores warnings from his people, and even from Zeus, until Achilles slays him. Zeus's Plan poses a third Problem, this one for the Greeks, who without Achilles suffer setbacks on the second and third days of fighting. They pursue Actions of two types: (1) they seek substitutes for Achilles, namely the fortifications they build, Diomedes and Odysseus in the night raid, and Patroklos in Achilles' armor (substitution series: trench, etc., in fig. 1.5), and (2) they try to persuade Achilles to rejoin them, first by sending the embassy, then when Patroklos visits Nestor's encampment, and finally when Patroklos himself pleads with Achilles (persuasion series: embassy, etc., in fig. 1.5). Problem^3 + Decision/Action$^{(1,2)}$ = Move^5 (Greeks). The *substitution series* and *persuasion series* each

from mine, may find in the following analysis aspects of the story they had not previously noticed. The claim of the systematic analysis is not that they should have noticed these aspects, but that they could have, and not capriciously, but in cooperation with the poem's legible indications.

5. To avoid clutter, a great number of minor embedded Moves have been omitted from the diagram. For example, Decision/Action^1 of Move^2 (Zeus helps Trojans) includes numerous Auxiliary Moves by Zeus (e.g., sending Dream to Agamemnon) that, in terms of the event trajectory, are completely subordinate to the goal of helping the Trojans. Thus they do not need to be explicitly represented at this stage of analysis.

6. Compare the general observation of Brooks 1984: 12, that "the organizing line of plot is more often than not some scheme or machination, a concerted plan for the accomplishment of some purpose which goes against the ostensible and dominant legalities of the fictional world, the realization of a blocked and resisted desire." Achilles' plan to win honor from Zeus represents the most obvious example of such a scheme in the *Iliad*; but the plans of Hera, Athena, and Poseidon to help the Achaians despite Zeus's wishes (discussed later), Hektor's plan to ride Zeus's favor to a complete victory over the Achaians (discussed later), and the Plan of Zeus itself are also schemes that meet resistance.

7. On the extension of Zeus's plans beyond the temporal frame of the *Iliad*, see Clay 1999 and Rousseau 2001, as well as the brief discussion in the conclusion here.

8. Pavel uses the term "polemical configuration" for this kind of tit-for-tat (or Move-for-Move) plot trajectory; see Pavel 1985: 29–30.

achieve some success, although not nearly enough to ameliorate the Problem. The most effective substitute for Achilles approaches unseen from a collateral line of the action, the exchange between Zeus and H-A-P (polemical configuration, fig. 1.5), when Poseidon helps the Greeks until Zeus stops him.[9] And it is also from a collateral line that a resolution unexpectedly arrives: Move^{6} (Achilles) resolves the Greeks' Problem when Achilles returns to battle to avenge his friend and somewhat incidentally also to save the Greeks.[10]

Zeus's Plan (Move^{2}) also poses a Problem for Achilles, whose closest comrade has been killed (Problem^{4}). His Decision/Action has three parts, killing Hektor (Decision/Action^{1}), honoring Patroklos with a splendid funeral (Decision/Action^{2}), and abusing Hektor's corpse (Decision/Action^{3}). Problem^{4} + Decision/Action$^{(1,2,3)}$ = Move^{6} (Achilles). Finally, Move^{6} poses a Problem for Zeus, for Achilles' abuse of Hektor's corpse offends most of the Olympians. Zeus's Decision/Action is to compel Achilles to return the corpse to Priam. Problem + Decision/Action = Move^{7} (Zeus).

It is clear from figure 1.5 that of the seven major Moves in the action of the *Iliad*, Move^{2} (Zeus) makes the most and biggest waves: four of the major Moves, involving four different character domains, develop in response to Move^{2} (Zeus). The one thing that Achilles, Hektor, the Greeks, and the Hera-Athena-Poseidon group have in common is that each must deal with a Problem posed for them by Zeus. Nor does any one of them ever create a Problem for the others: when Hektor kills Patroklos, he is merely an Auxiliary to Zeus's plan. It is Zeus's Decision/Action that creates the Problem to which Achilles must respond. Moreover, most of the Problems that arise from the Plan of Zeus are also resolved by Zeus. The *polemical configuration* pitting Hera-Athena-Poseidon against Zeus ends when Zeus combines threats with compromise and reveals to Hera that he plans the fall of Troy and even the death of his own son, Sarpedon.[11] The *testing configuration* involving Hektor ends when Athena, with Zeus's permission and according to Zeus's plan, prepares his death. Even the return of Achilles to the battle arises from the Plan of Zeus, since Zeus has predicted to Hera in book 8 that Achilles will return to the battle when Patroklos is killed.

In this regard Zeus—not Achilles—is the most influential agent in the *Iliad*, the hub around which the whole action turns. This fact has not been generally appreciated by critics,[12] perhaps because the conflicts between Zeus

9. On Poseidon as substitute for Achilles see Haubold 2000: 74.

10. Note that the rather minor role of the embassy in this series is not a measure of its importance in the story, but only an indication that its tremendous significance arises from the themes projected in its speeches, not from a powerful role in the shaping of events. Achilles is out of the battle when the embassy arrives and still out when it leaves, although he is perhaps slightly more sympathetic to the plight of his comrades than before. Here the analysis of action trajectories reaches its limit, and other approaches are needed; see my remarks at Heiden 2002b: 238–39.

11. Rousseau 2001: 149 notes that Zeus's plan to help Achilles also helps to destroy Troy, for Achilles' absence draws Hektor into a vulnerable position.

12. Homer's Olympians are generally taken less seriously than they should be; see my comments in Heiden 1997 (where I noted Erbse 1986: 228 as an important exception). Since then Clay 1999 and Rousseau 2001 have placed deserved emphasis on the importance of Zeus's plan.

and Achilles, and between Zeus and Hektor, never involve any face-to-face confrontations between the antagonists, or any expressions of animosity on either side. On the surface of the text conflict between Zeus and the mortal heroes approaches visibility in only a few passages; one thinks perhaps of 16.233–52, where Achilles prays for Zeus to help Patroklos but Zeus silently grants only part of his wish. In contrast, conflicts such as those between Achilles and Agamemnon, Achilles and Hektor, or Hektor and Poulydamas furnish some of the epic's most dramatic scenes and penetrating speeches; but in terms of the trajectory of events, they function as Auxiliaries to Zeus's plans, facilitating but not actually motivating the Decisions and Actions that address the story's major Problems. The conflicts between the mortal heroes and Zeus undergo displacement as the heroes Achilles and Hektor attempt to solve their Problems in conflict with one another rather than in conflict with their real antagonist, Zeus. The dramatic emphasis therefore does not redundantly highlight the progression of the action, and in this regard the *Iliad* illustrates a phenomenon Pavel terms "counter-plot emphasis" (1985: 37–38).

POLEMICAL CONFIGURATIONS

The basic action trajectory of the *Iliad* combines one dominant series of Moves, that in which Achilles and Zeus alternate in posing Problems for one another, with three lesser series or "subplots" (Bassett 1922: 52–62). The series of Moves in which Zeus opposes Hera-Poseidon-Athena furnishes a fairly straightforward example of what Pavel terms a "polemical configuration," a series of Moves divided between two characters or groups in which every Move is an answer to the Problem created by the previous Move (1985: 29–30). The polemical configuration opposing Zeus to Hera-Athena-Poseidon consists of about eleven Moves. (Since in fig. 1.5 the Move in which Hera-Athena-Poseidon oppose Zeus is labeled Move^{3} [Hera-Athena-Poseidon], in the following analysis its subordinate Moves will be labeled Move$^{3a,b,c \ldots k}$. The configuration of Moves can be understood easily without a diagram, so none is provided.) In Move^{3a} (Zeus), Zeus, faced with the Problem of how to fulfill his promise to Thetis, gets the Greeks and Trojans to meet on the battlefield (the action of book 2). This poses a Problem for the pro-Achaian Olympians, since the Greeks must fight without their best warrior, Achilles. Thus, when hostilities actually begin (end of book 4) after the detour of Paris's combat with Menelaos, Athena addresses this Problem by inspiring Diomedes, with the result that the first day of battle goes well for the Achaians: Move^{3b} (Athena) = Problem [Achaians must fight without Achilles] + Decision/Action [Athena enables Diomedes to take Achilles' place]. The next day Zeus makes a more forceful attempt to address the Problem of fulfilling his promise to Thetis (Move^{3c}). He warns the Olympians not to interfere in the battle (Decision/Action^{1}: 8.5–27), which Athena understands as meaning trouble for the Achaians (8.31–37); but initially the battle is a deadlock, and after placing unequal dooms on the scales, Zeus intervenes to help the Trojans (Decision/Action^{2}: 8.66–77). This provides the occasion for Move^{3d} when Hera perceives the Trojan success as a Problem and attempts two Actions. First she unsuccessfully incites Poseidon to help the Greeks in open opposition to his older brother, Zeus (Decision/Action^{1}: 8.198–207); when Poseidon demurs, she inspires Agamemnon to rally the Greeks. After he does so Agamemnon prays to Zeus on his own initiative, and Zeus responds to the prayer favorably and moderates the Greek rout (Decision/Action^{2}: 8.245–52). But Zeus still wants to put the Greeks in distress, and accordingly he again inspires the Trojans (Move^{3e}). This provides the occasion for Move^{3f}, in which Hera and Athena together prepare to help the Greeks (8.350–96). But before they can accomplish anything Zeus responds preemptively to this new Problem by sending Iris to stop them (Move^{3g}: 8.397–408). Next Athena works around Zeus's prohibition by helping Odysseus and Diomedes in their night expedition (Move^{3h}: 10.272–579).

As Zeus begins the third day of battle Hera and Athena do not assist the Achaians, blaming Zeus's plan to glorify the Trojans (11.75–79); but Zeus does not act to help the Trojans until Agamemnon has chased them back to the city, when Zeus sends Iris to Hektor (Move^{3i}: 11.185–94); this is perhaps best seen not as a polemical response to Athena, but as a renewed effort in the embedded series of Moves aimed at fulfilling the promise to Thetis. But when, after enabling Hektor to burst through the Greek wall, Zeus turns his eyes from the battle, Poseidon seizes the opportunity to help the Achaians (Move^{3j}, Decision/Action^{1}: 13.1–15.219). Hera's beguiling of Zeus (14.153–360), which aims to keep Zeus's attention distracted and thus facilitate Poseidon's interference (Decision/Action^{1}), can be regarded as a second Decision/Action (Decision/Action^{2}) addressed to the same Problem. The final Move of the series (Move^{3k}) occurs when Zeus awakens from his postcoital nap and realizes that Poseidon has been helping the Greeks; his Decision/Action has four parts: threatening Hera (Decision/Action^{1}: 15.13–77), revealing his Plan to Hera so that she can support him (Decision/Action^{2}), sending Iris to summon Poseidon from the battlefield (Decision/Action^{3}: 15.149–219), and sending Apollo to urge Hektor on (Decision/Action^{4}: 15.220–61). After this, Zeus's plan to help Achilles meets no further opposition.

The series of Moves in which Zeus and Achilles take turns in posing Problems for one another may likewise be described as a polemical configuration in which Achilles requests Zeus's help (Move^{1}), Zeus grants the request but in a manner that devastates Achilles, i.e., the death of Patroklos (Move^{2}), Achilles responds by killing Hektor and then abusing his corpse (Move^{6}), and Zeus responds to this final Problem by compelling Achilles to accept ransom for the body so that it can be buried properly (Move^{7}).

This polemical configuration displays considerably more subtlety than that opposing Zeus to Hera-Athena-Poseidon. For one thing, the structure's polemical shape is masked by the long intervals that separate the Problems from the Actions that then pose new Problems in turn: Achilles asks Zeus to help the

Trojans in book 1, Zeus brings about Patroklos's death in book 16; Achilles then does not kill Hektor until book 22, and he is still abusing his corpse at the beginning of book 24, when Zeus decides to stop him. The displacement of Achilles' opposition against Zeus onto Hektor also contributes to the same masking effect.

But more important, the exchange between Achilles and Zeus advances the epic thematically as the Problems that prompt the characters to action change in nature: in Move^1 the Problem posed for Achilles by the abduction of Briseis (which can be roughly thematized as *a king's responsibility for the property of his comrades*) is not the same as that posed in Move^6 by the death of Patroklos (roughly, *a man's responsibility for the life of a comrade*). In turn, Achilles' terrible vengeance against Hektor then poses in Move^7 a Problem for Zeus (whether a pious mortal should be preserved from absolute disgrace after death) that is thematically unlike that implied in Move^2 by Thetis's request (whether to compensate a mortal before death because he is related to a goddess to whom Zeus owes a favor). The basic tit-for-tat polemical structure supports a profound shift in the thematic content of the story. At this point in the analysis it is too early for a detailed discussion of the shift and its significance, except to indicate that in each pair of Moves[13] the shift follows a similar direction, a *thematic trajectory*.[14]

A "TESTING CONFIGURATION": ZEUS'S CONFLICT WITH HEKTOR

Like his conflict with Achilles, Zeus's conflict with Hektor hinges upon gaps in communication. Except that while the Achilles-action unfolds through Zeus's problematic response to Achilles' straightforward request, the Hektor-action unfolds through Hektor's straightforward response to Zeus's problematic signs. Thus the Move-analysis, by isolating the Hektor-action and its Problems, brings the communication between Zeus and Hektor into view as a theme. The following explication of the series of Moves in Zeus's conflict with Hektor will therefore include observations about this theme as well as about the events and their trajectory.

Zeus has several overlapping plans for the Trojans. He plans to give the Trojans short-term success to fulfill his promise to Thetis, but he also plans to destroy the city eventually,[15] and he has planned the death of Hektor by the middle of the third day of battle (15.68) if not before. Zeus spurs Hektor's battle-fury with encouragement in the form of signs (e.g. 8.170–83) and success. But he also sends warnings, as when Iris explicitly informs Hektor that he will have success only until he reaches the ships of the Achaians and the sun goes down

13. Pair (a) = Move^1 [Achilles] to Move^6 [Achilles], Pair (b) = Move^2 [Zeus] to Move^7 [Zeus].

14. See Heubeck 1958: 45–46 on the shift of plot in book 16. On Zeus see the insightful remarks of Erbse 1986: 227.

15. See Clay 1999 and Rousseau 2001: 148.

(11.185–209); or when Zeus[16] sends the omen of the eagle and the serpent that Poulydamas interprets as a warning against attacking the ships (12.211–29); and when Ajax boasts to Hektor that the end of his success is near, and the boast is followed by a portent from Zeus (13.809–32) (Schadewaldt 1966: 106–7).

In each case Hektor fails to heed the warning.[17] The series of warnings had already begun on the first day of battle, when Andromache begged Hektor to take a defensive position on the city wall (6.431–39). On the third day of battle Hektor is repeatedly warned by Poulydamas,[18] whose advice Hektor accepts when it calls for cautious advance (12.61–81, 13.723–53) (Redfield 1975: 144), but not when it calls for declining to attack the Achaian ships altogether, even though this advice is prompted by the portent (145).[19] Later when Apollo and Zeus help Hektor in the battle, he again takes courage from their assistance (15.253–70). But he is unmoved when Patroklos in his final breath prophesies his imminent death at the hands of Achilles (16.843–61) (Schadewaldt 1966: 107); and when Poulydamas warns the Trojans to retreat within the city walls now that Achilles has returned to the battle, Hektor once again rejects his advice, even though he was told by Iris that his success would last only until he reached the Achaian ships and the sun had set, both of which have by now occurred (18.254–309) (Taplin 1992: 158–60). Hektor's refusal to heed Poulydamas's advice costs many Trojan lives. Finally, as he awaits the attack of Achilles, Hektor disregards his father and mother as they plead with him to take refuge within the city wall (22.37–130). Thus the Hektor-action advances as an Auxiliary series of Moves in which Hektor is repeatedly tested to see whether he can hear and accept unfavorable signs, from Zeus and his surrogates, as well as favorable signs. This could be termed a *testing configuration*.

ERRANCY IN THE PROGRESSION OF EVENTS

It may accurately be said that the *Iliad* has one central action, Zeus's dubiously cooperative fulfillment of Achilles' request in book 1. Yet as noted, the conflict between Zeus and Achilles barely touches the surface of the narrative; indeed, Zeus refers to his fulfillment of Achilles' "hope" (ἐέλδωρ, 15.74); the narrator refers to Zeus's intention of "completely fulfilling the prayer of Thetis" (15.598–99); and finally Thetis reminds Achilles that Zeus has brought to pass what Achilles prayed for (18.74–77)—all as if Achilles' wishes and Zeus's accomplishments were simply identical. Nothing could be more ironic. Not only does a huge

16. One presumes it is Zeus. Poulydamas's warning does not actually depend upon certainty that the eagle and serpent were actually sent by Zeus. He makes inferences, about the occurrence and about the battle. So do readers of the *Iliad*. There might be a point in the narrator's reticence.

17. Schadewaldt 1966: 105–9; Reinhardt 1961: 179–80, 273; Schein 1984: 183; and Taplin 1992: 159–60.

18. On Poulydamas as warner, see Schadewaldt 1966: 104; Reinhardt 1961: 272–77; and Redfield 1975: 143–47.

19. Taplin 1992: 157 defends Hektor's rejection of Poulydamas's counsel. On the eagle-and-serpent portent and its multiple meanings in relation to the multiple plans of Zeus, see Schadewaldt 1966: 105, and especially Clay 1999.

gap open between the request of Thetis and Zeus's fulfillment: this very gap furnishes the ground of possibility for the action of the *Iliad*. When Agamemnon takes Briseis away, Achilles' response establishes what he must imagine to be a simple scenario. His goal is to make the Greeks suffer until they restore his honor; his means, to engage the participation of the supreme god. With Zeus behind his plan there would seem to be no obstacle to its swift fulfillment (Lattimore 1951: 30; Morrison 1992: 36–43). The example of Apollo's response to Chryses suggests that a virtually instantaneous solution could be expected.[20] If it had occurred, there would be no *Iliad*; but it did not, and the *Iliad* is the story of what happened *instead*, the underdetermined Plan of Zeus that frustrates and replaces the Plan of Achilles to determine the future through Zeus's power. Thus the action of the *Iliad* is built upon the folktale motif of the "backfiring wish": a mortal speaks words that magically determine the future, but the meaning of those words and the future they create is not what the mortal intended or desired.[21]

This misfiring of Achilles' plan, as well as his displaced conflict with Zeus and the shifting stakes that propel it, reveal a characteristic of the action trajectory that might be called "errancy." Errancy would also seem to be a theme of the action as well as a description of its direction. The words of Achilles' request, apparently clear in meaning and sure of fulfillment, expand and drift unpredictably as Zeus improvises his plan and the divine antagonists of Troy strive to obstruct it.[22] From the moment Thetis hears Achilles' prayer and must inform her son that Zeus is vacationing among the Ethiopians and cannot even be contacted for twelve days, until the death of Patroklos at the end of book 16, the *Iliad* traces the meandering path between Achilles' request and its surprisingly remote fulfillment. Moreover, Zeus's plan has also come to include a continuation—the death of Patroklos—that obscures the point at which fulfillment has been achieved. After wandering about before reaching its explicit goal, the narrative eventually overshoots it, producing an outcome Achilles never envisioned, and obviating his plan to receive honor before it has achieved its goal.[23]

Nevertheless, when Thetis tries to console her son by reminding him that Zeus has granted what he asked for, and Achilles replies that his wish has become meaningless since Patroklos has been killed, the "plot" of Achilles to win honor is still the main plot (i.e., action trajectory), if only in the sense that through the beginning of book 18 the *Iliad* progresses as the story of how

20. Rabel 1997: 50–54 argues that Achilles gets the idea for his plea to Zeus from Apollo's response to Chryses' prayer.

21. Compare Nagler 1974: 134 n. 6; Murnaghan 1997: 27; and Rousseau 2001: 146.

22. Compare Lynn-George 1988: 269 ("the narrative becomes a story in which direct linear progression is interrupted in a complicated space of reversals and deferred action, returns, counter-movements and collisions"); also 37–41 on the Plan(s) of Zeus; Morrison 1992 on misdirection; Murnaghan 1997: 23–28; and Rousseau 2001: 144–52. Brooks's analysis of the narrative middle as "the 'dilatory space' of postponement and error" is fundamental; see Brooks 1984: 90–108.

23. Compare Murnaghan 1997: 23.

Achilles' "plot" misfired. But at this very point the events of the epic spin even further off their original course as Achilles develops a new goal, that of avenging Patroklos by killing Hektor and many other Trojans. Achilles' indifference to Agamemnon's formal reconciliation in book 19 marks not the resolution of Achilles' plan to win honor but its irrelevance to a story that has now taken off in a new and previously only vaguely foreseen direction.[24]

But just as the apparently imminent goal of defeat for the Greeks and concomitant honor for Achilles could be approached only by a crooked path of delay, the new goal of vengeance against Hektor, apparently easy and swift for the mighty Achilles to achieve, immediately withdraws from the hero's grasp as he must impatiently tolerate the preparation of new armor by Hephaistos, Agamemnon's speech and offerings of reconciliation, the refreshments of the Achaian troops, and the disorganized interference of divinities on the battlefield.[25] The greatest of Greek heroes can only kill his opponent after two thousand more lines of narration, and even then he does it through the surprising ruse of Athena. But when this goal has been reached, it too turns out not to be a fulfillment after all, as the death of Hektor does not satisfy Achilles' anger, and he continues—without effect or completion—to abuse the Trojan's corpse.

Achilles' killing of Hektor was foretold by Zeus (15.68, 17.198–208) and Patroklos (16.852–55) and thus cannot be a total surprise to audiences when it becomes part of the action. (Although not everything foretold in the *Iliad* is narrated there: Zeus also foretells the fall of Troy [15.70–71], and Hektor foretells the death of Achilles [22.358–60].) But when after killing Hektor and interminably abusing his corpse Achilles remains unsatisfied, the action seems to have lost trajectory altogether.[26] The story has arrived at a unique moment: for the first time since Chryses supplicated Agamemnon, it does not advance toward the fulfillment of an explicit goal. When the story regains direction, the new goal is one that no previous foretelling of events has predicted: the ransoming of Hektor's corpse.[27] To be sure, Priam has mentioned that he would attempt to ransom the corpse (22.415–22), but since he has no means of bringing this about, and makes no effort to do so (not even praying for divine assistance), his longing does nothing to direct or advance the story. It is Apollo's spontaneous inclination to save the dead Hektor from abuse, and his sense that Achilles' conduct has transgressed the bounds of decency and must be checked, that now furnishes the goal that advances the story toward its conclusion. Thus for the last time the action of the *Iliad* strays from the goals that have previously guided it forward.

24. Compare Heubeck 1991: 471 and Scully 2003: 37.

25. Compare Morrison 1992: 43–48; on this and other long delays in the plot of the *Iliad*, also see chapter 3 (or Heiden 2000a: 46–48).

26. Compare Lynn-George 1988: 230 on the situation at the beginning of book 24.

27. See Morrison 1992: 83–93.

SOME PRELIMINARY THEMATIC IMPLICATIONS

The novelty and power of this final twist highlight thematic developments whose investigation would extend the analysis well beyond the immediate question of the trajectory of events. While in terms of character dilemmas the ransoming of Hektor's body carries the story line far from the goal that advances the action of the *Iliad* through most of its course (winning honor for Achilles from the Achaians), thematically the story's conclusion returns to a point like that where it began: a powerless, elderly man supplicates a powerful young warrior for the return of his child, and with the help of the gods achieves his wish.[28] After the middle of book 1, when Chryseis is returned to him, the priest Chryses never reappears in the story, or receives so much as a single mention. In terms of the action trajectory, his supplication of Agamemnon and its immediate aftermath serve as an Auxiliary, merely providing the occasion for the outbreak of conflict between Agamemnon and Achilles and Achilles' eventual withdrawal and prayer to Zeus (Clark 2001: 5). When viewed from the vantage point of, say, book 18, the old priest's supplication seems to be important as nothing more than a preparatory event in a story whose real subject is the misfired plot of the semidivine hero Achilles. But Homer has a surprise in store: when the *Iliad* concludes, it turns out that the story of the misfired plot of Achilles, now left completely behind, has after all been preparation for the majestic narration of an old man's successful supplication. Thus a thematic trajectory asserts itself at the very point where the trajectory of events seems to have been interrupted.[29]

This thematic trajectory merits further investigation. But since the themes of the epic emerge from the dilemmas and actions of the characters, the next chapter will continue analysis of the trajectory of events. So far our application of a provisional "single action" reading function has shown the poem's indications of an overarching event trajectory in which the central agency of Zeus creates or addresses all the dilemma-situations in which the other characters deliberate, plan, and act. This overarching event trajectory furnishes a degree of orientation to a reader who deploys an "orientation" function. But a practical orientation function might also seek relatively accessible points of orientation throughout the telling. Does the *Iliad* provide indications of such orientation? The next chapter will simulate an application of the Move-analysis that probes for shorter subtrajectories that might help the reader maintain orientation as the story proceeds.

28. Book 24 reprises many themes introduced in book 1. Many scholars have discussed the relationship between books 1 and 24; Whitman 1958: 257–60 is perhaps the best-known treatment, but it is hardly unique; the earliest I have found is Peppmüller 1876: xxiii–xxiv. Heiden 2000a: 34 n. 1 contains an extensive bibliography.

29. Compare Heubeck 1991: 473: "mit dieser äusseren Rückkehr zum Anfang zugleich ein innerer Fortschritt sich vollzogen habe, dass also die 'Ausbuchtung' des Geschehens mehr sei als ein Umweg, der ebensogut hätte unterblieben können."

2

Event Trajectories in the "Books" of the *Iliad*

In the analysis in chapter 1 the "orientation/single action" function found, in the problem of Zeus's promise to Thetis, a trajectory that relates all the epic's events to a single point of orientation. But the reader of such a long epic might well feel the need for more local orientation. To some extent the analysis in chapter 1 found local orientation in the major subordinate Moves, such as the polemical configuration that pits Zeus against Hera-Athena-Poseidon. But these Moves might not be enough; the events of the polemical configuration spread out discontinuously over about ten books (around six thousand verses), during which they also compete for attention with the testing configuration pitting Zeus against Hektor. So it is plausible that readers would want shorter and more continuous trajectories. To investigate whether the *Iliad* also indicates shorter trajectories, the heuristic model now postulates a "short event trajectory" reading function.

As we bring the "short trajectory" function into simulation, it seems—at least provisionally—to find certain definite indications in the transmitted articulation of the epic, the twenty-four so-called books of the *Iliad*. Numbered in a continuous series, in our printed editions these marked segments resemble the numbered "books" of epics like the *Aeneid* and *Paradise Lost*, whose development they influenced, as well as the "chapters" of novels, whose development they also influenced (Stevick 1970: 162–71). Since a reader of the *Iliad* is always reading a certain numbered "book," whose verses are also numbered with respect to the beginning of that book, the poem, through its marked articulation, does furnish a certain local orientation. Of course, if the orientation did not converge with any aspect of the poem's legibility, then it would be merely nominal, and of little practical use to the work of collaborative reading. This chapter will investigate the question of whether the marked articulation in turn indicates other indicators that offer practical orientation to a reader. There are a number of ways a system of articulation might orient a reader to a poem's legibility, but this chapter will investigate only one: whether the transmitted articulation provides orientation to trajectories that give direction to the events narrated in the respective segments.

The heuristic model will therefore implement "orientation," "marked articulation," and "event trajectory" functions in tandem. This simulation extends and develops an earlier study (Heiden 1998a) that was discussed in the introduction.

It found that all twenty-three segment markers in the *Iliad* occur between scenes of low consequence in the narrative (these end the marked segments) and scenes of high consequence (which begin marked segments). It also showed that the only low consequence/high consequence junctures are those marked: none occur within the transmitted segments, and thus no "book divisions" alternative to those transmitted could replicate the distinctive feature that all the transmitted marker placements have in common.[1] The marker placements in the *Iliad* cue attention to useful information about the organization of events in the epic. In this sense the markers cooperate with the poem's other legible signs, and readers who take guidance from the articulation therefore also work in legitimate collaboration with the poet's work. Of course, some scholars may wish to ignore the transmitted articulation, and they are free do so. But they run a substantial risk of disorientation and diminished cooperation with the poet's work in organizing the story.[2]

EVENT TRAJECTORIES IN THE MARKED SEGMENTS

The action trajectory of a "book" of the *Iliad* can be seen very clearly when the narrative is analyzed in terms of problems, goals, decisions, and actions. Again and again a character or character group confronts a *problem situation*; they take a *decision* to deal with that problem situation; they undertake an *action* in accordance with that decision; and a certain low-consequence *aftermath* follows that is distinct from the agent's explicit intention. Frequently the problem and the decision to deal with it are narrated together, in the same scene or even the same speech; the action and the aftermath are usually narrated separately. The trajectory therefore normally consists of three stages, a Problem/Decision stage, an Action stage, and an Aftermath stage, in that order. Occasionally, the Aftermath stage may be lacking. Each stage may comprise a subcomplex of several scenes. Since in the imaginary world of the *Iliad*, as in the real world, actions often confront some resistance that obstructs the path to the goal, most actions in the narrative when analyzed also display one or several Auxiliary substages. A complete sequence of a Problem/Decision stage, an Action stage, and an Aftermath stage will be referred to as a Problem/Decision-Action-Aftermath Trajectory (P/D-A-A trajectory).

Iliad 24 perfectly illustrates a P/D-A-A trajectory that is coextensive with a transmitted "book." The Problem/Decision stage identifies Achilles' abuse of

1. The Teichoskopia, for example, occurs in the middle of book 3, and it is similar to scenes that precede marked "book divisions" in that it has low consequence for the passages that follow it. However, the next passage after the Teichoskopia, in which the Trojan heralds summon Priam to the swearing of oaths, is not a "high-consequence" scene, since it only affects the scene that immediately follows it. Thus the junction is not like those that coincide with the segment markings. For further discussion see Heiden 1998a: 74–75.

2. This would be true whatever the provenance of the segment markings. But some scholars have allowed themselves to be distracted from the function of the markers by speculation about their supposed postcompositional origin. The weak grounding of this speculation is discussed at the end of this chapter.

Iliad **Book 24: $\text{MOVE}_{\text{Zeus}}$**

Problem/Decision	**Aux**	**Action**	**Aftermath**
[Ach abuses corpse; Zeus decides Ach must return corpse to Priam] 24.1–76	[Zeus arranges return of corpse] 24.77–321	[Priam retrieves corpse] 24.322–691	[Hektor lamented and buried] 24.692–804

FIGURE 2.1. Trajectory of the events in *Iliad* 24.

Hektor's corpse as a Problem for Apollo and other Olympians, and it narrates Zeus's Decision that Achilles should return the corpse to Priam. The Action stage (which includes Auxiliary preparations performed by Zeus and others) narrates Priam's journey to Achilles' encampment and his return with the corpse. The low-consequence Aftermath stage narrates the lamentation and funeral at Troy.[3] Figure 2.1 concisely analyzes the trajectory of the events in *Iliad* 24.[4]

Like the dactylic hexameter, this simple pattern can accommodate enormous variation without losing its basic shape. In one simple variant, especially common in "books" featuring a great deal of battlefield action, a single Problem situation generates two or more P/D-A-A trajectories that succeed one another. Book 2 presents an elementary example. The governing Problem situation calls for Zeus to renew the fighting so he can fulfill his promise to Thetis.[5] His Decision is to send Dream to Agamemnon and tell him to prepare the troops for battle. This leads to a pair of parallel Actions, each of which is itself a P/D-A-A trajectory. Action^1 narrates how the Greek army takes the field: Auxiliary = Agamemnon tests the troops (2.35–393); Action = the Achaians prepare for battle (2.394–483); Aftermath = the catalogue of Achaian ships (2.484–785). Action^2 narrates how Zeus got the Trojan army to take the battlefield: Auxiliary = Iris exhorts Hektor (2.786–806); Action = Trojans marshal on the plain (2.807–815); Aftermath = catalogue of Trojans and allies (2.816–77).

Some other variants of the basic P/D-A-A trajectory can be identified, but the best way to observe them is to analyze the actual "books," one at a time. The

3. Compare MacLeod 1982: 14: "The plot of Book 24 may be roughly divided into three parts: (a) the gods show pity, (b) a man accepts a supplication, (c) a lament and burial are achieved." Also compare Nicolai 1973: 116–17.

4. For detailed analysis of some of the stages, see the discussion of book 24 later, with figure 2.14.

5. Compare Kirk 1985: 48: "Book 2 can be seen as a whole as an elaborate and interrupted description of the process of carrying Zeus's oath into effect, at least to the extent of bringing the forces on either side to the point of engagement." Also compare Nicolai 1973: 93 on Zeus's initiative, which orients the expectation (*Erwartung*) of the listener. But Nicolai ends this "chapter" at 2.483, leaving the catalogues in a separate "chapter" which, he has to admit (94), seems to lack a "center" (*Kapitelzentrum*). My analysis shows that the catalogues attach to the trajectory of 2.1–483 as its Aftermath.

Nicolai's analyses of "chapters" usually do not coincide with the transmitted "books" and do not adequately explain their trajectories, mainly because Nicolai overlooks the Aftermath stage. Nicolai correctly recognized that in most "chapters" the motivations of the characters are not the sole organizing factor, and a role is also played by the "intention of the narrator," which leads the action toward a peak (*Höhepunkt*) that is not the same as the characters' goal (*Handlungsziel*). In my analyses, the scenes Nicolai would identify as the *Höhepunkte* function as "Aftermath" stages in their respective event trajectories.

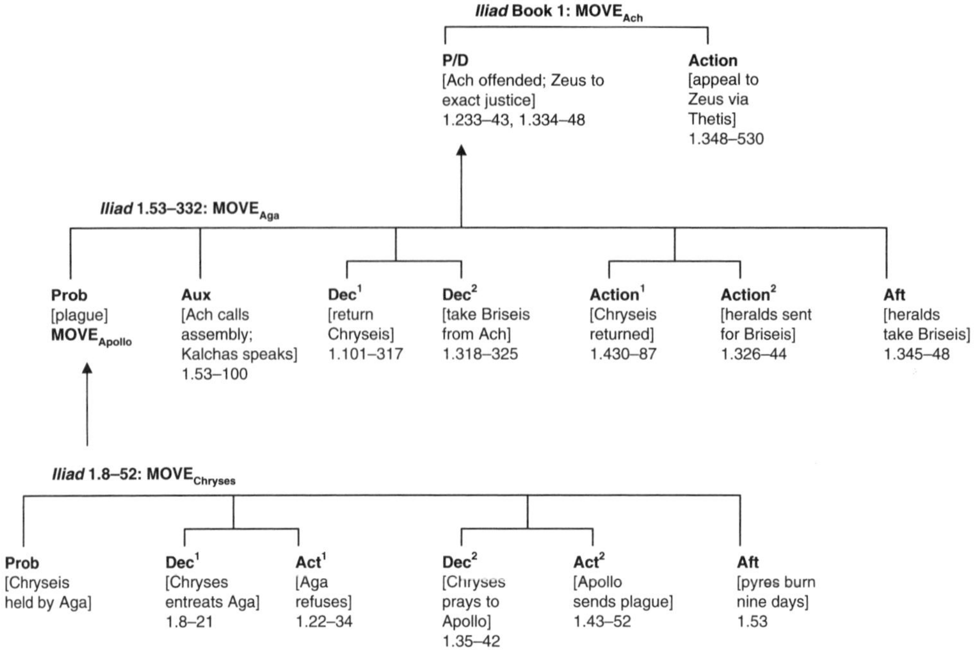

FIGURE 2.2. *Iliad* 1.8-348 Problem/Decision element (detail). Read starting from lower left.

analysis will show that each book does narrate a single, coherent P/D-A-A trajectory, and thus that it furnishes a reader with local orientation in the developing story. (Book 2 does not have a separate section in the analysis, since it has been discussed above.)

Book 1

In the proem, the narrator provides the reader with a clear outline of the trajectory of events to come in book 1. The epic will tell how multitudes of Greek heroes died through the wrath of Achilles and the Plan of Zeus (1.1–5). The wrath and the plan arise from the quarrel between Achilles and Agamemnon (1.6–7); that is, in the Action, the quarrel motivates Achilles' wrath and Zeus's Plan (Marks 2002: 13). As the unfolding narrative reveals, this means that the quarrel (1.8–348) furnishes the Problem situation in which Achilles makes the Decision to call upon Zeus.[6] Action = Achilles appeals to Zeus through Thetis (1.345–530); Aftermath = Hera complains to Zeus about Thetis (1.531–611).

Figure 2.2 analyzes the structure of the complex Problem/Decision stage (1.8–348), the quarrel that leads to Achilles' decision. Move (Chryses) is a

6. Latacz 2000b: 8–9 articulates book 1 into four parts: (1) the Proem (1–12a), (2) the Vorgeschichte des Streites ("Narrative Antecedent to the Quarrel," 12b–52), (3) the Quarrel (53–305), and (4) the first consequences of the Quarrel (306–611). The basic difference between Latacz's framework and mine is that Latacz makes no reference to the purposes articulated by the narrator and the characters, and the way these purposes impart forward direction to the action.

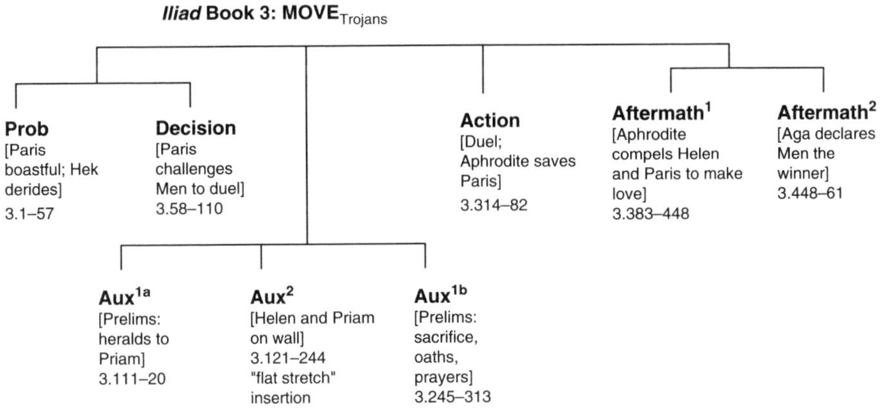

FIGURE 2.3. Event trajectory of book 3. Men = Menelaos, Prelims = Preliminaries.

subordinate stage that explains the quarrel, as the narrator indicates clearly when Chryses' appeal is introduced (1.8–11: "What god . . . set them together in bitter collision? . . . Apollo, who in anger at the king drove the foul pestilence along the host . . . since Atreus's son had dishonored Chryses, priest of Apollo").[7] The Problem situation that confronts the assembly—i.e., the plague—is labeled Move (Apollo) because the narrator initially presents the quarrel as if Apollo intended to instigate it. When the assembly is narrated, however, the critical agent is Agamemnon, for the assembly scene represents how Agamemnon reached his Decision for ending the plague. The Decision has two parts: (1) returning Chryseis to her father, and (2) taking Briseis for himself as compensation for Chryseis. The actual return of Chryseis (1.430–87) is the Action that fulfills the first Decision; the sending of the heralds for Briseis (1.326–48) fulfills the second Decision.

However, when the heralds come for Briseis, a new Problem exists, namely the offense to Achilles and what he will do about it: Achilles' appeal to Zeus is not a consequence of his *quarrel* with Agamemnon—i.e., the purely verbal confrontation—but of Agamemnon's actual *taking* of Briseis. Achilles' reply to the heralds explains his Decision: he will give up Briseis, but he considers the offense justification for allowing the Achaians to perish (1.338–44; also 1.233–43). Thus, the whole complex of scenes from 1.8 to 1.348 together frames the dilemma in which Achilles makes his decision.

Book 3

A straightforward P/D-A-A trajectory[8] is given variety by doubling the Aftermath stage, and by inserting a lengthy Auxiliary passage in which the preparations for the duel are split in two by the Teichoskopia (see fig. 2.3).

7. Compare Nicolai 1973: 91 (whose analysis is otherwise quite different). Also Clark 2001: 3–5.
8. Compare Nicolai 1973: 94–95.

Book 4

This book is even simpler than book 3. The Problem posed is that of restarting the war; Zeus decides that the Trojans should break the oath. Auxiliary: Athena persuades Pandaros to shoot an arrow at Menelaos. Action: Pandaros wounds Menelaos, breaking the truce (4.73–219).[9] The Aftermath stage is doubled: Aftermath^1 = Agamemnon rouses the Achaians (4.220–421); Aftermath^2 = armies clash on battlefield (4.422–544).

Book 5

Scholars who have investigated the functional narrative systems of the *Iliad* have usually felt that book 5 is not among them; several, such as Nicolai, have identified a *Diomedeia* beginning as early as 4.422 and ending as late as 6.136.[10] But the indecisive fighting begun at the end of book 4 conforms to the pattern whereby the events in a book of the *Iliad* move in the direction of an Aftermath that lacks forward momentum. Thus a new event trajectory begins exactly where book 5 begins.

Book 5 begins with Athena addressing the implicit Problem of Achilles' absence (suggested in Apollo's encouragement of the Trojans at 4.512–13) by putting strength into Diomedes, who will put the Trojans to rout and eventually also cause mischief for Aphrodite and Ares. So the basic action trajectory consists of Athena's Decision to help Diomedes, and Diomedes carrying out Athena's plan (the Action). But Athena's plan meets resistance from Apollo and the Trojans, and as a result her initiative must be renewed several times. The basic Problem/Decision-Action structure presented above is worked out as five P/D-A-A trajectories, the first three led by decisions of Athena, the fourth led by a decision of Apollo, and the last led by a decision of Athena and Hera acting together.

The first two Trajectories are relatively simple. Move^1 (Athena) = P/D: Athena inspires Diomedes (5.1–8); Action: Diomedes kills Phegeus (5.9–20); Aftermath^1: Hephaistos saves Phegeus's brother Idaios (5.20–24); Aftermath^2: Diomedes captures the horses of Phegeus and Idaios (5.25–26); Aftermath^3: Trojans become angry (5.27–29). Move^2 (Athena) = P/D: Trojans angry; Athena removes Ares from the battlefield; Action: Achaians kill many Trojans (5.37–84); Aftermath: general view of Diomedes scattering the enemy (5.85–94).

In Athena's third Move (5.95–454) the Action stage is developed into an elaborate polemical configuration. Figure 2.4 presents a detailed analysis.

In Apollo's Move (5.454–710) the Decision and Action stages are both developed. Apollo's Decision to help the Trojans (5.454–93) develops in three Auxiliary substages before the Trojan counterattack actually occurs (Aux^1 = Apollo rouses Ares, 5.454–59; Aux^2 = Ares rouses Trojans, 5.460–70; Aux^3 = Sarpedon rouses Hektor, 5.471–93). The Action (Trojan counterattack, 5.494–710) becomes a lengthy polemical configuration as the Greeks respond, the Trojans respond in turn, and so forth. The

9. Compare Nicolai 1973: 95. Again, after a good start, Nicolai's analysis goes astray by overlooking the Aftermath.

10. For a summary of such analyses, see Stanley 1993: 338 n. 4.

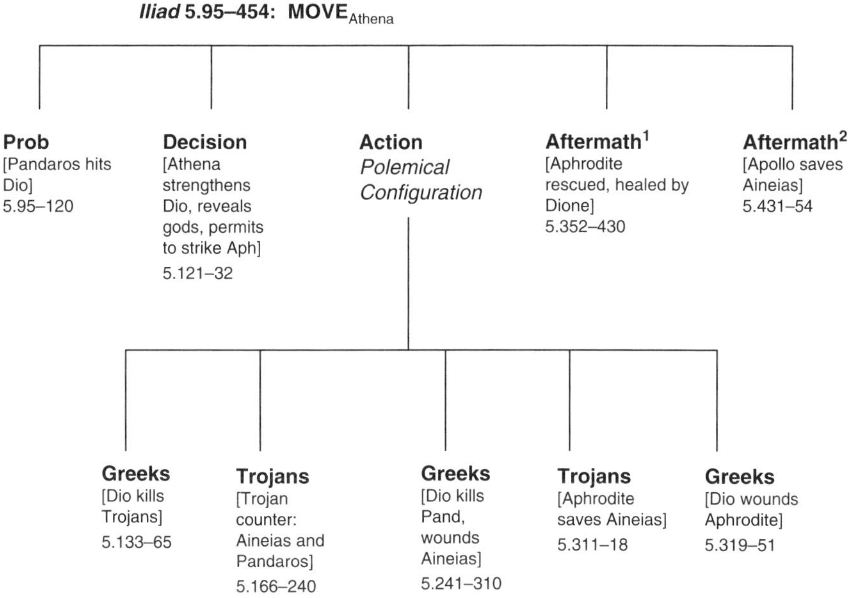

FIGURE 2.4. Athena's third Move in *Iliad* book 5. Aph = Aphrodite, Dio = Diomedes, Pand = Pandaros.

Aftermath stage in this Trajectory is the list of Hektor's victims (5.703–10), which follows the narrator's report of the effect of the counterattack on the battle.

Book 5 concludes with a simple P/D-A-A trajectory in which Athena and Hera decide to help the Greeks (5.711–834), Athena helps Diomedes attack Ares (Action, 5.835–63), and Ares flees to Olympus, where he whines to his father Zeus (Aftermath, 5.864–908). The Aftermath of this particular Move also concludes book 5 and serves as the Aftermath that completes the whole book's standard trajectory.

Book 6

In this book the Problem is the Greek rout of the Trojans (6.1–72), and the Decision, taken by Helenos, is to send Hektor to Troy to instruct the Trojan women to make a dedication to Athena and pray to her (6.73–101). The Action therefore has two parts: Hektor's transmission of the instructions and the ritual performance by the Trojan women (6.237–311).[11] In the Aftermath stage Hektor encounters Paris, Helen, Andromache, and then Paris again as they leave the city together (6.312–529).

Before Hektor can leave the Trojan fighters, however, he must rally them, so that they can continue the fight in his absence. This event, which is Auxiliary to

11. Compare Nicolai 1973: 88–90 on the "plot arc" (*Handlungsbogen*) that organizes *Iliad* 6: it begins with Helenos's counsel (6.73), for which the catalogue of deaths (6.5–65) prepares; the plot-goal (*Handlungsziel*) is winning Athena's help; and the arc concludes when Hektor returns to the battlefield. The catalogue of deaths and Helenos's counsel correspond to the Problem-Decision stage of my analysis, and the supplication of Athena corresponds to the Action stage. Nicolai's model lacks an Aftermath stage, but he identifies Hektor's meeting with Andromache as the *Höhepunkt* of book 6; on Nicolai's model, see further note 5 here.

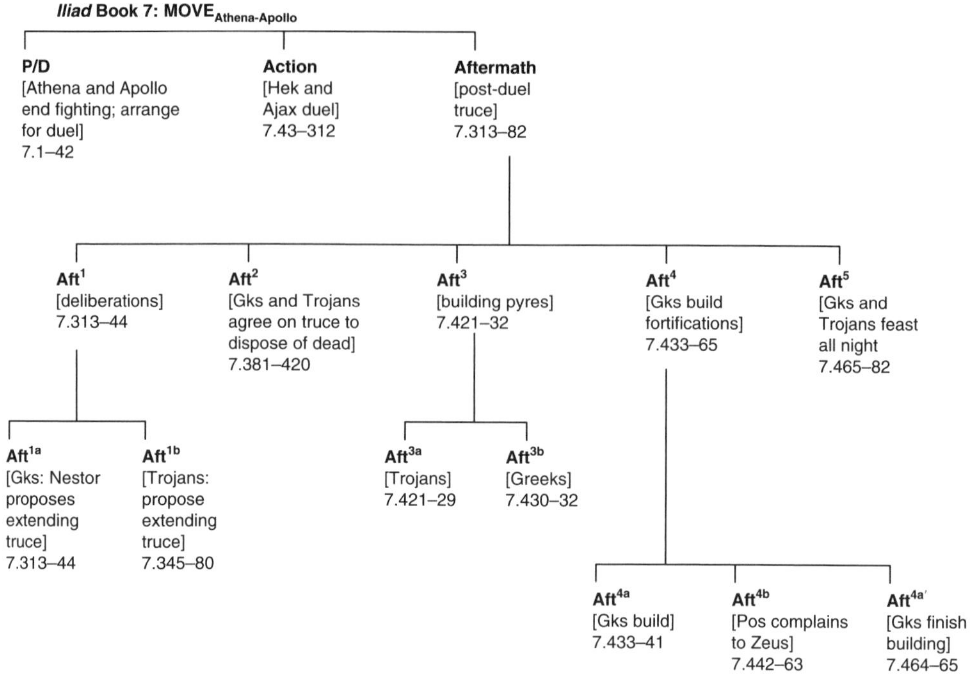

FIGURE 2.5. Trajectory of book 7.

the main Action, in itself develops in a standard action trajectory: P/D: Helenos advises Hektor and Aineias to rally the troops (6.73–82); Action: Hektor successfully rallies the troops and departs (6.102–18); Aftermath: Glaukos and Diomedes meet on the battlefield (6.119–236).

Book 7

In book 7 the Problem/Decision stage is the plan of Athena and Apollo to end the day of battle by having Hektor and Ajax fight a duel. The Action is the duel; the Aftermath is the truce that follows the duel. Five events occur during this truce, two of them further subdivided into parallel Greek and Trojan scenes (the deliberations and the pyres) and a third into parallel mortal and divine scenes (the Greeks build fortifications, while Poseidon complains to Zeus about them in the temporal "flat stretch" between the beginning of the building and its completion). The development of the Aftermath stage is somewhat busy, but it does not complicate the trajectory of events at all.[12] Figure 2.5 illustrates the whole trajectory.

12. Kirk finds book 7 less coherent than its predecessors. "So far every Book of the *Iliad* has contributed . . . to the monumental plan of the poem. . . . The seventh Book, by contrast, seems to falter slightly in its monumental role, as well as in the coherence of events generally—this is reflected in the clumsy Hellenistic title of the Book, *Ἕκτορος καὶ Αἴαντος μονομαχία. Νεκρῶν ἀναίρεσις*. . . . Hektor and Paris return to battle as indicated at the end of bk 6, but are soon interrupted by Apollo and the proposal for a second formal duel, curiously like that of bk 3 but without stated or accomplished purpose. It is bizarrely curtailed by the heralds, and Hektor survives" (1990: 230). Kirk sees in books 7 and 8 "a new kind of arbitrariness in the selection and preparation of topics."

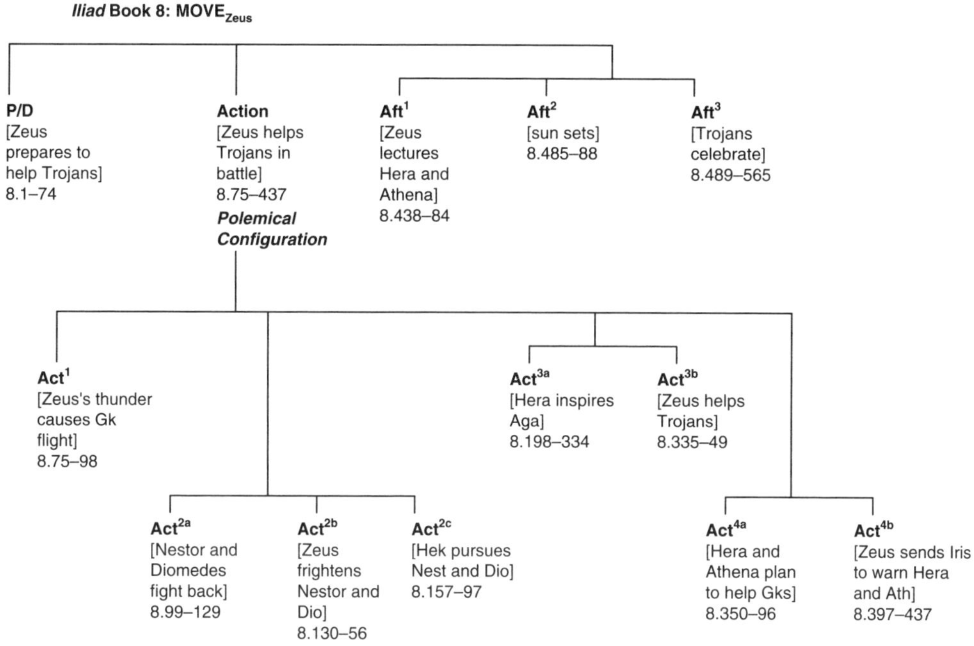

FIGURE 2.6. Polemical configuration in *Iliad* book 8. Ath = Athena, Nest = Nestor.

Book 8

Kirk (1990: 293) says of book 8: "It is characteristic of the Book as a whole that most of its actions and initiatives, whether divine or human, are soon abandoned or reversed. Only Zeus's initial determination is ultimately maintained." This formulation is correct with regard to Zeus's leading role, but otherwise it puts the relationships backward: the other initiatives are abandoned or reversed *because* they conflict with Zeus's, and Zeus *reverses them* in enacting his plan. The Action stage in which Zeus helps the Trojans develops as a polemical configuration, as the Greeks at first fight back on their own initiative, then with indirect help from Hera, and then Athena and Hera finally attempt to help them in person.[13] The Aftermath stage has three parts: Zeus's lectures to Hera and Athena (8.438–84); the setting of the sun (8.485–88); and the Trojans' celebration in the plain (8.489–565). Figure 2.6 includes a detailed analysis of the polemical configuration, revealing the clear, regular three-stage event trajectory.

Book 9

The Embassy has one of the simplest event trajectories of any book in the *Iliad*. The Problem is the threat to the Greeks of the Trojan encampment on the plain. The Decision is Agamemnon's offer of material compensation to Achilles if

13. Nimis 1999: 73–78 discusses "thresholds of decision-making" in *Iliad* 8.

he returns to the fighting. The Action is the embassy. The Aftermath is the report of the delegates to the Greek leaders.

Book 10
In this book the Problem/Decision stage is doubled: parallel councils, Greek and Trojan, each plan for the reconnaissance scene that begins at 10.338; P/D^1: Greek council sends Odysseus and Diomedes to reconnoitre (10.1–298); P/D^2: Trojan council sends Dolon to reconnoitre (10.299–337). The reconnaissance scene is also doubled. $Action^1$: Odysseus and Diomedes kill Dolon; $Action^2$: Odysseus and Diomedes kill sleeping Thracians (10.465–525). The Aftermath is the return of Odysseus and Diomedes to the Greek encampment.[14]

Book 11
In an elaborate Problem stage, a series of Greek setbacks accumulate to produce a problem situation for Achilles and the Greeks (11.1–594). Achilles' Decision to deal with this Problem by sending Patroklos to Nestor (11.595–615) furnishes the event trajectory for the rest of the book. $Action^1$: Patroklos confers with Nestor (11.616–54); $Action^2$: Nestor on behalf of the Greeks takes the opportunity to plead for Achilles' help (11.655–802). In the Aftermath stage, Patroklos pauses to take care of the wounded Eurypylos (11.803–47). Thus the action design of book 11 is actually a very simple, even routine trajectory, except that its Problem stage is developed to such extraordinary length that it can temporarily obscure the direction of the narrative.[15]

Book 12
In book 12 the Problem is that the Greek fortifications halt the Trojan advance.[16] The Trojans attempt several solutions, but their successes are only partial until Zeus helps Hektor complete the task.[17] Thus book 12 comprises multiple P/D-A-A trajectories, three to be exact. $Move^1$ (Trojans) = Problem: Trench halts

14. Hainsworth 1993: 155 divides book 10 into "almost exactly balanced halves" at 298/299. But the relevant principle of organization is the event trajectory, not balance of quantities.

15. Hainsworth's analysis of book 11 (1993: 212) loses the forest for the trees. After focusing predominantly on the narrative of fighting in 11.1–283, Hainsworth continues: "The climax of Agamemnon's *aristeia* is followed by a counter-*aristeia* of Hektor, briefly told (284–309). The pattern of the Book then settles into the theme of a fighting retreat culminating in the disablement of the hero: Diomedes 310–400, Odysseus 401–88, Aias and Makhaon 489–574, Eurupulos 575–95. This is interwoven with the successes of Paris as archer. Finally, by a neat linking into the episodes of Makhaon and Eurupulos, the narrative picks up again the story of Akhilleus and foreshadows the entry of Patroklos into the battle (596–848)."

16. Compare Nicolai 1973: 102.

17. According to Hainsworth book 12 is "one of the most weakly constructed Books of the *Iliad*" (1993: 313). Yet later in the same discussion he observes that "the twelfth Book is a well defined episode . . ." and refers to "the tremendous epic moment of Hektor standing in the open gate, a moment *towards which the poet is hastening* from the moment when he brought the Trojans up to the Achaean trench" (315; emphasis in original). The latter statement is basically correct, but it also explains Hainsworth's confusion, because while Hektor's breach of the wall is indeed the goal of the book—i.e., the goal of Zeus in the book—from beginning to end, the poet does not hasten toward it but creates resistances that must be overcome; this is part of his usual repertoire. Hainsworth does not see that resistance is built into the design of the story, both in book 12 and everywhere else in the *Iliad*. The "weakness" it entails, if any, is inseparable from the epic's themes and not merely technical.

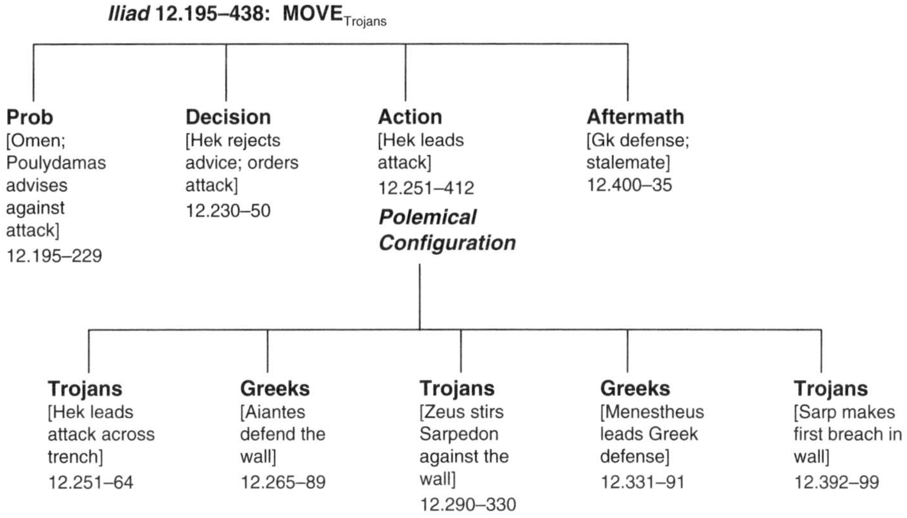

FIGURE 2.7. Analysis of Move^{2} in book 12. Gk = Greek, Sarp = Sarpedon.

Trojan advance (12.1–59); Decision: Poulydamas persuades Hektor to order a Trojan attack on foot (12.60–80); Action^{1}: the Trojans dismount and prepare to cross; Action^{2}: Asios, acting separately, charges across the trench, where the Lapithae repulse him (12.108–74); Aftermath: description of general fighting; the Lapithae kill some Trojans (12.175–94). In the second trajectory (12.195–435) the Action stage is developed into a lengthy polemical configuration. Figure 2.7 analyzes Move^{2} (Trojans) in detail.

In the last P/D-A-A trajectory, Zeus makes a Decision to help Hektor (12.437–38). The Action is Hektor breaking through the wall (12.439–70). The Aftermath is very brief, the narrator's general description of the panicking Greeks (12.470–71). This Aftermath also concludes the book.

Book 13

In this book, the P/D stage narrates how Zeus's inattention creates an opportunity for Poseidon to help the Trojans.[18] With his support, they halt the Trojan advance against the ships (the Action), and neither side can maintain momentum. The Aftermath stage is the exchange of taunts between Ajax and Hektor (13.808–37). Since, as is usual in the battle narratives, the divine initiative meets resistance (here from the Trojans), Poseidon's attempted Action must be repeated. Book 13 thus comprises two P/D-A-A trajectories, of which the second is much longer than the first, mainly because its Action stage is developed into a massive polemical configuration. Figure 2.8 illustrates the second subtrajectory, with detailed analysis of the polemical configuration in the Action stage.

18. Compare Nicolai 1973: 103.

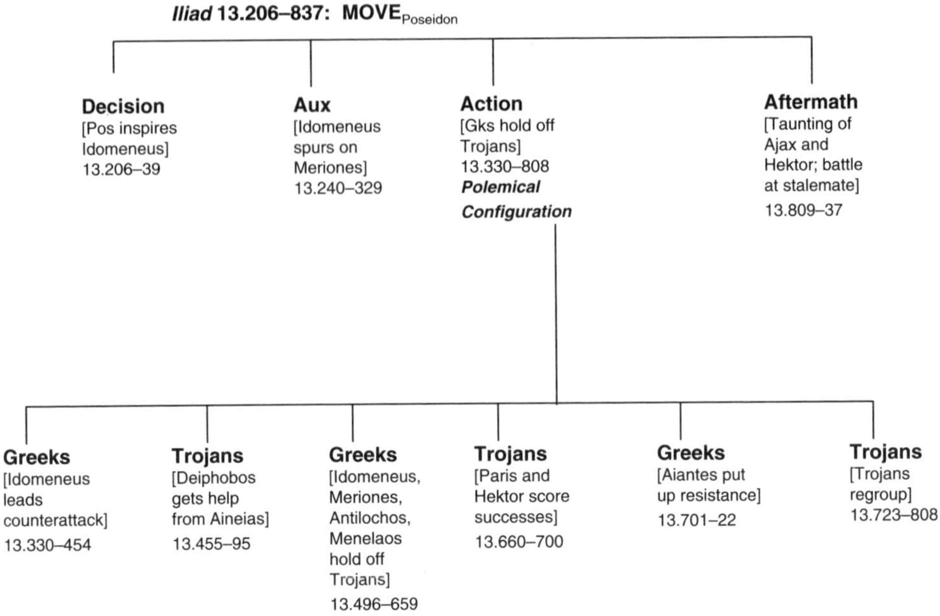

FIGURE 2.8. Second subtrajectory in *Iliad* book 13. Pos = Poseidon.

Book 14

In book 14 the success of the Trojans is a Problem for both the Greeks and their divine supporters, Hera and Poseidon. The Greek leaders and Hera both face the same Problem, but they plan to deal with it separately, so that two Problem/Decision stages prepare for one Action. In the first, the disabled Greek leaders confer and decide to encourage their men (14.1–152). In the second, Hera decides to help the Greeks by putting Zeus out of commission, so that Poseidon can support them more freely. Her seduction of Zeus is therefore Auxiliary to the main Action, the Greek counterattack that occurs with Poseidon's assistance. The Aftermath stage in this trajectory is the narrator's invocation of the Muses to recall the names of the most deadly Greeks (14. 508–22).

Book 15

In book 15, one major Problem/Decision stage (Zeus's plan to fulfill his promise to Thetis by helping the Trojans, 15.1–261)[19] governs a doubled action-aftermath trajectory. Action^{1}: Hektor, inspired by Apollo, leads a Trojan counterattack (15.262–389); Aftermath^{1}: Patroklos hears the Greeks' distress and rushes back to Achilles (15.390–404). Action^{2}: Hektor continues the counterattack (15.405–725); Aftermath^{2}: Ajax holds the Trojans off temporarily (15.726–46). The P/D stage includes several Auxiliary actions (Zeus sending Hera to summon Iris and Apollo; Zeus sending Iris to Poseidon and Apollo to the battlefield).

19. Compare Nicolai 1973: 105.

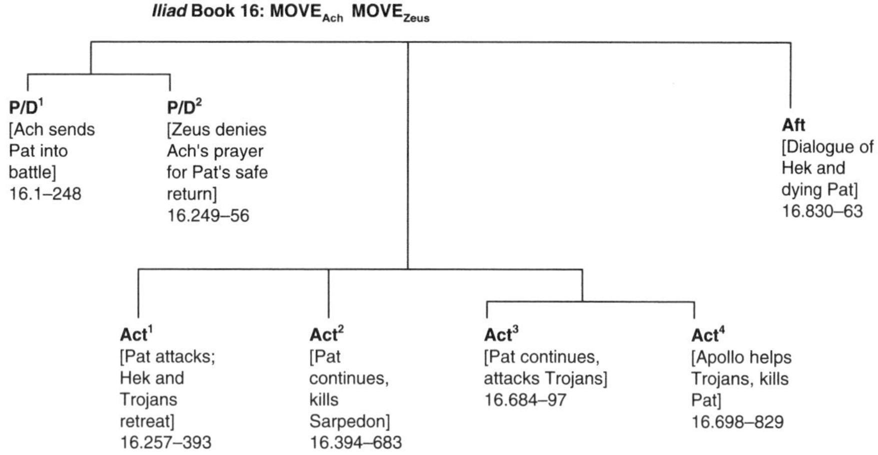

FIGURE 2.9. Event trajectory of book 16.

Book 16

This book displays an exceptionally complex trajectory of events, since its agenda is set by a doubled Problem/Decision stage in which Achilles and Zeus make decisions that do not coincide: P/D^1: Achilles sends Patroklos into battle to help the Greeks (16.1–248); P/D^2: Zeus declines to fulfill Achilles' prayer for Patroklos's safe return (16.249–56). In the Action stage that follows, Patroklos first fulfills the instructions of Achilles to put the Trojans to flight, giving the Greeks some breathing room in the battle (Action^1, 16.257–393), but then he continues fighting, extending the Action and fulfilling Zeus's plan for Sarpedon's death (Action^2, 16.394–683). Finally, the Action continues on to fulfill Zeus's plan for Patroklos's death (Action^3, 16.684–829). The Aftermath stage is the dialogue of Hektor and the dying Patroklos (16.830–63). Figure 2.9 analyzes the event trajectory that spans the whole book.

Action^2 (Patroklos kills Sarpedon) has its own internal trajectory. The P/D stage has three parts: Patroklos's persistence in fighting, in disobedience of Achilles' command (16.394–418); Sarpedon's decision to face Patroklos (16.419–30); and Zeus's decision not to rescue Sarpedon (16.431–61). The subtrajectory's Action stage also has three parts (Patroklos kills Sarpedon, Glaukos defends Sarpedon's corpse, and Patroklos leads the Greek rout of the Trojans). In the Aftermath stage, Apollo rescues Sarpedon's corpse.

Action^3 of the overarching trajectory (Zeus and Apollo bring about Patroklos's death, 16.684–829) also has a complete internal trajectory. In the P/D stage, Zeus impels Patroklos to continue fighting, toward his doom (16.684–91). The subtrajectory's Action stage has three parts: Patroklos attacks the Trojans (16.692–97); Apollo helps the Trojans (16.698–776); and finally Apollo brings about Patroklos's death (16.777–829). The dialogue of Hektor and the dying Patroklos provides the Aftermath stage of this subtrajectory and the whole book.

Book 17

The book narrating the battle over Patroklos's corpse consists of a series of P/D-A-A trajectories in which Greek and Trojan initiatives alternate. First Menelaos takes a stand over Patroklos's corpse and sustains the attack of Euphorbos (P/D: 17.1–42). Then he kills the attacker (Action: 17.43–60). As he begins stripping Euphorbos's body, the Trojans are helpless (Aftermath: 17.61–69). Next Apollo rouses Hektor against him (Problem: 17.70–89), and Menelaos decides to call on Ajax for assistance (Decision: 17.90–105). Menelaos gets Ajax to help repel Hektor (Action: 17.106–31). Ajax then stands over the body (Aftermath: 132–39). A Trojan initiative begins as Glaukos rouses Hektor, who answers the challenge (P/D: 17.140–82). But first he changes armor (Aux^1: 17.183–97) and Zeus inspires him (Aux^2: 17.198–212). Then he makes another attack (Action: 17.212–36). Ajax and Menelaos respond by summoning reinforcements (P/D: 17.237–55). Their defensive stand (Action: 17.352–65) leads to a stalemate, evoked by the narrator in a general description (Aftermath: 17.366–425).

The stalemate is broken when Zeus inspires another Greek initiative: P/D: Achilles' horses refuse to run, and Zeus inspires them; Action: Automedon, Achilles' charioteer, leads a Greek rally. This initiative is then answered when Apollo inspires a Trojan initiative. The P/D stage begins when Athena inspires Menelaos (17.543–81); then Apollo responds by inspiring the Trojans (17.582–96). The Action stage is the Trojan rally (17.597–625). The book concludes with two Greek initiatives: Antilochos is dispatched with a message to Achilles (P/D: Antilochos is sent; Action: he runs to Achilles). Ajax and Menelaos decide to retreat with Patroklos's corpse (P/D: 17.700–721). The Action is their slow retreat (17.722–34). The Aftermath stage is the general view of the inconclusive retreat (17.735–61).

Book 18

The initial Problem is that Achilles, having learned that Patroklos is dead, wishes to avenge him, but he has no armor. Thetis therefore decides to obtain new armor for him from Hephaistos (18.1–147). A long interval then separates Thetis's Decision from her Action, which begins at 18.368. An entirely different P/D-A-A trajectory is embedded in between: P/D: since the Greeks cannot retreat with the body, Iris advises Achilles to help by frightening the Trojans with a shout (18.148–201). In this trajectory, the Action is Achilles' shout, which allows the Greeks to rescue Patroklos's corpse (18.202–38). The Aftermath of Achilles' appearance, the end of the day of battle, is developed into four stages, the setting of the sun (18.239–42), the Trojan debate (18.243–314), the lamentation over Patroklos (18.314–55), and the discussion of Zeus and Hera (18.356–67). Then the initial trajectory is resumed as Thetis gets the armor from Hephaistos (18.368–614). The brief Aftermath stage is Thetis's dive from Olympus with the armor (18.615–16). Hephaistos's construction of the armor must be considered part of the Action stage, since until he has made it Thetis's mission is incomplete. But the elaborate description that concludes the Action stage is unnecessary to the advancement of the story, and it could be said to

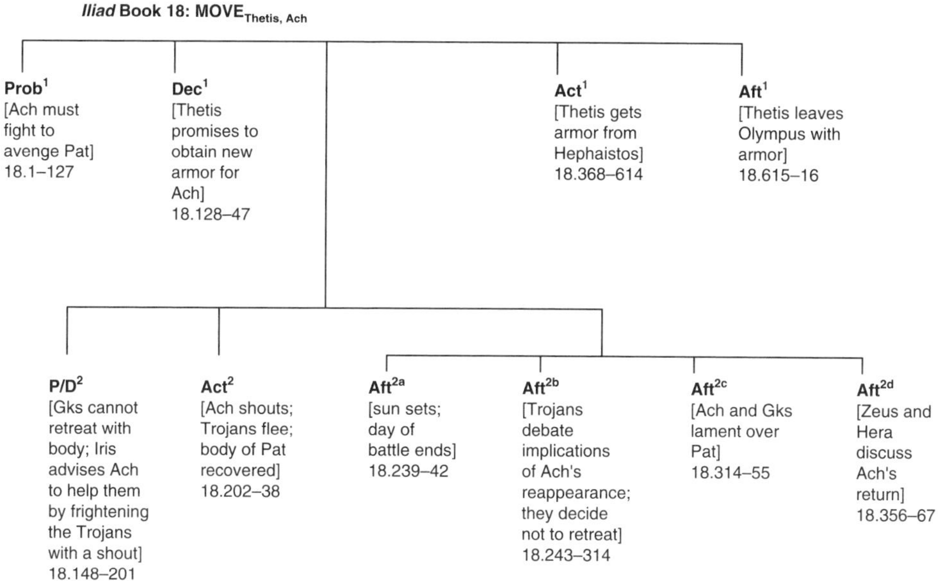

FIGURE 2.10. Event trajectory of book 18.

incorporate the Aftermath into the Action. Figure 2.10 illustrates the entire trajectory.

Book 19

When Thetis brings his new suit of armor, Achilles decides to return to the battle immediately. But the Action is delayed by two additional Problems: first Agamemnon must publicly disclaim responsibility for the offense against Achilles

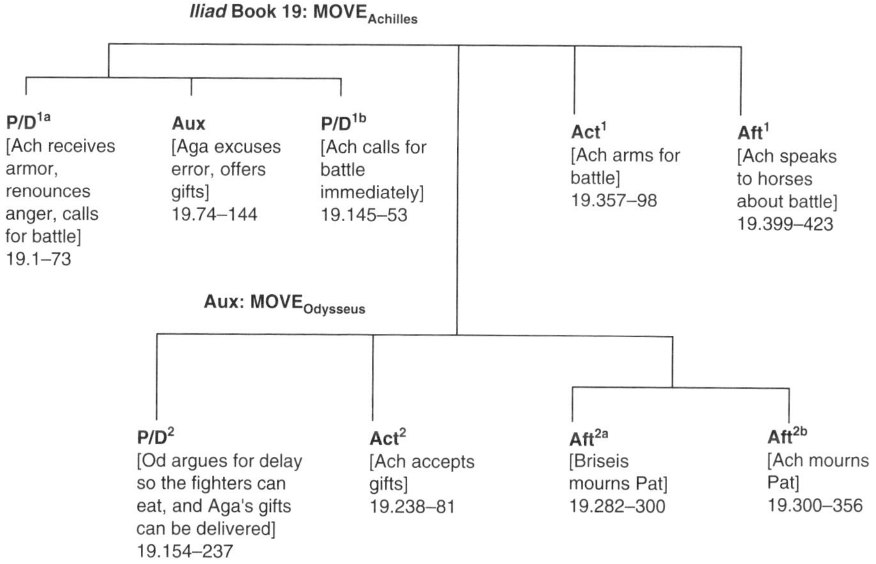

FIGURE 2.11. Event trajectory of book 19.

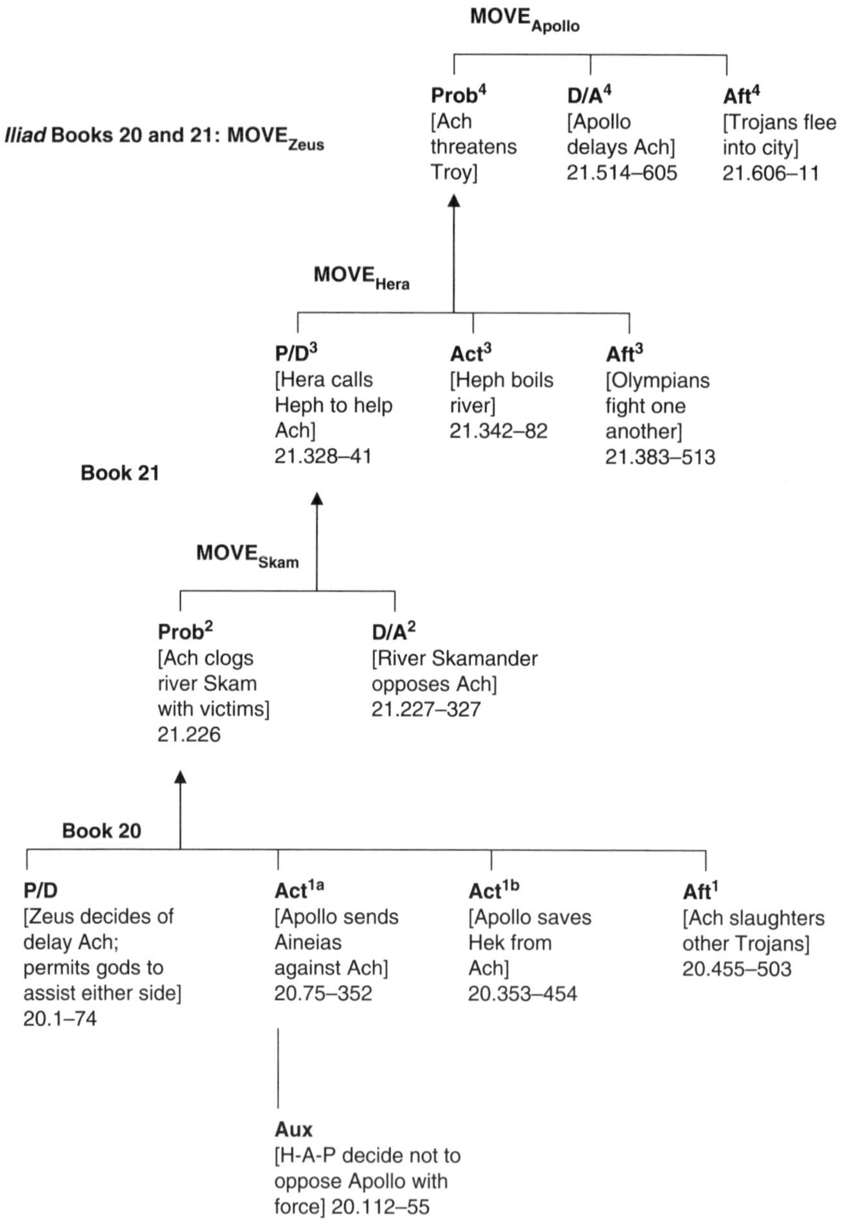

FIGURE 2.12. *Iliad* Books 20 and 21: $\text{MOVE}_{\text{Zeus}}$. Heph = Hephaistos, Skam = Skamander.

(19.74–153), and then Odysseus insists that the soldiers must eat before fighting (19.154–237). The second delay is developed into a complete P/D-A-A trajectory whose Action is Achilles' submission to Odysseus's behests, including acceptance of Agamemnon's gifts (19.238–81). The Aftermath is the period of waiting in which Briseis and Achilles mourn Patroklos (19.282–356). Then the initial trajectory resumes as Achilles arms for battle (Action, 19.357–98). The

Aftermath is the dialogue of Achilles with his horses (19.399–423). Figure 2.11 (p. 51) illustrates the whole trajectory.

Book 20

In his introduction to book 21, Richardson says:

> This Book cannot be considered separately from book 20. The framework of both consists in the scenes describing the Battle of the Gods. At the opening of book 20 Zeus urged the gods to intervene directly in the conflict . . . and a grandiose passage described the cosmic effects of their entry into battle (47–66). After this prelude to the Theomachy the theme of direct conflict between the gods was left suspended, while Akhilleus clashed with Aineias, skirmished with Hektor, and killed other Trojans. It is resumed at 21.328–514. (1993: 51)

These remarks are generally correct. But Richardson is less correct in his statement elsewhere that "the division [between books 20 and 21] cuts into what is better regarded as a single sequence of events" (1993: 1). The Problem/Decision stage at the beginning of book 20 (Zeus decides to delay Achilles; 20.1–74) does set an agenda that is carried out in books 20 and 21 together. Nevertheless this agenda does not take the form of a "single sequence of events," but rather of four action-aftermath trajectories, the first of which is coextensive with book 20 (Apollo delays Achilles through mortal intermediaries Aineias and Hektor; 20.75–454), while the latter three are coextensive with book 21. The action-aftermath trajectory of book 20 includes an important Auxiliary event in Poseidon's speech convincing Hera and Athena not to intervene directly against Apollo (20.112–55), which temporarily averts the violent conflict of gods that had seemed imminent as they prepared to help their favorites (20. 54–75). This conflict only breaks out in book 21, and the distribution of the Theomachy between the deferral in book 20 and the occurrence in book 21 is a functional distinction that the segment marker indicates.

Figure 2.12 (p. 52) analyzes the joint trajectory of books 20 and 21, showing both its continuity through the two segments and the articulation into subtrajectories that coincide with the marked segments. Figure 2.13 analyzes the trajectory of Action[1] in Book 20 in detail.

Book 21

Most of this book presents the battle of gods against gods promised at the beginning of book 20, but deferred while Apollo was permitted to delay Achilles by assisting Aineias and Hektor. A new Problem stage (21.1–226) reintroduces the Theomachy indirectly by motivating the conflict of Achilles with the divine river Skamander, an Action that develops into a polemical configuration as first Athena and Poseidon (21.284–97, not analyzed in fig. 2.12) and then Hera and Hephaistos (= Move [Hera]) intervene on Achilles' behalf. The river eventually succumbs to Hephaistos's flames and returns to his channel (21.377–82). In the Aftermath the conflict

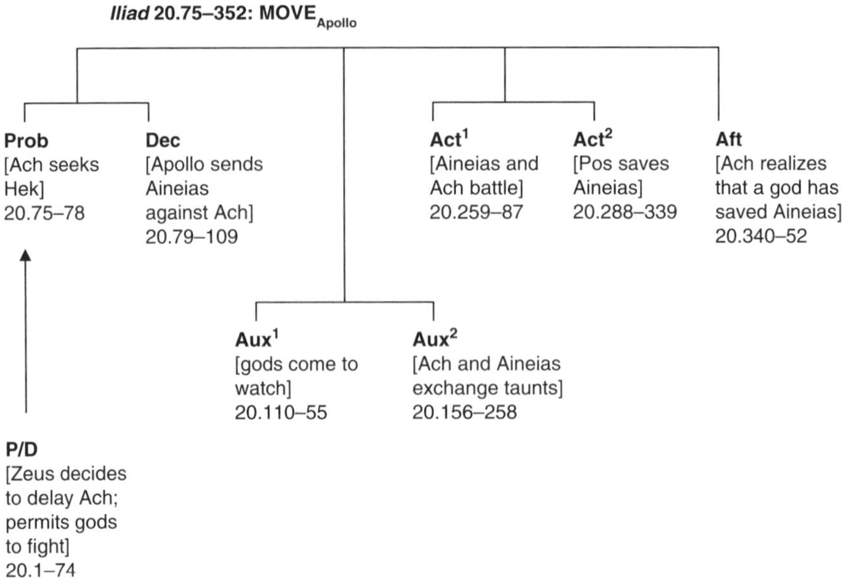

FIGURE 2.13. Trajectory of Action^1 in *Iliad* book 20.

spills over, and the anticipated fracas of Olympians versus Olympians finally takes place (21.383–513). Thus the event trajectory in which gods help Achilles against the divine Skamander offers a theomachy that furnishes thematic transition into a second theomachy, that of Olympians versus Olympians (Richardson 1993: 51; also compare Nicolai 1973: 113), which only begins at 21.383–90.

This Aftermath stage is developed into a P/D-A-A trajectory (not analyzed in fig. 2.12). The Problem/Decision stage (21.383–90; the gods feel hatred for one another) generates a three-part Action stage in which the Olympians battle one another. Action^1 pits Hera and Athena against Aphrodite and Ares (21.391–434). Action^2 concerns two unsuccessful efforts to draw Apollo into the brawling: first Poseidon taunts him (21.435–67) and then Artemis joins in. Hera then boxes Artemis's ears for her insolence (21.468–96). In Action^3, Hermes declines to fight Leto (21.497–504). In the Aftermath of the Theomachy trajectory, Zeus consoles Artemis (21.505–13).

But while the Olympians are fighting one another they are not addressing the Problem for which Zeus let them loose, that of delaying Achilles. The whole elaborate Action of delaying Achilles concludes with the P/D-A-A trajectory in which Apollo resumes the delaying tactic he used in book 20: P/D: Achilles attacks the Trojans, and Apollo sends Agenor to distract him while the other Trojans flee to safety (21.514–49). Action^1: Agenor confronts Achilles (21.550–94); Action^2: Apollo takes the form of Agenor and lures Achilles away from the city (21.595–605). In the Aftermath, the Trojans flee into the city (21.606–11).

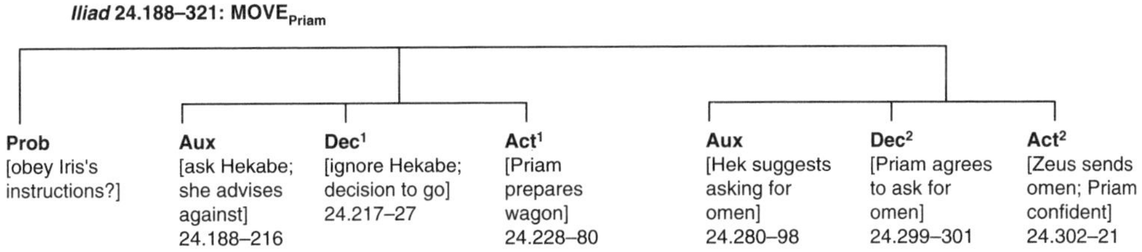

FIGURE 2.14. Priam's decision in *Iliad* book 24. Hek = Hekabe.

Book 22

The P/D-A-A Trajectory of this book is very straightforward, except that the Aftermath stage is doubled: P/D: Achilles attacks Troy; Hektor decides to face him (22.1–130). Action: Achilles pursues and kills Hektor (22.131–366). Aftermath^{1}: The Greeks and Achilles abuse Hektor's corpse (22.367–404); Aftermath^{2}: The Trojans lament Hektor (22.405–515).[20]

Book 23

Book 23 is as straightforward as book 22, except that here the Action stage is doubled, while the Aftermath is single: P/D: Achilles must honor and bury Patroklos (23.1–107). Action^{1}: Patroklos's corpse is burned, his bones are collected, and a mound is heaped for him (23.108–257); Action^{2}: Achilles honors Patroklos with funeral games (23.257–883). Aftermath: Achilles awards prizes to Agamemnon and Meriones without a contest (23.884–97).

Book 24

As we have seen, this book has a simple overarching event trajectory: P/D: Achilles abuses Hektor's corpse; Zeus decides that he should return it (24.1–76). Auxiliary: Zeus arranges the return of the corpse (24.77–321). Action: Priam retrieves the corpse (24.322–691). Aftermath: Hektor is lamented and buried (24.692–804).[21] Zeus's Auxiliary preparations can be analyzed as two Actions, each of which is prepared for by two Auxiliaries. In the first Action Zeus arranges for Achilles to cooperate. Aux^{1a}: Iris summons Thetis (24.77–102); Aux^{1b}: Zeus commands Thetis (24.103–19); Action^{1}: Thetis obeys and obtains Achilles' cooperation (24.120–40). Aux^{2a}: Zeus sends Iris to Priam (24.141–59); Aux^{2b}: Iris brings message to Priam (24.160–87); Action^{2}: Priam decides to go to Achilles (24.188–321). There is no Aftermath stage.

Priam's decision to trust the message from Iris and undertake the journey to Achilles, which is the last stage in Zeus's preparations, has a complex trajectory that Figure 2.14 analyzes in detail.

20. Compare Clay: "Book 22 of the *Iliad* has only one action: the death of Hector, its preparation, and its immediate aftermath" (2002: 7). Also compare Schadewaldt 1944: 23.

21. See note 3 here.

Overview

The foregoing analyses show that the narrative of the *Iliad* is articulated into distinct and coherent action trajectories, each of which arises from agenda-setting decisions and follows out the actions taken to fulfill those decisions. There are twenty-four such distinct subtrajectories, and their beginnings and ends coincide with the placement of the transmitted segment markers. The segment markers therefore cue or reinforce attention to an aspect of the narrative that is important to comprehension. They are, in this respect, signs that cooperate with the poet's other signs, just as punctuation marks indicate the immanent syntax that, in poetic recitations as in ordinary spoken discourse, would also be indicated by paraverbal cues of intonation, rhythm, and volume. From a reader's standpoint, the markers are as much the poet's work as any other features of the text.

"BOOK DIVISIONS" AND NARRATIVE DISCONTINUITY

As a historical matter it cannot be determined whether the poet physically added paraverbal cues in the recitational or graphic format, or left it to others to supplement the articulation he indicated in the story. A few passages of the *Iliad* and *Odyssey*, however, seem to assume that the segmentation was obvious to readers or audiences. In that case, cues of some sort would probably have been needed, and the composer of those passages would have known the cues and used them. The passages to which I refer present narrative discontinuities that are never found anywhere in Homeric poetry except in the immediate vicinity of transmitted segment markers.[22]

Most of the marked segments or "books" of the *Iliad* and *Odyssey* begin with formulaic phrases that establish continuity with the immediately preceding narration. These phrases belong to a few regular types,[23] of which I will here illustrate three, as follows. (All citations in the rest of this chapter are from the *Iliad* unless otherwise indicated.)

1. Summary of the previous action + transition to a new scene:[24] *Ὣς οἱ μὲν περὶ νηὸς . . . μάχοντο·/Πάτροκλος δ' Ἀχιλῆι παρίστατο . . .* (Thus they fought around the ship . . . but Patroklos came beside Achilles, 16.1–2).
2. Shift from a general scene to a "close-up" or the reverse:[25] *Ἄλλοι μὲν . . . ἀριστῆες . . . εὗδον παννύχιοι. . . . ἀλλ' οὐκ Ἀτρείδην . . . ὕπνος ἔχε* (Other leaders . . . slept through the night . . . but sleep did not hold the son of Atreus, 10.1–4).

22. The following discussion is a slightly revised version of Heiden 2000b.

23. See Stanley 1993: 249–59.

24. On such transitions see also Hölscher 1939: 40–41; van Groningen 1958: 42–45; Goold 1977: 29–30; and Wyatt 1989–90: 11–12.

25. Wyatt 1989–90: 12–13 analyzes this type slightly differently.

3. Bisection of continuous narrative of action by the same character(s): at the end of book 23 Achilles awards Agamemnon the prize for spear-throwing; book 24 begins *Λῦτο δ' ἀγών, λαοὶ δὲ θοὰς ἐπὶ νῆας ἕκαστοι/ ἐσκίδαντ' ἰέναι.* (The contest broke up, and all the people/Scattered to go to the swift ships, 24.1–2.)

Instances of all three types are often found in the middle of marked segments, i.e., in continuous narration (except that in these cases, type 3 would effect "reframing" rather than "bisection"). When the Homeric narrator shifts focus in the middle of a marked segment, his technique is scarcely distinguishable from that employed at most marked segment junctures.[26] The following typical transition occurs in the middle of book 16: *ὣς οἱ μὲν τοιαῦτα πρὸς ἀλλήλους ἀγόρευον, /Αἴας δ' οὐκέτ' ἔμιμνε·* (Thus they said these things to one another; / but Ajax no longer stood his ground, 16.101–2). Thus, while the language found in the first lines of the Homeric "books" generally follows certain regular patterns, these patterns in themselves cannot mark off the beginnings and ends of "books," because the patterns are not unique to first lines.

However, a small number of Homeric "books" begin with scene transitions that differ from those internal to the marked segments. When placed in immediate juxtaposition to the preceding lines, these transitions display unusual discontinuities whose awkwardness the segment markers seem to mitigate or conceal. In these exceptional passages it appears that the transmitted text presupposes that readers or audiences could notice the segmentation without special effort and thus would not mind the unusual discontinuity. Here are the last line of book 7 and the first of book 8, shown without the segment marker.

7.482 *κοιμήσαντ' ἄρ' ἔπειτα καὶ ὕπνου δῶρον ἕλοντο.*
8.1 *Ἠὼς μὲν κροκόπεπλος ἐκίδνατο πᾶσαν ἐπ' αἶαν.*

"They went to bed and took the gift of sleep. Dawn began to spread. . . ." The narrator has obviously skipped over a few hours between the time when the Greeks and Trojans fell asleep and the rise of Dawn.[27] This bald chronological discontinuity is unique in the two Homeric epics.[28] Of course many Homeric passages narrate characters going to sleep, and then narrate the next sunrise, but except for the transition from *Iliad* book 7 to book 8, Homer's narrator invariably indicates the passage of time during the night. The following lines are typical:

26. See especially Edwards 2002: 42–47; compare Edwards in Jensen et al. 1999: 52; also de Jong 1996: 25. Also compare Broccia 1967: 23, 56; and Hainsworth 1993: 57–58.

27. Stanley 1993: 255 notes the exceptional combination of temporal discontinuity and change of scene found at *Iliad* 7/8 and 10/11. These are the sole examples in his category (3). Compare also the remarks of Broccia 1967: 60–61, and those of West *ad* H 482/θ 1 in the apparatus of his Teubner edition.

28. Scholars at least since S.E. Bassett (1938: 42–56) have observed that the Homeric narrator scrupulously maintains the continuity of his narrative. Bassett (42) denies any temporal discontinuity in Homer, as do Richardson (1990: 20) and Edwards (2002: 37–61, esp. 58). Compare the remarks of the grammarian Nicanor (discussed below) about the alleged continuity of what would now be called the *récit* of the *Iliad*.

1.475 ἦμος δ' ἠέλιος κατέδυ καὶ ἐπὶ κνέφας ἦλθε,
1.476 δὴ τότε κοιμήσαντο παρὰ πρυμνήσια νηός·
1.477 ἦμος δ' ἠριγένεια φάνη ῥοδοδάκτυλος Ἠώς,
1.478 καὶ τότ' ἔπειτ' ἀνάγοντο μετὰ στρατὸν εὐρὺν Ἀχαιῶν·

"They went to bed. And *when* Dawn appeared. . . ." The temporal conjunction acknowledges that time has passed and thus preserves the narrative continuity by indicating the uneventful span. On rare occasions an independent clause in the middle of a marked segment does narrate the approach of dawn, but even then there is no discontinuity like that at the transition from book 7 to book 8, because in the immediately preceding lines characters have not been described as going to bed, but on the contrary as having already awakened (2.48 [Agamemnon]; 24.695 [Priam and Idaios]).

Besides *Iliad* 8, three other marked segments (*Iliad* 11 and 19, *Odyssey* 5) begin with an independent clause narrating the arrival of Dawn, but the characters in the preceding lines have not gone to sleep, so temporal discontinuity is avoided or rendered less obtrusive.[29] But the first lines of *Iliad* 11 do display a different kind of discontinuity, which is also found at *Iliad* 8.1: the sunrise introduces a new scene with different characters.[30] *Iliad* 10 ends with Odysseus and Diomedes pouring a libation to Athena in the Greek camp, but after the sunrise in *Iliad* 11 Zeus, from some unspecified place, sends Eris to the ships.

10.578 . . . ἀπὸ δὲ κρητῆρος Ἀθήνῃ
10.579 πλείου ἀφυσσόμενοι λεῖβον μελιηδέα οἶνον.
11.1 Ἠὼς δ' ἐκ λεχέων παρ' ἀγαυοῦ Τιθωνοῖο
11.2 ὄρνυθ' . . . ·
11.3 Ζεὺς δ' Ἔριδα προΐαλλε θοὰς ἐπὶ νῆας Ἀχαιῶν

drawing the sweet-hearted wine from the full
mixing-bowl they poured out an offering to Athene.
And Dawn rose from her bed, beside proud Tithonos. . . .
And Zeus sent Strife down to the Greeks' swift ships[31]

29. In *Iliad* 10 Odysseus and Diomedes are awakened when the night is almost two-thirds over (10.252–53), so they are somewhat rested when Dawn arises; at the end of *Odyssey* 4, the suitors do not go to sleep, because they are waiting in ambush for Telemachos (*Od.* 4.842–47). At the end of *Iliad* 18 Thetis is in transit from Olympus to the Achaian ships when Dawn rises (18.616–19.3); since she is a divinity, audiences need not be concerned about whether she caught any sleep while Hephaistos made Achilles' armor, and the narrator's silence is unsurprising.

30. The discontinuities at *Iliad* 3/4 and 10/11 are noted by Broccia 1967: 57, who cites earlier discussions of Bernhardy and Wilamowitz.

31. Lattimore trans., adapted. *Iliad* 7 ends on the plain of Troy, but after the sunrise in book 8 the setting is Olympus, where Zeus is about to address the other gods. If book 11 ever directly followed book 9, as many scholars have suspected, the discontinuity was of the same sort as that found at *Iliad* 7/8:

9.713 ἔνθα δὲ κοιμήσαντο καὶ ὕπνου δῶρον ἕλοντο.
11.1 Ἠὼς δ' ἐκ λεχέων παρ' ἀγαυοῦ Τιθωνοῖο κτλ.

No transitions of time/place/characters like those of the first lines of *Iliad* 8 and 11 are ever found within the marked segments.

The first lines of book 4 display a type of discontinuity similar to that just discussed, but without the change of time.

3.461	ὣς ἔφατ' Ἀτρείδης, ἐπὶ δ' ᾔνεον ἄλλοι Ἀχαιοί.
4.1	οἱ δὲ θεοὶ πὰρ Ζηνὶ καθήμενοι ἠγορόωντο
4.2	χρυσέῳ ἐν δαπέδῳ, μετὰ δέ σφισι πότνια Ἥβη
4.3	νέκταρ ἐῳνοχόει· τοὶ δὲ χρυσέοις δαπάεσσι
4.4	δειδέχατ' ἀλλήλους, Τρώων πόλιν εἰσορόωντες.

So spoke Atreus's son, and the other Achaians applauded him.
And the gods at the side of Zeus were sitting in council
over the golden floor, and among them the goddess Hebe
poured them nectar as wine, while they in the golden drinking-cups
drank to each other, gazing down on the city of the Trojans.[32]

In the typical transition to Olympus, the narrator immediately indicates the point of continuity with the preceding narrative: "and all the gods were watching" (22.166).[33] Here instead the topic shifts without warning to the gods around Zeus, and the narrator tells us what they were doing, where they were, and who was there, *before* indicating the link to the previous narration. And even this link is somewhat more tenuous than usual for Homer, since the gods are said to be watching the *city* of the Trojans, while the action in the previous scene was occurring in the plain.

Thus in the first lines of books 4, 8, and 11, we find transitions that would be anomalous in continuous narration and noticeably awkward. Similar awkward transitions also occur at *Odyssey* 3/4, 17/18, and 23/24. Since discontinuities avoided within marked segments occur only at segment junctures, it would appear that the junctures somehow mitigated the effect of discontinuity and rendered it tolerable to the composer's taste. The segmentation may have been perceived as setting the previous narration out of immediate focus, so that

32. Lattimore trans., adapted. A similar discontinuity occurs at *Odyssey* 23/24. Jensen 1999: 20 notes this discontinuity, but her analysis and mine differ. Hellwig 1964: 100 also notes the unusual abruptness at *Od.* 23/24, but she compares it to *Od.* 24.412–13, where the narrator shifts from Laertes' estate to the spread of rumor through the city. But the latter (book-internal) transition is much less abrupt, both because it employs a typical retrospective summary of the doings at Laertes', and because ὄσσα, whether or not personified, is not a real character like Hermes. Heubeck 1992: 356–57 compares the abrupt entrance of Hermes at *Odyssey* 23/24 to the narrator's shift from Hektor to Glaukos and Diomedes at *Il.* 6.119. But in *Iliad* 6 the abruptness is mitigated by the fact that Diomedes is already in the forefront of the audience's awareness as the very reason for Hektor's trip back to Troy, and he has been mentioned by Helenos scarcely twenty lines earlier (6.96–101).

33. Hellwig 1964: 91–92 points out that an unexplained shift to Olympus also occurs at *Il.* 15.1. Since this transition also coincides with a segment marker it reinforces the impression that such shifts do not occur in continuous narration. But *Il.* 15.1 has been omitted from this discussion because it reverts to a recently narrated scene (Zeus and Hera on Ida), making it less abrupt than the transition at *Il.* 4.1 and similar to some transitions in continuous narration.

smooth explicit transition was not required.[34] The composer of the six exceptional transitions would seem to have assumed that his collaborators (audiences, readers) would easily recognize that these positions were segment junctures.[35] In that case, they must have had some cues supplementary to the immanent trajectory of the story.

If these six transitions assumed the presence of the segment markers, it follows that either (1) the six cued segment junctures, as well as the verbal transitions, were coeval with the rest of the composition; (2) at a certain stage the composition featured segment markers in these positions, but with different transitions, and the present transitions were added later; or (3) both the six cued segment junctures and the anomalous transitions were added later; the markers may have been added first, or markers and transitions may have been added simultaneously.[36] Since there is no independent reason to doubt the authenticity of the passages in question, the most likely possibility is (1). But it is worth weighing the likelihood that the anomalous lines might have been later additions.

If the six anomalous transitions replaced other readings now lost, the earlier readings would almost certainly have presented transitions like those found in continuous narration. Of course, such transitions were perfectly acceptable—indeed regular—at marked segment junctures, so they would not have required replacement, whether the earlier text included segment markers already or whether it presented continuous narration into which the segment markers were added later. Indeed, since the regular transitions were retained in forty of the forty-six marker placements and all other scene transitions in the *Iliad* and *Odyssey*, there is no apparent reason why they should not have been retained as well at the six segment junctures in question. So the fact that transitions of the *ὣς οἱ μὲν κτλ.* sort or their like were not transmitted in these passages almost certainly means that they never existed there in the first place. Thus the first lines of *Iliad* 4, 8, and 11 and *Odyssey* 5, 18, and 24 would seem to be coeval with the rest of the work of composition.

Since the composer of these lines may already have had the segment markers in mind, it follows that in these six cases the transmitted segment markers not only cooperated with the composer's work, they may also have been incorporated into it by the composer himself. And if six of the transmitted segment markers were incorporated into the composition, then most likely all the others were, too,

34. Compare Mark Edwards's comment (1991: 63) that the "book-division" at *Iliad* 16/17 "obscures the diversion of our attention from Hektor . . . to the struggle for the body of Patroklos."

35. Broccia 1967 argued that the first lines of several books of the *Iliad*—*not* including books 4 and 11—presuppose an interruption in the continuity of rhapsodic performance. For Broccia it is usually the presence of a retrospective summary that indicates a pause immediately preceding that necessitated an explicit reminder of the previous action. I agree that the pauses may have been there and may indeed have prompted the use of the summaries. But since such summaries also occur in continuous narration, their presence cannot *prove* that a pause was presupposed. Broccia sees the "book divisions" as reflecting rhapsodic practice and unrelated to the composer's design (19).

36. Compare the view of Broccia 1967 that most of the transitions were supplied to facilitate continuous performance by competing rhapsodes; also the suggestions of Edwards 1991: 235 and Edwards (in Jensen et al. 1999: 53) that some of the smoother transitions might have been added or adapted after the insertion of the "book divisions."

since all the markers conform to the common principle of marking the beginnings and ends of event trajectories.

SUPPOSED ANCIENT EVIDENCE OF THE INAUTHENTICITY OF THE "BOOK DIVISIONS"

Of course, the conservative inference that the composition of the *Iliad* might have marked the immanent event trajectories by supplementary signs—an inference that, I reiterate, is not strictly necessary to the analysis in this chapter—would be much less conservative if there were testimony external to the text that indicated otherwise. Some scholars think there is.

Two bits of ancient testimony are directly relevant to the "book divisions." The better known is the statement of Ps-Plutarch (*Vita Homeri* B.4) that "the articulation of the epics into the number of letters in the alphabet was not the work of the poet, but of scholars associated with Aristarchus" (*διῃρημένη ἑκατέρα* [*ποίησις*] *εἰς τὸν ἀριθμὸν τῶν στοιχείων, οὐκ ὑπ' αὐτοῦ τοῦ ποιητοῦ, ἀλλ' ὑπὸ τῶν γραμματικῶν τῶν περὶ τὸν Ἀρίσταρχον*). It is hardly self-evident that this testimony merits credence. Ps-Plutarch's few historical assertions are undisguised reports of gossip ("Pindar says . . . the school of Aristarchus says . . . the school of Crates says . . . most people believe," B.3), and they give no reason to believe that he either possessed accurate information about Homer and Homeric scholars or thought his unadvanced readers would have expected it. Stephanie West has treated Ps-Plutarch's testimony about the "book divisions" with prudent skepticism.[37] Some scholars of my acquaintance are more credulous; but anybody who thought that the passage was reliable at face value would also have to agree that it resolved a disputed question much more important than that of the "book divisions": whether the *Iliad* had an author (since Ps-Plutarch refers to "the poet himself"). Ps-Plutarch may not have known much more about the "scholars associated with Aristarchus" than he did about the author of the *Iliad*: as West pointed out, his comment about the Homeric "book divisions" seems indebted to a convention that routinely attributed scholarly innovations to Aristarchus. Both the poet of the *Iliad* and the great Alexandrian scholar were objects of fictitious gossip and speculation. Ps-Plutarch's statement resembles some of the fiction. Whether true or not, its face value as testimony is essentially nil.

A second testimonium from a somewhat more respectable source has now been adduced by René Nünlist. In the scholia *ad Il.* 2.877 a comment attributed to Nicanor states: *ἡ κατὰ στοιχεῖα διαίρεσις γραμματικῶν ἐστιν, ὁ μέντοι ποιητὴς ζηλῶν πραγμάτων φύσιν ἑνοῖ τὸ σωμάτιον καὶ τὰ ἔπη ἐν εἱρμῷ· ἐπιφέρει γὰρ ὁ ποιητὴς σύνδεσμον τὸν "αὐτὰρ"* (*Il.* 3.1) *συνδήσας τοῖς προκειμένοις, καὶ τοῦτο ληπτέον εἰς τὸ μὴ κατὰ ῥαψῳδίαν γεγραφέναι.* (For the division by letters is the

37. "The statement in [Plutarch] is probably based on mere conjecture," West 1967: 19.

work of grammarians. The poet, however, in imitation of the nature of things, makes it one body, and the lines are in an uninterrupted sequence. For the poet adds as a conjunction the word *αὐτάρ*, thereby connecting <the verse> to the preceding lines. And this must be taken as an indication that he did not write <the poem> in separate books [Nünlist 2006: 47]). This testimonium, like Ps-Plutarch's, records something about its author, but nothing of substance about the origin or function of the "book divisions." Its assertion about "grammarians" does not even pretend to specific information about who inserted the markers, when, why, and how. Yet it could not have appealed to implicit common knowledge, or there would have been no need to make an argument for it (*τοῦτο ληπτέον εἰς κτλ.*).

Nicanor's argument was an inference from the poet's use of the conjunction *αὐτάρ* in *Iliad* 3.1. This inference is faulty, because it assumes that the conjunction could only join sentences that were read or recited in unmarked continuity. But syntactic, narrative, or metrical segmentation need not be absolute. Conjunctions *always* imply a degree of separation, which they mitigate and qualify. The poet's use of conjunctions at the beginning of marked segments is an indication to readers that *some connection* is to be understood between the continuing narrative and that which preceded. This is no obstacle to a system of marked narrative segmentation. Nicanor's testimony shows that the scholar was loathe to attribute the segmentation of the *Iliad* to its poet. It also indicates why: the segmentation conflicted with his idea that the poet maintained continuity *in imitation of nature*. This could hardly be true: in a poem the length of the *Iliad*, even a design that did seek to imitate nature must have allowed for some articulations, whether or not they enhanced the imitation.

Arguments for a terminus post quem for the transmitted "book divisions" usually rely on more indirect evidence. Signs have been detected in expressions like Herodotus's "in Diomedes' *aristeia*" (*ἐν Διομήδεος ἀριστείῃ*, Herod. 2.116.3; the citation accompanies quotation of *Il.* 6.289–92). These phrases are evidence of how the Homeric epics were cited, not of their articulation or its marking. The lines Herodotus places "in Diomedes' *aristeia*" concern the weavings from which Hekabe selected the dedication for Athena. Since the dedication accompanied a prayer that asked Athena to stop Diomedes' rampage, *ἐν Διομήδεος ἀριστείῃ* is a perfectly informative citation just as it stands. A reference to "book 6" or "*Z*" would have been much less informative to Herodotus's readers, even if their texts of the *Iliad* did have a segment so labeled.[38] The only thing Herodotus's phrase tells us about the segment markings is that there probably was no marked

38. Herodotus also quotes *Od.* 4.351–52, but he introduces the lines merely as something Menelaos told Telemachos (*τάδε ἕτερα πρὸς Τηλέμαχον Μενέλεως λέγει*), which was apparently a sufficient reminder of the pertinent general context. In quoting *Od.* 4.227–30 Herodotus says only that the passage is "in the *Odyssey*" (*ἐν Ὀδυσσείᾳ*). But a degree of context, apparently sufficient, is provided by the quotation itself, since the first line mentions the *Διὸς θυγάτηρ* (i.e., Helen), and Helen only appears in a few passages of the *Odyssey*.

segment of the *Iliad* that bore the *title* "Diomedes' *Aristeia*." Since this title was later applied to "book 5," the system of labeling the "books" by descriptive title probably did not exist in Herodotus's time.[39]

Informal citations like Herodotus's were obviously compatible with the segment marking, since they remained normal even in later periods for which the existence of the "book divisions" is attested.[40] Ps-Longinus, writing when the marked articulation was well known, refers to the "summoning of spirits" in the *Odyssey* (ἐν Νεκυίᾳ, 9.2) and "the battle of the gods" in the *Iliad* (ἐπὶ τῆς θεομαχίας, 9.6). He would not have improved his readers' understanding by sending them to a particular "book" of the *Iliad*. In fact, in quoting from the Theomachy, Ps-Longinus *conflates* lines from two different "books" of the *Iliad*, "books" 20 and 21. This shows that en passant references to the Homeric epics are unreliable evidence of what readers might have found in their texts. No manuscripts of the *Iliad* transmit the same conflation, and nobody would argue that either Ps-Longinus or his readers had it in their texts of Homer. The conflation merely indicates that the exact sequential position of the lines in question was irrelevant to the particular point Ps-Longinus was trying to illustrate. So, apparently, was the segment marking.

Stephanie West also brought a critical eye to other indirect "evidence" that had been cited to support terminus post quem arguments for late insertion of the Homeric "book divisions." She drew a critical distinction between "the system itself, and the way in which it was reflected in the format" (1967: 18) She discounted use of the Ionic alphabet to label the segments, because she recognized that the alphabetic labeling could have been adapted for a twenty-four-part segmentation that was already in existence (19): in other words, the use of the letters was evidence for the *labeling*, not for the segmentation.[41] She also discounted the absence of segment markers from many early papyri, pointing out that papyri were very unreliable records of segmentation and punctuation, and often failed to mark even the separation of distinct works (21–22). West herself posited a third-century terminus ante quem, adducing as positive evidence two early papyri that bear traces of familiar "book divisions" (22). She stated, "the evidence of the earliest papyri does not conflict with the view that the familiar system of division was already in use."[42]

39. Richardson 1993: 20. His further speculation about what this implies "taken by itself" should be considered with all the caution its wording invites.

40. The author of the Pseudo-Plutarchan *Vita Homeri*, who certainly knew of the "book divisions," never used them for citations. Citations of tragedy furnish a parallel phenomenon. Aristotle states that each tragedy consists of precisely distinguishable parts (*Poet.* 1452b), but he never refers to passages in tragedy by citing the *epeisodia* or *stasima* in which they occur.

41. It is also possible that the *Iliad* and *Odyssey* were written down in the twenty-four-letter Ionic alphabet before it became the standard; see Goold 1960: 272–91; Janko 1992: 34–37; and Erbse 1994: 82–97. This hypothesis has the merit of explaining the otherwise puzzling hegemony of the Ionic alphabet over many locally established competitors: it spread in copies of Homer.

42. West herself has speculated (1988: 39–40) that the "book divisions" derived "very probably" from Athenian rhapsodic practices in the late sixth century.

Historical discussion of the Homeric "book divisions," such as it is, focuses mainly on their alleged intrusion into a text that existed earlier. But their dissemination is what really should arouse curiosity, because, to quote West again (1967: 16), "there was no Alexandrian University Press." Actually, there was no press at all, so it is very puzzling by what means a recent innovation in the Homeric text, much less one as far-reaching as the segment marking, could have become canonical. By about 400 BCE at the latest, the *Iliad* and *Odyssey* had become quite stable. Written texts existed and circulated widely among readers, and recitations also occurred, but all this circulation tended to preserve a very large core of stability rather than to erode it. Four hundred years later the *Iliad* and *Odyssey* were still stable, and for the most part they were still the same stable poems they had been in 400 BCE, except that their stability included a uniform system of marked articulation, a numerical label for each "rhapsody," and often a descriptive title as well (West 1967: 23). The numerical labels were well known, and scholars, pedagogues, and ordinary people referred to them in informal discourse.[43] In such references the implicit assumption was that anybody who read the reference knew exactly how the *Iliad* and *Odyssey* were articulated.

Since the transmission of the *Iliad* and *Odyssey* resisted substantial verbal modification, why would it not have resisted the intrusion of segment markers? It is not likely that Alexandrian scholarship could have imposed them. The work of Alexandrian scholarship, even at its most ambitious, seldom if ever achieved the uniform acceptance that the Homeric "book divisions" eventually enjoyed. The marginal notations Alexandrian scholars added to their texts of the *Iliad* and *Odyssey* never became uniform standard accompaniments, and the lines the Alexandrian scholars athetized did not disappear from copies. Why would the supplementary "book divisions" have been more successful? And how could the work of Alexandrian scholarship serve to explain the acceptance of the "book divisions" with the nonscholarly reading public? The usage and spread of the "book divisions" would seem to indicate a strong extrascholarly factor.

The difficulty here framed would be considerably alleviated if the following hypothesis were true: the "book divisions" were not actually an innovation in the transmission of the *Iliad* and *Odyssey* at all, although their gradual appearance might be a symptom of innovation in the *uses* to which the epics were put. A system of segment marking might once have existed for one purpose only: for performances, let us say. In that case, most early written texts of the epics would indeed have contained no segment markers, and references to the epics in written and spoken discourses need not have mentioned them. Then let us suppose that as the epics came into use in schools, pedagogues found it convenient to assign pupils segments of the *Iliad* and *Odyssey*. There were many ways they could have segmented the epics. But one of the ways, and from several

43. "A mother who asked the teacher how her son was getting on . . . was told, 'He is studying the sixth'—τὸ ζῆτα—i.e., canto *Z* of the *Iliad*" (Marrou 1956: 162–63, citing *POxy*. 930, 15).

standpoints the easiest, would have been to adapt a system of segmentation that already existed, and was known to exist—except not for the purposes of pedagogy. In that case the intervention of the "book divisions" into the otherwise stable transmission of the *Iliad* and *Odyssey* would not have represented a unique manifestation of instability, but rather an *extension* of stability to include an aspect of the poems that existed before but had not previously been represented in the discourse of schools or in texts used in that setting. A preexisting system of segmentation could also have been adapted for use as a uniform system of citation, as scholarly discussion developed the need for one, without putting any scholars to the trouble either of inventing a new system or of figuring out how a new system could be disseminated so widely that it could serve as a uniform standard—which a system of reference virtually had to be if it was to be useful at all. This hypothesis would also relieve the need to explain why different purposes such as citation, reading, and pedagogy all eventually adopted the same system of segmentation: the system adopted was the only one already in existence, the only one already accepted (whether correctly or not) as authentically Homeric, and thus the only one that faced little resistance either as an interpolation or on other grounds such as relative inefficiency for one particular purpose or another.

But this historical speculation, which must remain inconclusive, is a digression from the business at hand in this study, which is the legibility of the *Iliad*. The internal evidence of the poem, as elicited by the "orientation" function, indicates that the twenty-four transmitted "books" constitute comprehensible articulations of the narrative. These articulations accommodate a reader's interest in clear orientation toward the local trajectory of events at any point in the story. The transmitted segment marking cooperates with the articulation of the story and makes it more noticeable and effective.

3

Orientation by Design

NAVIGATING THE STORY

The reader of the *Iliad* confronts an expansive but not shapeless poem. Its countless events share a common point of orientation in Zeus's decisions in dilemmas created by Achilles. Moreover the events advance through shorter subtrajectories of which twenty-four share a common general shape (P/D-A-A), vary only slightly in length,[1] and bear paratextual markings that draw the reader's attention to their articulative function. Thus readers of the *Iliad* who thought they should be able to hold the whole story in mind at once would not be deluded: the poem accommodates this interest to a considerable degree.

But some readers might desire even more orientation than this investigation has so far discovered. While each of the marked segments affords a pretty clear short-range perspective on the course of events, only a few of them cue the reader's attention toward the central dilemmas of the epic and Zeus's agency. As shown in the introduction, the six that do are book 1, in which the central Action is Achilles' request to Zeus for help; book 8, in which Zeus decides to intervene in the battle to fulfill his promise to Achilles, and then in the Aftermath reveals to Hera some further dimensions of his plan; book 9, in which the Greeks attempt to convince Achilles to end his refusal to fight (and Achilles assumes Zeus's agreement with his wishes); book 15, in which Zeus again decides to intervene to fulfill his promise to Achilles, and again reveals to Hera further dimensions of his plan; book 16, in which Patroklos appeals to Achilles to end

1. The shortest book of the *Iliad* (book 19) is 424 lines, and the longest (book 5) is 909. The difference of 485 lines is slightly more than 3 percent of the length of the entire epic. The average length of a book of the *Iliad* is 654 lines, and the difference between this and the book most variant in length from the average (book 5) is 255 lines, which is less than 2 percent of the total length of the epic. The lengths of the books cluster within a narrow range, as shown by the fact that no book differs from the next shorter or longer by more than ninety-seven lines (book 18 is 616 lines, while book 9 is 713). But the next highest difference is only forty-three lines (book 17 is 761 lines, book 24 is 804 lines). The other twenty-two books differ from the next shorter or longer by a maximum of only thirty-three lines. The maximum difference between any two neighboring books is 416 lines (book 2 is 877 lines, book 3 is 461), which is 2.65 percent of the total length of the epic. In seven places, the difference is 300 lines or more, in eleven places 148 lines or fewer. Thus in terms of the time of reading (or recitation) the reader would have a sense of variation in the length of books relative to one another, but also a sense that the variation occurred within a restricted range relative to the length of the whole.

his refusal to fight, and Achilles' response calls for making a second request of Zeus; and book 24, in which Zeus decides to end Achilles' unremitting desecration of Hektor's corpse. Three of these books focus upon decisions of Achilles (1, 9, and 16) and three upon decisions of Zeus (8, 15, and 24).[2]

The orientation provided by these books might have little effect, however, unless the other eighteen books somehow oriented the reader's attention to the six that in turn draw attention to the central dilemmas; otherwise the reader might oscillate violently between long periods of confusion and brief periods of orientation. Conceivably the eighteen books that do not directly orient the reader toward Zeus's dilemmas might provide orientation toward the six that do through narrative crossreferencing. However, adopting a provisional *narrative crossreferencing* function eliminates this possibility: the crossreferences are not there.[3]

However, as we have seen, two of the six orienting books are cued for attention by their transmitted positioning at the beginning and end of the epic, and the other four are positioned in such a way that without any rearrangement of sequence, the epic can be configured as three series whose three beginnings are the three Achilles-decision books and whose three ends are the three Zeus-decision books. Thus all six books would be cued for attention by relative positioning and minor supplemental punctuation. A reading function that articulated the *Iliad* in three series (I = 1–8, II = 9–15, III = 16–24) would gain a great deal in comprehension and lose nothing, because it simply enhances the visibility of the epic's own indications. The same cannot be said of any alternative configuration, including the transmitted linear sequence. From the standpoint of a reader of the *Iliad* who is following the story, the three-series configuration is uniquely optimal.

The experimental repertoire will therefore adopt the *three-series orientational design* as a provisional reading function. Adoption of this function in effect supplements the text with articulation-markers placed after books 8 and 15. These supplementary markers represent reader-work that collaborates with the poet's, which already provides (1) the overarching event trajectory, (2) the orienting books, and (3) the orientative sequence that the movement punctuators

2. Now and then skeptics have informally contested my observation that books 1, 8, 9, 15, 16, and 24 are uniquely suited to orient a reader's attention to the overarching event trajectory. I find these demurrals somewhat facile, because while claiming to adduce *additional* orientation to the epic's overarching event trajectory, they ignore what that trajectory is. One scholar, for example, has suggested to me that book 4, in which Zeus permits Hera and Athena to restart the war, offers just as much orientation as books 8, 15, and 24. Does it? The skeptic may wish to recall that in books 8 and 15 Zeus opposes Hera and declares modifications to the forward course of the epic's events, including, in both books, the death of Patroklos. In book 4, in contrast, Zeus *declines* to oppose Hera and modify the course of events by allowing the truce to hold. Book 18 has also been mentioned to me as deserving inclusion among the orientational books. Granted, Thetis clearly refers to Zeus's promise at 18.74–77. But the six orientational books do not merely mention the major crises of the story: in each one the whole action trajectory focuses on a major decision. The trajectory of book 18 as a whole does not focus attention on the dilemma of Achilles' request and Zeus's agency in fulfilling it. Thetis's own recapitulation of the events leading to Achilles' grief (18.444–56) is symptomatic: it makes no mention of the request she brought to Zeus and Zeus's promise.

3. Users of this book who suspect that any postulated reading function can automatically manufacture its own material, please take note.

emphasize. The addition of these markers is a *complement* to the text, a set of signs that redundantly indicate extraverbal signs the poem provides already.[4] Thus it is comparable to the well-accepted practice of inscribing each hexameter verse on a separate line.

ORIENTATION TO EVENT TRAJECTORIES, ORIENTATION TO THEMES

The localization of orientation in six books, so distributed in the transmitted linear sequence as to permit a consistent placement of the same books as beginnings and ends of three series, confirms the degree to which the *Iliad* accommodates a reader's interest in maintaining a clear orientation to the whole epic. Yet a reader could reasonably ask for even more. So far this study's cognitive repertoire has addressed a reader's interest in orientation to the trajectory of *events*. But a reader of the *Iliad* might well seek *significance* in the story, and as noted in the introduction, the epic's characterizations, speeches, and paradigm narratives offer considerable encouragement to a reader's thematic interest. The question then is whether this poem that accommodates a reader's interest in orientation to its events also accommodates a plausible interest in orientation to its themes.

It would be economical and cognitively efficient if the same arrangement that cued a reader's orientation to the epic's trajectory of events also cued attention to its themes. In fact this is the case, as far as the six orienting books are concerned, because while each orienting book in itself cues attention to the central agencies of the events, the positional analogies also cue attention to the relationships the orienting books bear *to one another*, and these relationships are in large part thematic. For example, books 8, 15, and 24 all hinge upon Zeus's management of conflict between himself and other Olympians. This represents a thematic analogy, not an event trajectory. A comparable observation has been made about books 1, 9, and 16, and the thematic implication of Achilles' decisions in them. The parameters Achilles-Zeus and beginning-end coincide, so that each hypothetical beginning is occupied by a book in which Achilles takes the initiative, and each ending by a book in which Zeus takes the initiative. The arrangement described is a type of parallel sequencing (A_1—Z_1, A_2—Z_2, A_3—Z_3).[5]

4. On redundant cuing, see Rubin 1995: 90–121 and Steinrück 1997a: 88.

5. Some users of this book may wish to compare this three-part articulation to those offered by Taplin 1992, Stanley 1993, and others, or to the many symmetrical two-part arrangements, of which the best known is Whitman 1958. They should bear in mind that the articulation presented in this study is the only one that marks a system of orientation toward the epic's overarching event trajectory. Taplin's three-day articulation marks the chronology of the narrative; Stanley's articulation marks "rings" that supposedly focus attention on whatever stands in the middle segment; Whitman's scheme is "purely and even abstractly architectonic" (1958: 255). Thus despite some areas of overlap, these arrangements are not fundamentally comparable. But those seeking grounds for preferring one arrangement to the others should ask themselves (1) what *function* does each arrangement perform? (2) how *important* is that function? and (3) how *efficiently* does the arrangement serve its putative function?

	A	B	C	M	X	Y	Z
I	1	2	3	4+5	6	7	8
II	9	10	11	12+13+14			15
III	16	17	18	19+20+21	22	23	24

FIGURE 3.1. Three-series orientational design in parallel alignment.

Within the three postulated series, every book occupies a certain position relative either to the beginning of its series or to the end. Since analogous positioning at the beginning indicates thematic analogy, and analogous positioning at the end does likewise, the next question to ask would be whether other positional analogies also cue thematic analogies. A preliminary sign that they do is the fact that books 6 and 22, whose thematic analogies have long been recognized (in both books Hektor returns to Troy and resists or ignores pleas to save himself),[6] stand in exactly analogous positions relative to the ends of their respective series: each is exactly two books from the end. If two such thematically analogous books did *not* stand in analogous positions, the hypothesis of a unique arrangement that optimally served the purpose of orienting a reader's attention would be weakened; but since they do stand in analogous positions, the hypothesis survives a significant test. In fact, as I shall show, examination of the comparably positioned books in the three series reveals many thematic analogies; the parallel arrangement of beginnings and ends extends to the interior segments of the series. Moreover, each series displays an *internal* arrangement of thematically analogous segments based on symmetrical reversal. These two systems (parallel-sequence relations between series, reverse-sequence relations within series) are coordinated and mutually reinforcing: the same position places a book in both systems of relationship without contradiction. Of course, any conflict between the two sets of cues would render the arrangement confusing, diminish its effectiveness, and cast doubt upon its optimality. But since, as I shall show, the cues do not conflict, the postulate of a three-series orientational design survives another test.

Accordingly, the heuristic model will adopt a new provisional function to explore the thematic orientation afforded by the three-series design. Before simulating the function and demonstrating the thematic analogies, an overview of the three series and their positional relationships will be helpful.

Figure 3.1 represents the three series in parallel alignment. The horizontal rows represent the whole *Iliad* arranged in temporal sequence of presentation. Each horizontal row represents a series. The vertical columns represent the epic's similarly positioned thematically analogous segments. The B and C columns are defined by their positional relationship to the A column; the X and Y columns are defined by their positional relationship to the Z column. The

6. For extensive discussion, see Richardson 1993: 152–54. Scully 1990: 42–43 also has good observations.

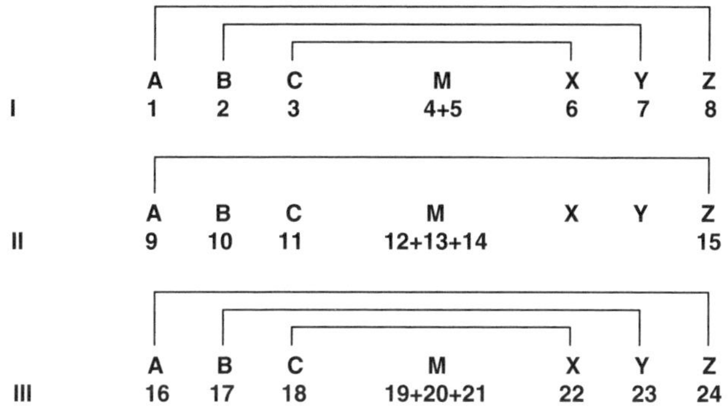

FIGURE 3.2. Relationships of thematically analogous segments.

M (= Middle) column consists of multibook segments defined by their proximity to the A column but not the Z column. This difference in counting is due to the fact that the second series lacks books that are thematically analogous to books 6 and 22 (X column books in series I and III) and to books 7 and 23 (Y column books in series I and III).[7]

Figure 3.2 shows the relationships of thematically analogous segments internal to each series.

The reverse-sequence correspondences suggest that the three series of the *Iliad* are actually three cycles, in each of which the reverse-sequence correspondences represent the sequence of themes returning along its original path, but in the opposite direction, as if the performance were proceeding along a racecourse with two legs and a turn.[8] Figure 3.3 shows the three series as cyclic configurations. In the diagram of cycle II, note the syncopation or "short-cut" that the narrative takes from the middle section of the cycle to the end.

Since the three cycles proceed continuously, the entire epic can be imagined as a spiral path that completes three revolutions. Figure 3.4 (p. 73) illustrates the three cycles as a continuous spiral.

The positional analogies I have described are, in themselves, underdetermined and arbitrary: in fact, the universally observed practice of numbering the "books" in a twenty-four-member series implies a rather different system of positioning, that of a single continuous straight line with one beginning and one end that do not converge. So there is clearly no necessity that determines that, for example, books 1, 9, and 16 should each occupy the initial position in a cycle. The very

7. This omission of analogy where it might have been expected introduces a variation that might cause a reader a moment of confusion, but it scarcely reduces the functional efficiency of the arrangement, which still cues all the major thematic analogies that are present. The omissions in series II are equivalent to a rhythmic syncopation; the regular positional analogy of the series ending, and its corresponding thematic analogy, arrive sooner than expected. But at no point does an actually existing book (or book group, in the case of the M segments) lack thematic analogy with the other books in the analogous position. The slight variation of rhythm might actually promote cognitive orientation, by avoiding mechanical repetition and affirming the poet's agency in fabricating the design.

8. On ring composition as dynamically following a *stadion*-like course out to a turning point, around it, and back, see Lohmann 1970: 15–18; Mueller 1984: 64; and Steinrück 1997a: 60–64.

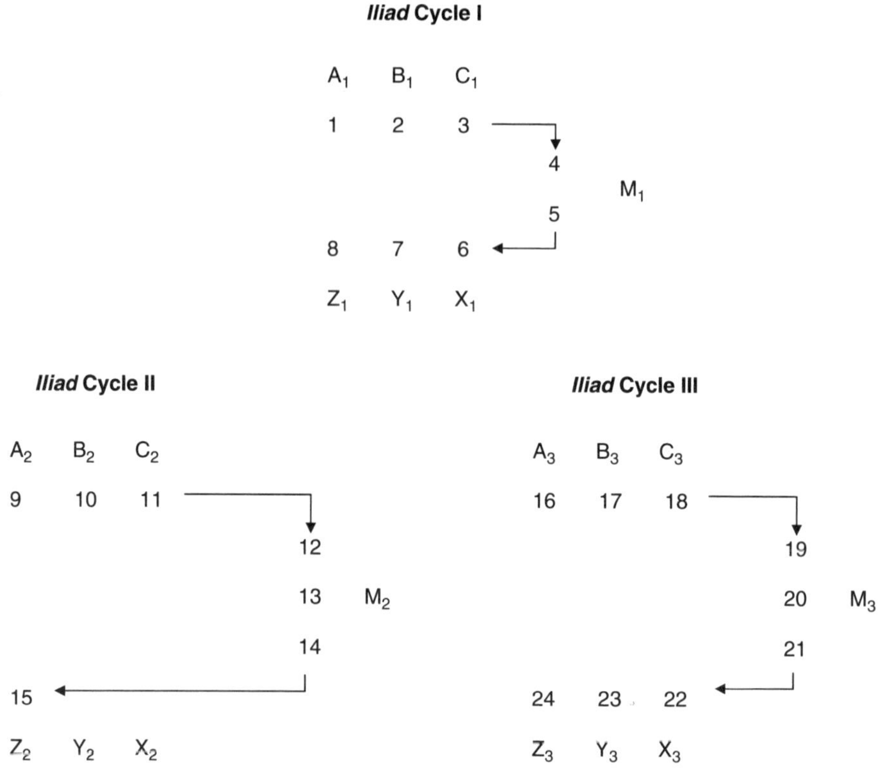

FIGURE 3.3. The three series as cyclic configurations.

arbitrariness of the positioning enhances its potential effectiveness as a cue, since it would compel a reader to *seek* a reason why books 1 and 9 in particular should be similarly positioned, and this reason lies solely in their thematic analogy.

The cyclic arrangement of the *Iliad* offers great clarity and functional economy as a mnemonic system. When adopted, it allows a reader easily and perhaps even intuitively to orient each of the twenty-four marked segments or "books" in relation to any of the others, by positioning them within nesting modules each of which comprises only three elements maximum: at any given point, the epic is traveling within a certain cycle, one of only three; at any given point within that cycle the epic is proceeding along either the beginning leg (A-B-C), the midpoint turn (M), or the back leg (X-Y-Z); and all but two of the legs have exactly three books, the two exceptions both having fewer. The system therefore accommodates the vast scale of the *Iliad* to the limitations of human working memory, which has great difficulty keeping track of more than about seven items at a time, and normally does so by putting them into groups.[9]

9. On the normal capacity of working memory, see Miller 1956: 81–93. Tatum 1993: 484–86 suggests, following R. Sorabji, that the mnemotechnic proposed by Aristotle in *De memoria* involves a system of organizing data into triplets. Also see Rubin 1995: 101–3.

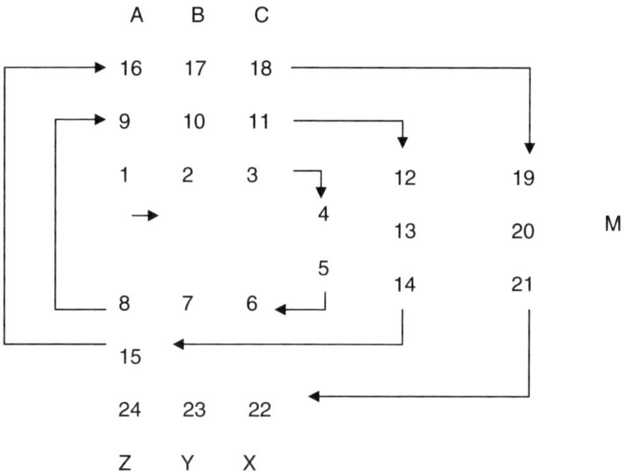

FIGURE 3.4. The three cycles as a continuous spiral.

The immediately following pages will implement the three-cycle/thematic analogy function and present the systemic thematic analogies it encounters converging with it. The simulation will then present the analogies observed between the segments in reverse sequence within each cycle (i.e., A_1—Z_1, etc.)

	A
I	**1**
II	**9**
III	**16**

The segments of the A column, books 1, 9, and 16, each narrate a trajectory in which Achilles makes a decision about the fate of the Greeks that assumes Zeus's critical cooperation. This comprehensive thematic analogy is carried into many details, any of which might provide additional cues to the reader. Many of these details will furnish subjects for interpretation in chapters 5 and 7.

	A	**B**
I	1	**2**
II	9	**10**
III	16	**17**

The segments of the B column, books 2, 10, and 17, all narrate parallel Actions on the Greek and Trojan sides in order to get fighters onto the battlefield.[10] In book 2 the Decision of Zeus to incite the Greeks and Trojans to battle

10. In cycle II, the B column includes the much maligned and often bracketed *Doloneia* (book 10). It is impossible to reargue here the stylistic evidence brought against its authenticity. For the purposes of this

initiates two action-aftermath trajectories in which subordinate decisions are taken by Agamemnon and Hektor, the respective leaders of the two sides. After hearing the message brought from Zeus by Dream in the guise of Nestor, Agamemnon awakens before dawn and convenes a council of the Greek leaders to announce his plan to arm the Greeks, but also to test them first (2.1–83). The eventual marshaling of the Greek fighters is followed by the narrator's catalogue of the Greeks who had originally marshaled at Aulis (2.441–785). This in turn is followed by the parallel assembly of the Trojans. Zeus sends Iris, disguised as Polites, to Priam and Hektor, to urge them to adjourn the assembly and marshal the troops for battle (2.786–806). Hektor issues a call to arms, and the catalogue of Trojans and their allies follows (2.807–77).

Book 10 has a very similar trajectory, except that the initial Decision is not taken by Zeus. Agamemnon, still awake after all the other Greeks have gone to bed, decides to rouse the other leaders and convene a council to devise a plan (10.1–71). Nestor promises great glory to whoever volunteers to reconnoiter the Trojan camp (10.203–17). Meanwhile, on the Trojan side, Hektor has also called a council and promised the horses of Achilles to Dolon for reconnoitering the Greek camp (10.299–337).

The thematic analogy between book 17 and books 2 and 10 might at first glance seem limited, since while the first two B column books each begin with the Problem of putting troops onto the battlefield, in book 17 all the participant characters are already in combat. Nevertheless, after he has killed Euphorbos at the very start of book 17, Menelaos is the only fighter on either side who is present at the particular site that must be fought over, the corpse of Patroklos; and this circumstance determines that in book 17, as in the previous B column books, the event trajectory starts from the Problem that both sides must summon forces to go to the place where they are needed to fight. As in the previous B column books, where both sides marshaled for battle and both sides sent spies, in book 17 the Greeks and Trojans engage in parallel efforts directed at the corpse of Patroklos, which the Trojans aim to desecrate and the Greeks to preserve from desecration.

An overview of the B column segments also indicates that they are related by an archsystemic topos, the disjunctive relationship between conventional heroic risk and military success. Book 2 displays conventional heroism without success when Agamemnon is enticed to lead the troops into battle by the thought that they will conquer the Trojans and their city that very day. On the other hand, Odysseus's success in stopping the flight of the Greeks to their ships, which is indispensable to the Greeks' eventual victory at Troy, can be regarded as an

discussion, it is sufficient to accept the amply supported conclusion of Hainsworth (1993: 151–55; see Danek 1988: 11–13) that the poet of the *Doloneia* did adapt the episode specifically for inclusion in the *Iliad* (i.e., in the transmitted *Iliad*, which is the only *Iliad* known). The observations made here will add elements to our picture of the degree and type of adaptation the poet performed. Improved understanding of the place the *Doloneia* holds in the *Iliad* is relevant to assessment of whether or not it could have been composed as part of the ensemble.

example of "differently heroic" conduct, since Odysseus does not confront a dangerous adversary; in fact, when the troops hail his punishment of Thersites as "the best thing he ever accomplished" (2.272–77), their words ironically indicate the difference between what Odysseus has done and a conventional heroic *aristeia*.[11] In book 10, the Trojan Dolon undertakes the heroic risk of seeking to win a glorious prize, but he fails. In contrast, Diomedes and Odysseus give all the glory to Athena (10.556–57), and they kill a number of very unimpressive adversaries, the sleeping Thracians and the hapless Dolon; but for the Greeks this is a significant success. In book 17 Hektor follows Dolon on the path of unsuccessful heroism by fruitlessly pursuing the horses of Achilles (see the invective of Apollo, 17.75–81) and self-destructively donning the armor of Patroklos (see Zeus's reflections, 17.198–208); while Menelaos, Ajax, and their helpers follow Diomedes and Odysseus on the path of "differently heroic" success by working together as a team to rescue the corpse of Patroklos.

	A	B	**C**
I	1	2	**3**
II	9	10	**11**
III	16	17	**18**

In book 3, the Problem/Decision stage that orients the trajectory of events narrates Paris's challenge to the Greeks, his retreat before Menelaos, Hektor's rebuke, and Paris's decision to meet Menelaos in a duel (3.15–75). The Problem and the Decision to address it therefore imply a systemic theme, the relationship between heroic shame and military tactics. Although neither book 11 nor book 18 exhibits a trajectory that is governed by a Decision exactly like that of Paris in book 3, they do revisit the theme that decision implied. In the Problem stage of book 11, while Agamemnon is putting the Trojans to rout, Zeus sends Hektor a message that as long as he sees Agamemnon fighting in the forefront, he should stay back from the fighting and urge on his troops (11.203–5), but that after Agamemnon is wounded he can take the offensive (11.206–8). The first part of Zeus's instructions tell Hektor *to do* much the same thing Hektor *reproached Paris for doing* in book 3. After Agamemnon departs the battle (wounded by the undistinguished fighter Koön), Diomedes and Odysseus make a stand against Hektor, and Diomedes hits Hektor in the head and sends him fleeing back to the protection of his troops (11.360). But immediately after Hektor's retreat, Paris shoots an arrow from a distance and deals Diomedes a nonlethal wound in the foot (11.368–400). Diomedes ridicules the vaunting Paris much as Hektor had (11.384–95), but the brave spearman's words are empty, for Paris's arrow has incapacitated him, and he must leave the fighting. In book 11 Paris is no less heroic than Diomedes or

11. Also see the pertinent remarks of Haubold 2000: 59.

Hektor—both of whom retreat to cover just as Paris did in book 3—but Paris, fighting from cover, is more effective than they in the forefront, for it is Paris and not Hektor who actually chases the dreaded Diomedes from the battlefield.

On the other hand, the stance articulated by Hektor in book 3, that a fighter should maintain his position in the forefront whatever the risk, immediately reappears in book 11 on the Greek side: when Diomedes is wounded and leaves the battlefield, his companion Odysseus remains alone, and must decide whether to flee or fight. Odysseus decides to fight, because honor demands it (11.408–10) and flight is cowardly: this is exactly the reasoning Hektor articulated when he rebuked Paris in book 3 (3.39–57). But Odysseus cannot prevail in the fighting, and eventually Menelaos and Ajax must lead him away to safety (11.461–88). The opponent who betters Odysseus is not a hero, but a multitude of Trojan fighters without special distinction as individuals. Thus the entire sequence of scenes from Zeus's message up to Odysseus's retreat narrates an anti-*aristeia* in which heroes fight ineffectively and, notwithstanding the inhibitions of shame, retreat before less heroic fighters who attack en masse or from a protected position.

The relationship between heroic shame and military tactics also appears as a theme in the final book of the C column. The interior P/D-A-A trajectory of book 18 (see P/D^2 in fig. 2.10) begins with the Problem that Hektor is about to drag Patroklos's corpse away from Menelaos and the other rescuers (18.165–68). But Iris, at the behest of Hera, comes to Achilles and shames him into taking action to retrieve the corpse (18.178–80). Iris and Achilles, therefore, occupy the roles played in book 3 by Hektor and Paris respectively. Achilles, however, cannot go out to fight the Trojans, because he has no armor (Paris also changes armor in book 3; see 3.332–33); but Iris suggests that Achilles merely show himself from behind the trench, to frighten the Trojans off. This tactic proves effective, though it is exactly contrary to the maximum-exposure-to-risk tactic Hektor urged on Paris in book 3. Then, immediately after the Trojans flee and Patroklos's corpse is brought to the ships, the narrator turns to the Trojan assembly, where Poulydamas advises the Trojans to retreat behind the city wall, but Hektor shames Poulydamas and insists that he himself will meet Achilles in combat (18.243–313). The narrator explicitly says that Poulydamas's counsel was sensible and Hektor's was not. This exchange between Hektor and Poulydamas reenacts that between Hektor and Paris in book 3, except that the whole Trojan army and not Paris alone are now put at stake.

In the C_2 and C_3 books the trajectory-shaping Problems are analogous. In book 11, the rout of the Greeks presents itself to Achilles as a Problem when, from his observation point on his ship, he sees a Greek fighter taken wounded from the battlefield and wonders whether this means that the conditions for his return to the battle have arrived. To find out, he sends Patroklos to learn the identity of the wounded man and bring back the message (11.595–616). In book 18, the Problem that orients the event trajectory occurs when Achilles, again overlooking the battle and again seeing the Greeks in flight back to the ships, receives from Antilochos the message that Patroklos has been killed. This time

Achilles decides that the conditions for his return to battle have indeed arrived (18.88–93), though they are not the conditions he originally imagined. A similar theme is also implied in book 3, when Priam, overlooking the battlefield, expresses curiosity about the identities of the Greek fighters he sees and receives news that his own son Paris is about to fight Menelaos—a report that frightens him and also requires him to come down to the battlefield himself (3.166–263).

The Aftermath stage of book 18 is the description of the shield of Achilles (18.478–607). This passage displays numerous analogies with passages in the other C column books. The most immediately obvious analogue is the description of Agamemnon's arming that preceded the beginning of the third day of battle (11.15–44).[12] Since Thetis's arrival on Olympus and the manufacture of Achilles' armor occur during the evening immediately following the end of the same day of battle, the two armor descriptions together frame the third day of battle, and likewise frame books 11 and 18 taken as a pair. Cycle I also includes an ecphrasis in the C column, the tapestry woven by Helen with depictions of the Trojan War itself (3.125–28).[13]

While the shield as such is similar to ecphrases in the other segments of the C column, the scenes depicted *on* the shield are also analogous to scenes *narrated* elsewhere in the C column.[14] The shield of Achilles depicts a trial by hearing (18.497–508). Book 3 depicts a trial by ordeal in the arranged duel between Paris and Menelaos, in which it is agreed that the winner should be allowed to take Helen and all her possessions.[15] The shield depicts a city in which weddings are taking place (18.491–96) as well as a kind of courtship dance (18.590–605); in book 3 the wedding night of Paris and Helen is explicitly recalled in the Aftermath stage, when Aphrodite forces Helen into bed with Paris (3.383–448, esp. 443–46).[16] Notice that Aphrodite describes Paris as resembling a man just come from dancing, or about to go dancing (3.393–94). The shield also depicts a battle in which cattle and sheep are raided and a city besieged (18.499–540); in book 11, in the Aftermath stage after Patroklos has fulfilled his mission of learning what Achilles sent him for, Nestor regales Patroklos with a story of how in his youth he won fame in a sequence of cattle raids and battles

12. Schadewaldt 1966: 36; Edwards 1987: 278; Edwards 1991: 200; and Stanley 1993: 189.

13. A few skeptics have objected to me that the three ecphrases are of very unequal scale. They are; but this fact does not negate the observations that the ecphrases are thematically analogous (inasmuch as they are all ecphrases) and occur in analogously positioned segments. Analogy neither implies nor requires identity of all features. Of course, readers who do not wish to perform the cognitive work of synairesis are not compelled to do it. In this study, passages are deemed analogous because the poet's work appears to converge and collaborate with the hypothetical reader's, not to obviate it.

14. See Andersen 1976: 5–18 and Aubriot 1999, as well as the conclusion here.

15. See Leaf 1900: 1.296; Kirk 1978: 19. Rousseau 1990: 347–48 also brings the "pre-judicial" procedure in *Iliad* 3 together with the trial depicted on the shield.

16. This resonance is noted emphatically by Andersen 1976: 11. Elsewhere in the *Iliad* only Hera's seduction of Zeus (14.159–351) evokes a wedding in such detail. But as a divine rather than mortal union it may not be directly comparable to those in the C column.

between the Pylians and Epeians (11.669–761); nowhere else in the *Iliad* do we find internal narratives of raiding and battling such as these.[17]

	A	B	C	**M**
I	1	2	3	**4 + 5**
II	9	10	11	**12 + 13 + 14**
III	16	17	18	**19 + 20 + 21**

The segments of the middle branches (column M), unlike those of the beginning and end branches, combine several "books." Yet while each "book" has its own systemic event trajectory,[18] the combinations that make up the M segments are not merely agglomerations of unrelated "book" trajectories. In each combination the systemic event trajectories of the "books" constitute a system organized by a trajectory even higher in the cognitive hierarchy. In each M column branch, the orienting Problem is that a certain event is about to occur sooner than it should. At the beginning of book 4, the Trojan War is about to end before Troy has fallen; in book 12, the Trojans are about to storm the Greek wall, which Zeus has planned to destroy with Poseidon and Apollo after the Greeks have left (7.459–63, 12.10–33); and in book 19, Achilles is about to kill Hektor and lead the storming of Troy. But in each case the imminent event is subjected to a series of delays. In book 4 Zeus contrives that a Trojan break the oath of truce, so that the war does not end; while in book 5 the involvement of gods on both sides prevents victory for either. In book 12 the Trojan approach to the Greek wall is delayed at first by the trench; then, after Zeus has helped Hektor breach the wall, Zeus's inattention allows Poseidon to prevent further Trojan advance, until Zeus again takes charge in book 15. In cycle III, Achilles is ready to charge out after Hektor as soon as he has received his new armor and publicly put aside his anger (19.68), but he must cool his heels while Agamemnon ceremoniously excuses himself of responsibility, delivers the promised gifts, and swears he never touched Briseis, and while the Achaians take refreshments (19.74–351).[19] When the Achaians finally go forth, another delay occurs as Zeus releases all the Olympians to intervene in the battle, explicitly to prevent Achilles from storming Troy prematurely (20.30). As the gods obstruct and baffle Achilles in his attack on Hektor and the city, the fatal confrontation of the heroes is delayed for over one thousand lines of recitation.[20]

17. Schadewaldt 1944: 352; Andersen 1976: 9; Edwards 1991: 218; Haubold 2000: 70. Andersen 1976: 9–11 also compares certain details of the shield's battle scene to other passages in the *Iliad*. Andromache's recollection of how Achilles killed her father and brothers (6.414–24) is arguably comparable to Nestor's narrative and that on the shield.

18. E.g., book 4 = actual hostilities between Greeks and Trojans begin; book 5 = Diomedeia; book 12 = battle for the wall.

19. See Owen 1947: 190–93 and Taplin 1992: 205.

20. See especially Bremer 1987: 33–37; also Owen 1947: 199–202; and Stanley 1993: 201. Edwards 1991: 286 emphasizes expanded scale of presentation rather than retardation of action.

	A	B	C	M	X
I	1	2	3	4 + 5	**6**
II	9	10	11	12 + 13 + 14	
III	16	17	18	19 + 20 + 21	**22**

In book 6 the Problem is that the Greeks have put the Trojans to rout. Helenos proposes to his brother Hektor that he (with Aineias) station himself behind the Trojans to prevent them from fleeing into the city, and then that Hektor go to the city and instruct his mother to lead the Trojan women in making a dedication to Athena (6.73–101). In book 22 the Problem is that Achilles has put the Trojans to rout, and all those not slaughtered have fled into the city, except Hektor, who waits outside the gate to meet Achilles alone, disregarding the pleas of his father and mother to take refuge inside and survive to save the city (22.1–97). In book 6 the Action stage narrates the dedication and prayer of the Trojan women and Athena's refusal to subdue Diomedes on their behalf. In book 22 the Action stage narrates Achilles' pursuit of Hektor, and the scheme of Athena that enables Achilles to defeat him (22.214–305). In book 6 the Aftermath stage narrates Hektor's visits with Helen, Paris, and Andromache; in book 22, the Aftermath stage narrates the lamentation of the Trojans, and especially Priam, Hekabe, and Andromache, because Hektor is dead and will return to them no more.[21]

	A	B	C	M	X	Y
I	1	2	3	4 + 5	6	**7**
II	9	10	11	12 + 13 + 14		
III	16	17	18	19 + 20 + 21	22	**23**

The Problems in the Y column books are different, but the themes are analogous. In book 7 Athena and Apollo face the Problem of ending the day of battle, which they decide to accomplish through the duel of Ajax and Hektor (7.29–42). The Aftermath of the duel is the truce in which both sides collect the remains of their dead and grieve. In book 23 the Problem is that Achilles cannot finish grieving for Patroklos and put him on the pyre. But the ghost of Patroklos tells him that he must, and he does (23.69–92). In the Aftermath of Patroklos's cremation Achilles sponsors the magnificent funeral games that honor his dead companion. The Action stage of book 7 (the duel) is analogous to the Aftermath of book 23 (the games), while the Aftermath of book 7 (the truce for collecting and mourning the dead) is analogous to the Action stage of book 23 (the cremation of Patroklos). Thus the events of the Y column books follow similar trajectories, but in opposite directions. They also share in developing an archsystemic theme, the various relationships between death and glory. Despite fully intending to kill one another, the duelers Ajax and Hektor actually win glory for themselves without

21. For bibliography on books 6 and 22 see note 6.

death, so that their duel is equivalent to a tournament *avant la lettre*. The contestants in the funeral games of book 23 also win glory without death, this time by design. But the occasion of the games is the glorification *in* death of Patroklos, whose funeral the games celebrate.[22] In the Aftermath stage of book 7, the mass cremations of unnamed dead, hard to identify and heaped many to a single pyre (7.421–36), display death *without* glory. The Aftermath stage of book 7 also includes the dialogue of Poseidon and Zeus, in which Zeus agrees to preserve the glory of Poseidon's Trojan wall by destroying that of the Achaians (7.442–63). This scene adds to the topos another permutation: glory with immortality.

	A	B	C	M	X	Y	**Z**
I	1	2	3	4 + 5	6	7	**8**
II	9	10	11	12 + 13 + 14			**15**
III	16	17	18	19 + 20 + 21	22	23	**24**

As mentioned previously, the segments of the Z column (books 8, 15, and 24) each present Zeus confronting a Problem posed by Achilles, proclaiming a plan, and compelling others to cooperate in effecting it (Heiden 1996: 19–21).[23] Thus once again the systemic thematic and event trajectories are analogous.

As we conclude this stage of the simulation, we pause to note that a degree of blurring occurs in the X, Y, and Z columns, as certain subsystemic trajectories offer analogies with subsystemic trajectories in the neighboring column. For example, the dialogue of Poseidon with Zeus at the end of book 7 (7.443–63, Y column) is analogous to the dialogue among Apollo, Hera, and Zeus at the beginning of book 24 (24.31–76, Z column).[24] In each case Zeus hears and resolves divine complaints of mortal impiety and claims of divine self-interest. Such blurring obscures the pattern of analogies slightly, but hardly enough to cause disorientation.[25] The blurring makes for good poetry,[26] and might even assist the orientative function indirectly by avoiding an appearance of mechanical regularity and thereby affirming the poet's agency in creating the design.[27]

22. Kirk 1978: 38–39 shows that the conclusion of the duel between Ajax and Hektor extensively deploys language and motifs apparently borrowed from narratives of funeral games. See also MacLeod 1982: 32–33; Kirk 1990: 249–51, 254, 256–57, 259, 269; Taplin 1992: 258; and Richardson 1993: 213–14, 228, 237, 244, 247.

23. Also see Janko 1992: 234 on Zeus's summaries of the coming action here and at 8.470–76; see also Schadewaldt 1966: 114–15.

24. This analogy does not detract from the passage's participation in the thematic and action trajectories of book 7. In terms of action, the dialogue occurs during the pause in fighting arranged by Apollo and Athena at the beginning of the book, which ends only when the next day of battle begins (book 8). In terms of theme, it extends the archsystemic topos of glory/death into the realm of the immortals, who still enjoy glory but for whom death is impossible.

25. In degree it is not comparable to the serious and numerous inconsistencies that vitiate the schemas of Whitman 1958 and Stanley 1993.

26. "Rien de plus cher que la chanson grise / Où l'Indécis au Précis se joint" (Verlaine, "Art Poétique").

27. Some other examples of blurring in this vicinity are discussed in Heiden 2000a: 50.

THEMATIC SEQUENCES INSIDE CYCLES

The simulation so far has elicited the major thematic analogies among the segments of corresponding position in each cycle. A simplified overview of the major themes indicates that within each cycle they unfold in approximately the following sequence:

A: Achilles decides
B: Disjunctive relationship of heroic risk and military success (abstracted from ["differently heroic" achievement] + [conventionally heroic delusion])
C: Retreat wrongly rejected; warrior identified to onlooker; ecphrasis; trial; wedding; raiding (last three in only two cycles)
M: Delay
X: Hektor returns to Troy; why fight/why not fight (omitted from cycle II)
Y: Uncertain relationship between death and glory (abstracted from [symbolic combat] + [disposal of dead]) (omitted from cycle II)
Z: Zeus decides

This sequence suggests that each cycle follows its initial presentation of Achilles' decision with events that enact typical heroic errors: overconfidence; excessive shame; detachment; lust; and greed.[28] The segments immediately after Achilles' decisions (i.e., B column), however, also display successes achieved somewhat unheroically: Odysseus (and Athena) halting the flight to the ships; Odysseus and Diomedes (and Athena) ambushing the sleeping Thracians; Menelaos retreating from the body of Patroklos (17.90–105) but eventually (with Athena's assistance, 17.543–81) helping to rescue it in a notably collective effort. After the middle section of delay, the sequence turns toward its conclusion by presenting alternatives to heroism: the extemporaneous guest-friendship of Glaukos and Diomedes; the beautiful city and family that Hektor's longing for glory puts at risk; the ghastly consequences of battle and the possibility of honor won without bloodshed; the supremacy and ultimate benevolence of Zeus.

The major themes of each cycle therefore share not only a common sequence but also a common direction: the concluding segments thematically complement the initial ones. In other words, the inner structure of beginning, middle, and end in each cycle—identifiable from the rhythmic phrasing of the cycles (three book-length segments [A, B, C] followed by a multibook segment [M], followed [in cycles I and III] by three book-length segments [X, Y, Z])—also has a certain thematic dimension. This relationship indicates a second system of analogies that operates *within* each cycle. In this system, the three segments leading away

28. The shield readapts some of these errors by correcting them; thus lust is transformed into the civically legitimated sexuality of marriage.

from the M segment (in cycles I and III) complement those leading toward it, in reverse order: X complements C, Y complements B, and Z complements A. In cycle I the relationship of these analogies can be visualized as shown in figure 3.2. The C_1 segment (book 3) displays the Trojan royal males taking the battlefield (systemic event trajectory = Hektor compels brother Paris to help the city on the battlefield, in a man-to-man fight; systemic theme = heroic shame). The X_1 segment (book 6) displays the royal family at home (systemic event trajectory = Hektor's family appeals to him to help the city off the battlefield; systemic theme = heroic shame). The B_1 segment (book 2) narrates the beginning of the first day of battle (systemic event trajectory = Zeus begins day of battle) in a delusory pursuit of glory, while also displaying glory won without heroic risk when Odysseus halts the Achaian flight (systemic theme = disjunctive relationship of heroic risk and military success). The Y_1 segment (book 7) narrates the end of the same day of battle (systemic event trajectory = Athena and Apollo end day of battle) in the grim reality of anonymous mass death (7.421–32; compare the images of anonymous masses assembling for battle in book 2),[29] while also offering the prospect of glory won without bloodshed in the combat of Ajax and Hektor (systemic theme = varying relationship of death and glory). The A_1 and Z_1 segments (books 1 and 8) each present the topic of "decision," focusing attention upon a critical difference: the initiative of Achilles in A_1 as against that of Zeus in Z_1.

The relationships of the analogous segments within cycle III may be visualized as shown in figure 3.2. In the C_3 segment (book 18) Achilles announces his determination to return to battle specifically to kill Hektor (18.92–93, 18.114–15) and to make a Trojan wife shed tears of lamentation (18.122–24); the systemic event trajectory of the book is the preparation for Achilles' revenge. In the X_3 segment (book 22) Achilles takes his revenge, killing Hektor and, as Achilles had predicted, causing the lamentation of a Trojan wife, Andromache. The B_3 segment (book 17) narrates the Achaian effort to recover Patroklos's corpse for honorable burial and Hektor's effort to stop them and desecrate it (systemic trajectory = Greeks/Trojans battle to honor/dishonor Patroklos's corpse), while the Y_3 segment (book 23) narrates the obsequies performed for the same corpse (systemic event trajectory = Patroklos's corpse honored). Achilles' distribution of prizes (which include spoils of war) at the funeral games in the Y_3 segment offers a peaceful alternative to Hektor's delusory pursuit of the spoils of war in B_3, while the peaceful resolution of conflicts at the games recalls the cooperative effort that rescued the corpse whose burial the games solemnize (systemic theme = various relationships between heroic risk and success).[30] The A_3 and Z_3 segments (books 16 and 24) share the dominant theme of "decision," again, as in cycle I, focusing the difference of initiative between Achilles in A_3 and Zeus in Z_3.

29. On suggestions of lamentation in the Greek and Trojan catalogues of *Iliad* 2, see Heiden 2008a: 149–52.

30. Note the involvement of Menelaos and Antilochos in both episodes. On the resolution of conflict at the games see Taplin 1992: 253–60; Richardson 1993: 165–66; Stanley 1993: 225–29.

In cycle II the sequence is syncopated, as we have seen, since the X and Y segments are lacking. Therefore segments B_2 and C_2 have no counterparts in the internal articulation of the cycle. Segments A_2 and Z_2 ((books 9 and 15), like the other A and Z segments, share the topic of "decision," again focusing the critical difference of initiative between Achilles and Zeus. The internal relationship of analogous segments in cycle II may be visualized as shown in figure 3.2.

Application of the provisional three-cycle/thematic orientation function has confirmed that in the *Iliad* thematically analogous segments occupy analogous positions in three successive cycles. This system of coordinating similar themes with similar positions redundantly cues attention to the themes, and thereby suggests synairetic comparisons between distant segments of the epic. A reader of the *Iliad* who seeks to cooperate with its author may reasonably suppose that he purposely sought the effect here observed. Apparently the poet did not expect his reader's work to remain at the concrete level of the narrative description, or fixed solely at the present moment of reading.[31] But rather than supplying an explicit interpretation of his themes, the poet supplied a design that indicated where thematic analogy was to be found. This design is a kind of thematic map for the memory, using cues of temporal sequence.

31. Nor would readers collaborate well with the poet's work on the *Iliad* if instead of attending to analogies among particular passages in the poem, they construed each passage as a *pars pro toto* reference to the whole "tradition," as connoisseurs contemporary with the poem's composition are supposed to have done, according to Foley 1999 and other interpreters of Homer à la "oral poetics." Foley's "traditional referentiality" and some other premises of traditional oral poetics receive astute critique in Scodel 2002: 1–41.

4

Paths of Thought—*Iliad* Cycle I

The preceding three chapters have investigated how the *Iliad* cooperates with a postulated reading function of maintaining a sense of orientation toward the epic's event trajectories and important themes. Among other things, it was found that the *Iliad* lends itself to a cyclic arrangement that, when adopted, cues attention to thematically analogous segments by placing them in analogous positions. In this way the poem guides its reader toward a sense of its major themes and the passages where they are developed.

Readers who benefited from this orientation to the whole epic might also expect it to enrich their understanding of shorter passages. Accordingly, I shall next postulate a reading function that seeks thematic significance in the *relationship* between thematically analogous segments. If it should occur to anyone to wonder why a reader would do this, the story of the *Iliad* itself suggests a reason: the practice of drawing analogies between sequences of events is an elementary form of wisdom that can yield useful information. When Poulydamas interprets the omen of the eagle and the serpent (12.200–229), or when Phoinix tells Achilles the story of Meleager (9.529–605), or when the narrator makes a simile, they are all constructing thematic analogies. Poulydamas and Phoinix each draw upon a sequence of events outside his situation in the story to instruct an addressee about the probable direction of comparable events inside the story.[1] The poet, by narrating analogous passages and placing them in analogous positions within the shape of the poem, has in effect offered his audience a prepared exercise in finding material for analogies, with the help of some discreet cuing. As Hesiod told Perses, a man is good if he follows good advice, but "best of all is the man who perceives everything himself" (*Works and Days* 293).

Of course it is also quite possible that further analysis of the relationships between thematically analogous segments will reveal nothing more than the

1. On paradigm narratives and other forms of "mirroring" in Homeric poetry, see especially Lohmann 1970: 183–212. Lohmann's formulation of "paradigmatische Spiegelung" as a purposeful technique in which "Umkehr und Parallelismus . . . erweisen sich als dialektisch einheitliches Begriffspaar" (185) looks back to the seminal work of Reinhardt 1961, to whose perspectives my analysis here is also indebted. Recent important discussions of paradigmatic or specular narratives in Homer include Létoublon 1983: 24–27; de Jong 1985; and Andersen 1987; as well as Alden 2000 and Collins 2002. Much has been written about the narratives that Glaukos and Diomedes exchange; for especially worthwhile observations, see Scodel 1992 and Harries 1993.

system of orientation itself. In that case the experiment will have identified a certain limit to the epic's convergence with a reader's search for meaning. To investigate the proposed hypothesis, this chapter takes as specimens the three cued pairs within the first cycle: books 3 and 6, 2 and 7, and 1 and 8. Chapter 5 will turn to books 1 and 9, which are the A column books in cycles I and II. Chapter 6 will extend the examination to books 8 and 15, the Z column books in cycles I and II, and to books 9 and 15, the A and Z pair in cycle II. In each case the analysis will begin by taking an "aerial survey" that observes the thematic development of each book alongside its counterpart. The purposes of this stage are (1) to ascertain whether there is enough data to sustain a reader's interest in thematic analogy, and (2) to make a preliminary assessment of the nature of the data. Accordingly, in the surveys interpretation will be kept to a minimum. But as we shall see, the data is more than sufficient to confirm the hypothesis. Each survey of the data will therefore be followed by interpretive discussion.

ILIAD BOOKS 3 AND 6

Books 3 and 6 are the first two comprehensively related segments that one encounters when reading the *Iliad* in sequence. Book 3 (C_1) is the last segment before the turn of the first cycle, book 6 (X_1) the first after the turn (see fig. 3.3). Readers will recall that book 3 tells of the Trojan royal males taking the battlefield, as Paris challenges the Greek heroes but withdraws in fear before Menelaos. Hektor challenges his brother to avoid disgrace; Paris then confronts Menelaos man-to-man; and Priam comes out to swear an oath and sacrifice before the duel. Book 6 tells of the Trojan royal family at home, as Hektor's relatives (brother Helenos, mother Hekabe, sister-in-law Helen, and wife Andromache) variously call on him to serve the city off the battlefield.[2] In each book the whole trajectory of events is informed by the archsystemic theme of heroic shame. So much is clear as soon as we disengage these segments from their immediate narrative context and compare them to one another. A closer look, however, reveals that besides the archsystemic theme of heroic shame, many subsystemic themes in book 6 are also analogous to subsystemic themes found in book 3.[3] In the following "aerial survey,"

2. Books 3 and 6 are also compared in general terms by Kirk 1990: 155.

3. Readers should note that the following investigation of subsystemic analogies is an extension of the analysis of archsystemic analogies presented in the previous chapter. In other words, the analogies between given scenes (which are subsystemic modules) implicitly include those scenes' occurrence in systemically analogous marked segments (in the present specimens, books 3 and 6), as well as their internal (i.e., scene-to-scene) features of convergence. Therefore, this analysis cannot be tested and found trivial simply by asserting that, e.g., similarities among "typical scenes" are found throughout the *Iliad*, so that there is no reason to pick out the scenes in books 3 and 6 as worthy of special attention. This kind of reductio ad absurdum would overlook the shared characteristic of scenes in books 3 and 6 that derives from the unique and multidimensional comparability of *those particular books* that my analysis has already observed. It would also overlook the difference between the conceptual analogies here adduced and the formal similarities of "typical scenes." Conceptual analogies are much rarer than formal similarities (which in Homeric style are of course quite common), and because they are conceptual their thematic significance cannot be doubted (except from the standpoint of a postulated reader whose repertoire has no capacity for edification).

passages in book 6 will be mentioned before those in book 3, to simulate the activity of a reader who in reading book 6 recognizes analogies to book 3 in retrospect.

Thematic Analogy: Aerial Surveys

Book 6 begins with a short series of confrontations in which Greeks kill Trojans. The series ends as Menelaos encounters the Trojan Adrestos, who has been thrown from his chariot in the flight. The helpless Adrestos appeals to Menelaos to take ransom for his life, and Menelaos is about to accept the offer when his brother Agamemnon berates him for softness and convinces him to take the Trojan's life (6.37–65). A scene analogous to this occurs near the beginning of book 3, where Menelaos encountered the Trojan Paris, Paris withdrew to safety, Paris's brother Hektor berated him for not fighting, and Paris accepted his brother's criticism (3.21–75). The two scenes are analogous, in that in each Menelaos attacks a Trojan and one royal brother berates another for being insufficiently aggressive.[4] Note also that while in book 6 Adrestos is lying on the ground helpless when Menelaos approaches him (6.43), in book 3 a simile compares Menelaos approaching Paris to a lion that has discovered an animal already killed by hunters (3.23) and so obviously lying on the ground and unable to flee.

Continuing in book 6: shortly after Menelaos heeds Agamemnon and kills Adrestos, the narration switches to another pair of royal brothers, the Trojans Hektor and Helenos (6.73–115). This second royal-brother scene in book 6 is also analogous to the scene of Hektor and Paris in book 3 (3.30–75).[5] In book 6 Helenos urges his brother Hektor to help the Trojans by leaving the battle and doing something better, i.e., arranging for the women of Troy to pray to Athena and make a dedication to her; in book 3 Hektor taunts his brother Paris *for* leaving the battle (by retreating to safety before Menelaos) and thus disgracing the Trojans.[6]

As book 6 continues, Hektor takes Helenos's advice and travels back to Troy to arrange an offering to Athena, who eventually rejects the prayer of the Trojan women (6.116–18, 237–311). This sequence of scenes recalls a similar sequence in book 3, where after Paris and Menelaos agree to duel, heralds travel back to Troy to summon Priam for a sacrifice before the duel, and the Greeks and Trojans pray to Zeus, who rejects their prayers (3.116–20, 245–302). Figure 4.1 summarizes the analogous scenes in the respective sequences.

In book 6, while Hektor is on his way to Troy, the narration switches to the Greek Diomedes and the Trojan ally Glaukos, whose meeting fills the so-called flat stretch in the temporal continuity (6.119–236).[7] In book 3, there was a

4. For a diagrammatic summary of the analogies, see Heiden 2003a: 165.

5. For a diagrammatic summary of the analogies, see Heiden 2003a: 166.

6. A friendly reader has suggested that the thematic analogy between the scenes is disturbed by their "polarity," since Hektor in book 3 and Helenos in book 6 urge opposite courses of action. I suggest in reply that this reader's sense of disturbance arises from a faulty understanding of polarity. Polarity is itself a kind of analogy, for in order for things to be opposites they must share the criterion with respect to which they are opposed. The urgings of Hektor and Helenos can be seen as "polar" precisely because their frames of reference share many parameters: relationship of brothers, what's good for the Trojans, location of "battle station" relative to the site of engagement.

7. On parallel actions that conceal "flat stretches" in Homeric narration, see Bassett 1938: 39–40.

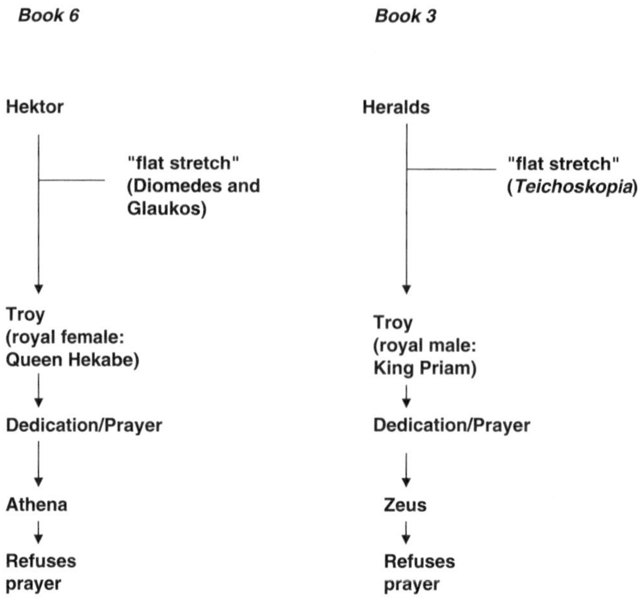

FIGURE 4.1. Analogous sequences in *Iliad* 6 and 3.

similar "flat stretch" while the heralds were on their way to Troy, and this was filled by the scene of the Trojans and Helen on the city wall, the Teichoskopia. These two "flat stretch" insertions display four thematic analogies:[8]

1. Diomedes encounters an unknown enemy fighter (Glaukos) whose identity he seeks and learns (6.119–211); in the Teichoskopia, Priam seeks and learns the identities of several unknown Greek fighters (3.161–244).
2. Glaukos's reply to Diomedes begins with the story of his grandfather Bellerophontes, who was made very handsome by the gods but who rejected the adulterous advances of Anteia, wife of Proitos, whom Zeus had endowed with the scepter of kingship over the Argives (6.156–62);[9] in the Teichoskopia, Helen (former wife of a king of "Argives," though not in Argos) begins her reply to Priam's query about Agamemnon (king of Argos) by expressing regret that she did commit adultery with a guest in her home, the handsome Paris (3.171–76).
3. In book 6, the adversaries Diomedes and Glaukos find they are united by an old bond of hospitality, and they agree not to fight one another (6.212–36); in book 3, the Trojan Antenor recalls when Menelaos and Odysseus, adversaries of the Trojans, were his guests on a embassy on behalf of Helen, i.e., to retrieve the casus belli and thus obviate the

8. For a diagrammatic summary of these analogies, see Heiden 2003a: 168.

9. Bellerophontes is probably to be thought of as a guest in the home of Proitos and Anteia when the incident occurred; see Bouvier 2002: 335 n. 35.

Trojan War (3.203–24; note especially 3.207: *τοὺς δ' ἐγὼ ἐξείνισσα καὶ ἐν μεγάροισι φίλησα*, I hosted them and treated them as friends in my home).

4. In book 6, Glaukos exchanges his more valuable golden armor for Diomedes' bronze, thus confirming their peaceful bond and obviating fighting between them (6.230–36); in book 3, the Trojan elders on the wall wish they could give up the beautiful Helen lest she cause grief for their city in the fighting (3.154–60).

The scene of Glaukos and Diomedes is also thematically analogous to the duel of the Greek Menelaos and the Trojan Paris, which is narrated in book 3 shortly after the Teichoskopia. There are four thematic analogies:[10]

1. Diomedes meets Glaukos on the battlefield, and is confident of his chances if the unknown warrior is a mortal, as he appears to be, but still approaches with caution lest the stranger prove to be a god (6.123–43); in book 3, Menelaos meets Paris on the battlefield, and the narrator compares Menelaos to a lion who stops to scavenge found prey. The lion's scavenging is confident but incautious, because hunters are approaching (3.21–29).
2. Glaukos and Diomedes meet as enemies but forge a bond of hospitality and forgo their expected duel. In book 3, Menelaos and Paris, formerly host and guest, duel as enemies.
3. In book 6, Glaukos and Diomedes ratify their friendship by exchanging armor; in book 3, Menelaos and Paris exchange weapons in hostility by hurling them at one another.
4. The meeting of Glaukos and Diomedes ends when the god Zeus steals Glaukos's wits, so that he agrees to the exchange of armor (6.234–36); this in effect saves a warrior's life, since without the bond of hospitality Diomedes and Glaukos would have fought to the death. It is not clear which warrior would have perished, for while Diomedes is the better fighter, his spear is stuck in the earth, where he plunged it when he realized his connection to his adversary (6.213): the opponent Glaukos faces is already partially disarmed.[11] In book 3, the duel of Paris and Menelaos ends when Aphrodite physically separates Paris from his helmet, which is left in Menelaos's hand, and she snatches Paris from the battlefield, thus saving him from Menelaos's attack (3.373–82).

After the meeting of Diomedes and Glaukos, Hektor arrives at Troy and visits with noncombatants and members of his family. (For the time being, the analysis will leave aside the analogies between the sequence of scenes in book 6 leading

10. For a diagrammatic summary of the analogies, see Heiden 2003a: 169.

11. Alden 2000: 307 correctly notes that Zeus's intervention rescues Glaukos from a dangerous confrontation with Diomedes. She does not note that the situation is also dangerous for Diomedes.

to the dedication of the peplos to Athena and the sequence in book 3 leading to the sacrifices before the duel.) After the narration of the dedication to Athena, Hektor visits the home of his brother Paris, then meets his wife Andromache at the Skaian gate, and finally, with his brother Paris, leaves the city and returns to the battlefield. These scenes are analogous to the scenes in book 3 of noncombatant Trojans both at Troy and on the battlefield.[12]

1. Hektor finds Paris and Helen in their bedchamber together while the fighting continues on the battlefield (6.321–31); this is exactly where the narrator left them the last time they appeared in the story, at the end of book 3 (3.421–48).[13]
2. In book 6, the visitor Hektor reproaches Paris for not fighting (6.325–31), a speech that obviously recalls the beginning of book 3, where the same Hektor taunts the same Paris for not fighting Menelaos (3.38–57); but it also recalls the scene of Helen and Paris in the bedchamber at the end of book 3, where Helen taunts Paris and urges him to fight Menelaos (3.426–36). Book 3 contains two scenes in which Paris is taunted for not fighting, one at the beginning and one at the end; and in fact book 6 also has two, since at the end of book 6, when Hektor and Paris are leaving the city together, Hektor again chides his brother for staying back from the fighting (6.521–25).

Continuing in book 6: after Paris replies to Hektor, Helen then speaks to her brother-in-law (6.343–58), saying she wishes she had died before getting involved in "this trouble" (*τάδε ἔργα*, 6.348); and in book 3, in the Teichoskopia, Helen tells her father-in-law Priam that she wishes she had died before running off with Paris (3.171–76). In book 6, Helen tells her brother-in-law Hektor that the evil destiny she shares with Paris was inflicted on them by Zeus (6.357–58), while in book 3 father-in-law Priam says to Helen that he blames the gods for the war, not her (3.164–65).

Still continuing in book 6: after Hektor leaves Paris and Helen, he meets his own wife Andromache at the Skaian gate; this is the penultimate scene in book 6; in a similar position in book 3 the spouses Helen and Paris are reunited inside Troy.[14] Each wife evaluates her husband as a substitute for family members she has lost, Andromache characterizing Hektor as a substitute for her whole family (6.413–30), Helen taunting Paris because he is inferior to her former husband Menelaos (3.428–29). And each wife gives her husband advice about fighting: Helen first urges Paris to challenge Menelaos again, and then warns him not to, lest Menelaos kill him (3.432–36); Andromache, also concerned that her

12. For a diagrammatic summary, see Heiden 2003a: 170.

13. Some of the analogies between these scenes have been noted by Heitsch 2001: 205–9. Also see Wyatt 1989–90: 19; Scully 1990: 42–43; and Di Benedetto 1998: 191–94.

14. For a diagram representing the following analogies, see Heiden 2003a: 173.

husband may dare too much and be killed, urges him to defend the city wall with the whole army (6.431–36).

Finally, in book 6, after Hektor and Andromache part, Paris comes running after Hektor enthusiastically to rejoin the battle (6.503–19), a scene analogous to that at the beginning of book 3 when Paris runs out in front and challenges the Greeks (3.16–20); and in each scene Paris gets a scolding from his brother Hektor (3.38–57; 6.521–25). The scene at the end of book 6 is analogous to that at the beginning of book 3, as if the two scenes framed the two books taken as a pair.

Retroview

The experiment has shown that if a reader of *Iliad* book 6 were ever to follow the cues to recall book 3, the effort would not be wasted. Virtually every scene in book 6 converges with a counterpart in book 3, and vice versa, and the thematically analogous themes even proceed in approximately parallel order, so that even within the books the ordering of the thematically analogous scenes furnishes redundant cues to their comparability. Interestingly, two scenes that are indispensable to the action trajectory of book 3, Hektor's taunting of Paris and the duel of Paris and Menelaos, converge with Auxiliary scenes in book 6 that could have been omitted altogether without much affecting the trajectory of events, Menelaos's killing of the minor character Adrestos and Diomedes' meeting with Glaukos. Moreover, the analogy between Menelaos's encounter with Adrestos and his earlier encounter with Paris is enhanced in book 3 by a simile that is obviously an unnecessary addition to the narration of the events themselves. Thus, there is no reason to suppose that these thematic analogies might have arisen merely as unintended byproducts of the poet's narration of the action.

It is also very unlikely that the thematic analogies could have arisen as coincidental byproducts of traditional composition repetitively availing itself of a repertoire of scene-types and verbal formulas,[15] because the analogies have little to do with repetitions of either description or language. Menelaos and Paris duel, but Glaukos and Diomedes do not, and analyses of "typical scenes" in Homeric poetry have never to my knowledge observed any connection between the two encounters. The features of "typical" or traditional dueling scenes could scarcely have guided the composition of the aborted duel in book 6 toward analogy with the enacted duel in book 3; and if such "typical" features had actually played a significant role in the composition, they would necessarily have produced a very different encounter between Glaukos and Diomedes from the one narrated in the *Iliad*. The analogies between the Menelaos-Paris duel and the Glaukos-Diomedes cancellation are primarily conceptual rather than linguistic (in terms either of phrases or "speech genres"); they exist *despite* the scenes'

15. Contrast the linguistic explanation of Andersen 1987: 10: "One should perhaps explain such correspondences less by maintaining the 'freedom' of the poet, or his proclivity to invent details, than by counting on a certain thematic steering rooted in the technique of thematic composition and in the employment of parallelism and repetition on a small scale as well as on a grand one. That may be why and how patterns soak through, as it were."

respective features of generic typicality, which align the passages with different types and thus tend to differentiate them rather than draw them together.

There is, in other words, a significant lack of alignment between the *linguistic* formulas (of variable scale) of the *Iliad* and the *concepts* the poem suggests, which in this study I call *themes* in accordance with familiar literary usage. It is very important not to confuse these conceptual "themes" with the "themes" referred to by ethnolinguists, which are defined in large part by linguistic grounding. Gregory Nagy (1979: 78) refers to these linguistically grounded themes when he writes that "in Greek poetry, as also elsewhere in traditional poetry, inherited themes are expressed by inherited forms which are highly regulated by the formulaic system of the genre." The conceptual themes observed in this analysis are not expressed by inherited forms; they are not, properly speaking, expressed at all, since they make their appearance largely through a reader's *apperception* of the characters' Problems and Decisions and the trajectory of events, in cooperation with the poem's linguistic indications. The design of analogous events is perhaps *affected* by a system of verbal formula, but hardly regulated by it. Even Helen's speeches at *Iliad* 3.171–76 and 6.343–58 display surprisingly little repetition of formulaic phrases, although it might have been compositionally efficient and semantically unobjectionable in view of the topoi shared by both passages.[16] The regularities are such as to indicate genre as only one of several factors affecting the composition. The conceptual and positional analogies suggest deliberation and choice rather than regulation, because concepts and poetic shaping are less likely than diction to be a matter of habit; but even more important, because as analogies they involve differences as well as similarities. The analogous passages are too different to be described as regulated by anything other than some personal intention. It is by no means obvious what this intention might be; but it is a legitimate object of a reader's interest. In other words, the thematic analogies between *Iliad* books 3 and 6 invite interpretation.

Thematic Analogy and Thematic Transformation: Interpretations

When Aphrodite rescues Paris from Menelaos, the event looks like a particular, one-time occurrence, the more so because of the special personal connection between Paris and Aphrodite; but when the pairing of books 3 and 6 implicitly juxtaposes Aphrodite's rescue of Paris with Zeus's rescue of Glaukos and/or Diomedes, both events appear as instances of a more general kind of occurrence, a god rescuing a mortal.

At the same time, however, the analogous scenes do not lose their particularity, since in each the role of "god who saves a mortal" is played by a different god, who saves a different hero in a different way for a different reason and with different

16. Compare Russo 1968: 288: "The fact that in the similes the same need, and often the same general content, is expressed through new language, new formulaic phrases, each time is to me a clear sign that . . . orally derived strict economy . . . is no longer really operative in the creation of the *Iliad* and the *Odyssey* as we have them."

results. By implying that narrative situations do belong to certain recurrent kinds, but that the same kind of situation does not always proceed in the same direction or toward the same conclusion, the thematic counterparts indicate that a given narrative situation may after all be open to a broader range of potential choices than those immediately evident to the characters who are in it. This broader range of potential choice is also relevant to the omens, paradigm narratives, and similes of the *Iliad,* for these miniature narratives, like the analogous scenes in books 3 and 6, also display certain significant disparities with the situations they are called upon to model.[17] These disparities are seldom pointed out explicitly, and in the case of the omen interpretations and paradigm narratives the silence is understandable, because the speakers are using the analogies to advocate one particular course of action, not to prompt creative reflection.

The Homeric narrator, however, does highlight the difference between a simile and the target narrative in at least one prominent passage (22.157–61). When he compares Achilles' pursuit of Hektor to a competitive footrace, the simile hinges upon a point of contrast between the pursuit of hero by hero and of racer by racer: in a race, the prize is not a contestant's life:

> *τῇ ῥα παραδραμέτην, φεύγων, ὁ δ' ὄπισθε διώκων·*
> *πρόσθε μὲν ἐσθλὸς ἔφευγε, δίωκε δέ μιν μέγ' ἀμείνων*
> *καρπαλίμως, ἐπεὶ οὐχ ἱερήιον οὐδὲ βοείην*
> *ἀρνύσθην, ἅ τε ποσσὶν ἀέθλια γίγνεται ἀνδρῶν,*
> *ἀλλὰ περὶ ψυχῆς θέον Ἕκτορος ἱπποδάμοιο.*

> There they ran by, one in flight, his pursuer behind.
> Excellent he who ran in front, fleeing, but a far better man pursued him;
> and he ran at full tilt, for they were not competing to win
> an animal for sacrifice, or the hide of an ox—the kind of things
> that men win as prizes in footraces—
> no, the stake was the life of Hektor, tamer of horses.

This difference indicates not only one more potential outcome for a spectacle of footspeed, but a potential outcome of a different kind, in which the victor's superiority to the vanquished is represented by a *symbol* that is arbitrarily related to the loser and the condition of his defeat, rather than by the physical remains of the defeated warrior's insufficiently fast and ultimately motionless body.

17. The often slim—or subtle—connections between the Homeric similes and their narrative comparanda has been noted since the ancient scholiasts; see Clausing 1913. In recent times this phenomenon has been ascribed to the technique of extemporaneous oral composition by Scott 1974: 126–27. Various rhetorical effects of contrast between similes and their comparanda have been emphasized by Bassett 1938: 165–72; Porter 1972: 11–21; Foley 1978: 7–26; Ben-Porat 1992: 737–69; and Heiden 1998b. On the inappropriate and/or ironic relationships between Phoinix's story of Meleager and Achilles' situation in the *Iliad*, see Brenk 1986; Andersen 1987: 4–7; and Heiden 1991: 8–9.

The situations in book 6 often differ from their analogues in book 3 in just the way competitive racers differ from running warriors; that is, the episode in book 6 frequently varies from that in book 3 by introducing one or several elements of arbitrary, symbolic substitution, which open the possibility not only that in a given type of problem situation a plurality of solutions can be found, but also that the possibility of fabricating such solutions is limited only by the imaginative choices—one might say, the poetic imaginations—of the participants. The interpretive discussion in this chapter will largely restrict itself to illustrating this one point, in order to ease the reader's entry into the unusual intertextual analyses that are this study's next experimental trials.[18]

1. In book 3, Hektor berates Paris for retreating from combat (3.39–57), while in book 6, Helenos urges Hektor to help the Trojans precisely *by* retreating from combat (6.86). Hektor's reproach already involves an element of symbolic substitution, since he does not blame Paris for failing to kill his adversary Menelaos, but rather for *representing* the Trojans badly, for the Greeks would think them all laughingstocks if Paris were their champion just because of his pretty looks (3.43–45). Still, Hektor encourages Paris to live up to his boasting, not to replace it with boasting about something else. In the analogous passage in book 6, Hektor's individual physical prowess is dispensable because it can be *replaced*, first of all by Hektor's leadership: Helenos tells Hektor that he and Aineias should strengthen the Trojan ranks by encouraging them, and it is with this encouragement that the rest of the Trojans can replace Hektor in battle while he goes to the city (6.83–86):

> αὐτὰρ ἐπεί κε φάλαγγας ἐποτρύνητον ἁπάσας,
> ἡμεῖς μὲν Δαναοῖσι μαχησόμεθ' αὖθι μένοντες
> [. . . .]
> Ἕκτορ, ἀτὰρ σὺ πόλινδε μετέρχεο . . .
>
> When you two rally the troops throughout the battle-lines
> we will hold our position and fight the Greeks. . . .
> Meanwhile, Hektor, your mission is to go to the city

Once in the city Hektor is to get another substitute: the Trojan women, who are to attempt by sacrifice and prayer the repulse of Diomedes that the Trojan men cannot achieve by arms (6.86–101). Or more precisely, the women ask Athena to accomplish what their menfolk cannot. Thus the poem spins out a long series of substitutions: leadership of a group replaces individual physical prowess (6.77–82); group discipline replaces individual courage (6.83–86); the group of noncombatant women replaces the group of combatant men (6.86–94); the priestess Theano substitutes for the group of noncombatant women in making the dedication and

18. These analyses draw general inspiration from the pioneering *Odyssey-Iliad* intertextual interpretations of Pucci 1987. The specifics, however, are quite different.

prayer (6.297–310); the dedication of a valuable artifact (dyed fabric) substitutes for blood sacrifice (6.90–94, 271–78, 302–10; blood sacrifice is itself a form of substitution for the life of the community); and finally, the immortal Athena is asked to substitute for the mortal Trojan fighters (6.94–101, 271–78, 305–10). In the passage in book 3 substitution is largely deplored; in book 6, it is developed.

2. In book 3 (3.90–94), Menelaos and Paris agree to settle their disagreement on the basis of a contest in which the original disputed property is put at stake between the same original parties (3.92–93):

> *ὁππότερος δέ κε νικήσῃ κρείσσων τε γένηται,*
> *κτήμαθ' ἑλὼν εὖ πάντα γυναῖκά τε οἴκαδ' ἀγέσθω·*

> Whoever prevails in the contest and proves the stronger,
> let him take possession of all the goods and the woman,
> and transport them home.

Notably, the resolution of the conflict is not displaced onto a third party who could make a judgment of guilt or innocence relative to an agreed-upon standard of conduct. In fact, the insistence of both Hektor and Menelaos that the duel will free the Greeks and Trojans from fighting on behalf of Paris and Menelaos (3.83–85, 98–102) implies that the hostile armies *have* served as substitutes for the aggrieved parties up to this point, but will do so no longer. In book 6, when Menelaos encounters the Trojan Adrestos, Adrestos offers Menelaos valuable property (gold, bronze, and iron, 6.46–50) in exchange for his life. Menelaos is inclined to accept the offer (6.51–52), until Agamemnon urges him to reject it in order to exact punishment for the violation of his home by Trojans (6.56–60):

> *σοὶ ἄριστα πεποίηται κατὰ οἶκον*
> *πρὸς Τρώων; τῶν μή τις ὑπεκφύγοι αἰπὺν ὄλεθρον*
> *χεῖράς θ' ἡμετέρας, μηδ' ὅν τινα γαστέρι μήτηρ*
> *κοῦρον ἐόντα φέροι, μηδ' ὃς φύγοι, ἀλλ' ἅμα πάντες*
> *Ἰλίου ἐξαπολοίατ' ἀκήδεστοι καὶ ἄφαντοι.*

> . . . I suppose that was excellent treatment you got at home
> from the Trojans! I hope not one of them outruns the doom
> our hands will deal them, not even some child a mother
> still bears in her womb, not even he should escape; no, but all in Troy
> should perish together, unwept, without a trace.

But Menelaos's home was actually violated by one Trojan, who was not Adrestos, not the unborn Trojan babies Agamemnon would like to see killed in the womb, and needless to say not the pregnant Trojan women who would also have to be killed in order to exterminate their offspring. Agamemnon's merciless counsel employs tropes (litotes + synecdoche: "Did you get the best treatment in your home from the Trojans?") to arbitrarily extend Paris's guilt to every Trojan whatsoever, and to make blood compensation for property.

3. In book 3, Menelaos and Paris fight husband against husband to decide who shall keep the possessions, including Helen, that Paris took with him from Menelaos's home (3.90–93); in book 6, Diomedes and Glaukos, who are emphatically complete strangers when they meet on the battlefield (τίς δὲ σύ ἐσσι; says Diomedes: "who are you?" 6.123), become guest-friends because their grandfathers were guest-friends, and they elect to transfer this relationship to themselves (6.216–25).[19] As noted already, while in book 3 Menelaos and Paris hurl their arms at one another in violence (Menelaos gets to keep Paris's fancy helmet as booty, 3.376–78), in book 6 Glaukos and Diomedes also exchange armor, but in friendship. In book 3, interestingly, the unequal prowess of the combatants is nullified in part by the equal ineffectiveness of their weapons, which break when used (Paris's spear, 3.348; Menelaos's sword, 3.362–63; Paris's helmet-strap, 3.375): the weapons substitute for the warriors, and the effectiveness of the weapons is unrelated to the prowess of the warriors who use them. In book 6 the practical value of weapons is even more attenuated, as the narrator's specification of the grossly unequal cattle-exchange-value of the two sets of arms (6.234–36; the exchange is so unequal that it could not have happened without divine intervention) emphasizes precisely that the value of the armor as a symbol of friendship is wholly arbitrary with respect to its value in a commercial transaction.[20]

4. In book 3, in the Teichoskopia, Priam asks Helen about the identities of the Greek fighters, because he admires their appearance (3.166–70, 191–98, 225–27). For example (3.166–67), he begins the discussion by asking

> *ὥς μοι καὶ τόνδ' ἄνδρα πελώριον ἐξονομήνῃς*
> *ὅς τις ὅδ' ἐστὶν Ἀχαιὸς ἀνὴρ ἠΰς τε μέγας τε.*

> [Sit down here] so you can tell me the name of this man here,
> this giant of a man—who is he?—
> this Greek, a man so big and impressive.

19. When Diomedes treats his friendship with Glaukos as if the friendship of their grandfathers entailed it automatically (μοι ξεῖνος πατρώϊός ἐσσι . . . , "You are my ancestral friend," 6.215), his imagination has run away with him; having just thrust his spear into the ground, he is lucky that Glaukos lets him tell his story before attacking him. If the friendship of Diomedes and Glaukos were already in effect, they would not need to exchange armor, nor would Zeus's intervention be needed to make the exchange possible.

20. The compact between Glaukos and Diomedes employs the same transformation of material into symbol that Menelaos's rejection of Adrestos's offer does, but with the opposite effect. In both cases the issue is guest-friendship. Adrestos did not violate Menelaos's home, but Agamemnon persuades his brother to treat Adrestos as if he had, because of his association with the actual offender. Glaukos was not Diomedes' guest-friend either, but Diomedes treats him as if he were, because of his association with the guest-friend of Diomedes' grandfather. Adrestos offers Menelaos an exchange that is economically very favorable to Menelaos, who would acquire valuable metals and give up nothing of economic value at all. But Agamemnon persuades Menelaos that the violation of his

In book 6, Diomedes inquires about the identity of Glaukos, in spite of his unintimidating mortal appearance (*τίς . . . καταθνητῶν ἀνθρώπων*, 6.123), because Diomedes associates the imminent confrontation with the mythical paradigm of Lykourgos, who attacked the (unintimidating) nurses of Dionysos and put the (unintimidating) infant god to flight, but later suffered for it (6.132–40). Priam, therefore, is impressed by the physical appearance of the heroes he sees right before him, while Diomedes substitutes a story about others, indeed a story about misleading appearances. And Diomedes eventually avoids the approaching combat with Glaukos by taking a detail from Glaukos's genealogical story (which is intended to threaten Diomedes) and connecting it to a detail of his own genealogy of which Glaukos himself is apparently unaware. By this appropriation Diomedes *transforms* the meaning of Glaukos's speech into the reverse of what its speaker intended.[21]

5. In book 3, Paris tells Helen that eros blankets his mind even more than it did when he took her from her home in Lakedaimon (*οὐ γάρ πώ ποτε μ' ὧδε γ' ἔρως φρένας ἀμφεκάλυψεν, κτλ.*, 3.442). In book 6, Glaukos tells Diomedes how Anteia, maddened by lust, propositioned the good-looking Bellerophontes, who rejected her because he had a perceptive mind (*δαΐφρονα*, 6.162) and kept it on good things (*ἀγαθὰ φρονέοντα*), that is, not on the temptation right before his eyes. For Paris, eros is a force that surrounds and immobilizes thought, even buries and implicitly kills it, while Bellerophontes' thought *evades* the erotic madness around him and eventually *removes* Bellerophontes himself (if only via banishment) from subjection to execution—that is, from the absolute material necessity and immobility that is physical death.

6. In book 3, Helen tells her husband Paris that he is no match in combat for the strong Menelaos (*ἀνδρὶ . . . κρατερῷ*), the husband he has replaced (*ὃς ἐμὸς πρότερος πόσις ἦεν*, 3.428–29). In book 6, Andromache tells Hektor that he replaces her dead father, mother, and brothers (6.411–30), because he is her only *comfort* (*θαλπωρή*, 6. 412). For Helen, the replacement husband is evaluated against the physical properties of his predecessor, and she deems the replacement unsatisfactory. For Andromache, Hektor does not replace her family physically, but instead by fulfilling their roles as providers of material and emotional security. In the same pair of scenes, Helen at first urges Paris to fulfill his boasting literally and go back to fight Menelaos, and then advises him to stay home and save his neck

home calls for a punishment that exceeds computation in economic terms. Similarly, Glaukos and Diomedes solemnize their guest-friendship by a symbolic exchange that calls for economic considerations to be ignored by everybody—except Zeus and the narrator, who calls the audience's attention to what has happened.

21. Mackie 1996: 67–71 and 96 has suggested that Glaukos tells the story of his grandfather Bellerophontes as a crafty stratagem to distract Diomedes from fighting him. This cannot be squared with the text, where the narrator, far from even hinting that Glaukos plans to forge a bond with Diomedes, says instead that Zeus has to take Glaukos's wits away to gain his cooperation. But Mackie's discussion usefully observes that Glaukos's speech does in fact have the effect of distracting Diomedes, and that the speech itself follows a rather erratic course and narrates unpredictable movements as part of its subject matter. That the encounter with Diomedes does not go according to Glaukos's plan actually reinforces the theme of distraction that Mackie has noticed.

(3.432–36); while Andromache (who is afraid that Hektor *will* fulfill his boasting and get himself killed doing it) pleads with her heroic husband to lead the whole army in defending the city wall (6.431–34). She explains that the wall needs defense; but the wall also lessens Hektor's personal risk, because in effect it furnishes an artificial substitute for the front line of fighters.

In view of these differences between the counterpart passages, the thematic analogies might be more precisely described as thematic transformations.[22] And since the transformations follow a similar direction, they describe a trajectory to be added to the other trajectories observed so far: a trajectory of *thematic transformation*. In book 3, when characters face problem situations, they envision solutions that involve either direct action upon the very person or thing implicated, or a very close substitute. In book 6, similar problem situations evoke a different potential, the potential for symbolic substitution. This trend of opening a possibility for symbolic thought accords with the synairetic nature of the thematic pairings themselves, and indeed with the underdetermination of the cyclic design that cues the contemplative juxtaposition of books 3 and 6. The potential for imaginative choice is thus a significant theme in the *Iliad*, as well as a basis of its poetic technique.

BOOKS 2 AND 7

In the hypothetical three-cycle arrangement of the *Iliad*, book 7, the penultimate segment in the first cycle (Y column), has an analogous position to book 2, the second (B column) segment in the same cycle (see fig. 3.3). Recall from chapter 3 that the archsystemic event trajectory of book 2 narrates the beginning of the first day of battle, as the sun rises and the Greek and Trojan armies move from camp and city to battlefield; while the archsystemic event trajectory of book 7 narrates the end of the same day of battle as the sun sets and the two armies cease fighting and return to camp and city. The narrative archtrajectories of these two books are thus clearly linked by a synaptic relationship. But, as with books 3 and 6, closer examination of books 2 and 7 reveals many thematic analogies.

Thematic Analogy: Aerial Surveys

To begin with, the respective event trajectories of books 2 and 7 are not only synaptically linked, but they also follow similar directions, since the day of battle begins in book 2 with the instigation of a new battle, and in book 7 the same battle ends—rather counterintuitively—also through the instigation of a new battle, the duel of Hektor and Ajax.[23] In book 7 the gods Apollo and Athena confront the Problem of ending the day of battle by deciding that Hektor should challenge

22. See Reinhardt 1961: 15 on the principle of "Verwandlungen in der Wiederkehr des Gleichen" in the poetry of the *Iliad*; also Pucci 1987 *passim*; and Heiden 2000a: 53, with the other works there cited.

23. See chapter 2 for discussion of the event trajectory of book 2.

one of the Greeks to a duel (7.29–42). The message reaches Hektor supernaturally through his brother the seer Helenos, who tells him that the time is favorable for him to fight (7.47–53). At the beginning of book 2 Zeus faces the Problem of how to instigate battle between the Greeks and Trojans, and he sends a message with Dream to the Greek leader Agamemnon urging him to arm the Greek fighters and assuring him that the time is favorable for the conquest of Troy (2.1–34). Later, Zeus sends Iris to the Trojans with a message that the Greeks are approaching and action must be taken (2.786–87). Iris in the form of Hektor's brother Polites commands Hektor to place the allies under their own leaders.

After Agamemnon awakens from his dream and consults with the other Greek leaders, he tries to rouse his troops to battle by making a speech, but the Greeks flee to their ships instead (2.110–54). In book 7, after taking the advice of Helenos, Hektor tries to rouse a Greek hero to fight by making a speech (7.67–91), but the Greek heroes are afraid of him and do not accept the challenge (7.92–93). Both speeches, Agamemnon's in book 2 and Hektor's in book 7, attempt to arouse the Greeks by threatening them, except that in the "testing speech" the threat is communicated to the Greeks by their own leader, who proclaims that the Trojans have put them to shame. Agamemnon essentially makes the Greeks hear the boasting speech of their enemies, and in this way he challenges his men to prove that the Trojans cannot defeat them after all; but the Greeks are so demoralized that this boasting speech without a boaster throws them into a rout without pursuers.

The speeches themselves also develop similar themes. Both Agamemnon and Hektor begin by pointing to Zeus's failure to give expected help, and his bad intentions for the addressees (2.111–15, 7.69–72). Both speakers propose a course of action whose effects will explicitly be remembered by men far into the future (2.119–33, especially 119; 7.73–91, esp. 87–91). Both speakers propose returning bodies to the women and children who wait for them at home: Agamemnon insincerely proposes that the Greeks should return their bodies while they are alive (2.134–41), while Hektor stipulates that his own dead body should be returned to his family if he should lose the duel (7.77–80). The narrator precedes Hektor's speech by a description of the armies sitting down, elaborated with an image of the sea's surface ruffled by wind (7.63–66), while he follows Agamemnon's speech with a description of the Greek army rising up, elaborated by similes of winds buffeting seas and fields (2.143–52).

In book 2, after the Achaians rush to the ships and Odysseus halts the flight, Thersites rises, rebukes Agamemnon and the Achaians for cowardice, and calls upon the Achaians to sail home with him (2.211–42). In this passage Thersites speaks explicitly on behalf of Achilles (2.239–42), and he serves as Achilles' substitute in opposing Agamemnon and shaming the Achaians for tolerating his leadership. In book 7, when no Greek hero rises to accept Hektor's challenge, Menelaos rebukes the Achaians for cowardice, and offers to fight Hektor himself (7.94–102). This too amounts to a replacement for Achilles, who would have been the obvious candidate to face Hektor (as Agamemnon acknowledges,

7.113–14). Neither Thersites nor Menelaos can replace Achilles, and each is rudely and forcibly put in his place, Thersites by Odysseus, Menelaos by Agamemnon (2.243–69; 7.103–22).

In book 7 no satisfactory opponent to Hektor volunteers until Nestor makes a speech shaming the Greeks (7.123–61). In book 2, the Greek army is not eager to fight until they have heard speeches by Odysseus and Nestor, the latter putting them to shame (2.336–68).

The selection of Hektor's opponent and the duel have no counterpart in book 2.[24] But the scenes in book 7 that follow in the aftermath of the duel have many analogies with scenes in book 2.

When the duel ends, the narrator describes sequences of events occurring on the Greek and Trojan sides in parallel: the Trojans go from the battlefield to Troy, the Greeks from the battlefield to camp (7.294–312); then celebrations, followed by assemblies, take place on both sides (7.313–78). Book 2 similarly represents the Greeks and Trojans acting in parallel: Zeus sends Dream to Agamemnon, and later sends Iris to Hektor (2.1–34, 2.786–810); both sides conduct assemblies that conclude with orders to marshal for battle (Greek assembly 2.84–440; Trojan assembly 2.786–808); each side marches out (Greeks 2.780–85; Trojans 2.808–15).

The particular postduel events in the Greek camp in book 7 are also analogous to the immediate premarshaling events in the Greek camp in book 2. Taken in broad outline, these events present similar sequences that proceed in opposite directions: in book 7 from fighting to feasting to deliberation, in book 2 from deliberation to feasting to marshaling for fighting. At the end of the duel Hektor accepts the suggestion of heralds to discontinue it. He makes a speech to Ajax proposing they make a reconciliation satisfactory to each, and then retire to celebrate with their people (7.287–312). At the end of the assembly in book 2 Agamemnon states in a speech that he regrets his quarrel with Achilles and wishes the Greeks could end their division; then he calls for a meal (2.370–81). In each book these overtures are followed by scenes in which Agamemnon dedicates an ox, and the Greeks feast (7.313–22, 2.398–431).

After the feast in book 7, Nestor addresses the Greek leaders in council (7.323–35). After the feast in book 2, Nestor advises Agamemnon (2.432–40), and in the assembly that has preceded the feast he has addressed the Greeks deliberatively (2.354–68). The topics of Nestor's advice after the feast in book 7 are analogous to those of the post-feast and pre-feast speeches of book 2. Nestor's first topic in book 7 is the need for a pause in the fighting to recover the bodies of those killed in the battle (7.327–32); in book 2, after the feast, Nestor advises Agamemnon that there should be no further delay in sending the troops into battle (2.434–40).

24. Once again, I especially call this omission of analogy to the attention of skeptics who imagine that the postulated cognitive function of thematic analogy can simply manufacture analogies at the reader's will. It requires the cooperation of the poem.

Nestor's second topic in book 7 is the need to cremate the dead, so that later those who return from the war can bring back their bones (7.333–35); in the assembly in book 2, Nestor tells the Greeks it is their duty to return only after raping the wives of the Trojans, and that anyone who wishes to return sooner will die before the others (2.350–59). Finally, in book 7 Nestor advises building fortifications to defend the Greek encampment (7.336–43); in book 2, Nestor concludes his speech to the assembly by advising Agamemnon to arrange his troops in battalions, so that he can identify the cowardly warriors who are keeping the Greeks from victory (2.360–68). Both tactics aim at strengthening the Greeks, in book 7 by adding defensive materiel, in book 2 by subtracting weak offensive manpower.

The Trojan assembly of book 7 replays the start of the war, when Antenor proposes ending the war by returning Helen. Paris refuses, and Priam decides that the Trojans will fight (7.347–78). In book 2 the start of the war is recalled from the Greek side, when Odysseus (2.284–332) and Nestor (2.350–52) remind the Greeks of the marshaling at Aulis, and the narrator recalls the gathering of ships (2.484–785).

After the Trojan assembly of book 7, the herald Idaios goes to the Greek camp to propose a formal truce so that both sides can gather their dead, and Agamemnon accepts the Trojan proposal (7.405–32). In book 2, in the testing speech, Agamemnon himself envisages a formal truce in which the living Greek and Trojan fighters will be gathered and counted (2.123–28). In book 7, during the truce, the unindividuated dead bodies of fallen fighters are burned in sorrow and silence (7.423–32). In book 2, after the assembly, the narrator describes the unindividuated Achaian fighters marching out for battle joyfully and noisily. He compares them to fire (2.455–58) and swarms of noisy birds or insects (2.459–73). The troops' feet make a loud roar as they march (2.465–66); and the prospect of fighting is sweeter to the warriors than the prospect of returning home (2.454–55).[25]

After the truce, book 7 includes a second Aftermath stage, in which Poseidon complains to Zeus that the wall the Greeks are building will obscure the fame of the Trojan wall that Poseidon and Apollo built. Zeus promises Poseidon that he can destroy the Greek wall, so that mortals will not think that they can achieve fame without divine help; but Poseidon's fame will last forever (7.442–63). The corresponding scene in the Aftermath stage of book 2 is the narrator's invocation of the Muses before the recitation of the catalogue of ships (2.484–93). The narrator calls upon the Muses because they preserve the memory of past men, and without their help he could not name the heroes.

As book 7 ends, Zeus's thunder keeps the Greeks and Trojans awake most of the night, but eventually they go to sleep (7.478–82). This scene of mortal

25. In book 2 the march out is followed immediately by the Greek and Trojan catalogues, which associate the armies with their homelands and convey a tone of lamentation for their deaths; for further discussion see Heiden 2008a.

sleeplessness corresponds to the scene of Zeus's sleeplessness that begins book 2 (2.1–34). Thus books 2 and 7 taken as a pair are framed by scenes of sleeplessness and Zeus's planning of troubles for both sides.

Trajectories of Thematic Transformation

Almost every scene in book 7 has a counterpart in book 2, and vice versa, although the duel of Ajax and Hektor in book 7 has no counterpart in book 2. Like the analogous passages of books 3 and 6, those of books 2 and 7 display differences that reveal an unforeseen potential in problem situations. The first day of battle begins with hope, but its aftermath is sorrow and fear. In the morning Agamemnon receives a message from Zeus that convinces him victory is imminent, and later Odysseus and Nestor remind the Greeks that at Aulis Zeus sent them omens that clearly seemed to promise victory (2.299–332, 2.350–53). But at the end of book 7, Zeus's thunderbolts portend evil against both sides (7.478), and they inspire fear rather than hope. In book 2 the common Achaian fighters rush to the ships, and need to be rallied by Odysseus and Nestor (2.283–359); in book 7 the Greek leaders themselves are afraid to meet Hektor's challenge, until Nestor exhorts them (7.123–60). In the morning, Nestor tells the troops that before they can return to their homes they are obligated to exact symbolic vengeance for the rape of Helen by raping the wives of the Trojans (2.354–56); but by the evening he declares that those who return will do so with the actual bones of their dead companions (7.334–35). In the morning Nestor advises offensive tactics that should remove the bad fighters who are keeping the good ones from victory (2.360–68); in the evening he advises building defensive works to augment the Greeks' physical power (7.336–43). The optimistic outlook of the huge armies as they take the field in the morning (2.454–73) gives way by nightfall to thoughts of the large numbers of dead whose corpses must be burned (7.423–32).

In these cases the trajectory of transformation seems to reverse that observed in books 3 and 6: the work of the imagination is undone, and symbols are replaced by material, or at least by less arbitrary symbols. The advancing Achaian army was said to shine *like* fire (2.455–58: synairetic image), while the next day the bodies of the dead are actually burned by fire (7.421–32: synaptic image). The fear inspired by Zeus's thunderbolts in book 7 is closely linked to their actual physical nature, while the hopeful omens in book 2 are related to what they signify much more arbitrarily.

In other cases, however, the added potential derives from the extension of arbitrariness in substitutions. Zeus begins the day of battle planning all alone; his plan already involves a certain symbolic substitution, since Achaian deaths are to bring honor to Achilles (i.e., they are not just deaths, but are to symbolize Achilles' importance to the Greeks). Through Dream Zeus sends Agamemnon exactly the message he wants to send him, almost verbatim (note Zeus's instruction at 2.10, and the nearly exact repetition of 2.11–15 in 2.28–32; but Dream exceeds Zeus's instructions and adds a few lines at the beginning and end of his message). In book 7, at the end of the day of battle, two gods, Athena and Apollo, meet in opposition, but instead of supporting their respective favorite sides, they agree on a plan to suspend hostilities temporarily, so that each accepts a temporary defensive achievement instead of a decisive offensive victory. Apollo's idea for suspending the battle is not actually to stop the fighting, but rather to encourage Hektor to propose a duel; thus one duel substitutes for the general fighting. Unlike Zeus, Apollo does not send a messenger with precisely dictated instructions; instead he lets the seer Helenos mentally grasp his plan, although what Helenos thinks he has heard is not exactly what Apollo has proposed, since Helenos adds that Hektor is not about to die (7.52–53), which Apollo did not say to Athena (7.38–42).

In book 2 Agamemnon tells the Achaians that Zeus has disappointed his hopes for conquering Troy, and he urges them to return home without glory, since they have failed of their objective (2.110–41). In book 7 Hektor tells the Achaians and Trojans that Zeus has disappointed their hopes of ending the war in accordance with the oaths sworn before the combat of Menelaos and Paris (*ὅρκια . . . Κρονίδης . . . οὐκ ἐτέλεσσεν*, 7.69); but Hektor suggests a *substitute* duel. Whereas in the first duel the prize at stake is the actual property stolen by Paris and the lives of Helen's two husbands, in the replacement duel the prize is glory (*κλέος*, 7.91). This prize is exclusively symbolic, since Hektor specifies terms for the return of the loser's corpse to his own people for burial, so that the victor's glory can be represented only by the loser's armor and burial marker—symbols, but not physical remains, of the loser (7.76–91).

In book 2 Thersites stands forth as a substitute for Achilles, but he is rejected, and no further substitute emerges to oppose Agamemnon. In book 7 Menelaos stands forth as a substitute for Achilles when no other Greek will oppose Hektor; Menelaos too is rejected as unqualified to replace Achilles in fighting Hektor, but nine acceptable candidates stand forth subsequently, of whom one, Ajax, is selected by lottery, that is, by random selection of a symbolic token (7.161–90).

In book 2 Nestor complains that the Greeks are all talk and no fight (2.336–43, esp. 2.342, *αὔτως. . .ἐπέεσσ' ἐριδαίνομεν*), and he reminds them of their solemn undertakings to destroy Troy, and Zeus's visible omen of support. Of course Nestor himself is part of the Greek army and will share in the fighting. But the terms of Nestor's exhortation in book 7 are rather different. He thinks better of talk, reminding the Greeks of the good reputation they once enjoyed with Peleus (7.125–31; *μέγ' ἐγήθεεν . . . / πάντων Ἀργείων ἐρέων γενεήν τε τόκον τε*, he really rejoiced . . . when he asked me about each Argive's family and ancestry 7.127–28). Now Nestor himself is mere talk, since he cannot be the one to take on Hektor, and he exhorts the Greeks to replace him, not to join him. Instead of offering himself as an opponent for Hektor, Nestor offers himself as a symbol of an opponent, telling the story of how he once distinguished himself in a challenge fight against Ereuthalion, a physically larger adversary; in other words, the fight had a symbolic purpose to begin with, and the victory did not represent physical superiority but its opposite (7.132–56). In fact, Nestor devotes more of his narrative to the story of the armor he won from Ereuthalion than to the actual duel, and this armor itself was once won by Ereuthalion's lord Lykourgos in an encounter where he used craft to overcome the superior weaponry of his opponent Areithoos and kill him (7.136–45):

> *τοῖσι δ' Ἐρευθαλίων πρόμος ἵστατο, ἰσόθεος φώς,*
> *τεύχε' ἔχων ὤμοισιν Ἀρηϊθόοιο ἄνακτος,*
> *δίου Ἀρηϊθόου, τὸν ἐπίκλησιν κορυνήτην*
> *ἄνδρες κίκλησκον καλλίζωνοί τε γυναῖκες,*
> *οὕνεκ' ἄρ' οὐ τόξοισι μαχέσκετο δουρί τε μακρῷ,*
> *ἀλλὰ σιδηρείῃ κορύνῃ ῥήγνυσκε φάλαγγας.*
> *τὸν Λυκόοργος ἔπεφνε δόλῳ, οὔ τι κράτεΐ γε,*
> *στεινωπῷ ἐν ὁδῷ, ὅθ' ἄρ' οὐ κορύνη οἱ ὄλεθρον*
> *χραῖσμε σιδηρείη· πρὶν γὰρ Λυκόοργος ὑποφθὰς*
> *δουρὶ μέσον περόνησεν, ὁ δ' ὕπτιος οὔδει ἐρείσθη.*
>
> Ereuthalion, a god's equal, arose as their champion.
> On his shoulders he wore the armor of lord Areithoos,
> Areithoos the godlike, known to men and fashionable women
> by the nickname "Slugger," because he never fought
> with bow and arrow, or the heavy spear. No, he used
> an iron club to smash the enemy ranks.
> Lykourgos killed this man, and did it with finesse, not strength,
> in a narrow pass, where the iron club couldn't deal
> a fatal blow. For Lykourgos beat him to the punch,
> slipped beneath his guard, nailed his spear into his middle.
> Areithoos crashed upon the earth, belly up.

Nestor then explains that Lykourgos won Areithoos's armor because "brazen Ares" *gave* it to him (7.146). In other words, Ares replaced Lykourgos's prowess and armor, and the metaphorical metal of Ares' epithet replaced physical metal.[26] Later, when Lykourgos grew old, he made Areithoos's armor a gift to Ereuthalion (*δῶκε δ' Ἐρευθαλίωνι φίλῳ θεράποντι φορῆναι*, 7.149), so that Ereuthalion acquired it without having to defeat its former owner or anybody; Lykourgos chose to bring Ereuthalion and Areithoos's armor together, and thereby to make the armor a symbol of Ereuthalion's chosen service to him rather than of his prowess.[27]

Nestor's background story therefore follows a thematic trajectory of synaireses that become ever more underdetermined. In fact, Nestor's decision to attach the

26. And if one were to suppose that in ascribing Lykourgos's victory to Ares Nestor deployed a "figure of speech," that figure would not reduce the role of arbitrary substitution in Nestor's story, but enhance it.

27. Citing N. Van Brock and others, Nagy 1979: 292 discusses the Greek lexeme *θεράπων* as bearing a prehistoric concept of a "ritual substitute." This trace seems to illuminate the relationship between Lykourgos and Ereuthalion. Like Patroklos, Ereuthalion dies in armor bestowed by his master.

background story is itself underdetermined, a narrative synairesis. When Nestor returns to the main story, his combat with Ereuthalion, he repeats the thematic trajectory implied by the background story. Ereuthalion wore Lykourgos's gift, Areithoos's armor, when he fought Nestor, but in the contest its strength helped Ereuthalion no more than the strength of his hand: according to Nestor it was Athena who gave him the victory over Ereuthalion (δῶκεν δέ μοι εὖχος Ἀθήνη, 7.154). Thus, as Nestor tells it, the whole contest was a symbol of Athena's superiority to both combatants. Ereuthalion, who acquired his special armor because of his *assistance* rather than his prowess, lost to Nestor, who had Athena's assistance.

The selection of the Greek combatant has no counterpart in book 2, but it does contribute to the emphasis upon symbolic substitution, since by using a lottery the Greeks actually select not a warrior but a token of a warrior, and even the warrior chosen fights as a representative of the honor of the group, not as a seeker of honor for himself. The actual duel is ultimately settled not by the combatants Ajax and Hektor, but by the heralds, whose very role is that of human symbols, substitutes for their masters; they step between the fighters and offer both of them recognition that substitutes for a final victory of one combatant over the other ("You're both good spear-fighters, and everyone knows it" 7.281). Ajax and Hektor then exchange words, and finally arms; the contest is resolved in the story that others will tell, that Ajax and Hektor fought in hate but joined in friendship (7.301–2). The exchange of arms is unequal, since Hektor gives three valuable items to Ajax's one (7.303–5); Zeus is not needed to steal Hektor's wits, which at the moment are apparently wiser than Glaukos's were earlier.

In book 2, the narrator asks the Muses to help him tell who assembled at Aulis, since he could never do it without them (2.484–92). This request implies that many mortal achievements have been lost to fame because the Muses did not preserve them: mortal achievements either cease to exist altogether, or the Muses' memory allows a poet to supply a replacement in the medium of synaptic reporting by divine informants ("you know all things" says the narrator, 2.485). In book 7 the Greeks construct a great fortification without making sacrifices to the gods, that is, without seeking divine help, and Poseidon worries that the glory of the Olympians will be diminished by the continued existence of the Greek structure. In particular he worries that it will obscure the fame he and Apollo enjoy for building the Trojan Wall (which is destined to fall and not be replaced) (7.451–53):

> τοῦ δ' ἤτοι κλέος ἔσται ὅσον τ' ἐπικίδναται ἠώς.
> τοῦ δ' ἐπιλήσονται τὸ ἐγὼ καὶ Φοῖβος Ἀπόλλων
> ἥρῳ Λαομέδοντι πολίσσαμεν ἀθλήσαντε.

> I tell you [their fortifications] will be famous wherever the sun shines,
> while people will forget the wall that Apollo and I constructed
> for the hero Laomedon, when we served him as laborers.

Zeus, however, assures his brother that as a powerful god his fame will be undiminished (7.456–58) and he gives Poseidon permission to destroy the Greek fortification and cover it over with sand (7.461–63):

> *τεῖχος ἀναρρήξας τὸ μὲν εἰς ἅλα πᾶν καταχεῦαι,*
> *αὖτις δ' ἠιόνα μεγάλην ψαμάθοισι καλύψαι,*
> *ὥς κέν τοι μέγα τεῖχος ἀμαλδύνηται Ἀχαιῶν.*
>
> Break up the wall and shove it entirely into the sea;
> then cover the whole coast in sand,
> to obliterate the Greeks' great wall.

Thus the medium of Poseidon's fame is not to be any visible object or signifier that bears the synaptic trace of his presence, but precisely the absence of such a signifier. Poseidon does not even need the memory of the Muses, because unlike mortals and their works, gods do not cease to exist. Since Poseidon's power exceeds his visible deeds, his glory must be evoked in symbolic story, rather than reported from memory. And this symbolic story is also the only medium through which the vanished Greek fortifications are remembered.[28]

BOOKS 1 AND 8

The last pair in the first cycle are the A and Z books (see fig. 3.3). These books are clearly linked by a synaptic relationship, since in book 8 Zeus takes steps to fulfill the promise he made to Achilles in book 1. They also share the archsystemic theme of decision, with Achilles deciding in book 1 and Zeus in book 8.

Thematic Analogy: Aerial Surveys

In the Problem/Decision stage of book 8, Zeus decides that to fulfill his promise to Thetis he must prevent the other Olympians from interfering in the coming day's battle.[29] Later, when Hera and Athena prepare to defy him and go down to the battlefield, Zeus sends Iris to hale them back to Olympus, where he threatens them with physical punishment and warns Hera that she cannot make him change his plan. Book 8 therefore has two Olympian scenes (Problem/Decision and Aftermath[1]), in both of which Zeus warns the other gods against trying to disrupt his plan.[30] These scenes taken together recycle and transform many themes from the Aftermath stage of book 1, where Zeus rebuffs Hera's inquiries about his planning with Thetis.

In the Problem/Decision stage of book 8 (8.1–40), Zeus warns the gods not to interfere with his plan and threatens physical punishment if they disobey him:

28. Well noted by Taplin 1992: 140.
29. For the event trajectories of book 1 and book 8, see chapter 2.
30. On the correspondence of the two Olympian scenes, see Schäfer 1990: 71 and Stanley 1993: 105.

he says he will throw any offender down to Tartarus (8.13–16).[31] In the Aftermath stage of book 1 (1.531–611), after Hera complains to Zeus about his plan to help Achilles, Zeus threatens her with violence, and Hephaistos recalls when Zeus tossed him bodily off Olympus (1.560–94).

The Aftermath stage of book 8 begins as Zeus returns to the assembly of the gods and takes his throne (8.438–43). Two gods, Hera and Athena, sulk silently, and Zeus warns them that he could toss them from Olympus permanently with the violence of his thunderbolt (8.444–56). Hera replies, asserting that she respects Zeus's strength, and will not help the Greeks physically, but with counsel alone (8.457–68). Zeus then reveals part of his plan to Hera, but warns her that there is nothing she can do to alter it (8.469–83). Hera does not answer, and then the sun sets (8.485–86). In book 1, the Aftermath stage also begins as Zeus returns to the assembly of the gods and takes his throne (1.533–36). Hera then angrily accuses Zeus of keeping secrets from her, and Zeus replies that he can withhold from Hera anything he wishes (1.536–50). Then Hera explains that she fears he has planned with Thetis to destroy many Greeks (1.551–59), and Zeus replies that whatever he has planned, she can do nothing to stop him, and that if he laid hands on her none of the Olympians could help her (1.560–67). Hera does not answer, but Hephaistos then reminds her that Zeus could toss all the Olympians from their homes, and that he once tossed Hephaistos himself down into the sea (1.571–94). The Olympians then party until the sun sets (1.595–611). Figure 4.2 summarizes this sequence of analogous passages in the two Aftermath stages.

The Action stage of book 8 narrates the short battle in which Zeus helps the Trojans. Intervention by other gods is very limited, since Zeus has prohibited it, but some does occur, and Zeus himself helps the Greeks at one point when the battle threatens to swing too far in the Trojans' favor. No battle occurs in book 1, but even so, many passages in the battle in book 8 transform themes in the Problem/Decision and Action stages of book 1, which narrate the quarrel between Agamemnon and Achilles and the action Achilles takes to bring Zeus onto his side.

In the first part of the Action stage in book 8 (8.68–197) Zeus helps the Trojans in the battle, fulfilling the promise he made to Thetis in the Action stage of book 1 (1.407–12, 1.503–30). But Hera does not accept Zeus's dispensation contentedly, and she calls on Poseidon to join her in helping the Greeks, telling him that all the gods together could overcome Zeus (8.198–211). Book 1 contains an analogous event: Achilles tries to overcome Agamemnon by forming an alliance with his divine mother Thetis and Zeus. In appealing to Thetis to obtain Zeus's cooperation against Agamemnon, Achilles recalls the time Hera, Poseidon, and Athena allied

31. Schäfer 1990: 63–64 observes that in boasting that the other gods all together could not pull him down from Olympus by a rope (8.18–27) Zeus does not issue a threat of violence but a challenge to a kind of athletic contest, an Olympian tug-of-war. The demonstration of strength would be symbolic.

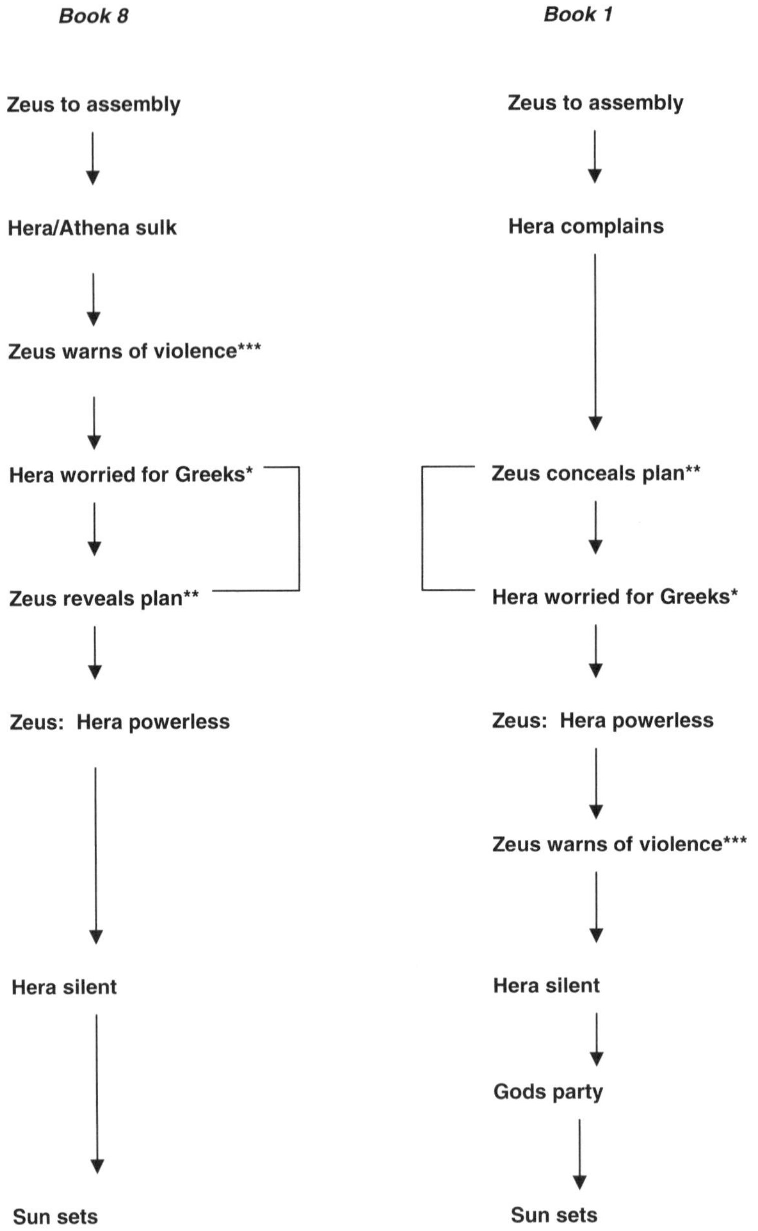

FIGURE 4.2. Aftermath stages. Brackets indicate counterpart pairs. Elements marked with one or more asterisks are out-of-sequence counterparts to similarly marked elements.

themselves against Zeus but without success, because Thetis and Briareus allied themselves with Zeus and frightened his adversaries away (1.393–406).[32]

32. Willcock 1964: 144 suggests that Homer chose the three plotters named at 1.400 to coincide with the pro-Achaian trio of the *Iliad*.

In book 8, when Poseidon rejects Hera's proposition, Hera takes the only type of action permitted to her, that of giving the Greeks counsel: she inspires Agamemnon to rally the Greeks, and he then prays to Zeus, reminding Zeus of his regular sacrifices (8.212–52). The prayer is successful: Zeus responds by showing the Greeks a sign that inspires them to counterattack (8.247–52). This counterattack is led by nine named heroes, but the outstanding defender is the unlikely Teukros (8.273–99). Agamemnon offers Teukros prizes, including a concubine, if the Greeks conquer Troy (8.287–91):

> *αἴ κέν μοι δώῃ Ζεύς τ' αἰγίοχος καὶ Ἀθήνη*
> *Ἰλίου ἐξαλαπάξαι ἐυκτίμενον πτολίεθρον,*
> *πρώτῳ τοι μετ' ἐμὲ πρεσβήιον ἐν χερὶ θήσω,*
> *ἢ τρίποδ' ἠὲ δύω ἵππους αὐτοῖσιν ὄχεσφιν*
> *ἠὲ γυναῖχ', ἥ κέν τοι ὁμὸν λέχος εἰσαναβαίνοι.*

> If Zeus who holds the aigis and Athena grant me
> the well-built citadel of Troy to sack,
> first prize—after mine—will go to you. I'll hand you
> a tripod, or a pair of horses, complete with gear,
> or a woman, to share your bed with you.

But Teukros rejects the offer, since he is already fighting (*με σπεύδοντα καὶ αὐτὸν*, 8.293) and needs no additional incentive to continue.

This sequence closely follows the sequence of Moves that begins the Greek assembly in book 1 and culminates in the quarrel between Agamemnon and Achilles. When Apollo is decimating the Greeks with plague, Hera inspires Achilles to call the assembly; Achilles suggests to Agamemnon that the Greeks might have angered Apollo by neglecting a sacrifice, and he recommends consulting Apollo's seer (1.53–67). Through the seer, Apollo indicates to the Greeks that they will all be safe from his anger if Agamemnon returns Chryseis to her father without ransom (1.92–100). When Agamemnon refuses to save the Greeks by surrendering Chryseis unless he receives a substitute, Achilles, the Greeks' most effective warrior, offers to replace Agamemnon's concubine later, with other rewards added as well, if the Greeks conquer Troy (1.128–29):

> *τριπλῇ τετραπλῇ τ' ἀποτείσομεν, αἴ κέ ποθι Ζεὺς*
> *δῷσι πόλιν Τροίην εὐτείχεον ἐξαλαπάξαι.*

> We'll repay you three and four times over, if Zeus ever
> grants us Troy, the well-walled city, to sack.

But Agamemnon rejects Achilles' offer, insists on immediate compensation, and threatens to seize it by force (1.116–40). Agamemnon, however, does ultimately follow the seer's instructions, and by propitiating Apollo brings the plague to an

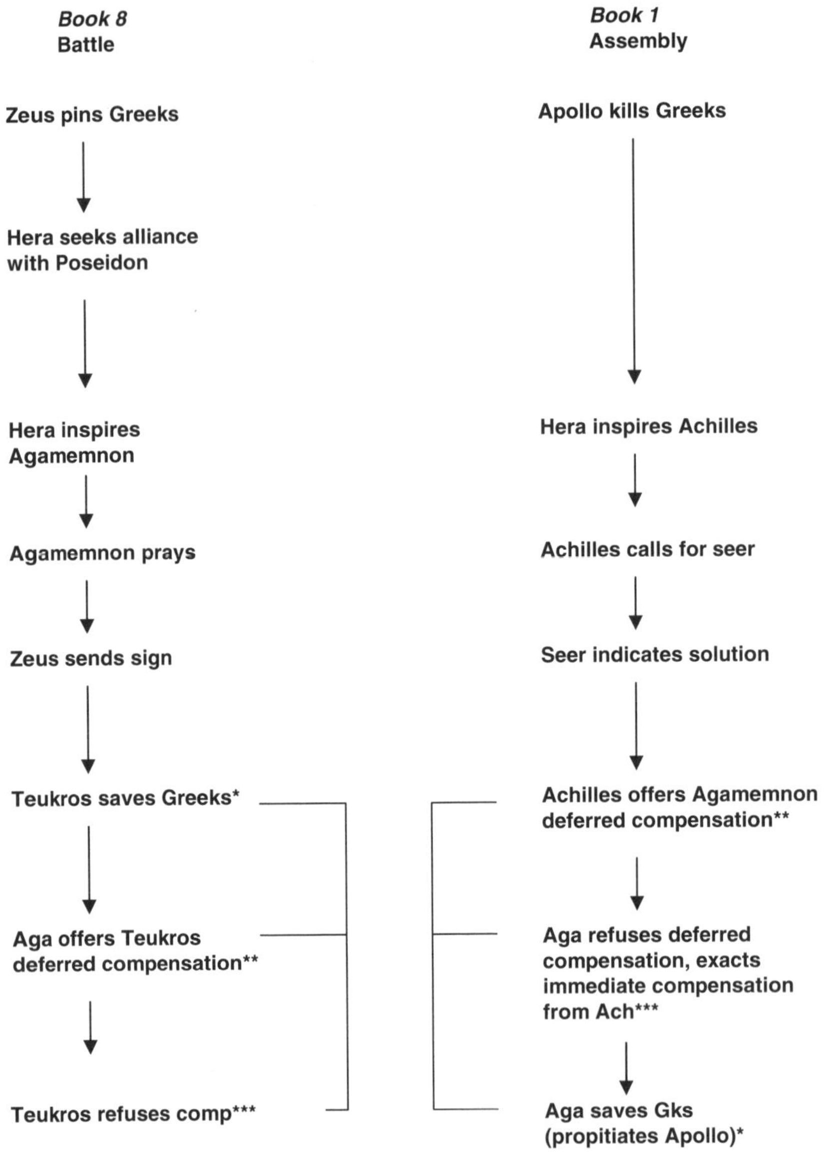

FIGURE 4.3. Analogous Sequences in battle of book 8 and assembly of book 1. Brackets indicate counterpart triplets. Elements marked with one or more asterisks are out-of-sequence counterparts to similarly marked elements.

end. Figure 4.3 illustrates the similar sequences of events that transpire in the battle of book 8 and the assembly of book 1.

Notice that after the reception of the divine sign, the order of events in book 8 reverses that in book 1: Teukros fights to save the Greeks before receiving an offer of compensation, while Agamemnon does not act to save the Greeks until after he has decided what compensation he will receive.

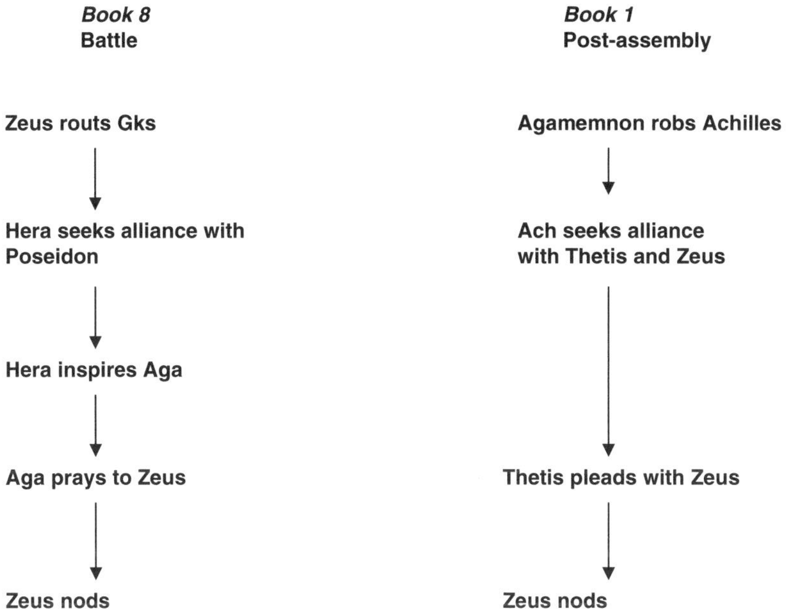

FIGURE 4.4. Sequence following assembly in book 1 alongside Zeus's rout of the Greeks in book 8.

Agamemnon's prayer in book 8 transforms five different divine appeals made in book 1. The reason for this asymmetry may simply be that only one of the appeals in book 1, the appeal of Thetis, is made to Zeus himself. (The other four are the two occasions when Chryses prays to Apollo, Achilles' proposal that Apollo's seer be consulted in case the Greeks have angered Apollo by neglecting a sacrifice, and Achilles' appeal to Thetis to intervene with Zeus on his behalf.) Agamemnon's prayer in book 8 is particularly analogous with the plea of Thetis, and, although Agamemnon does not know it, the object of his prayer is the modification of Zeus's agreement to Thetis's plea. In Agamemnon's prayer in book 8, he asks Zeus whether his intention is to strip one of the Greek kings of honor; he reminds Zeus of the sacrifices he has never failed to make; and he prays to Zeus to let the Greeks escape. Zeus pities Agamemnon, nods his head, and allows the Greeks to rally (8.236–52). When Thetis appeals to Zeus in book 1, she reminds him of the favors she has done him (1.503–4); asks him to help the Trojans and thus correct the dishonor done to Achilles by Agamemnon (1.505–10); and then, when Zeus does not reply, tells him that his refusal would do her dishonor (1.515–16). After some resistance, Zeus nods his approval (1.524–30).

The analogy of Agamemnon's prayer in book 8 with the plea of Thetis in book 1, and the analogy, noted earlier, between Hera's effort to make an alliance against Zeus in book 8 and Achilles' plan in book 1 to draw Zeus into an alliance against Agamemnon, together indicate a second sequence in book 1 that, like the quarrel in the assembly, is recycled into the battle in book 8. Figure 4.4 shows the sequence following the assembly in book 1 alongside the sequence following Zeus's rout of the Greeks in book 8.

In book 8, the Trojans counterattack after Hektor hits Teukros with a rock and puts him out of the battle, ending his *aristeia*. With the Greeks again on the defensive, Hera again tries to interfere on their behalf, this time seeking the cooperation of Athena (8.350–56). Athena responds favorably to Hera's overture, complaining that Zeus forgets how she often saved his son Herakles; she says that Zeus hates her and listens to Thetis instead. But Athena predicts that in time Zeus will again fawn upon her (8.357–72). Hera and Athena then arm themselves and prepare to descend to the battlefield, but before they can get anywhere Zeus dispatches Iris with a warning (8.397–408). Iris reaches Hera and Athena before they can leave the gates of Olympus, and she delivers Zeus's admonitory message (8.424–31). Hera accepts her impotence to obstruct Zeus's wishes, and she and Athena return to the assembly of gods on Olympus (8.425–37).

This sequence transforms the sequence of scenes that occur in the assembly of book 1, when the quarrel breaks out between Agamemnon and Achilles. The analogous scenes call for similar roles to be played by different characters, even though two characters, Hera and Athena, appear in both sequences. Achilles, angry at Agamemnon's threat to take Briseis from him, declares that Agamemnon has forgotten or does not care about the services Achilles has performed for him and Menelaos (1.148–71, esp. 158–60). When Agamemnon replies that he is honored by Zeus and does not care if Achilles takes his men back to Phthia, and that he will take Briseis from Achilles (1.172–87), Achilles prepares to draw his sword to attack him (1.188–94). But before Achilles can do anything against Agamemnon, Hera dispatches Athena, who physically halts Achilles (1.194–214). Achilles accepts Athena's warning (1.215–22). After Athena leaves and Achilles resheathes his sword, he warns Agamemnon that in time the Greeks will long for Achilles, and Agamemnon will repent the wrong he has done him (1.223–44); this corresponds to Athena's prediction that in time Zeus would fawn on her. These analogous sequences are illustrated in figure 4.5.

The return of Hera and Athena to Olympus leads to the first Aftermath stage in book 8, which, as we have seen, offers many analogies with the Aftermath stage of book 1. But after Zeus reveals part of his plan to Hera (8.470–76) he adds that he does not care what Hera thinks about it or where she may go to sulk (8.477–83), a speech analogous to the first part of Agamemnon's reply to Achilles' threat to return to Phthia (1.172–81). In fact it might be said that in this speech in the assembly Agamemnon declares his authority to execute a "Plan of Agamemnon" (taking Briseis) without Achilles' agreement, while later in the Aftermath stage Zeus declares to Hera his authority to execute a "Plan of Zeus" without Hera's agreement, and that Zeus's declaration to Hera in the first Aftermath stage of book 8 offers analogies to both passages.

The second and final Aftermath stage of book 8 transforms the initial Problem/Decision stage of book 1. At the end of book 8, Hektor addresses the assembly of Trojans. He tells them that he expected to destroy the Greeks and their ships and return to Troy victorious, and orders the Trojans to remain encamped in the plain ready to attack the Greeks the next day. Hektor also

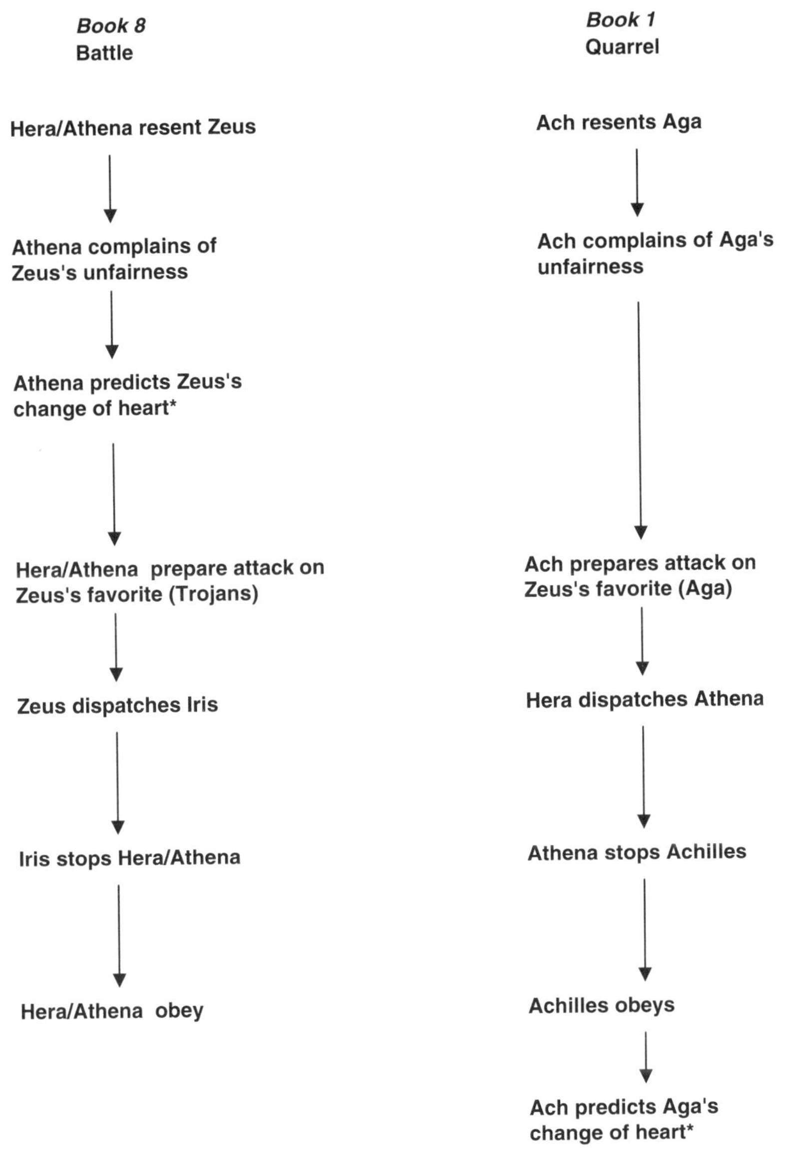

FIGURE 4.5. Divine interventions in books 1 and 8.

prays that Zeus will let him destroy the Greeks, and that he may then be honored as Apollo and Athena are honored. The Trojans offer sacrifices to the gods, but the gods reject them.[33] Numberless fires burn on the plain (8.489–565, end of

33. Kirk, West, and other editors omit 8.548 and 550–52. These lines are not transmitted in the vulgate, but supplied from Pl. *Alcib.* 2.149d, where they are quoted in this context. In rejecting the lines Kirk 1990: 340 cites a number of (apparent) anomalies, but neither individually or cumulatively would they sustain a case for excluding lines that were better attested. Whoever inserted these lines seems to have recognized that the Trojan assembly of book 8 transformed themes from the first Greek assembly of book 1. The interpolation, if such it be, was hardly "Cyclic" (as claimed by Wilamowitz, whom Kirk cites) but "Iliadic" to a very subtle degree.

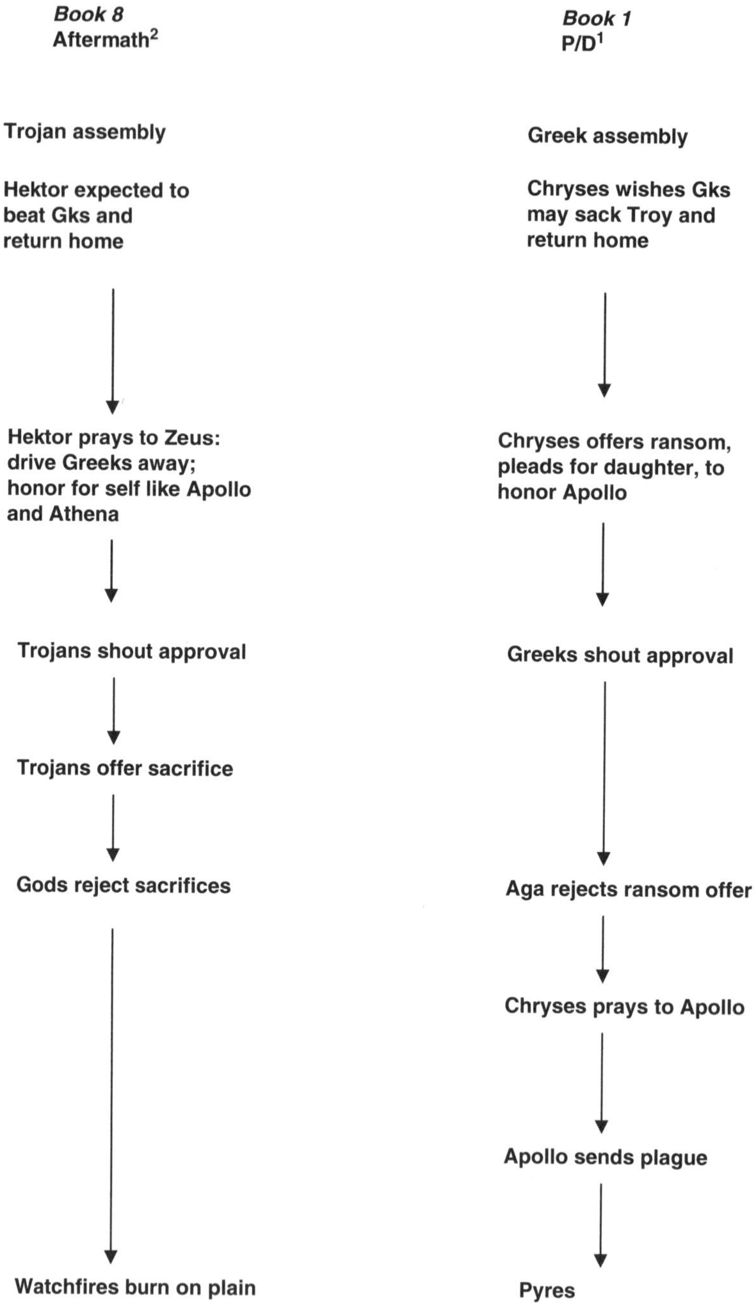

FIGURE 4.6. Assemblies in books 1 and 8.

book). At the beginning of book 1, immediately following the proem, Chryses comes before the Greek assembly and declares a wish that the Greeks may return home safely after capturing Troy, if they honor Apollo by accepting ransom and returning his daughter. The Greeks shout approval, but Agamemnon rejects Chryses' offer. Chryses then prays to Apollo, who accepts Chryses' prayer and sends a plague upon the Greeks. Corpse-fires burn Achaian dead for nine days, and the Achaians think they may have to flee (1.8–61, beginning of book). The analogous events follow similar sequences (see fig. 4.6), except that the sequence of *offering–rejection of offering–prayer* in book 1 is reversed in book 8 to *prayer–offering–rejection of offering*. The two passages enclose books 1 and 8 taken as a pair, and the first cycle as a whole.

Thematic Transformation: Interpretations

Book 8 effects thematic transformations of book 1. In these transformations, as in those that occur between books 3 and 6 or books 2 and 7, the later passages suggest unexplored potentials in the earlier situations, and in particular a potential for ever more arbitrary substitution. In book 1, when Thetis pleads with Zeus on behalf of Achilles, Zeus responds with his nod, which, because it promises fulfillment of Thetis's words without modifying them in any way, leaves the impression that they will be fulfilled exactly as Thetis expects them to be. Yet the nod itself is already a symbolic substitute for Zeus's thought, and thus it implies Zeus's capacity to replace Thetis's words with equivalents of his own choosing. (Thetis herself had in fact already rephrased Achilles' request: compare 1.407–12 and 1.503–10.) When challenged by Hera, Zeus affirms that he can plan as he wishes (1.564–68), which in the immediate context seems to further guarantee the fulfillment of Thetis's plea. Between book 1 and book 8 Zeus does very little to fulfill his promise, a substitution of inaction for action that might arouse more suspicion if its negativity, like Zeus's inarticulate nod, did not seem to leave the specifications of Zeus's promise undisturbed and clear. When Zeus addresses the Olympians at the beginning of book 8 and warns them not to interfere with the speedy accomplishment of his plans, he reiterates (though not verbatim) the declaration of his authority he made to Hera in the Aftermath stage of book 1, and thus the speech implies that he will fulfill his promise to Thetis after all and not somehow replace it. Yet after Zeus has forcefully prohibited the gods from helping on either side, he surprisingly accepts a compromise: Athena says that she will help the Greeks with counsel (*βουλὴν δ' Ἀργείοις ὑποθησόμεθ', ἥ τις ὀνήσει*, 8.36), and Zeus indulges her in this (8.38–40) (Schäfer 1990: 64). Counsel, therefore, replaces arms, and Athena's wish to help the Greeks replaces Zeus's wish to harm them.

The same replacement of arms by counsel occurs later, when Hera wants to help the Greeks in the battle. She appeals to Poseidon to join her so that together they can resist Zeus's force. When Poseidon demurs, Hera adopts a substitute plan, that of giving Agamemnon counsel to stir the Achaians (*ἐπὶ φρεσὶ θῆκ' Ἀγαμέμνονι πότνια Ἥρη/αὐτῷ ποιπνύσαντι θοῶς ὀτρῦναι Ἀχαιούς*, 8.218–19). Agamemnon rallies the Greeks as Hera inspires him to do, but then he chooses to do something else as well: he prays to Zeus, and he reminds Zeus of the oxen he has sacrificed in the hope of conquering Troy (8.236–44). But in this prayer the words about sacrifices take the place of the sacrifices, and a new wish takes the place of the old one: instead of asking Zeus to let him sack Troy, Agamemnon asks that his men not perish.

Agamemnon's prayer occurs at exactly the moment when it appears that Zeus is about to fulfill his promise to Thetis, since Agamemnon himself says that the rout of the Greeks appears likely to put him in dishonor (*τιν' . . . ὑπερμενέων βασιλήων/ . . . μέγα κῦδος ἀπηύρας*; 8.236–37), which is what should have resulted from Achilles' request. Zeus's promise should have meant, at the very least, that when the Greeks and Agamemnon were in distress he would not spare them and save Agamemnon's honor, especially not in response to a prayer from Agamemnon himself, the very man who dishonored Achilles. Yet Zeus heeds Agamemnon's prayer, acting in effect as a substitute for his own adversary (Hera) and substituting Agamemnon's prayer for Thetis's.

Zeus's manner of fulfilling the prayer also involves substitution; whereas Thetis asks Zeus to repay a debt he owes her (though not to repay it in kind), and Agamemnon's reminiscence of his sacrifices implies the same transaction, the narrator explains that Zeus responds favorably for a different reason: when he sees Agamemnon weeping he pities him like a father (*πατὴρ*, 8.245). Zeus's relationship to Agamemnon is not that of a king to a loyal subject, but that of a father to his child. Zeus, however, is not actually Agamemnon's father, while Thetis *is* actually Achilles' mother: in this way too the scene of Agamemnon's prayer in book 8 displays a more arbitrary symbolism than a thematically analogous scene in book 1.

But the revision in Zeus's plan implied by his response to Agamemnon's prayer is minor compared to the one that occurs by the end of book 8. For there Zeus reveals to Hera the plan that he refused to reveal in the Aftermath stage of book 1 and that Hera has not asked about since.[34] Zeus, therefore, has changed his mind about his relationship to Hera, and he has also changed his mind about his plan to fulfill his promise to Thetis, since the plan he reveals to Hera says nothing about either honoring Achilles or disgracing Agamemnon, but proclaims instead that Achilles will return to the fighting for a reason other than the repayment of his honor, namely the death of his comrade Patroklos (8.470–77), and that when Achilles returns Hektor will be stopped (8.473). Patroklos therefore will replace Briseis as the loss Achilles must recoup, and Hektor will replace Agamemnon as the object of Achilles' anger.

Hera's inspiration of Agamemnon in book 8 also recalls her action in book 1 when she stirred Achilles to convene the assembly, an intervention that, unlike her inspiration of Agamemnon in book 8, was not a substitute for another she had abandoned. In the assembly Achilles calls on the seer of Apollo to tell the Greeks if they have omitted a sacrifice, so that they can propitiate Apollo by supplying the omission; Kalchas then tells the assembly in plain Greek that Agamemnon must return the daughter of Apollo's priest, and do it without compensation (*ἀπριάτην ἀνάποινον*, 1.99): Apollo would accept no substitute

34. Schäfer 1990: 72 notes the concession to Hera implicit in Zeus's disclosure.

for Chryseis, and Agamemnon can expect none either. Agamemnon, however, insists upon receiving compensation if he surrenders Chryseis to save the Greeks, and when Achilles offers Agamemnon a minimally symbolic substitute—the *promise* of compensation later when Troy is taken—Agamemnon insists that such a substitution is tantamount to deception, and declares that if the Greeks do not give him a substitute prize of equal worth (ἀντάξιον, 1.136) he will take one himself (αὐτὸς ἕλωμαι 1.137). And eventually he does this, although not by himself but through his representatives.

In book 8, a similar sequence involves a much more liberal play of substitution. As already noted, Agamemnon does not offer Zeus sacrifices, nor does he imply that any sacrifices have been omitted that might need to be replaced; on the contrary, his prayer implies that Zeus's hostility is completely undeserved ("I burned the juicy thighs of cattle on every one of your altars," 8.240). Zeus, in heeding Agamemnon's prayer, is moved emotionally by his relationship to Agamemnon (τὸν δὲ πατὴρ ὀλοφύρατο, 8.245) rather than by Agamemnon's sacrifices, and this relationship, as noted, is symbolic and elective, not biological and necessary. Zeus responds with an omen (αἰετὸν ἧκε, 8.247), not with words, as Apollo's seer Kalchas did in book 1. When the Greek rally begins it looks like the strength of Achilles is to be replaced in kind by that of Diomedes (8.253–60). But it soon transpires that the Greek success depends on nine warriors, not one (8.261–66), and that the most successful of these is Teukros, a man only half-heroic, since he is of less noble birth than his father, he strikes his enemy at a distance with the bow, he needs the shelter of Ajax's shield, and Ajax guards him as a mother does her child (πάις ὣς ὑπὸ μητέρα, 8.271), although he is actually Teukros's half-brother.[35] The paradigm of an artificial hero, Teukros is an arbitrary substitute who requires additional substitutes upon additional substitutes to supplement his physical insufficiency.

Yet it is Teukros who does more to save the Greek cause at this moment than any other Greek fighter, and Agamemnon, who saved the Greeks in book 1 by heeding the instructions of Kalchas, approaches Teukros to offer him material compensation for his heroism, to be delivered when the Greeks conquer Troy (8.281–91).[36] Like Achilles' offer in book 1, Agamemnon's is symbolic insofar as it promises rewards rather than delivering them; unlike Achilles' offer, Agamemnon's is not even remotely a promise of compensation in kind, since in defending the Greeks Teukros is not giving up any of his property. Teukros, however, rejects Agamemnon's offer altogether, declaring that even without compensation or the promise of compensation he is already fighting and eager to continue (8.293–94). Teukros has some motivation to fight other than the desire for material compensation. He does not say what that motivation might be, although Agamemnon, before offering prizes, suggested a few: helping the Greeks, and glorifying his father to compensate for his care (8.282–85):

35. On illegitimacy and its associations, with reference to Teukros in this passage, see Ebbott 2003: 37–40.
36. For a somewhat different interpretation of Teukros's *aristeia* and Agamemnon's offer, see Stanley 1993: 107.

> *βάλλ' οὕτως, αἴ κέν τι φόως Δαναοῖσι γένηαι*
> *πατρί τε σῷ Τελαμῶνι, ὅ σ' ἔτρεφε τυτθὸν ἐόντα,*
> *καί σε νόθον περ ἐόντα κομίσσατο ᾧ ἐνὶ οἴκῳ.*
> *τὸν καὶ τηλόθ' ἐόντα ἐυκλείης ἐπίβησον.*

> Keep shooting, so that you can be a light to the Danaans
> and to your father Telamon, who reared you when you were little
> and accepted you into his family, even though you were a bastard;
> set him in glory, even though he is far away.

Both forms of compensation are nonmaterial, and both compensate Teukros by establishing him in a relationship to others whom he helps: the relationship is Teukros's compensation. In the case of Teukros's relationship to his father Telamon, this is an underdetermined relationship, because Telamon might have disavowed Teukros but chose to raise him in his home as a son; in the case of Teukros's relationship to the Greeks, the tie of blood is even more attenuated, since his half-brother Telemonian Ajax is the only one to whom Teukros has any kin relationship at all.

The comparable sequences in which, in book 1, Athena stops Achilles from killing Agamemnon, and in book 8, Iris stops Hera and Athena from descending to the battlefield, display the same trajectory of transformation, from less arbitrary substitution toward more. In the assembly in book 1, Achilles explains that he did not come to Troy to seek compensation for some loss the Trojans dealt him, but for Agamemnon and Menelaos (who of course came to take back Helen) (1.152–54, 158–59):

> *οὐ γὰρ ἐγὼ Τρώων ἕνεκ' ἤλυθον αἰχμητάων*
> *δεῦρο μαχησόμενος, ἐπεὶ οὔ τί μοι αἴτιοί εἰσιν.*
> *οὐ γάρ πώ ποτ' ἐμὰς βοῦς ἤλασαν* [*κτλ*].
> *ἀλλὰ σοί, ὦ μέγ' ἀναιδές, ἅμ' ἑσπόμεθ', ὄφρα σὺ χαίρῃς,*
> *τιμὴν ἀρνύμενοι Μενελάῳ σοί τε, κυνῶπα . . .*

> I didn't come here to fight on account of the Trojans;
> they've never done me any harm, never raided my cattle [etc.] . . .
> No, we came with you—shameless ingrate—to do you favor
> by getting your due for you and Menelaos—you dog

This implies that Achilles substitutes the Atreidai and their property for his own. But Achilles complains that Agamemnon has forgotten or neglected the service Achilles has rendered (*τῶν οὔ τι μετατρέπῃ κτλ.*, 1.160), since Agamemnon threatens to confiscate the property awarded to Achilles for his labors. This property is actually symbolic, since as Achilles stresses, it is very small (*ὀλίγον*, 1.167) in comparison to the amount of labor he performs (*πλεῖον*, 1.165). But Achilles still likes his compensation (it is *φίλον*, 1.167), and he is very angry that it should be taken from him. In book 8 the stakes for Hera and Athena are rather different; it is the Greeks and not they who suffer because of Zeus's plan, and the goddesses are angry because they want to help the Greeks and harm the Trojans (8.350–80). Athena complains that Zeus has forgotten the services she performed when he commanded her to save his son Herakles (*οὐδέ τι τῶν μέμνηται κτλ.*, 8.362), an affair of substitution all around, since Hera persecuted Herakles as a substitute for Zeus, Athena substituted for Zeus in saving Herakles, and Herakles substituted for Zeus as the beneficiary of Athena's services. In book 1, when Achilles is enraged by Agamemnon's threat, he draws his sword to kill Agamemnon himself (1.194), while in book 8 Hera and Athena take up arms to attack the Trojans, not Zeus himself (8.376–80). In book 1, Athena halts Achilles physically by grabbing his hair, and offers him material compensation for his obedience (1.197, 212–14), while in book 8 Zeus sends Iris to stop Hera and Athena with words, so that he will not have to confront them physically (*οὐ γὰρ καλὰ συνοισόμεθα πτόλεμόνδε*, 8.400). While Zeus offers them no material incentive to obey him, he declares that he is not very angry at Hera. The reason is not that Hera has done something to mitigate his anger, but just the contrary, that she hasn't, since for Hera disobedience is normal behavior (8.407–8):

> *Ἥρῃ δ' οὔ τι τόσον νεμεσίζομαι οὐδὲ χολοῦμαι·*
> *αἰεὶ γάρ μοι ἔωθεν ἐνικλᾶν ὅττι κεν εἴπω.*

Zeus's indulgence is a free gift, a repayment to Hera *not* in her own coin.

PART II

Reading Thematic Trajectories

5

Replacements and Representatives

The Quarrel (Cycle I, Column A) and the Embassy (Cycle II, Column A)

SYNOPSIS: THE THEME OF "THEMES"

The last chapter's experiment simulated a function that methodically performed synairetic comparisons between scenes in books 3 and 6 of the *Iliad*, books 2 and 7, and books 1 and 8, which were selected as specimen pairs of discontiguous segments whose promise of thematic edification was indicated by their arch-systemic analogies and analogous positioning within cycle I. The experiment found that the analogies between the paired books extended into many thematically significant details. Moreover, analysis of the analogies indicated that they were amenable to a higher-level synairesis, an analogy of the analogies that might be called an arch-analogy or master theme. This master theme was synairesis itself: the underdetermined joining of one thing to another (including substituting one thing for another) by an act of choice; or to phrase the same idea another way, interested agents improvisationally fabricating underdetermined relationships. Thus the thematic implications of the characters' choices in the story's action (including its speeches) was analogous to (and this does *not* mean identical to) the choices of a reader in thinking *how to put the story together* as intelligible actions and themes.

Yet while the joinings—action sequences, themes, and analogous positions in the postulated three-cycle design—are underdetermined, they are not simply *un*determined, for they are not underdetermined absolutely and equally. They appear to be semidetermined. Things are put together that accept connection without either compelling or preempting it; they give a certain appearance of synapsis, but they also give an appearance of resistance. They are, therefore, available to synairesis, the active intervention of interested agents, including readers. This observation touches upon the issue of aesthetic unity that has bedeviled appreciation of the *Iliad* and merits a brief expatiation. The semidetermined—and therefore underdetermined—connections of the *Iliad* guarantee that no principle of "organic" unity can ever be found in this poem, because truly organic connections are highly determined. Actually, no poem can have "organic" unity unless "organic" is given a special limited definition that is very far from the ones it bears in most discourse. In comparing poems to organisms Aristotle did about as much good as Homer when he compared Achilles to a lion; both comparisons are illuminating in certain respects, but taken anatomically they are positively misleading. Rarely would anybody give a real natural organism as an example of a work of art, or vice versa, and this is so even though works of art may often bear resemblance to natural organisms, or their materials may have *been* organisms before they became art. What accounts for this virtually unfailing distinguishability between organisms and art? The critical discriminator is probably the degree and kind of determination that governs their respective existences.[1] Organisms are understood as belonging to nature, and belonging to nature is understood as participating in processes that are very highly determined. Works of art, on the other hand, exhibit choices, and in the realm accorded to "nature" these choices are just impossible. Art therefore intervenes upon "nature," and this intervention is constitutive of art's existence, recognizability, and value. Art intervenes upon nature even when it imitates nature, because while nature *reproduces* itself, it does not (as "nature" is usually understood) *imitate* itself.

But art's imitations of nature, while not especially confusing to art-fans, have sown much confusion among many philosophers and critics of art, in part because systematically minded folk (or all folk when thinking systematically) are more interested in nature/necessity than in art/underdeterminism. The commonsense assumptions that "nature" = "everything" and that "natural" = "good" serve us well in many aspects of deliberation, but art is not one of them, and when extended to the consideration of art these assumptions have fostered the erroneous impression that works of art must be, or should be, subject to the same necessities as "everything" else. Thus for a long time it was commonplace for art critics to disparage works of art on grounds of *artificiality*.[2] But to say that a work of art is bad because artificial is like saying that it is bad because it is art. Works of art *are* artificial, all of them, because they are artifacts. No philosopher or critic has ever been able to point to any object agreed to be art in which an element of artifice is lacking. Organisms are something else. The notion that the value of a poem was to be found in a *perfection* like that of natural organisms, that is, things that come into existence by necessity, put investigations of art and poetry on a wrong track.

Appreciation of the *Iliad* has been very ill served by the misguided notion of "organic unity." Many so-called imperfections have been found in the *Iliad*, and since the presence of "imperfection" has generally been regarded as a diminution of poetic quality, explaining "imperfections" became, and still remains, one of Homeric scholarship's primary disciplinary tasks. The "imperfections" of the *Iliad* and *Odyssey* have been approached by (on my count) four general routes: scholars conclude that (1) the *Iliad* and *Odyssey* are primitive, infantile, bad poems (common in the eighteenth century, rarely heard now); (2) the *Iliad* and *Odyssey* are not poems at all, but compilations of shorter and more perfect poems (philological "Analysis"); (3) the perceived imperfections of the *Iliad* and/or the *Odyssey* have

1. On "causal history" as a distinction between art and non-art, see Danto 1981: 33–53; on artifacts and nature, see Dipert 1993.

2. Abrams 1953: 184–225 analyzes the sources of organicism in nineteenth- century aesthetics. His discussion of Carlyle (217) illustrates the antipathy to artifice at its starkest.

been misunderstood, and the epics' perfection would be appreciated if their rhetorical basis were correctly grasped (the view of Aristotle and the so-called Unitarians of the nineteenth and twentieth centuries);[3] and (4) the *Iliad* and *Odyssey* are perfect, qua specimens of a perfect oral/cultural tradition (the view of evolutionary ethnolinguistics, e.g. Foley 1999). Common to all these approaches is the premise that "perfection" and "imperfection" are criteria relevant to the quality of poems. I submit that this premise is false, and that the features identified as "imperfections" in the Homeric poems should be recognized as instances of underdetermination, which is a condition of artistry and can be a symptom of it. The preceding chapters have shown that the *Iliad* does not have "unity" in the sense of a single *logos* that pervades, determines, and explains the poem's every detail. What the *Iliad* does appear to have—I err on the side of caution—is design, that is, a purposeful system of semideterminants, *degrees* of organization, and only degrees, since if the poem were too "perfect" (supposing that were even possible) it would be nature rather than art, and it would not invite the interested engagement of readers, that is, it would not be legible or enjoyable as a poem. The poet of the *Iliad* is sometimes quite flagrant in his display of choice. Every Homeric simile exults in forcing and fabrication. Some have regarded this as bad poetry, or good oral poetry, but I think it is just good poetry in the most fundamental way: synairesis. The "forced" or "errant" Homeric similes intriguingly invite an audience's interest and reward it, but avoid leaving it satisfied. Thus they invite audiences to apply some mental force of their own, the force of deliberation. This is also what the thematic and positional analogies do.

To recognize the analogies the *Iliad* suggests, therefore, is entirely consistent with recognizing the poem's resistance to analogy; in fact a reader *must* recognize the resistance, at least intuitively, in order to apperceive analogy rather than simple identity. In the last chapter, the study of the paired books of cycle I observed resistance consistently, in that the joining was underdetermined and partially arbitrary. In other words, the master theme of synairesis includes by implication the theme of resistance to thematizing. More succinctly: themes are constitutively underdetermined, constitutively chosen, and that is a theme of the *Iliad*.

The theme of synairesis appeared in book 3, and it also appeared in book 6. It was the same theme, but also not the same. However, in observing the differences across the range of specimens, that is, in gathering them together and treating them as a theme, we also observed that the differences too were semidetermined, in that the synaireses of the later books were consistently less determined than those of the earlier. This theme—the thematic trajectory toward less determination (more arbitrariness) in choices—will be kept in mind as the study proceeds to its next specimen pair, where the reading encounters, among other things, Agamemnon's offer of rewards to Achilles in exchange for his participation in the war against the Trojans, and Achilles' story of his choice of dooms.

3. Or in many cases of "Unitarians" as caricatured by "Analysts."

THEMATIC ANALOGY: AERIAL SURVEYS

Book 9 begins a new cycle, and for the first time the cyclic design returns to a position analogous to that in a previous cycle. This chapter will mainly examine and interpret indications of thematic analogy between the A column books in cycles I and II (A_1 = book 1, A_2 = book 9). Since, as the study of the cued pairs of cycle I confirmed, books that head up cycles (A column books) offer many thematic analogies with books that conclude cycles (Z column books), I will secondarily examine indications of thematic analogies between book 9 (A_2) and book 8 (Z_1).

Readers of the *Iliad* will recall that in book 1 the archsystemic trajectory led to Achilles' decision to withdraw from fighting and engage Zeus to punish the Greeks on his behalf. In book 9 Achilles revisits that decision, and reaffirms it. In this regard it is clear enough that books 1 and 9 are counterparts, and like other paired books I have examined, their thematic analogies extend into many details.[4] Unsurprisingly, a great many of these concern the issues disputed between Achilles and Agamemnon in the assembly scene of book 1. But comparison of book 9, the Embassy book, and book 1, often thought of as the Quarrel book, exposes the less obvious fact that book 1 itself is packed with embassies, whose various features are combined and transformed in the embassy Agamemnon sends to Achilles in book 9.

Desperation, Again

At the end of book 8, Zeus's help for the Trojans has brought the Achaians back to where they were when Apollo sent the plague on them: forced to flee Troy unless some relief for their distress can be found. In the earlier situation, Achilles called an assembly and said that the Achaians might have to return home, and he proposed asking Kalchas what made Apollo angry (1.54–67). In book 9, as the second cycle begins, Agamemnon calls an assembly, and simply advises that the Greeks go home, without any investigation of another possible solution (9.9–28). Diomedes, already Achilles' substitute on the battlefield, now also replaces Achilles as Agamemnon's critic in the assembly, dismissing his suggestion of flight on the grounds that if necessary he and his companion Sthenelos could conquer Troy alone, since they came with divine support (9.49).[5] Diomedes claims the right of reply to Agamemnon on the grounds that Agamemnon has insulted him publicly (9.32–36), and he accuses Agamemnon of cowardice (9.39–44), turning back on him the same insult Agamemnon insinuated against Achilles in the assembly when Achilles threatened to sail back home (φεῦγε μαλ', 1.173; ἔρχεο, 9.43) (Aubriot 1985: 262).

Nestor, however, is less confident than Diomedes that Agamemnon's despair can simply be dismissed. He comes between Diomedes and Agamemnon, as he did

4. See Aubriot 1985: 261–66.

5. On Diomedes as Achilles' replacement, see Taplin 1992: 135–36.

between Achilles and Agamemnon in book 1 (1.254–84, 9.53–78). Now, however, instead of reproving Agamemnon publicly, as he did in book 1 (*μήτε σὺ τόνδ' . . . ἀποαίρεο κούρην, κτλ.* 1.275–76; *Ἀτρεΐδη, σὺ δὲ παῦε τεὸν μένος, κτλ.*, 1.282–84), Nestor calls for Agamemnon to host a meeting of the chiefs in his personal quarters (9.69–72) and there, after tactfully establishing his right to be heard and Agamemnon's responsibility to listen (9.96–103),[6] he plays the role Kalchas played in book 1,[7] explaining that Agamemnon caused the Greeks' distress by taking a girl and angering her relation, a mortal with divine protection (9.104–13).

In book 9, therefore, the Achaians' problem-situation casts Achilles and Zeus in the role that Chryses and Apollo together played in book 1. Agamemnon's embassy to Achilles is analogous to the embassy he sent to Chryses in book 1, to return Chryseis and offer hecatombs to Apollo.[8] Actually, book 1 also features three other scenes where repayment is offered: Chryses' offer of ransom in the Greek assembly (1.20–21), Achilles' promise of deferred compensation to Agamemnon for returning Chryseis (1.127–29), and Athena's promise of deferred compensation to Achilles for refraining from violence against Agamemnon (1.212–14).[9] Another analogous scene also occurs in book 8, when Agamemnon promises deferred compensation to Teukros (8.287–91).

Embassies and the Embassy

In the council in book 9, after Agamemnon has finished reciting the goods he will offer Achilles, Nestor proposes selecting some of Achilles' friends to bring the offer. By selecting Achilles' surrogate father Phoinix to join Odysseus, Ajax, and two heralds, Nestor combines features of four embassies that were narrated in book 1, as well as a fifth narrated in book 8: (1) Agamemnon's embassy to Chryses, led by Odysseus; (2) Agamemnon's embassy to Achilles, i.e., the two heralds sent to fetch Briseis; (3) Achilles' embassy to Zeus, i.e., his mother Thetis; (4) Hera's embassy to Achilles, when she dispatches Athena to stop him from killing Agamemnon; (5) Zeus's embassy to Hera and Athena in book 8, when he dispatches Iris to order the renegade goddesses not to interfere in the battle.

These five embassies may be classified as sent by stronger parties to weaker or vice versa. In embassies 2, 4, and 5 a stronger party (Agamemnon, Hera, Zeus) sends an envoy to command a weaker (Achilles, Achilles, Hera + Athena); in embassies 1 and 3 a weaker party (Agamemnon, Achilles) seeks help from a stronger party (Chryses + Apollo, Zeus). The embassy in book 9 combines both types: Agamemnon needs Achilles' help, and thus appeals from a position of

6. Compare Kalchas's concern about a king's anger (*ὀίομαι ἄνδρα χολωσέμεν*, 1.78–79), Diomedes' injunction to Agamemnon not to get angry at him when he speaks (*σὺ δὲ μή τι χολωθῇς*, 9.33), and Nestor's injunction to Agamemnon that it is his responsibility *as king* to listen to others (9.98–100). Haubold 2000: 63 has pertinent remarks on Nestor's shaping of Agamemnon's role as king.

7. Some analogies between Kalchas's speech in book 1 and Nestor's in book 9 have been noted by Wilson 2002: 48–49.

8. See Rabel 1997: 115.

9. On these and other examples of repayment in the *Iliad*, see in general Wilson 2002.

relative weakness. But he also expects Achilles to accept a position of inferiority, and thinks that Achilles can be commanded to accept his offer (see especially 9.160–61). Achilles believes that he holds the position of strength, because the Greeks cannot prevail without him and Zeus (9.419–20), but he also complains that he is a suffering mortal who has been victimized by Agamemnon and must protect himself against further victimization (9.321–35, 367–77).

Godlike Agamemnon and His Envoys

The embassy of book 9 recycles and transforms details from all five embassies narrated in books 1 and 8. For the sake of simplicity, the following analysis will compare the embassy in book 9 to only one precursor at a time, and most of the examples of thematic analogy will be drawn from the embassies of Hera to Achilles (envoy Athena) and Achilles to Zeus (envoy Thetis).

1. In book 1, Achilles is about to kill Agamemnon when Hera sends Athena to stop him. In book 9 Achilles is about to kill the whole Greek force by his inactivity, when Agamemnon sends the embassy to stop him.
2. Just as Hera sends Athena to Achilles with an offer of future material compensation for not harming Agamemnon (1.210, 212), Agamemnon sends a similar offer through his envoys (Odysseus, reporting for Agamemnon, 9.299).
3. Athena's arrival puts Achilles into a state of amazement (*στῆ δ' ὄπιθεν . . . θάμβησεν*, 1.197, 199); so does the arrival of the embassy in book 9 (*στὰν δὲ πρόσθ' αὐτοῖο· ταφὼν δ' ἀνόρουσεν Ἀχιλλεὺς*, 9.193).
4. When Achilles sees Athena he at first thinks she has come to witness his punishment of Agamemnon (1.200–205), but she informs him otherwise. In book 9 the warm reception Achilles gives the embassy indicates that he welcomes them as his friends (9.197–98); but they inform him that they are Agamemnon's emissaries.
5. Athena explains to Achilles (1.208–9) that Hera feels equal love and care for him and Agamemnon (*ἄμφω ὁμῶς*). Although in book 9 Agamemnon's messenger Odysseus cannot make a similar declaration, he adds a message from someone who does love Achilles, his father, Peleus (9.252–58).
6. In book 1, when Achilles is about to use his strength to kill Agamemnon, Hera and her emissary Athena counsel him to control himself. In the embassy in book 9, Odysseus says that Peleus told Achilles that Hera and Athena would give him strength, but that Achilles himself would have to remember to control his anger (9.254–56).
7. In book 1, Achilles concludes that if he obeys the gods, he will benefit, for they will heed his wishes in turn (*ὧς γὰρ ἄμεινον*, 1.217). In book 9, Odysseus relates that Peleus advised Achilles to avoid quarrel because by doing so he would benefit, gaining more honor from the Achaians (*φιλοφροσύνη γὰρ ἀμείνων*, 9.256). Odysseus himself promises Achilles that if he repels Hektor he will win great honor from the Achaians (9.301–6).

Godlike Achilles Sends His Reply

In the second category of embassies, a weaker party appeals to a stronger (Agamemnon to Chryses + Apollo; Achilles to Zeus).[10]

1. In book 1, Achilles appeals to Zeus through Zeus's old friend and ally, Achilles' mother Thetis. In book 9, the Greek army likewise chooses Achilles' friends to appeal to him.
2. Thetis appeals to Zeus to remember what she has done for him (Ζεῦ πάτερ, εἴ . . . σε . . . ὄνησα, κτλ., 1.503–4). In book 9, each of the envoys reminds Achilles of the relationships that should incline him to help the Greeks: Odysseus reminds Achilles that he has been Agamemnon's guest (9.225–26), Phoinix reminds Achilles that he nursed him as a baby (9.485), and Ajax reminds Achilles that the Greeks have honored him as a friend (9.631).
3. Thetis implies that her friendship to Zeus exceeds anyone else's, since if Zeus were to refuse her request it would signify that she was the most dishonored of gods (μετά πᾶσιν ἀτιμοτάτη θεός εἰμι, 1.516), while Ajax tells Achilles that the envoys are his best friends among the Achaians (κήδιστοί τ᾽ ἔμεναι καὶ φίλτατοι, 9.642).
4. In asking Zeus to pity her son, Thetis refers to Achilles as the "most swift-fated" of all others (1.455). In asking Achilles for help, Odysseus and Phoinix claim that death is near for the Greeks unless Achilles comes to their aid (9.230–43, 9.601–2).
5. Thetis has to make multiple appeals to Zeus (two); the embassy has to make multiple appeals to Achilles (three).

10. A friendly critic has posed the question whether "these [are] real parallels between 1 and 9, or rather general *topoi* of embassies? Or even of requests in general . . . ?" The phrasing of the question (I myself scrupulously avoid the term "parallels" when referring to thematic analogies) suggests a certain misunderstanding of the analysis. My experiment seeks convergences *between* the poem and postulated reading functions. The pertinent question, therefore, is not whether the analogies are "real" or meaningless in themselves, but whether or to what degree they cooperate with the postulated reading function and thus accommodate a reader's attribution of meaning. I would agree with the critic's implication that the generality of topoi is unfavorable to the ascription of meaning. But I would deny that the passages analyzed here are general at all. They are, in fact, each quite particular, as the analysis shows, and it is precisely the particularity of the comparable passages that permits their common themes to be viewed as poetically meaningful abstractions, rather than rhetorical formulas or social routines. (On the particularity of so-called typical scenes see Fenik 1978b.) The many features that distinguish the passages here in question from general topoi (or *typoi*) include their unique occurrence in the particularly marked "orientational books" of the *Iliad* where they are. A premise of the present simulation is that a reader seeking thematic edification would compare scenes in books 1 and 9 because that reader had *already* been cued by the postulated cycle-punctuators that mark those books as heads of cycles, and by the archsystemic themes that align them. These are characteristics of specific passages in the *Iliad*, not of topoi that by definition are available for use in an indeterminate range of cases.

Users of this book should bear in mind that the postulated reading functions in these experiments are all functions of reading the *Iliad* (i.e., that whole poem); they are not functions of reading "epic scenes," or of reading one passage *from* the *Iliad*, then another passage, etc. I am well aware that a reading function that approached each passage separately might find fewer promising thematic analogies. However, I do not myself read the *Iliad* as an accumulation of passages, and I doubt that anyone else does either (talk of "parataxis" notwithstanding). Cognition always deploys a frame of reference. For example, when reading Greek we do not need to ponder whether the symbol ω is the Greek "omega" or the English "double-u" (w). We know the symbol is "omega," not because the Greek and English characters are so unlike physically that nobody could confuse them, but because the Greek/English frame of reference is part of each symbol's respective signification.

Thetis appeals to the greatest of the gods, the embassy to the greatest of heroes, and Achilles' godlike stature is stated or implied at many points in the embassy scene.[11] The narrator describes him playing the lyre as the embassy approaches (9.186–87), and the only other lyrist in the *Iliad* is Apollo, who in book 1 accompanies the Muses during the feasting after Zeus and Hera have reconciled (1.603–4). Agamemnon's message compares Achilles to Hades (9.158–59) and promises that if Achilles accepts the offer he will be honored "like a god" by his vassals in Pylos (9.153). Odysseus adds that the Achaians will also honor Achilles "like a god" (9.302–3). Achilles' reply to Odysseus assumes the tones Zeus used to dismiss Hera: in book 8, when Zeus reveals part of his plan to Hera, he insists that he does not care what she thinks about it (*οὐκ ἀλεγίζω*, 8.477). When Achilles replies to Odysseus, he too says that he speaks "without concern" (*ἀπηλεγέως*, 9.309). He insists that he will tell all he thinks and all that will come to pass (9.309–10), attributing to his speech the same kind of authority Zeus attributed to his nod (1.526–28). Achilles' reply to Odysseus also recalls the speech Zeus makes to the assembled gods at the beginning of book 8, when he demands their attention so that he can speak out what his heart commands (*τά με θυμὸς ἐνὶ στήθεσσι κελεύει*, 8.6; see 9.312–14). Near the end of his reply, Achilles actually speaks as Zeus's mouthpiece, when he explains to the embassy that the Greeks cannot destroy Troy, because Zeus is protecting it (9.418–20). The embassy receives Achilles' reply to Odysseus with silent amazement, just as the other Olympians receive Zeus's speech at the beginning of book 8 (see 8.28–30, 9.430–31).

Achilles' godlike posture is thus analogous to that of the gods who received embassies in book 1, Apollo and Zeus. His reply to Odysseus also offers thematic analogies with book 1 by retrieving and amplifying the themes of the quarrel in the assembly.

1. In the assembly, Achilles complains that he was poorly compensated for the work he did in fighting (1.161–68). In his reply to the embassy, Achilles complains that he is poorly compensated for fighting, which includes much suffering and risk of life (9.314–33).
2. Assembly: Achilles denounces Agamemnon for not fighting, and for taking the possessions of others (1.225–31). Embassy: Achilles denounces Agamemnon for holding back from fighting, while taking the possessions of others (9.323–36).
3. Assembly: Achilles says that the Myrmidons came to win honor for Agamemnon and Menelaos (1.158–59). Embassy: Achilles says that the Achaians fight for the sake of Helen (9.336).
4. Assembly: Achilles swears that the Achaians will miss him when Hektor goes on a rampage (1.240–44). Embassy: Achilles says he will not fight Hektor despite the danger he poses to the Achaians (9.346–56).[12]

11. On Achilles as godlike, also see Parry 1956: 5 n. 11; Blickman 1987: 7–9; Martin 1989: 187–91; and Heiden 2002a: 431.

12. Compare 1.241–42 and 9.351–52; notice that even where verbal similarities occur they are not formulaic.

5. Assembly: Achilles threatens to return to Phthia (1.169). Embassy: Achilles threatens to return to Phthia (9.357–63) (Aubriot 1985: 262).[13]
6. Assembly: Achilles says that in returning to Phthia he will cease wasting his wealth on Agamemnon (1.169–71). Embassy: Achilles says he has left much wealth behind in Phthia (9.364–67).

Kingly Achilles

Achilles' reply to Odysseus also throws Agamemnon's own arguments back at him—or at least back in his direction.[14]

1. In book 1, Chryses offers Agamemnon ransom for Chryseis, and a prayer to Apollo for the Greeks' success and safe return, but Agamemnon refuses, telling Chryses that he would enjoy living with Chryseis back at his home in Argos (1.29–31). In book 9, Agamemnon and his envoys offer Achilles compensation for saving the Greeks, but Achilles gives Agamemnon a taste of his own medicine and refuses their offer, telling them that he will enjoy living with a wife at his home in Phthia (9.398–99).
2. Assembly: Agamemnon compares his concubine Chryseis favorably to his legitimate wife, Clytemnestra (1.113–15; *κουριδίης ἀλόχου*, 1.114). Embassy: Achilles speaks of his concubine Briseis as a legitimate wife (9.336–43; *ἄλοχον θυμαρέα*, 9.336) (Aubriot 1985: 265).
3. Assembly: Agamemnon deplores that he alone should be without a prize (*ὄφρα μὴ οἶος/Ἀργείων ἀγέραστος ἔω*, 1.118–19). Embassy: Achilles complains that of all the Achaians only he has lost his prize (*ἐμεῦ δ' ἀπὸ μούνου Ἀχαιῶν/εἵλετ'*, 9.335–36).
4. Assembly: Agamemnon threatened Achilles publicly, to teach all a lesson in obedience (*στυγέῃ δὲ καὶ ἄλλος/ἶσον ἐμοὶ φάσθαι κτλ.*, 1.186–87). Embassy: Achilles wants his reply announced publicly, so that the other Achaians will learn a lesson in their rights (9. 369–72; *ὄφρα καὶ ἄλλοι ἐπισκύζωνται Ἀχαιοί*, 9.370).[15]
5. Assembly (1.173–80): Agamemnon dares Achilles to go home (*φεῦγε*), saying that he does not need Achilles because he (Agamemnon) has honor from Zeus (*ἄλλοι/ . . . με τιμήσουσι, μάλιστα δὲ μητίετα Ζεύς*, 1.174–75), that Achilles is hateful to him (*ἔχθιστος*), and that he takes no account of Achilles (*οὐκ ἀλεγίζω*, 1.180). Embassy (9.376–78): Achilles says Agamemnon can "go to hell" (*ἐρρέτω*), that Zeus has taken Agamemnon's wits from him (*ἐκ γάρ εὑ φρένας εἵλετο μητίετα Ζεύς*, 9.377), and that he hates Agamemnon's gifts (*ἐχθρὰ . . . δῶρα*) and takes no account of Agamemnon (*τίω δέ μιν ἐν καρὸς αἴσῃ*).

13. Also see Lynn-George 1988: 115.
14. See the rich discussion of Lynn-George 1988: 108–22.
15. Again notice how the reappearance of the theme occurs without verbal similarity.

At the end of his reply to Odysseus, Achilles also recycles themes from the speeches he made at the beginning of the assembly, before the quarrel broke out. The same section of Achilles' reply to Odysseus also recycles themes from speeches Achilles made after the assembly.

1. Assembly: Achilles asks the seer Kalchas to explain why the Greeks are dying (1.62–67). Embassy: Achilles speaks as a seer, explaining why the Greeks are dying: because Zeus is protecting Troy (9.418–20).
2. Assembly: Achilles says the Greeks might have to go home unless they can find a solution to the plague (1. 59–61). Embassy: Achilles advises the Greeks to give up the war and go home (9.417–18).
3. Assembly: Achilles through his mother asks Zeus for honor in compensation for his life (1.352–53). Embassy: Achilles says that possessions such as those offered by Agamemnon cannot compensate him for the loss of his life (9.401).
4. Assembly: Achilles complains to Thetis that he deserves honor (*ὄφελλεν*) because he is destined to have a short life (1.352–53). Embassy: Achilles says that Thetis has told him that his glory is linked inversely to the length of his life (9.410–16).
5. Assembly: Achilles wishes for Zeus to help the Trojans (1.407–12). Embassy: Achilles reports to the emissaries that Zeus is helping the Trojans (9.419–20).

Achilles' reply also adapts themes from book 8, the Z book in cycle I. These thematic analogies contribute to the impression that in receiving the embassy Achilles adopts the position of Zeus.

1. Book 8: Zeus says he will not bend from his plan whatever Hera may do (8.478). Embassy: Achilles says he will not bend from his announced plan whatever Agamemnon may offer him (9.379).[16]
2. Book 8: The Trojans make sacrifices, but the gods hate Troy and do not accept them (8.548–52; *σφιν ἀπήχθετο Ἴλιος*, 8.551).[17] Embassy: Agamemnon offers gifts, but Achilles hates them and refuses to accept them (*ἐχθρὰ δέ μοι τοῦ δῶρα*, 9.378).

Phoinix's Intimate Appeal

When Achilles concludes, the envoys are shocked and remain silent, exactly as the Olympians did after Zeus's threatening declaration at the beginning of book 8 (8.28–29). Then it was Athena who broke the silence with a speech that began by assuring her father of her complete obedience (*ὦ πάτερ . . . / εὖ νυ καὶ ἡμεῖς*

16. Compare 8.477–83 (Zeus to Hera) and 9.378–79 (Achilles about Agamemnon); 8.470–71 (Zeus to Hera) and 9.357–59 (Achilles to Odysseus); 8.473–74 (Zeus to Hera) and 9.386–87 (Achilles about Agamemnon).

17. On the disputed authenticity of these lines, see note 33 in chapter 4 here.

ἴδμεν ὅ τοι σθένος οὐκ ἐπιεικτόν, 8.31–32); here Phoinix, Achilles' substitute father but as much Achilles' dependent as a daughter, likewise begins by assuring Achilles that disobedience is unthinkable (πῶς ἂν ... ἀπὸ σεῖο, φίλον τέκος, αὖθι λιποίμην / οἶος, 9.437–38). Moreover, Athena and Phoinix both want the same thing, safety for the Achaians. Athena proposes to help them by providing counsel (βουλήν, 8.36), and Phoinix, after reminding Achilles that he accompanies him as a teacher (διδασκέμεναι, 9.442), gives him counsel.

Phoinix's reply to Achilles' speech obviously recalls Nestor's attempt at reconciliation in the assembly in book 1; both speeches appeal in terms of the harm to be done by continued conflict, and both begin with prefatory tales about the speaker's past that authorize his counsel in the present (1.259–74, 9.447–95) (Aubriot 1985: 263–64). As already pointed out, Phoinix's appeal to Achilles also recalls Thetis's appeal to Zeus in book 1, since both pleaders enjoy a personal relationship to a powerful figure that allows them to serve as intermediaries. Thetis is Achilles' mother, and Phoinix is also a kind of parent to Achilles (9.485–95). Phoinix also lived in exile with Peleus, and so, in a manner of speaking, did Thetis, since she was compelled to marry Peleus and live with him. Phoinix was forced into exile when he did his mother the favor of sleeping with his father's concubine, to make the older man less desirable to her and presumably faithful to his wife. For this impertinence Phoinix's father cursed him, and this led to his exile in Phthia. According to the *Kypria* (fr. 2 Davies), Zeus condemned Thetis to marry the mortal Peleus because she spurned Zeus's sexual advances, not wishing to dishonor Hera, who was virtually Thetis's foster mother (see *Iliad* 24.59–60) as well as Zeus's legitimate spouse.[18]

Phoinix's prologue, in which he tells the story of how he came to Peleus's home and adds the parable of the Litai (9.434–512), also recalls themes from Athena's mission from Hera to Achilles in book 1. Phoinix says that after his father Amyntor cursed him, he wanted to kill Amyntor, but his anger was checked by some immortal (τὸν μὲν ἐγὼ βούλευσα κατακτάμεν ὀξέι χαλκῷ · /ἀλλά τις ἀθανάτων παῦσεν χόλον, 9.458–59), who made him mindful that killing his father would hurt his reputation (9.459–61); similarly, in the assembly Achilles is about to kill Agamemnon when Athena checks him (1.188–222).[19] In Phoinix's parable the Litai, like Athena, are daughters of Zeus (Διὸς κοῦραι, 9.502); Phoinix tells Achilles that they listen to the appeals of those who respect them (ἔκλυον εὐχομένοιο, 9.509), and when Achilles obeys Athena in book 1, he says he does so because the gods listen to those who obey them (ἔκλυον αὐτοῦ, 1.218). Phoinix also says that whenever anyone rejects the Litai,

18. It is quite likely that the poet of the *Iliad* knew this version of Thetis's story, and fairly likely that he assumed it as background to the *Iliad*, since, as Finkelberg 2002 has shown, *Iliad* 7 seems to be modeled on and allude to a version of the *Kypria*. On the version—apparently the only one many scholars have heard of—in which Zeus compelled Thetis to marry Peleus to ensure that her son would not overthrow him, see note 45 here.

19. The verses 9.458–61 are absent from the MSS and are supplied from a citation in Plut. *Mor.* 26; see the discussion of Hainsworth 1993: 123, who accepts the verses' authenticity. Wilson 2002: 201 n. 77 suggests that "the lines are surely designed to echo 1.188–205." Griffin 1995: 130 notes the "striking similarity." Heubeck 1984: 135 and Schein 1984: 111 mention it too.

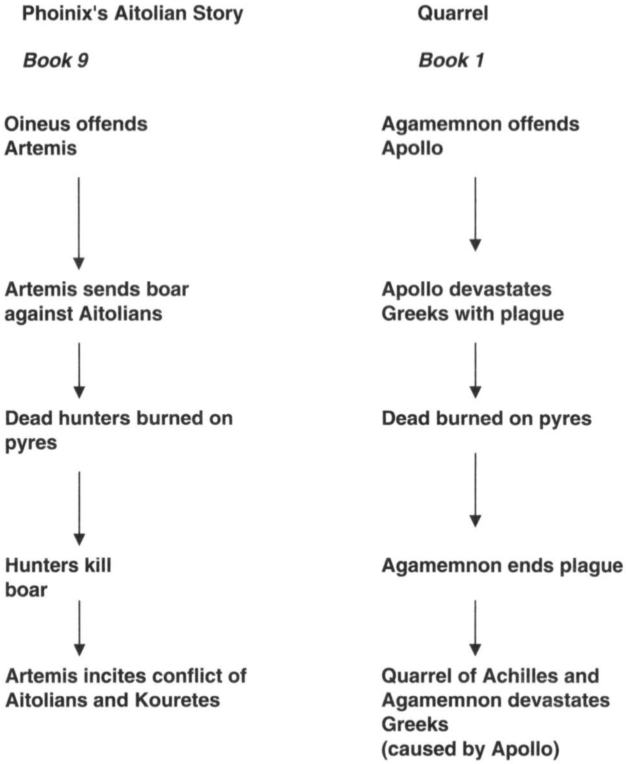

FIGURE 5.1. Artemis's Move in book 9 and the quarrel in book 1.

they appeal to Zeus, who sends Ate as punishment upon the refuser (9.510–12); in book 1, not long after Athena leaves Achilles, he calls upon a different goddess, Thetis, to intercede with Zeus on his behalf and ask that Agamemnon be punished (1.407, 1.500–510).[20]

Phoinix's fable of Meleager has long been recognized for its analogies to the situation of Achilles, to whom, after all, it is addressed as a negative paradigm of Achilles' own conduct and its probable trajectory.[21] These obvious analogies concern Achilles' present situation, in which the embassy appeals for his help in battle just as the Aitolians appealed to the recalcitrant Meleager to save them from the Kouretes; the analogies also foreshadow events to come, when Achilles will bend to the pleas of his comrade Patroklos as Meleager did to those of his wife Kleopatra.

But Phoinix's fable actually begins long before the Aitolians appeal to Meleager. The war between the Aitolians and the Kouretes arose from a prior problem situation, the Kalydonian boar that Artemis sent to ravage the Aitolian lands (9.532–46). Artemis's Move and the conflict it generated recall the quarrel in book 1 and its beginning (see fig. 5.1).

20. Compare 1.500, 502, 509–10 and 9.511–12.

21. Schadewaldt 1966: 139–40; Howald 1946: 132; Kakridis 1949: 21–25; Whitman 1958: 191; Rosner 1976: 322–27; Willcock 1978: 1: 281–82; Nagy 1979: 104–6; Schein 1984: 112–13; Brenk 1986: 77–86; Edwards 1987: 226–29; and Heiden 1991: 8–9.

Agamemnon dishonors the priest of Apollo by taking his daughter as booty and refusing to return her, and in punishment the god uses his arrows to cause a devastating plague among Agamemnon's people (1.8–12), whose dead bodies are burned in great numbers on pyres (1.52). Achilles eventually makes it possible to end the plague when he calls an assembly and suggests seeking the advice of Apollo's seer, since he thinks that Apollo may be angry at the Greeks for omitting an offering to him (1.65–67). Although Agamemnon reluctantly takes Kalchas's advice and Apollo remits the plague, the very measures taken lead to the circumstances in which the devastating quarrel between Agamemnon and Achilles arises; and this, as the narrator clearly says in book 1 at the beginning of the whole sequence, was ultimately caused by Apollo (1.8).

Phoinix's story begins when King Oineus omits to offer sacrifice to Artemis from the first fruits of his orchard (9.533–35), and in anger the goddess, the sister of Apollo and like her brother an archer (*ἰοχέαιρα*, 9.538), sends a monstrous boar to rip up the Aitolians' plantings and their fruits. Meleager gathers a big force against the boar, who still kills many of the hunters, and their bodies are burned on pyres (*πολλοὺς δὲ πυρῆς ἐπέβησ' ἀλεγεινῆς*, 9.546). But when the hunters do eventually kill the boar, Artemis finds another way to punish Oineus and his allies, by inciting conflict between the Aitolians and the Kouretes over the division of the trophy (9.547). Meleager helps the Aitolians in their war with the Kouretes, until he withdraws from fighting in anger at his mother, Althaia (9.550–56).[22]

In his anger at Althaia Meleager remains beside his wife, Kleopatra, to whose family history Phoinix devotes about ten lines (9.555–65), which are extremely confusing because of several ambiguous pronouns and one ambiguous common noun. (The lines are here provided for convenience of reference and thus left untranslated.)

> *ἤτοι ὁ μητρὶ φίλῃ Ἀλθαίῃ χωόμενος κῆρ*
> *κεῖτο παρὰ μνηστῇ ἀλόχῳ, καλῇ Κλεοπάτρῃ,*
> *κούρῃ Μαρπήσσης καλλισφύρου Εὐηνίνης*
> *Ἴδεώ θ', ὃς κάρτιστος ἐπιχθονίων γένετ' ἀνδρῶν*
> *τῶν τότε—καί ῥα ἄνακτος ἐναντίον εἵλετο τόξον*
> *Φοίβου Ἀπόλλωνος καλλισφύρου εἵνεκα νύμφης·*
> *τὴν δὲ τότ' ἐν μεγάροισι πατὴρ καὶ πότνια μήτηρ*
> *Ἀλκυόνην καλέεσκον ἐπώνυμον, οὕνεκ' ἄρ' αὐτῆς*
> *μήτηρ ἀλκυόνος πολυπενθέος οἶτον ἔχουσα*
> *κλαῖεν ὅ μιν ἑκάεργος ἀνήρπασε Φοῖβος Ἀπόλλων—*
> *τῇ ὅ γε παρκατέλεκτο χόλον θυμαλγέα πέσσων . . .*

Kleopatra, Phoinix explains, was the daughter of nice-ankled Marpessa, whose father was Euenus (9.557). Marpessa's husband and Kleopatra's father was Idas,

22. Phoinix never explains Meleager's reasons altogether clearly, and he does not explain them at all until later in the story. On the difficulties in the story of Meleager, see Hainsworth 1993: 130–32 and Griffin 1995: 134–36.

the mightiest mortal (*κάρτιστος ἐπιχθονίων*, 9.558) of his time—by way of illustration, Phoinix mentions that Idas even drew his bow against the lord Apollo (*ἄνακτος*, 9.559) on behalf of a "bride" (*νύμφης*, 9.560). On first reading one naturally assumes that *νύμφης* refers to Idas's own bride, his wife Marpessa, especially since other versions of Idas's story[23] say that he and Apollo were rivals for Marpessa (Hainsworth 1993: 136; Griffin 1995: 138). But the arrangement of Phoinix's discourse suggests that *νύμφης* refers to Idas's daughter Kleopatra, for Phoinix's next word is the feminine demonstrative pronoun (*τὴν*, 9.561), which in its clause must refer to Kleopatra, Idas's daughter, abductee of Apollo (*μιν . . . ἀνήρπασε*, 9.564) and the antecedent of the demonstrative *τῇ* in 9.565 (which must also refer back to *μιν* in the preceding line).[24] Coming as it does immediately after *νύμφης*, *τὴν* would naturally take *νύμφης* as its antecedent (i.e., "on account of a bride; and she . . ."). In that case the bride would have been Kleopatra. So Phoinix gives the impression that Idas drew his bow against Apollo on behalf of Apollo's bride, not his own: Apollo must have come to take Idas's daughter Kleopatra *as* a bride.[25] Despite Phoinix's confusing pronouns, it seems pretty clear that Apollo abducted Kleopatra for his sexual enjoyment. One must also infer that Apollo eventually surrendered possession of Kleopatra/Alkyone, because otherwise she could not have married Meleager.

Kleopatra's background story sounds like the stories of Chryseis and Briseis in book 1, both of whom are abducted by Agamemnon, Chryseis for his sexual enjoyment explicitly. Idas, who takes up his bow to prevent lord Apollo from abducting his daughter, recalls Chryses, whose daughter was taken by Agamemnon (e.g., *ἄναξ*, 1.7); and he also recalls Achilles, who was prepared to take up arms against lord Agamemnon to prevent his taking Briseis (1.194; see 1.298–304). But Idas also recalls Agamemnon himself, since Agamemnon, as the *possessor* of Chryseis, aims to keep her and threatens Chryses when he asks Agamemnon to surrender her (1.26–32).[26] Finally, Idas as maiden-defender recalls Apollo, whose bow (*τόξ'*, 1.45) protects Chryseis from her abductor Agamemnon (1.43–52).

In Phoinix's story, which in the narrative chronology takes place long before the events of *Iliad* book 1, Apollo is something of an Agamemnon himself, seizing the daughters of mortals for his own pleasure and their parents' grief. Moreover, since Phoinix's story implies that Apollo eventually returned Kleopatra to her normal life, Apollo appears in book 9 as the *rescuer* of a maiden abducted from her father, as he does in book 1, where he rescues Chryseis from Agamemnon.

After filling in the background on Kleopatra, Phoinix returns to Meleager, who remained beside his wife in anger at his mother's curses (9.565–72):

23. Simonides 563P, Paus. 5.18.2 on the chest of Kypselos, Apoll. 1.7.8.

24. Willcock 1978: 1:282: "*τὴν δέ*: This must be Kleopatra."

25. Willcock 1964 showed that Phoinix's story of Meleager probably differed from traditional versions in other respects as well. He argued that mythical paradeigmata in Homer did not slavishly repeat familiar versions but modified them as needed to suit the rhetorical context.

26. Wilson 2002: 50 suggests that in comparing Chryseis to his wife Clytemnestra, Agamemnon implies that "the loss of Chryseis would be no less than the loss of a wife." From Agamemnon's perspective, therefore, he is the victim of a predatory raid on his family, and Apollo is the implicit predator.

τῇ ὅ γε παρκατέλεκτο χόλον θυμαλγέα πέσσων,
ἐξ ἀρέων μητρὸς κεχολωμένος, ἥ ῥα θεοῖσι
πόλλ' ἀχέουσ' ἠρᾶτο κασιγνήτοιο φόνοιο,
πολλὰ δὲ καὶ γαῖαν πολυφόρβην χερσὶν ἀλοία
κικλήσκουσ' Ἀΐδην καὶ ἐπαινὴν Περσεφόνειαν,
πρόχνυ καθεζομένη, δεύοντο δὲ δάκρυσι κόλποι,
παιδὶ δόμεν θάνατον· τῆς δ' ἠεροφοῖτις Ἐρινὺς
ἔκλυεν ἐξ Ἐρέβεσφιν, ἀμείλιχον ἦτορ ἔχουσα.

he lay beside her [Kleopatra] nursing anger that pained his heart,
enraged at the curses his mother kept calling out to the gods,
in deep grief at her brother's slaying;
repeatedly beating on the fertile earth with her hands,
prostrate along the ground, and drenching her bosom in tears,
she appealed to Hades and revered Persephone
to give her son death; and Erinys, who goes in misty darkness,
she whose heart never yields, heard her from Erebos.

Phoinix explains that Althaia cursed her son in grief at the murder of her brother, asking Hades and Persephone to take Meleager's life. The Erinys heard Althaia's prayer, and this was why Meleager refused to fight for his city. Notice the following analogies between Meleager-Althaia and Achilles-Thetis: like Meleager, Achilles stays out of the battle because he has a mother whose prayer has been heard by a powerful divinity. Althaia's prayer and Thetis's both have to do with the short lives of their sons: Althaia asks the gods to make Meleager's life short (9.571), while Thetis assumes that her son's life will be short and requests compensation for its shortness (1.505–6). The appeal to Zeus in book 1, however, consists of two stages (Achilles to Thetis, Thetis to Zeus), and the appeal of Althaia transforms elements from the first stage as well as the second: Agamemnon deprived Achilles of a companion, Meleager deprives Althaia of a brother; Achilles wept and called upon Thetis (a sea-goddess) to punish the offender, Althaia weeps and calls upon chthonic gods to punish the offender; Thetis heeded Achilles, and the chthonic gods heed Althaia (compare 1.348–58 and 9.566–72).

We have already noted that Phoinix, as Achilles' intimate and Agamemnon's intermediary, transforms the role of Thetis as Achilles' intermediary to Zeus in book 1, and that in the embassy scene Achilles occupies the role of Zeus. In replying to Phoinix Achilles continues this role, telling Phoinix that he risks becoming hateful to Achilles by speaking in favor of Agamemnon (*ἵνα μή μοι ἀπέχθηαι*, 9.613–14). In book 1 Zeus similarly warns Hera that her query about his meeting with Thetis is alienating him (*ἀπὸ θυμοῦ/μᾶλλον ἐμοὶ ἔσεαι·*, 1.562–63). In fact, Hera and Phoinix are both trying to help the Achaians, and Zeus and Achilles have both been consulting with Thetis.

We have also seen that Achilles' role in the embassy transforms the role of Agamemnon as king in book 1; and his reply to Phoinix continues this pattern of transformation: Achilles' threat to Phoinix recalls Agamemnon's threat to Chryses (1.32; 9.614), and Achilles' statement that he needs no honors from Agamemnon, since he already has honor from Zeus (9.608), also recalls Agamemnon's similar statement to Achilles in the assembly (1.174–75), when he dares Achilles to carry out his threat of returning to Phthia, exactly the threat Achilles has just repeated to the envoys in the embassy scene, and exactly the course of action from which Phoinix wishes to dissuade him (Aubriot 1985: 264).

Setting Terms

Of the three envoys, Ajax is the only one who does not appeal to Achilles as a god or as god-like. He does not expect Achilles to pity the Achaians, but rather to respect them as his friends, equals who share a roof with him. His statement that Achilles does not care about their relationship (*οὐδὲ μετατρέπεται φιλότητος ἑταίρων*, 9.630) recalls Achilles' complaint in the assembly that Agamemnon did not care about the favor Achilles and the other Myrmidons were doing him by fighting on his behalf (*τῶν οὔ τι μετατρέπῃ*, 1.160). Ajax contrasts Achilles' intransigence with the flexibility of a man who accepts compensation from the murderer of a brother or child (9.632–38).[27] Although Agamemnon has neither admitted any breach of law nor submitted his dispute with Achilles to the arbitration of a third party, Ajax's comparison apparently envisions a dispute that is publicly arbitrated (perhaps like that depicted on the shield of Achilles, 18.497–508),[28] since the murderer is allowed to remain in his district (*ἐν δήμῳ*, 9.634). In the assembly in book 1, Achilles characterizes his quarrel with Agamemnon as one calling for a legal judgment, when he swears an oath on the scepter borne by the judges (*δικασπόλοι, οἵ τε θέμιστας/πρὸς Διὸς εἰρύαται·*, 1.238–39).

In his reply to Ajax Achilles gives the delegates the conditions under which he will fight the Trojans: he promises he will fight when Hektor reaches his own ships (*ἀμφὶ . . . τῇ ἐμῇ κλισίῃ καὶ νηὶ*, 9.654). This formulation is consistent with his threat to Agamemnon in book 1 that he will give up Briseis but fight to defend his own property if Agamemnon tries to take it (*ἅ μοί ἐστι . . . παρὰ νηὶ κτλ*, 1.300–3). In conceding that he will eventually fight Hektor, and specifying when he will do it, Achilles also echoes the tones of Zeus at the end of book 8, when Zeus makes a similar concession to Hera, explaining when Hektor will be stopped: not before Achilles rises up beside the ships, in the fighting over the corpse of Patroklos (8.473–76).[29]

The dialogue with Achilles concluded, libations are poured from the two-handled cup; the envoys, minus Phoinix, return to their own encampment; and Achilles and Patroklos go to bed beside their respective mates (9.656–68). In book 1, the quarrel of Zeus and Hera ends when Hephaistos brings the cup to

27. Wilson 2002: 105 notes that Ajax's comparison implies that he does not recognize the affective relationship between Achilles and Briseis that Achilles claims was violated (9.342–43).

28. See Wilson 2002: 105.

29. Compare 8.473–75 (Zeus) and 9.650–53 (Achilles).

Hera, and after the partying the gods all go back to their own homes, and Zeus goes to bed beside his mate Hera (1.601–11).

THEMATIC TRANSFORMATION: INTERPRETATIONS

Bodies and Representations

Interpretation of the thematic transformations between books 1 and 9 might begin with the general observation that in book 1 many gods appear as characters (Apollo, Hera, Athena, Thetis, Zeus, and eventually the whole Olympian family), while in book 9 no god ever appears as a character (except within the embedded story told by Phoinix). When the problems and themes of book 1 return in book 9, the gods have been replaced by surrogates, many of them mortal: Agamemnon as embassy-sender replaces Hera (who sent Athena to Achilles in book 1); Agamemnon's delegates replace Athena and Thetis; Achilles as the object of appeals replaces Apollo and Zeus. The gods are also replaced by speeches: Achilles reports Zeus's (alleged) plan to protect Troy, while Phoinix reports the parable of the Prayers, as well as the story of Meleager, in which Artemis, Apollo, and the Erinys all figure. In one case the gods are displaced by a speech that is then displaced by another: Odysseus's speech quotes (i.e., replaces) a speech by Peleus, in which the hero supposedly told his son that he must keep control of the strength that Hera and Athena will give him (9.254–56):

> *τέκνον ἐμόν, κάρτος μὲν Ἀθηναίη τε καὶ Ἥρη*
> *δώσουσ', αἴ κ' ἐθέλωσι, σὺ δὲ μεγαλήτορα θυμὸν*
> *ἴσχειν ἐν στήθεσσι· φιλοφροσύνη γὰρ ἀμείνων·*

> Son, Athena and Hera will provide you with strength
> if they want to; your job is to check the proud temper
> in your breast. It's better to have team spirit.

Since in book 1 the characters Hera and Athena actually did check the anger of Achilles themselves, in Odysseus's speech they are replaced first by Peleus, whom Odysseus in turn replaces; and Odysseus's counsel is, optimally, to be replaced and enacted by Achilles himself.

In addition to these replacements, in book 9 Agamemnon communicates with Achilles only through representatives, and these representatives are chosen more arbitrarily—with respect to Agamemnon—than the heralds Agamemnon sent to Achilles after the assembly in book 1: in book 1 Agamemnon sent his own herald and official representative Talthybios (1.320), while in book 9 Agamemnon's representatives are chosen for him by Nestor, and they do not include Talthybios (9.168–70).[30] Taken together, the replacement of Agamemnon by representa-

30. On the tactful omission of Talthybios, see Hainsworth 1993: 82–83.

tives and the replacement of the gods by mortals and speeches both indicate that in book 9 the action acquires a very oblique and synairetic ("together by choice") character.

Possessions and/or Relationships

The matter of synairesis is of course very significant in all the scenes concerning delegations and offers of compensation, since these always imply judgments about what can compensate for what and who can represent whom. In the initial Problem situation of book 1 and the whole *Iliad*, Chryses comes before the Greek assembly with an offer of symbolic compensation for his daughter (*symbolic* = "thrown together"). The narrator emphasizes the symbolic character of Chryses' appeal by his vivid description of the symbols of Apollo that the priest bears (1.14–15) and his perfunctory description of the ransom itself, which evidently does not include any young girls to substitute for Chryseis, and is therefore rather arbitrarily related to the object it is to replace. The appeal also includes a prayer for the success of the Greeks, which qua prayer is even more symbolic than the ransom. Moreover, Chryses casts the entire proposed exchange between himself and the Greeks as the symbol of another exchange, in which the Greeks are to display reverence for Apollo (ἁζόμενοι Διὸς υἱὸν κτλ., 1.21).

Agamemnon's reply rejects not only Chryses but the very possibility of symbolic/synairetic substitution. He addresses Chryses as "old man" (γέρον, 1.26) and threatens him with physical punishment if he does not immediately leave Agamemnon's presence (1.26–28, 32). In this way Agamemnon identifies Chryses as one particular physical body of one strength in one place and at one time; the narrator, in contrast, previously denoted Chryses by his *role* as priest (ἀρητῆρα, 1.11). Agamemnon specifically dismisses the symbols of Apollo as powerless matter (μή ... οὐ χραίσμῃ σκῆπτρον καὶ στέμμα θεοῖο, 1.28). In refusing to release Chryseis he emphasizes the physical mastery he will take of her in his bed (ἐμὸν λέχος ἀντιόωσαν, 1.31), the physical labor she will perform (ἱστὸν ἐποιχομένην, 1.31), and the necessity of aging to which she is physically subject (γῆρας ἔπεισιν, 1.29). Agamemnon values Chryseis as a *body*, and from that standpoint it is hardly surprising that he rejects an exchange that does not replace her body, that he threatens the weak body of her father, and that he scorns the pieces of stuff that represent Apollo.[31]

Chryses' strength, however, is not limited to that which he can exercise through his physical body in Agamemnon's presence. He prays to Apollo, without sacrifices but with words to remind Apollo of sacrifices he has made in the past (εἴ ποτέ τοι χαρίεντ' ἐπὶ νηὸν ἔρεψα κτλ., 1.39–41). Nor does he ask Apollo to retrieve his daughter, but to use his arrows to make the Greeks repay

31. Van Wees 1992: 124 (and elsewhere) correctly recognizes that in the *Iliad* conflict more often concerns symbols than material. However, in seeking to discover a single ideology that governs the society of the warriors in the *Iliad*, Van Wees obscures the scale of relative materiality and relative symbolism along which the stakes of conflict fall. There is no single ideology: different characters in different situations may describe the stakes differently.

his tears (τείσειαν Δαναοὶ ἐμὰ δάκρυα σοῖσι βέλεσσιν, 1.42). Apollo heeds the prayer and sends his arrows against the Greeks, and these afflict the Greeks with plague (1.10). A thread of symbolic substitutions leads from the feeble body of Chryses to the pyres that burn the corpses of the Greeks.

Soon afterward, Kalchas reveals that Apollo wishes Agamemnon to return Chryseis to her father "without price and without ransom" (1.99), a stipulation that ensures the transaction will be a symbolic exchange between Agamemnon and *Apollo* and not in any sense a material exchange between Agamemnon and *Chryses*. To emphasize the point, Kalchas adds that Agamemnon is to send along a sacred offering for the god (1.99–100). Agamemnon, however, cannot be enlightened so easily. First of all, he insults Kalchas, as if the seer were speaking only for himself and not as a representative of Apollo (τοι τὰ κάκ' ἐστὶ φίλα . . . μαντεύεσθαι, 1.107). Then he explains that he wants to keep Chryseis because she is better looking than his wife Clytemnestra, and a better worker (οὔ . . . χερείων/οὐ δέμας οὐδὲ φυήν, οὔτ' ἂρ φρένας οὔτέ τι ἔργα, 1.114–15); in other words, the symbolic relationship Clytemnestra bore toward him did not compensate for her deficiencies as a material object.[32] Finally, he agrees to return Chryseis because he does not want to lose something else, the army (βούλομ' ἐγὼ λαὸν σῶν ἔμμεναι, 1.117). But he insists that the Greeks give him a replacement for Chryseis. Here Agamemnon inches ever so slightly toward symbolism, since he demands a replacement for Chryseis not as concubine but as prize (γέρας, 1.120) and he counts the potential loss if he lacks a replacement as one of propriety and not material (οὐδὲ ἔοικε, 1.119). Still, he identifies the symbolism of the prize with its physical presence in his possession, inviting the Greeks to see (λεύσσετε, 1.120) the departure of his prize. Agamemnon cannot understand that by surrendering a girl to Apollo to save the troops he would actually enhance his stature as their leader, for he is essentially in the position of needing to make a sacrifice on their behalf: ceremonial loss of material would yield gain of symbolic prestige.[33]

Achilles is hardly tactful when he addresses Agamemnon as "most loving of possessions" (φιλοκτεανώτατε πάντων, 1.122), but the epithet is deserved, because possessions are what Agamemnon wants, and his desire to possess material objects, including persons, blocks virtually any potential he might have for conceptualizing value symbolically, and particularly for conceptualizing the value of symbolic/synairetic ("thrown together"/"chosen together") relationships like the relationship between a leader and his followers or between a husband and his wife.[34] Achilles has no illusions about Agamemnon's limitations, and he does not even dispute Agamemnon's claim that it is improper for him to be

32. Wilson 2002: 49–50 suggests that Agamemnon wishes to claim compensation from the Achaians for the loss of a wife-equivalent (Chryseis). Perhaps; but the terms he uses actually reduce the wife to the status of slave-equivalent.

33. See Haubold 2000: 37–40 on the relationship in early Greek epic between a leader's prestige and the welfare of the group.

34. Haubold 2000: 60–61 notes that in the catalogue of ships Agamemnon's greatness is explicitly based on the number (i.e. quantity) of people he leads.

without a prize, since he offers Agamemnon many more prizes to be delivered later (1.127–28).[35] But he calls on Agamemnon to recognize a competing propriety, the right of the followers to keep what has become their own property (λαοὺς δ' οὐκ ἐπέοικε παλίλλογα τά τ' ἐπαγείρειν, 1.126). Since at the moment there is no material to be given Agamemnon without violating this propriety, Achilles offers Agamemnon a minimal substitution: a verbal promise of replacement property, "with interest," later, when it became available. But for Agamemnon this substitution is unacceptable; he considers it a worthless lie intended to leave Achilles himself physically possessing a prize and Agamemnon without one (1.132–34), and he demands a replacement "of equal value" (ἀντάξιον, 1.136). What he ends up taking is Briseis, Achilles' prize and concubine. Superficially, Briseis is the closest thing to a substitute for the material Agamemnon has lost, a replacement of almost the least arbitrary relationship to what it replaces, girl for girl. But in fact, Agamemnon chooses Briseis more because of what she symbolizes as Achilles' possession than because she is a desirable young woman like Chryseis ("Is that what you want, to have a prize yourself, while I sit here without one . . . ?" 1.133–34).

Near the end of the first cycle, in book 8, Agamemnon approaches Teukros, who at the moment is successfully holding off the Trojans with his bow, and offers him a reward to be paid when the Greeks capture Troy (αἴ κέν μοι δώῃ Ζεύς . . . /'Ιλίου ἐξαλαπάξαι ἐυκτίμενον πτολίεθρον κτλ., 8.287–91). Teukros replies with a question: why should Agamemnon spur him on, when he is fighting eagerly already? (8.293–94) Teukros does not welcome Agamemnon's offer, even though it would have made him materially richer, because it conveys to him a symbolic implication: that he does not already have enough incentive to fight. Teukros does not explain to Agamemnon why he already has incentive enough, but Agamemnon himself has suggested that Teukros's success might make him a "light to the Greeks" and to his father Telamon, whose care Teukros could repay by bringing him glory (8.282–85). The nature of these rewards is that they would sustain a community to which Teukros belongs; they would not

35. Although Agamemnon declares (1.287–89) that Achilles intends to usurp his power as leader of the Achaians, Achilles never says a word that would confirm this. Many scholars, however, have taken Agamemnon's claim at face value and tortured Achilles' statements to find in them an ambition to Agamemnon's position; for a recent example see Wilson 2002: 63, 69. This view rests on the premise that the values of the Homeric warriors were determined by their culture, and that in this culture all warriors competed to maximize their status (see especially Adkins 1960 and Van Wees 1992). With regard to their aspirations to status, therefore, Agamemnon and Achilles are indistinguishable, and necessarily so. But the *Iliad* tells a different story. Achilles *acknowledges* Agamemnon's role as leader of the Greek force; he affirms that he came to Troy only to serve Agamemnon (σοί . . . ἅμ' ἑσπόμεθ' κτλ., 1.158–59). What Achilles disputes is *how* Agamemnon exercises his position as leader; he expects Agamemnon to show gratitude for Achilles' favors *as a follower*: according to Achilles, therefore, Agamemnon is not so much undeserving of his superior status in the expedition as abusive of it. In Homer honor (τιμή) is often understood as acknowledgment of an affectionate and trusting relationship, rather than deference as Van Wees constantly claims. Thus in the *Odyssey* the narrator says that Laertes honored his *slave* Eurykleia as much as he honored his wife (ἶσα . . . κεδνῇ ἀλόχῳ τίεν, *Od.* 1.432) and that Antikleia honored her slave Eumaios (*Od.* 15.365). In the *Iliad,* when Achilles says that Zeus honors him (*Il.* 9.608) he cannot mean that Zeus is showing deference to him. On honor in the *Iliad* and *Odyssey* as an expression of generosity between the parties of a relationship, see the important article of Riedinger 1976. On Achilles' expectation of generosity from Agamemnon, also see Gill 1996: 139.

make him wealthier. In this respect they are symbolic, not material like the tripod, horses, and woman from which Agamemnon invites Teukros to take his choice. By promising to put Teukros's award "right in his hand" (ἐν χερὶ θήσω, 8.289) and listing a tripod along with a woman for use in Teukros's bed (8.291), Agamemnon demonstrates graphically his inability to distinguish between symbolic and material value.

The embassy in book 9 develops the consequence of Agamemnon's insensitivity. When Nestor counsels him to take responsibility for alienating Achilles and to undo the damage, he voices a hope that Achilles can be persuaded by "gentle gifts and soothing words" (9.114). Of course, Nestor does not mean that Agamemnon should offer Achilles things that are materially gentle and soothing in themselves, like wine or incantations, but things symbolic of a pleasant affective relationship between giver and receiver.[36] Nestor's proposal in this respect resembles Kalchas's proposal to propitiate Apollo, except that Kalchas, who is Apollo's seer, explains rather specifically what Agamemnon is to send the god, while Nestor, who speaks without divine guidance and authority, leaves the details to Agamemnon. But with typical shallowness Agamemnon fails to see the point of Nestor's advice; his offer to Achilles is symbolic only to the minimal extent that it is conveyed by words and not the immediate delivery of material. Even the words themselves are limited in meaning to the denotation of material objects, and when Odysseus reports them to Achilles he repeats them—thirty-nine lines in Agamemnon's speech—almost verbatim, for a message such as Agamemnon's cannot be replaced by paraphrase: it means only what it says. As for the offer itself, the value of the things promised is purely material: they are things that can be counted, and Agamemnon's enumerations—seven tripods, twenty talents of gold, twelve horses, seven women of Lesbos, twenty Trojan women, one bride chosen from among three daughters, seven citadels—in their very insistence upon specific quantities stress that the value of the gifts is exactly what can be measured: they are goods, not symbols. They are not even symbols of a relationship in which Agamemnon would exchange material for Achilles' labor, since the things Agamemnon offers Achilles are the same things he and Agamemnon acquire from sacking cities. What Agamemnon offers Achilles is return of goods: if Achilles helps the Greeks sack Troy, he will give Agamemnon material spoil, and Agamemnon will give back to Achilles a major share of the same spoil.

Agamemnon's offer to give Achilles a daughter in marriage, and thus make him his son-in-law, is no exception to this: on the contrary, it illustrates that Agamemnon does not even recognize his own family relationships as symbolic of loving affect. His own son, Orestes, is being brought up far away from his father, but amid much material abundance (θαλίῃ ἔνι πολλῇ, 9.143). Agamemnon plans to bestow one of his daughters upon a man who, if things go right, will come home in

36. Wilson 2002. 74 obscures Nestor's point in explaining that when Nestor says δῶρα (gifts) he means ποινή (payback). Gifts are offered freely and warmly to a friend; payback is taken from a defeated enemy. Achilles does not demand payback; in 9.387 he does not use the word ποινή or any word related to it. Wilson similarly confuses compulsory payback with freely offered gifts in her gloss on Ajax's speech (Wilson 2002: 105).

possession of twenty Trojan women slaves selected for their beauty! A young woman would not choose a husband with twenty beautiful concubines—think of Phoinix's mother or Odysseus's—nor would a loving father choose him for a son-in-law. And Agamemnon offers Achilles all three of his daughters to choose from—Achilles can choose a wife, but Agamemnon's daughters cannot choose their husbands, any more than women taken in conquest, like the seven women of Lesbos or twenty Trojan beauties, can choose their masters. This shows what it means to be Agamemnon's son or daughter (not to mention his wife). In offering to make Achilles a member of his family, Agamemnon offers Achilles a relationship devoid of symbolism and affect even where it is most to be expected.[37]

Odysseus seems to understand that Agamemnon's offer holds nothing to mollify Achilles, and he precedes and follows it with affective descriptions of the situation that confronts Achilles: the Greeks are afraid, Hektor is raging, Achilles hates Agamemnon, and even if he does not soften toward Agamemnon he should pity the Greeks and rescue them. Odysseus also reminds Achilles that his own father advised him to increase his honor by avoiding quarrel (*ληγέμεναι δ' ἔριδος . . . ὄφρα σε μᾶλλον/τίωσ'* 9.257–58), and he promises him that if he returns the Greeks will honor him like a god (*σε θεὸν ὣς/τείσουσ'* 9.302–3). These supplements to Agamemnon's offer resemble the nonmaterial incentives (being a beacon for the Greeks, bringing glory to father Telamon) Agamemnon mentioned to Teukros, incentives Agamemnon apparently thought were insufficient, since he then immediately promised material rewards in addition. In Odysseus's speech, however, it is the material offer that is deficient, and the relationships he adds are more symbolic: where Agamemnon encouraged Teukros to repay the sustenance he received from his father Telamon, Odysseus encourages Achilles to remember and fulfill the teaching he received from his father Peleus, and where Agamemnon encouraged Teukros to save the Greeks, Odysseus encourages Achilles to pity them (*ἐλέαιρε*, 9.302).

In his reply to Odysseus Achilles essentially ignores all this and addresses Agamemnon's offer alone. He rejects the offer explicitly because it is merely material and not symbolic of an affective relationship (*οὐκ . . . τις χάρις ἦεν*, 9.316). This rejection continues and develops the perspective that Achilles has already articulated in the quarrel in the assembly in book 1, where he explained to Agamemnon very clearly that he did not come to Troy either to defend his own material possessions in Phthia or to acquire more, but to *please* Agamemnon (*ὄφρα σὺ χαίρῃς*, 1.158), and expressed outrage that Agamemnon did not reciprocate his generous affect (*οὐδ' ἀλεγίζεις*, you don't care at all, 1.160).

37. The references to Iphianassa (9.145, 9.287) do not necessarily mean that audiences of the *Iliad* were to imagine that Agamemnon never had a daughter named Iphigeneia whom he sacrificed (*pace* Griffin 1995: 92). According to the *Kypria* (fr. 17 Davies) Iphianassa and Iphigeneia were both Agamemnon's daughters. The absence of Iphigeneia from Agamemnon's list, where she might have appeared *with* Iphianassa, could therefore tacitly mark the death that her father inflicted on her. If anybody thinks this reading of absence is too subtle, remember that Odysseus, in reporting Agamemnon's speech, omits the final four lines (9.158–61) and replaces them with a new ending of his own (9.300–306). On the likelihood that the poet of the *Iliad* knew and adapted a version of the *Kypria*, see Finkelberg 2002.

Agamemnon's threat to take Achilles' reward symbolizes this deficiency of affect. Achilles reminds Agamemnon that his prize symbolizes his relationship to the Greeks, who gave it to him (1.162), that he suffered a lot to win it (1.162), and that he felt an affective relationship toward it (φίλον, 1.167) even though it was materially insignificant (ὀλίγον, 1.167) and not remotely equivalent to the effort expended for it. To Achilles, Briseis is symbol, not spoil; but to Agamemnon, Achilles declares, all gains are merely material wealth (ἄφενος καὶ πλοῦτον, 1.171), because they do not symbolize anything to Agamemnon and particularly not the good feelings of the allies who helped win them.

In replying to Odysseus Achilles immediately brings forward his desire for an affective relationship symbolized in speech and his conviction that Agamemnon has violated the very principle of such a relationship. When he proclaims his hatred of anyone "who hides one thing in his heart (ἐνὶ φρεσίν, 9.313) but speaks another," Achilles shows that for him speech mediates a relationship between hearts, and that if a speaker abuses positive affect (trust) to harm a friend, the relationship must become one of negative affect (hatred). Agamemnon and the Greeks cannot persuade Achilles to rejoin him because they have not given him *gratitude* (χάρις, 9.316); this is a kind of caring affect, not material wealth and not even status. Achilles explains that he has endured pain in fighting (πάθον ἄλγεα, 9.321) and risked his life (ψυχὴν παραβαλλόμενος, 9.322); life, as he explains later (9.398–416), is not an object, but the very possibility of feeling pleasure (τέρπεσθαι, 9.400). Achilles illustrates his pain in fighting by the simile of the mother bird who sacrifices to feed her chicks (9.323–27); but there is an implicit difference: the mother bird sacrifices unstintingly as part of her relationship to *her own young*, while Achilles bears no such relationship to Agamemnon and the Greeks, the proof being that Agamemnon has taken back from Achilles the prize that symbolized their relationship, while the other princes have kept their prizes and their relationship to Agamemnon (9.335–36).[38]

Achilles knows perfectly well the difference between persons who are possessions and persons with whom one has an affective relationship, *philoi*. Achilles has brought back possessions for Agamemnon (κειμήλια, 9.330), but the Trojans are fighting for their own wives (ὀάρων ἕνεκα σφετεράων, 9.327). The prize Agamemnon took from Achilles was a bedfellow (ἄλοχον, 9.336) but not a mere object; she suited Achilles' heart (θυμαρέα, 9.336).[39] This is not the way Agamemnon describes his own preference for Chryseis over Clytemnestra (1.113–15), and the asymmetry between the two heroes is clear in the difference. Achilles does not seek material possessions in the war on Troy, nor did he think the Greeks sailed to Troy to regain a *possession* stolen from Menelaos, but to restore the affective, marital relationship between Menelaos and his wife (φιλέουσ' ἀλόχους, 9.340). Agamemnon, however, is so alienated from other mortals as not to understand that they too feel affection and care for their

38. See Bassett 1938: 198–99.

39. Wilson 2002: 87–89 notes that Achilles redefines Briseis as family, not "prestige goods," but she then characteristically translates Achilles' expression back into a demand for "status."

women, as Achilles proclaims he did for Briseis, despite the fact that she was his property (ἐκ θυμοῦ φίλεον, δουρικτητήν περ ἐοῦσαν, 9.343). Achilles actually gives Agamemnon too much credit when he asks whether the Atreidai alone love their wives (9.340), since Agamemnon measures his own wife Clytemnestra according to the same material standard he applies to his concubine Chryseis. Nor does Agamemnon love his daughters, any one of whom he would compel to marry Achilles if he accepted Agamemnon's offer and chose her. Achilles treats his relations differently: he declares that he will not compel Phoinix to follow him home (ἢν ἐθέλῃσιν· ἀνάγκῃ δ' οὔ τί μιν ἄξω, 9.429).

Achilles does not even think of the military aspect of the expedition as purely one of force. He derides Agamemnon's unsuccessful attempt to keep off Hektor's strength (σθένος, 9.351) by putting massive material defenses around the camp (9.349–50). Previously Hektor did not even venture beyond his own gates (9.353–54), because his fear of Achilles made him unwilling (οὐκ ἐθέλεσκε, 9.353). Achilles refuses to "put his mind together" with Agamemnon's, either for planning or action (οὐδέ ... συμφράσσομαι ... 9.374), because Agamemnon's theft has destroyed the basis of a cooperative relationship. When Achilles enumerates the enormous quantities of material that would still be insufficient to pacify him, the quantification does not measure the enormity of Achilles' anger but on the contrary indicates the absolute incommensurability between material objects (which if countable are unsymbolic) and feelings of any degree whatsoever. In rejecting Agamemnon's offer of a daughter in marriage, Achilles proclaims that he would reject a daughter of Agamemnon's no matter how beautiful her body or how skillful her works (9.389–90). When he explains what he will do for a wife instead, he shows immediately that what he wants in a wife is a *family relationship*: his father will arrange it (9.394), he can choose from daughters of good families (9.396), he will make one his own beloved bed partner (φίλην ... ἄκοιτιν, 9.397).[40] Agamemnon is offering his daughter to Achilles as a concubine; Achilles rejects her because a concubine, even the best, does not symbolize the bond Achilles requires to put his life at risk.

Achilles prefers Peleus's possessions to Agamemnon's because to Achilles Peleus's possessions are symbols of his home and his family. The pleasure Achilles longs to take in these objects is not the pleasure of mere use but the pleasure of belonging to the community that shares them. The life of a community, in which possessions symbolic of communal life pass between god and mortal, husband and wife, parent and child, and guest and host, is not measurably long or short, like the life span of an isolated individual. When Achilles denies that the loss of a man's life can be compensated for in material (οὐ γὰρ ἐμοὶ ψυχῆς ἀντάξιον οὐδ' ὅσα κτλ., 9.401) he is referring to the finite life of an individual man, his own life, which must have a definite end and will be measurably long or short depending upon how he chooses to spend it (9.410–16):

40. *Pace* Wilson 2002: 94, who explains that "prestige goods" await Achilles in Phthia.

μήτηρ γάρ τέ μέ φησι θεὰ Θέτις ἀργυρόπεζα
διχθαδίας κῆρας φερέμεν θανάτοιο τέλοσδε.
εἰ μέν κ᾽ αὖθι μένων Τρώων πόλιν ἀμφιμάχωμαι,
ὤλετο μέν μοι νόστος, ἀτὰρ κλέος ἄφθιτον ἔσται·
εἰ δέ κεν οἴκαδ᾽ ἵκωμι φίλην ἐς πατρίδα γαῖαν,
ὤλετό μοι κλέος ἐσθλόν, ἐπὶ δηρὸν δέ μοι αἰὼν
ἔσσεται, οὐδέ κέ μ᾽ ὦκα τέλος θανάτοιο κιχείη.

For my mother, the goddess Thetis of the silver feet, tells me
that two divergent destinies carry me toward my end in death.
If I stay here and fight over the city of the Trojans,
I lose my return home, but my glory shall be unfading;
but if I make it home to the beloved land of my fathers,
I lose my fine glory, but my life will last long,
and the conclusion of death will not overtake me swiftly.

But the context of Achilles' denial suggests more than he seems to intend. Immediately after his acknowledgment of Peleus's advanced age (*γέρων*' 9.400), and immediately before his statement that if he remains at Troy he will die there (9.413), Achilles explains that a man's life breath cannot be seized and possessed (9.408–9):

ἀνδρὸς δὲ ψυχὴ πάλιν ἐλθεῖν οὔτε λειστὴ
οὔθ᾽ ἑλετή, ἐπεὶ ἄρ κεν ἀμείψεται ἕρκος ὀδόντων.

but a man's life does not come back again, neither by theft
nor capture, once it gets outside the teeth that fence it in.

These lines iconically separate the dying father from his dying son, so that the sequence of Achilles' argument emphasizes the disruption of his community in the physical separation of its members at the point of death. As the rhetorical presentation of this disruption, Achilles' description of the irrevocable final passage of the life breath through the dying man's teeth (9.409) evokes the normative deathbed scene when a man's final breath or symbolic final word is caught and preserved by a loving survivor[41]—the same scene whose nonoccurrence Andromache regrets near the close of the epic when she laments that Hektor did not die in bed with her nearby (*οὐδέ τί μοι εἶπες πυκινὸν ἔπος, ὅ τέ κεν αἰεὶ/μεμνήμην κτλ.*, 24.744–45).[42]

41. On the custom of a relative catching the last breath of the dying, see Onians 1951: 171–73.

42. Lynn-George 1988: 122 suggests that in 9.408–9 the word *ψυχή* replaces the word *ἔπος* ("word"), which in a familiar Homeric phrase characteristically escapes the *ἕρκος ὀδόντων* ("enclosure of the teeth"). Lynn-George identifies this implicit *ἔπος* with the immortal *κλέος* ("glory") for which the hero gives his life, concluding that "the *Iliad* thus structures itself as a question in celebration: does *kleos* ever balance the loss?" Andromache's regret for Hektor's unspoken last word (24.744) confirms that Achilles' word *ψυχή* does imply *ἔπος*, but it also shows that this *ἔπος* is not the same thing as *κλέος*: the word Andromache desired from Hektor was personal, while *kleos* is public.

Thus for Achilles to say that he wants to go home to his family (9.400) because no quantity of possessions can compensate him for the value of life (οὐ . . . ψυχῆς ἀντάξιον' 9.401) implies not only that he wants to increase the length (i.e., material quantity) of his individual life span, but also that he needs to *transmit* life from Peleus to another generation, and that no material can compensate him for this interrupted transmission.[43] This inference is supported by the development of the same theme as the poem progresses. When in mourning for Patroklos, Achilles will lament that he intended for Patroklos to transmit his legacy to his son Neoptolemos, and wonder whether his son and father are even still living (19.327–37). Later, before Patroklos is to be cremated, Achilles will cut a lock of the hair he had grown long for a dedication to the river Spercheios in his fatherland (23.141–51): such dedications symbolized a repayment of life to the source that gave and nourished it.[44]

In articulating Achilles' contempt for Agamemnon's materialism and his own consciousness of affective relationships and their symbols, Achilles' reply to Odysseus also represents an advance beyond Achilles' own understanding of symbolism and relationships as expressed in book 1. There he lamented the shortness of his individual life (1.352) and demanded that Zeus compensate him with honor (1.353). The solution Achilles sought was conceptualized symbolically, but the problem was brutely material, the insufficient quantity of his life as determined by the necessity of his birth (ἔτεκες, 1.352).[45] In book 9, Achilles says he has a choice: all by itself this possibility of choice transforms the transition between Achilles' past and future from necessity to arbitrariness. Moreover, at stake in this choice is not simply the quantity of life Achilles is to have, but its quality: death at Troy means not *short life*, but *return home lost* and *fame gained* (9.413); longer life is life lived *in his own beloved ancestral homeland* (φίλην ἐς πατρίδα γαῖαν κτλ., 9.414–17). In book 1 Achilles and Thetis imagine his "life" as a uniform material of limited measurable quantity, like a length of thread; in book 9 Achilles' "life" has become the signifier of two radically

The *Iliad* is speech, but whether Achilles' evaluation of ψυχή calls the value of the *Iliad* itself into question depends upon what kind of speech it is: is the *Iliad* κλέος (public) or πυκινὸν ἔπος (personal)? Either conclusion seems possible to me.

43. On death as the moment when life becomes transmissible, and the origin of story in that moment, see Brooks 1984: 28.

44. On offerings of hair to river-gods, see Onians 1951: 230–31. See Mackie 2002 on the associations between Homeric Phthia and the notion of perishing in the φθι - root (φθίνω/φθίω/φθινύθω).

45. The influential claim of Slatkin 1991 that Achilles expects compensation for denial of cosmic dominance rests on very thin textual evidence. There is no testimony earlier than Pindar for the story that Zeus condemned Thetis to marry a mortal because she was destined to bear a son greater than his father. The *Kypria* had a different story, that Zeus punished Thetis for refusing his advances. If the story of the cosmic destiny of Thetis's son was relevant to the *Iliad*, it is unclear why Achilles would never mention it (while it is easy to see why Zeus, Thetis, and Hera would never want to mention the story about Zeus's desire to have a harem and include Hera's nursling Thetis among his paramours). Even supposing that the reference to Briareus as "better than his father" (1.404) could have evoked a story touching upon Achilles' cosmic destiny, it is entirely unclear what the significance of the allusion would be. The narrative of the *Iliad* runs in an altogether different direction; the poet's allusion, if such it be, more likely marks his exclusion of the story than his inclusion of it via elliptical footnoting. Slatkin too readily eclipses the *Iliad* itself behind the epic's putative sources. See Scodel 2002: 140–42, a somewhat different critique of Slatkin's thesis.

different experiences (διχθαδίας κῆρας) that are linked by arbitrary symbolism (i.e., synairesis) to the same physical material, the man Achilles.

Choosing Self-Transformation: Personal Testimony

The next word in the embassy scene goes to Achilles' comrade Phoinix. His lengthy speech, like those of Glaukos and Diomedes in book 6, is marked as arbitrary in multiple ways: tenuous synairetic ("chosen together") relationship to its immediate pragmatic situation and objectives (Heiden 1991: 8–9), errant progression (Phoinix's autobiography—> allegory of the Litai—> appeal to Achilles—> parable of Meleager with inserted biography of Kleopatra—> final appeal to Achilles), and errancy of subject matter (Phoinix's flight into exile, the travels of Ruin and Prayers from one country to another and from mortals to Zeus).[46] And while Phoinix's speech scarcely tries to convince Achilles that Agamemnon's offer is symbolically sufficient, it develops the theme of arbitrary symbolism to a very high degree.

Before Phoinix even begins to speak he displays affect, as tears well up in his eyes (9.433). He also acknowledges Achilles' emotions (χόλος ἔμπεσε, 9.436). Climactically, he affirms that he and Achilles have an affective relationship and that they cannot be separated (πῶς ἂν . . . ἀπὸ σεῖο, φίλον τέκος . . . λιποίμην κτλ., 9.437–38). This relationship was forged by Achilles' father, Peleus, who sent Phoinix away with the youthful Achilles to be his teacher (προέηκε διδασκέμεναι, 9.442). The nature of this relationship, therefore, is synairetic, since Peleus chose Phoinix to be his substitute as father, chose teaching to substitute for nurture, and chose a site outside the homeland where Achilles' rearing was to occur. Phoinix also affirms that his relationship to Achilles is beyond material value, for he would not permit its rupture even if a god could restore his youth (γῆρας ἀποξύσας θήσειν νέον ἡβώοντα, 9.446). This draws out a bit further what was implied by Achilles' decision to reject Agamemnon's promise of booty and return home instead: Achilles said that no booty was worth the value of a man's *individual* life (9.401–9), while the context implied that Achilles' individual life belonged to a community of lives that would *also* die if Achilles remained at Troy to fight for booty; Phoinix now says that even the extension of his own *individual* life would not be worth the loss of his *communal* life with Achilles.

The thought of the youth whose restoration Phoinix would not choose leads him via a simile (οἷον ὅτε, 9.447)—that is, via an underdetermined assertion of imagined similarity—to a narrative of his own lived youth. In this youth, Phoinix fled into exile from his own father Amyntor, with whom he had a relationship that was natural but not affectively satisfactory (νείκεα, 9.448). The reason was that Amyntor had affection (φιλέεσκεν, 9.450) for a concubine with physically pleasing hair (καλλικόμοιο, 9.449), and in this way he devalued his symbolic relationship to his legitimate wife (ἄκοιτιν, 9.450), who was Phoinix's mother.

46. For analyses of the structure of Phoenix's speech, see Lohmann 1970: 245–71; Rosner 1976: 314–27; Scodel 1982b: 128–36; and Wilson 2002: 96–97.

Phoinix's mother came up with a plan to correct the situation by changing the way the concubine felt about her master (ἵν' ἐχθήρειε, "so that she would hate him" 9.452)—an interesting idea, since it assumed that Amyntor's pleasure in his concubine depended on her affection as well as her physical compliance with his wishes. But Phoinix's mother still conceived of the relationship as fundamentally physical, as her plan for changing the concubine's feelings shows: she urged her son to physically replace his father in the concubine's bed, so that the concubine would prefer the physically younger lover to the older one (γέροντα, 9.452). Phoinix agreed to help his mother and slept with the concubine, but the plan had an unexpected outcome: Amyntor laid a curse upon his son, that no son of his own would ever be born to him (9.453–56). Amyntor did not effect this punishment himself, but Zeus of the Underworld and Persephone did it as intermediaries (9.456–57).

Phoinix's anger at his father was so great that he planned to kill him with his sword (ὀξέι χαλκῷ, 9.458), and like Achilles in the assembly in book 1, Phoinix was stopped by a god (9.459). Yet while Achilles was stopped physically by Athena, Phoinix was stopped by "some god" (τις ἀθανάτων) whom he could not identify, who affected his mind (παῦσεν χόλον, 9.459). While Athena promised Achilles measurable material compensation (τρὶς τόσσα . . . δῶρα, 1.213) for his suffering, Phoinix's god made him mindful of the speeches of men, which would brand him as a parricide (ἐνὶ θυμῷ /δήμου θῆκε φάτιν . . . /ὡς μὴ πατροφόνος μετ' Ἀχαιοῖσιν καλεοίμην, 9.459–61). Phoinix therefore refrains from violence against his father because it would affect the symbolic currency of a synairetic relationship, his relationship to the Achaians, his non-kin.

Rather than kill his father, Phoinix fled his family altogether, acquiring a new home in the land of Peleus, a stranger who loved Phoinix as a father loves an only son (μ' ἐφίλησ' ὡς εἴ τε πατὴρ ὃν παῖδα φιλήσῃ /μοῦνον κτλ., 9.481–82). In this new, arbitrary relationship, Phoinix also took care of Peleus's actual only son Achilles (better care than Peleus did himself!) and made Achilles a replacement for the son Phoinix could never have (οὔ τι θεοὶ γόνον ἐξετέλειον /ἐξ ἐμεῦ· ἀλλὰ σὲ παῖδα . . . /ποιεύμην κτλ., 9.493–95). As Achilles' surrogate father, Phoinix fed the infant Achilles. He did not do this out of obligation to Peleus, but out of love for Achilles (ἐκ θυμοῦ φιλέων, 9.486), who would only accept food willingly from Phoinix himself (9.486). Caring for Achilles was a lot of work for Phoinix (9.492), but he did it, in the expectation that Achilles would pay him back by defending him against ruin (ἵνα μοί ποτ' ἀεικέα λοιγὸν ἀμύνῃς, 9.495). Thus Phoinix cared for Achilles as the mother bird in Achilles' simile cares for her young: except that in the simile it is never stated, or even implied, that the mother bird helps her young in expectation of reciprocated service, while Phoinix expected reciprocation from Achilles. This reciprocation is only slightly arbitrary (Achilles is to help Phoinix survive as Phoinix helped the infant Achilles survive), and it also diminishes the role of affect in Phoinix's relationship to Achilles. But in applying this tale and its conclusion to Achilles' response to Agamemnon, Phoinix has implicitly *extended* the scope of Achilles' obligation from Phoinix himself to the whole Greek army: Achilles could actually protect Phoinix himself quite well just by taking him home, as he has already proposed doing (9.427–29).

As noted earlier, the story of how Phoinix became Achilles' symbolic parent bears comparison to a story in the *Kypria* that told how Thetis (one of the pleaders of book 1, and like Phoinix a companion of Peleus in Phthia and parent of Achilles) became Achilles' biological mother: she had been nursed by Hera, Zeus's sister and wife, and in loyalty to Hera she resisted Zeus's sexual overtures. Zeus then punished Thetis by compelling her to marry the mortal Peleus, and Achilles was the offspring of their union. Thetis did not love Peleus, and when he grew old she left him to live beneath the sea, with her immortal father and sisters in the home of her birth. Thetis, therefore, was cast by Zeus into arbitrariness, that is, into a relationship that could never have existed if Zeus had not chosen it for her. But in almost every other respect Thetis's marriage to Peleus is defined by the material necessity of mortal aging and death, which Thetis finds unbearable and flees. Phoinix's case was different: the physical punishment of sterility liberated him into choice.

Choosing Self-Transformation: Prayer, Allegory, and God

After telling the story of his care for Achilles, Phoinix then urges Achilles to change his feelings by acting as the gods do (*οὐδέ τί σε χρὴ/νηλεὲς ἦτορ ἔχειν· στρεπτοὶ . . . καὶ θεοὶ αὐτοί*, 9.496–97). The gods, therefore, provide a synairetic model that Achilles can substitute for himself. According to Phoinix, the gods cannot be compelled to change their minds, since their power, honor, and excellence are so great (*μείζων ἀρετὴ τιμή τε βίη τε*, 9.498); but they change them anyway, by choice, when mortals appeal to them with symbols of kind feelings (*θυέεσι καὶ εὐχωλῇς ἀγανῇσι*, 9.499). To explain to Achilles why he should do likewise, Phoinix describes the conflicts among mortals in the form of an allegory: the gods are not the only ones to receive prayers; mortals receive them too, and while these prayers seem to come from other mortals, they actually come from gods, for the Prayers are the daughters of Zeus (*Λιταί εἰσι Διὸς κοῦραι*, 9.502) and have the power to benefit a mortal or persuade Zeus to punish him (9.508–12). Therefore, according to the allegory, when a mortal receives an appeal for reconciliation from another mortal, he is actually hearing from a divinity, and in accepting the appeal he would honor the divinity (*αἰδέσεται κούρας Διὸς ἆσσον ἰούσας*, 9.508), as he should. And so Phoinix advises Achilles to honor the Prayers (*πόρε καὶ σὺ Διὸς κούρῃσιν ἕπεσθαι/τιμήν*, 9.513–14) by accepting the gifts promised by Agamemnon (9.513–23).[47]

This part of Phoinix's appeal develops themes from three different scenes in book 1: Chryses' appeal to Agamemnon, Athena's appearance in the assembly to prevent Achilles from killing Agamemnon, and Thetis's appeal to Zeus. When Chryses appeals to the Atreidai, he says explicitly that accepting his ransom and

47. Wilson 2002: 100 correctly notes that the embassy does not constitute an act of supplication to Achilles, although Phoinix's allegory implies that it does.

returning Chryseis would symbolize reverence for Apollo (*ἁζόμενοι Διὸς υἱὸν κτλ.*, 1.21). Agamemnon dismisses the symbols of Apollo (*μή ... οὐ χραίσμῃ σκῆπτρον καὶ στέμμα θεοῖο*, 1.28) and refuses to pay the god the symbolic reverence that Chryses called for. As a result, Chryses prays to Apollo to punish the Greeks, and the god hears him. In this scene in book 1, Chryses indicates that he, his addressees, and their transaction all stand in a symbolic relationship to another party, a divinity whose involvement is only symbolized. This is a particular divinity, Apollo, with whom Chryses already has a special relationship. The Prayers in Phoinix's allegory are a little different; they are involved in prayers as such, not only in those made by some hypothetical "priests of Prayers." Those who make appeals for reconciliation—like Odysseus and Phoinix—do not come bearing special symbols of the Prayers, nor can they normally advise the addressee that his acceptance will symbolize reverence for the Prayers, since it is not generally understood that the Prayers actually are goddesses—that is why Phoinix has to explain them to Achilles (while Chryses did not have to explain to the Atreidai who Apollo was). The relationship of the divine Prayers to mortal pray-ers is therefore much more arbitrary than that of Apollo to Chryses, since the Prayers may extend their relationship to anybody who appeals for reconciliation, without the pray-er himself even knowing it.

As daughters of Zeus, the Prayers are also comparable to Athena, the daughter of Zeus who came to Achilles in book 1. In that scene, Athena comes to Achilles personally (albeit as a surrogate of Hera), stops him physically, and offers him an explicit promise of material (countable) compensation (*τρὶς τόσσα ... δῶρα*, 1.213). She leaves Achilles free to decide whether to accept the offer, but he has no choice about whether to hear it, or opportunity to doubt who is making the offer or what it is. In accepting the offer, Achilles says that the gods heed whoever obeys them (1.218).[48] Unlike Athena, the Prayers are not generally recognized as divinities, nor do they even look like divinities: they resemble the powerless, pitiable mortals who make prayers (*χωλαί τε ῥυσαί τε παραβλῶπές τ' ὀφθαλμώ*, 9.503). The physical appearance of the Prayers is therefore at wide variance from their divinity and power. They do not physically compel a mortal to listen, announce their presence, make promises, or give commands; mortal pray-ers are their chosen symbol, through which they "come near" (9.508), and the recipient of an appeal is free to decide whether the mortal pray-ers are just the pitiful mortals who are physically before him, or whether they might symbolize something else deserving of reverence.

The Prayers heed and help mortals who cooperate with them, but not exactly in the way Achilles imagines the cooperation of god and mortal after Athena's departure in book 1. In that case Achilles is directly addressed and instructed by a particular divinity who offers a promise and is in a position to fulfill it; this exchange illustrates his general conception that gods and mortals perform reciprocal obedience (1.218). But the help of the Prayers cannot operate in

48. Compare 1.218 (Achilles) and 9.508–9 (Phoinix).

quite that way, first of all because they do not make commands themselves and so cannot be obeyed: one shows respect for the Prayers by listening to mortal pray-ers, not to the Prayers themselves. Moreover, while the Prayers do listen to the prayers of one who respects them, and help him a lot (9.509), they may not help him themselves, but instead by acting as intermediaries with Zeus. At any rate, this is what happens when someone does not respect them (λίσσονται ... Δία ... κιοῦσαι, 9.511). And when Zeus punishes someone who disrespects the Prayers, he does not do it himself but through another intermediary, Ruin (Ἄτην, 9.512), who like the Prayers represents (and is represented by) a form of human conduct, and who therefore must act through a human intermediary: the guilty person, afflicted with Ruin, brings his punishment upon himself.

Phoinix's allegory of the Prayers also recycles and transforms Thetis's appeal to Zeus on behalf of Achilles. In book 1, shortly after Achilles agrees to Athena's terms and articulates his view of reciprocal obedience between gods and mortals, he calls on Thetis to intercede with Zeus on his behalf. Thetis, of course, is his mother, and as her only son, Achilles is apparently the sole mortal who can expect her assistance: Thetis's care for Achilles is based on their unique biological connection. Moreover, Achilles expects that Thetis *can* help him with Zeus because he believes that his mother once did Zeus a favor for which she can claim reciprocation. The favor Achilles wishes from Zeus is, in Achilles' eyes, itself an obligation Zeus owes him (ὄφελλεν, 1.353), because he is the son of an immortal (ἐπεί μ' ἔτεκές γε, 1.352) who did not inherit his mother's immortality (μινυνθάδιόν περ ἐόντα). Achilles wishes Zeus to correct the dishonor Agamemnon has done him by making Agamemnon learn "his mad mistake" (ἣν ἄτην, 1.412) in dishonoring the best of the Achaians.

The transaction between Achilles and Zeus through Thetis involves a number of symbolic aspects. Achilles believes Zeus owes him compensation for something—immortality—that was never his to lose or surrender, that he has not given to Zeus, and that Zeus has not received. Moreover Achilles does not expect compensation in kind: he does not ask Zeus to make him immortal, or to effect the return of Briseis herself. Instead, Achilles demands symbolic compensation: the symbols of honor. This honor is to come to Achilles indirectly, through the embarrassment of Agamemnon that Zeus is to cause by the suffering of the Greeks. Achilles also believes that Zeus can be expected to repay his debt to Thetis in any currency she chooses, so that while *Thetis* saved Zeus from bondage, *her son* may receive the repayment. It is by an arbitrary act of imagination that Achilles constructs Zeus's debt to him and then links it to Zeus's debt to Thetis; so Thetis is chosen quite arbitrarily as Achilles' delegate to Zeus. Finally, when Thetis appeals to Zeus, she substitutes a slightly different request for the one she has heard from Achilles (compare 1.408–12 and 1.503–10).

These features of symbolism notwithstanding, Thetis's mediation between Achilles and Zeus is much less symbolic than the one the Prayers effect between mortals and Zeus in Phoinix's allegory. Achilles calls on Thetis because she is his mother in the biological sense. The Prayers do not have children at all; the mortals they listen to are the ones who treat them with respect by respecting their surrogates, the mortal pray-ers. Phoinix does not say what kind of benefit the favored mortals receive from the Prayers (see 9.509); the notion of compensation consists solely of a friendly relationship between the Prayers and their favorites, and what passes between them might be anything that is consistent with their friendship. When mortals alienate the Prayers by disrespecting their surrogates, the Prayers appeal to their father Zeus. Apparently they do this whether or not the rejected pray-ers ask them to; they do not appeal to Zeus as intermediaries for the rejected pray-ers, but on their own behalf. The harm a man does in scorning Prayers is not the same as that he does in scorning mortal pray-ers: immortal Prayers can suffer no material harm at all, only symbolic harm. In these cases, therefore, the Prayers do not act as intermediaries for any victims they are related to, neither sons nor friends, and they do not even act as advocates for themselves: they act on behalf of their *dishonored symbolism*. Therefore they take the place of *both* Achilles and Thetis, the victim of dishonor and his intermediary, except that the Prayers do not appeal to Zeus to reciprocate a debt he owes *them*, or for any repayment of honor *to themselves* such as Achilles expects from Agamemnon. The rejected Prayers ask Zeus to send Ruin on the offender so that he will make repayment (ἀποτείσῃ, 9.512) through suffering harm (βλαφθεὶς, 9.512). Whether the harm itself repays the Prayers (Schadenfreude?), or they are compensated through some other repayment the offender makes, or are repaid when in the wake of Ruin the offender must himself seek reconciliation through reliance on them (see 9.504–7), these repayments are all much more symbolic ("thrown together") with respect to the Prayers than Agamemnon's repayment to Achilles could ever be.

While the Prayers are the daughters of Zeus, the favorable hearing they can expect from their father is apparently not ordinary parental indulgence, since they only appeal to Zeus in matters of mortals' petitions for reconciliation. The Prayers are, after all, less anthropomorphic than Apollo and Athena, since they exist as divinities solely as symbols of a specified aspect of human conduct, so any appeal they make to Zeus automatically concerns the conduct they symbolize. Therefore if Zeus loves and heeds the Prayers, it can only be because he loves the mortal pray-ers whom they symbolize in his presence. In effect, the Prayers transform Zeus's relationship to his children from a necessary material bond with particular offspring (a synaptic bond) into a symbolic-synairetic bond that propagates itself into infinitude: Zeus's paternal care potentially extends to *any* mortals who repent of their wrongdoing and pray for reconciliation.

Of course, Phoinix's speech about the Prayers is an allegory. It does not mean that prayers are actually Zeus's daughters or that they are lame, or that Ruin actually runs on fast feet. The speech itself is a rather arbitrarily imagined analogue of the narrative situation in book 9, one Phoinix may be supposed to have invented himself for the occasion,[49] since he doesn't refer Achilles to

49. See Hainsworth 1993:129 on the explanatory conjunction οὕνεκα, "a hint that Phoinix himself should be understood as the author of this piece of allegorical theology."

existing story as he does when he begins the tale of Meleager (*κλέα ἀνδρῶν*, 9.524). But if the Prayers are not really Zeus's daughters, then Zeus is not really their father. The question then arises whether Phoinix's symbolic gods—who include Zeus—*supplement* the putatively divine gods, whether alternatively they imply that the putatively divine gods are *only* symbolic and not "really" divine, or whether on the contrary they imply that the symbolic itself *is* after all the divine. The technique of allegory might in itself suggest any of these three, but Phoinix's specific allegory suggests the last, because its precise subject is the mediation between divinity and mortality through symbol—prayer. As the addressees of prayer, gods are the sanction of hope, and especially of hope against the force of apparent necessity. Since symbols are not given by nature but created by choice, their very existence displays the power to overcome necessity.

Choosing Self-Transformation: Myth as Model

Phoinix's appeal to Achilles moves from the allegory of the Prayers to the paradigmatic story of Meleager.[50] It is obvious that, qua paradigm, the story is symbolic, and indeed doubly so, since it furnishes a trajectory Phoinix hopes Achilles will *avoid* copying, so that it takes one act of imagination for Phoinix to bring the story of Meleager to bear on Achilles' case, and a second to suggest the alternative ending that Phoinix hopes Achilles will actually follow. The story itself, however, follows a course in which the characters form emotional attachments with ever more symbolic objects. Phoinix's story begins when Oineus fails to make a first-fruits offering to Artemis (9.533–36):

> *καὶ γὰρ τοῖσι κακὸν χρυσόθρονος Ἄρτεμις ὦρσε,*
> *χωσαμένη ὅ οἱ οὔ τι θαλύσια γουνῷ ἀλωῆς*
> *Οἰνεὺς ῥέξ'· ἄλλοι δὲ θεοὶ δαίνυνθ' ἑκατόμβας,*
> *οἴῃ δ' οὐκ ἔρρεξε Διὸς κούρῃ μεγάλοιο.*
>
> For Artemis of the golden throne drove this trouble upon them,
> enraged that Oineus did not dedicate
> the first fruits to her in a special part of his plantation;
> the rest of the gods had a share of sacrifice,
> but to her alone, this daughter of great Zeus, he dedicated nothing.

This offering was symbolic but only slightly arbitrary, since it consisted of a part of Oineus's crop, the very material he was thankful for receiving: the gods get back the same things they gave, but only a symbolic part of them. Oineus's neglect made Artemis angry (i.e., it ruined their affective relationship), and she punished him by destroying his crop, a punishment that reciprocated Oineus's crime by depriving him of crops as he deprived her (9.538–42):

50. On the story of Meleager as paradigm, see Alden 2000: 229–53.

ἡ δὲ χολωσαμένη δῖον γένος ἰοχέαιρα
ὦρσεν ἔπι χλούνην σῦν ἄγριον ἀργιόδοντα,
ὃς κακὰ πόλλ' ἔρδεσκεν ἔθων Οἰνῆος ἀλωήν·
πολλὰ δ' ὅ γε προθέλυμνα χαμαὶ βάλε δένδρεα μακρὰ
αὐτῇσιν ῥίζῃσι καὶ αὐτοῖς ἄνθεσι μήλων.

and in anger at his distinguished family the arrow-pouring goddess
sent upon them a wild boar, fierce, with shining tusks,
who, naturally, kept doing a lot of damage to Oineus's plantation.
For he ripped up many tall trees by their trunks and strewed them on the ground,
everything from the roots to the blossoming fruits.

Artemis's punishment was less symbolic than Oineus's offense, since Oineus's trees were a source of necessary sustenance for mortals, while offerings to the gods are not food for the gods but symbols of mortals' gratitude for their relationship to the divine. Artemis did not destroy Oineus's trees herself, but she sent a monstrous boar as her surrogate.

Eventually the boar was killed by Oineus's son Meleager, with the help of many hunters from other cities (9.544–45). The defeat of the boar was therefore due to a force that was in part related directly to the king and the land that Artemis was punishing, but also significantly to a force whose participation was elective. Phoinix does not even identify Meleager's helpers as personal friends of the Aitolian royal household, but as the residents of "many cities" (*πολλέων ἐκ πολίων*, 9.544), that is, they are identified only in terms of synairetic relationships. The boar was killed, therefore, by a substantially non-Aitolian force that replaced the force of Meleager alone, which, as Phoinix emphasizes, could not have killed the boar (*οὐ μὲν γάρ κε δάμη παύροισι βροτοῖσι*, 9.545).

When the boar was dead, its carcass became the symbol of the relationship among those who had collaborated in his killing. But apparently the nature of this relationship was not clear to all, for a dispute arose between those directly threatened by the boar, the Aitolians, and the Kouretes who had come to help them and had lost many comrades doing so (9.547–49). The issue at stake was whether the hunting force was a synaptic community (Aitolians protecting Aitolia) or a synairetic community (men gathered from no particular place). In this fight over the symbolic carcass, Meleager (Oineus's son: synaptic relationship) killed one of the hunters from abroad (synairetic relationship), who happened also to be the brother of Meleager's mother Althaia (9.567). The marriage of Meleager's parents, Oineus and Althaia, was therefore already a synairetic union between a man and woman of different cities (and it implicitly furnished a tenuous synaptic basis for the Kouretes to join the Aitolians against the boar). In grief at her brother's death, Althaia cursed her own son (9.569–71). From one standpoint, Althaia's curse manifested a preference for full kin (Althaia and her brother had the same biological parents) over half-kin (her son was also the son of Oineus, her husband, who was not her kin), and thus an adherence to a relatively more synaptic bond over a relatively more synairetic bond. This is confirmed by the fact that Althaia's curse was heard by the Erinys, avenger of offenses against kindred (9.571). From another standpoint, however, Althaia's curse also adumbrated the more synairetic relationship between the citizens of different cities, since Althaia's brother was after all not just a member of her family but a resident of a different city, and the conflict over the boar pitted two communities against one another and not just two hostile families. By siding with her brother, Althaia was in effect also siding with his *community* in its hostile relationship to the Aitolians.

The curse of Althaia converted Meleager from the enemy of the Kouretes to a neutral observer, since it alienated him from his family, and up to this point in the story Meleager's whole effort had been on behalf of his family. But instead of continuing to fight the Kouretes Meleager chose to stay with his wife (9.556), who of course was not his kin and not from Aitolia either. With the city under attack, the elders sent the priests as emissaries to Meleager and offered him great wealth in land if he would defend the city (9.577–80); this was material compensation that did not symbolize the repair of his relationship to his mother. Meleager refused this offer. He also refused the appeals of his father (9.581–83), brothers, and mother (9.584–85), who apparently did not (or could not) revoke her curse. Nor did he heed the appeals of his own companions (9.585–86).[51] But Meleager did finally heed the appeal of his wife (9.590–96).

> *καὶ τότε δὴ Μελέαγρον ἐύζωνος παράκοιτις*
> *λίσσετ' ὀδυρομένη, καί οἱ κατέλεξεν ἅπαντα*
> *κήδε', ὅσ' ἀνθρώποισι πέλει τῶν ἄστυ ἁλώῃ·*
> *ἄνδρας μὲν κτείνουσι, πόλιν δέ τε πῦρ ἀμαθύνει,*
> *τέκνα δέ τ' ἄλλοι ἄγουσι βαθυζώνους τε γυναῖκας.*
> *τοῦ δ' ὠρίνετο θυμὸς ἀκούοντος κακὰ ἔργα.*

> And then Meleager's fair-cinctured wife
> made a pitiable appeal to him. She told over
> all the sorrows that befall the people of a captured town:
> they kill the men, and fire obliterates the city,
> and strangers abduct the children and the deep-gowned wives.
> And his heart was moved as he heard this suffering.

According to Phoinix, Kleopatra did not ask Meleager to save *her*, and it is conceivable that she was not personally in danger, because Meleager might all along have planned to defend her when the Kouretes brought the battle to his door (as Achilles plans to defend his own ships when the Trojans reach them, 9.654–55). Instead of seeking her own safety, Kleopatra asked Meleager to take pity on the anonymous men, women, and children of the city who would suffer if the Kouretes captured it. The appeal that moved Meleager, therefore, was an

51. Kakridis 1949:18–42 is a famous discussion of the appeals to Meleager from a neoanalytical standpoint.

appeal to an emotional and highly synairetic relationship, his membership in the civic community itself.

It is very clear that Phoinix's story of Meleager narrates a series of choices whose thematic trajectory moves from relatively greater materiality to relatively more arbitrarily chosen symbolism. The comparable narrative in book 1, the quarrel between Achilles and Agamemnon, follows a similar thematic course, except that in the earlier passage the degree of synairesis seems to be comparatively greater at every corresponding stage (e.g., beginning with Chryses' symbolic appeal). Thus while the thematic trajectory of the *Iliad* usually displays synaireses of greater arbitrariness as the poem proceeds, in the story of Meleager that trajectory is reversed: synairesis in the later passage is less arbitrary than in the earlier. The reason for this reversal may simply be that Phoinix's story, while it is *narrated* later in the sequence of the epic performance, concerns events that are earlier in the *mythic chronology*. Thus in thematizing synairesis as relatively less arbitrary than in the quarrel of book 1, the story of Meleager still conforms to the general trajectory of thematic transformation in the *Iliad*, in which relative earliness accords with relatively less arbitrary choice.

Agamemnon's refusal of Chryses' offer of ransom, which implied refusal of honor to Apollo (1.21), is analogous to Oineus's refusal of first fruits to Artemis (9.534–37), but Agamemnon's refusal was more symbolic. The plague Apollo sends on the Greeks is a more symbolic response to Agamemnon's offense than Artemis's sending the boar to devastate Oineus's plantings. Agamemnon's solution, the propitiation of Apollo, is more symbolic than Oineus's solution of getting hunters to kill the boar. In the conflict between Agamemnon and Achilles, Achilles represents the participation of the allies as a favor to the Atreidai (1.158–60), while in the defense of Oineus's land the involvement of the Kouretes was implicitly motivated, at least in part, by the blood relationship between Oineus's wife and her brother. Agamemnon took Briseis from Achilles explicitly as a symbol, to warn any *other* ally against equating himself to the commander (*στυγέῃ δὲ καὶ ἄλλος κτλ.*, 1.186–87); in Phoinix's story the conflict erupted between the Aitolians as a group and the Kouretes as a group, that is, between the *same* groups who killed the boar. The substitute Agamemnon took was also arbitrarily chosen (Agamemnon mentions Ajax and Odysseus as others from whom he might take a substitute, 1.137–39),[52] while in Phoinix's story the symbolic object of contention was the same one particular boar the hunters had killed.

In Phoinix's story, Meleager's mother beat the earth and cursed her son with death (9.568–72):

> *πολλὰ δὲ καὶ γαῖαν πολυφόρβην χερσὶν ἀλοία*
> *κικλήσκουσ' Ἀίδην καὶ ἐπαινὴν Περσεφόνειαν,*
> *πρόχνυ καθεζομένη, δεύοντο δὲ δάκρυσι κόλποι,*
> *παιδὶ δόμεν θάνατον· τῆς δ' ἠεροφοῖτις Ἐρινὺς*
> *ἔκλυεν ἐξ Ἐρέβεσφιν, ἀμείλιχον ἦτορ ἔχουσα.*

52. In 1.137 the sense of "choose" cannot be excluded from *ἕλωμαι*.

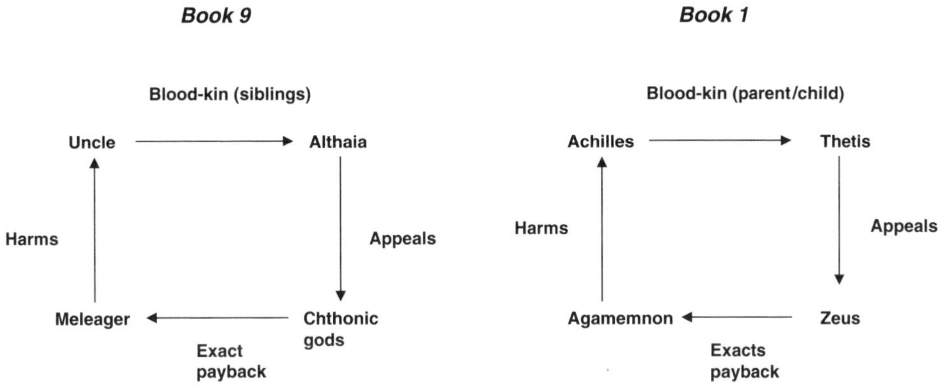

FIGURE 5.2. Appeals for payback in book 9 and book 1.

> repeatedly beating on the fertile earth with her hands,
> prostrate along the ground, and drenching her bosom in tears,
> she appealed to Hades and revered Persephone
> to give her son death; and Erinys, who goes in misty darkness,
> she whose heart never yields, heard her from Erebos.

The analogous situation in book 1 was the two-step appeal to Zeus (Achilles to Thetis, Thetis to Zeus) to punish Agamemnon on Thetis's son's behalf. Therefore while appellant-mother Althaia is analogous to appellant-mother Thetis, Meleager is analogous to Agamemnon, and Althaia's brother is analogous to Achilles. Figure 5.2 summarizes these analogies.

Althaia, apparently in close sympathy with her brother, invoked the chthonic gods without first being asked, while Thetis, apparently unaware of her son's distress (1.362–63), appealed to Zeus only after Achilles invoked her first. Althaia's brother's life had ended; Achilles' had not, but the end was supposed to be near, since Achilles was "short-lived" (*μινυνθάδιον*, 1.352), which quantified his life span more indefinitely and with more potential for arbitrariness than Althaia's brother's life span. Althaia beat the earth physically with her hands (*γαῖαν . . . χερσὶν ἀλοία*, 9. 568), while Achilles at the seashore extends his hands gesturally to his mother (*χεῖρας ὀρεγνύς*, 1.351), and Thetis likewise uses her hands gesturally in appealing to Zeus (1.500–501). Althaia called on the gods to avenge her brother's life by taking the life of his killer (*θάνατον*, 9.571); Thetis calls on Zeus to compensate for Achilles' destined short life by forcing Agamemnon, to whom Achilles has a purely symbolic relationship, to give him honor (*τιμῇ*, 1.510). The Erinys in heeding Althaia displayed an unappeasable heart (*ἀμείλιχον ἦτορ ἔχουσα*, 9.572); Thetis in heeding Achilles displays her affection (1.361), and Zeus in heeding Thetis yields to her entreaties (1.511–30).

Althaia, however, as Meleager's mother, bore the same relationship to Meleager that Thetis does to Achilles, and each mother is involved in determining her son's fate. Althaia's curse established that her son would die very soon, but apparently left him free to choose how he would die, whether defending his city or only his own house. According to Achilles (9.410–16), Thetis told him that he had a choice of two destinies, a short life extended by glory or a longer life lived with his family in Phthia and implicitly extended by it. In the later episode (in mythical chronology) the son's scope of choice is much wider, in terms of both quantity and quality. I shall return to Achilles' choice for further discussion before long. But for the time being let us take leave of the A column books and turn attention to the first two books in the Z column, books 8 and 15.

6

Zeus's Changing Plans

Cycles I and II, Column Z (Books 8 and 15)

The analysis in chapter 1 of the overarching event trajectory of the *Iliad* showed that the epic's central agent is Zeus, whose most important Decisions address Problems created for him by Achilles. But scholars, following a long tradition of discomfort with the Homeric gods, have by and large characterized the story of the *Iliad* as "Achilles' Wrath" (possibly supplemented by "Hektor's Tragedy") and demoted the Olympians to background color. The previous chapter, which focused on the first two A column books (1 and 9), devoted a customary big share of attention to the embassy, where heroes declaim of heroes and heroism, and gods are absent from the action. But by systematically comparing book 9 (A_2) to its thematic/positional counterparts in cycle I (book 1 = A_1, book 8 = Z_1) we saw that while Zeus, Hera, and other gods remained aloof from the embassy, their places were taken in the roles the heroes assumed. We turn now to portions of the *Iliad* less attractive to critics, book 15 (Z_2) and its counterpart in cycle I, book 8 (Z_1), where the Olympians themselves are overtly the main characters. As finales of their respective cycles, books 8 and 15 invite close attention and reward it. They emphasize Zeus's dominant agency in the story, as well as the resistance he faces and the means by which he and his adversaries negotiate cooperation. The Olympians, like the heroes, face off in conflict, but as we shall see, the Olympians prove wiser at transforming their differences into symbolic terms that facilitate compromise. Mortals like Glaukos and Diomedes, not to mention we who are Homer's readers, might consider trading wits with Zeus when he gives us the chance. The *Iliad* loses nothing in thematic complexity and significance when Homer spotlights the Olympians in the Z column books.

THEMATIC ANALOGY: AERIAL SURVEYS

With book 15 the analysis comes for the first time to a book that the design links to *two* previous books: as the Z column book in cycle II, the position of book 15 is analogous to that of book 8 (Z column in cycle I) and book 9 (A column in cycle II). The thematic analogies between books 15, 9, and 8 are very numerous and important, like those already observed between books 1 and 9 and books 3 and 6.

But the quantity of relationships is approximately doubled, and even more than doubled, since some relationships between 15 and 8, or 15 and 9, develop thematic relationships between 8 and 1 or 9 and 1; for example, Zeus threatens Hera physically for disobeying him at the beginning of book 15 (15.15–16), he threatens her near the end of book 8 (8.453–56), and he threatens her near the end of book 1 (1.565–67) (Erbse 1986: 213; Stanley 1993: 162). And the threats are all a little different. The effect on the attentive mind might be something like that of musical chords on the ear, and like musical chords, the thematic-positional analogies can produce an impression of great complexity by accumulating just a few simple relationships. For the sake of clarity, the analysis will generally examine the Z column analogies (15 with 8) and the A-with-Z analogies (15 with 9) separately, although of course the cues are actually intermingled in the poem. However, since the Zeus-Hera scene at the beginning of book 15 suggests a number of analogies with scenes in book 1, some of these will also be included in the following discussion.

Book 15 (Z_2), Book 8 (Z_1), Book 1 (A_1)

At the beginning of book 8, Zeus's Problem is that Athena, by helping Diomedes, has prevented the Trojans from dealing much damage to the Greeks in the previous day's fighting, and thus she has obstructed Zeus's fulfillment of his promise to Thetis. To forestall a similar occurrence, Zeus warns the gods against interfering on either side (Problem/Decision stage) and throws his own weight behind the Trojans, up to a point (Action stage, including polemical configuration); but when Hera and Athena decide to disobey his prohibition and help the Greeks, Zeus sends Iris to warn them back to Olympus ($\text{Action}^{4a,b}$).[1] Book 15 has a similar trajectory: in violation of Zeus's prohibition, Poseidon has been helping the Greeks and obstructing fulfillment of Zeus's promise to Thetis, and when Zeus realizes this he sends Iris to warn Poseidon back to the sea (Problem/Decision stage); then with Poseidon gone, Zeus and Apollo help the Greeks ($\text{Action}^{1,2}$).[2]

Books 8 and 15 also display many sequences of analogous subthemes. The Problem/Decision sequence in book 15 (from Zeus's awakening to Poseidon's departure from the battlefield) combines themes from two sequences in book 8, Zeus's initial warning to the gods (Problem/Decision) and his suppression of the rebellion of Hera and Athena ($\text{Action}^{4a,b}$ + Aftermath^{1}). Comparison of the Problem/Decision sequence of book 15 with that of book 8 reveals the following analogies.

1. 15.1–8: Zeus awakens and realizes that Poseidon is on the battlefield helping the Greeks. 8.1–12: Zeus commands the gods not to interfere in the battle on either side.

1. For the event trajectory of book 8, see chapter 2.
2. For the event trajectory of book 15, see chapter 2.

2. 15.9–33: Zeus threatens Hera with physical punishment for cooperating with Poseidon to help the Greeks. 8.10–27: Zeus threatens the gods with physical punishment if they disobey his order and interfere in the battle.
3. 15.18–33: Zeus illustrates his power by reminding Hera of an old feat, when he suspended her from the sky by a golden rope. 8.18–27: Zeus illustrates his power by challenging the other gods to pull him down from the sky by a golden rope.
4. 15.34–46: Hera swears she did not disobey Zeus's command. 8.28–37: Athena promises not to disobey Zeus's command.
5. 15.45–46: Hera says she will give Poseidon counsel. 8.35: Athena says she will give the Greeks counsel.
6. 15.47–48: Zeus is not angry at Hera. 8.38–40: Zeus tells Athena he is not angry at her.

The Problem/Decision sequence of book 15 also transforms themes from the rebellion of Hera and Athena in book 8.

1. 15.1–3: The Trojans flee back across the trench, away from the ships. 8.343–45: The Greeks flee back across the trench, toward the ships.[3]
2. 15.4–13: Zeus on Ida sees that Poseidon and Hera are helping the Greeks. 8.397–98: Zeus on Ida sees that Hera and Athena are about to help the Greeks.
3. 15.9–12: Zeus sees Hektor lying on the plain, and pities him. 8.337–50: Hera sees Hektor pursue the Greeks, and pities them.
4. 15.13–33: Zeus threatens Hera with physical punishment (*πληγῇσιν ἱμάσσω*). 8.438–56: Zeus threatens Hera and Athena with physical punishment (*πληγέντε κεραυνῷ*).
5. 15.34–46: Hera succumbs to Zeus's threats. 8.457–88: Hera succumbs to Zeus's threats.
6. 15.47–58: Zeus tells Hera that her cooperation can help his plan. 8.478–83: Zeus tells Hera that her opposition cannot impede his plan.
7. 15.58–77: Zeus reveals part of his plan to Hera. 8.469–77: Zeus reveals part of his plan to Hera.

Figure 6.1 schematizes points 4–7.

In book 15, the sequence of events that follows Zeus's revelation of his plan corresponds to the sequence in book 8 that precedes Zeus's warning to Hera and Athena.

3. This is one of the rare occasions when thematically analogous passages display a few lines of nearly verbatim repetition; compare 8.343–45 and 15.1–3.

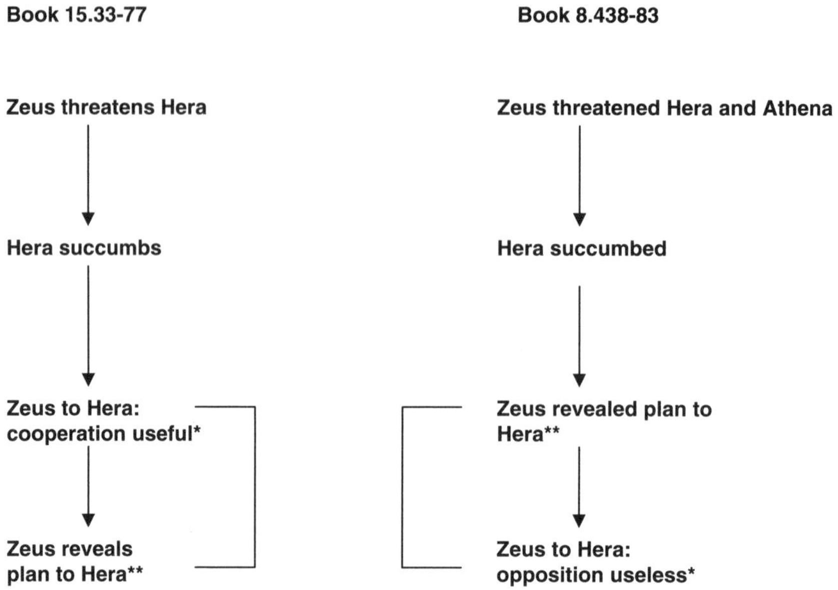

FIGURE 6.1. Zeus's threats in books 15 and 8, points 4–7. Brackets indicate counterpart pairs. Elements marked with one or more asterisks are out-of-sequence counterparts to similarly marked elements.

8. 15.78–103: Hera goes back to Olympus. 8.425–37: Hera and Athena return to Olympus.
9. 15.104–20: Hera incites Ares to disobey Zeus and help the Greeks. 8.350–96: Hera incites Athena to disobey Zeus and help the Greeks.
10. 15.121–41: Athena, warning of Zeus's anger, stops Ares before he can leave Olympus. 8.397–424: Iris, warning of Zeus's anger, stops Hera and Athena before they can leave Olympus.
11. 15.142–217: Zeus sends Iris to Poseidon with orders to leave the battlefield. 8.397–424: Zeus sends Iris to Hera and Athena with orders not to descend to the battlefield.

Figure 6.2 schematizes points 8–11.

Several themes that occur in these sections of books 15 and 8 also occur in the Aftermath stage of book 1.

1. 15.72–77: Zeus tells Hera that he will not cease from his anger until he fulfills the hope of Achilles, as he promised Thetis. 8.473–76: Zeus tells Hera that Hektor will not stop killing Greeks until Achilles returns to the battle. 8.370–72: Athena tells Hera that Zeus is helping the Trojans because he is fulfilling the promise he made to Thetis, to honor Achilles. 1.528–30: Zeus nods to Thetis's request that he honor Achilles by supporting the Trojans.

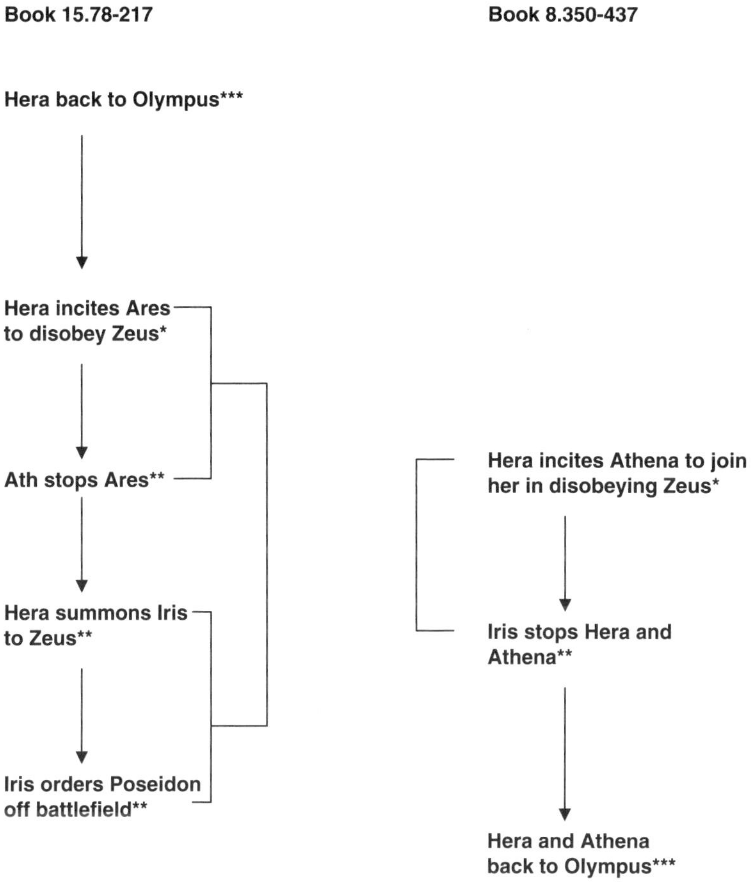

FIGURE 6.2. Zeus's threats, points 8–11. Brackets indicate counterpart pairs. Elements marked with one or more asterisks are out-of-sequence counterparts to similarly marked elements.

2. Zeus threatens Hera with physical punishment: 15.14–24, 8.444–56, 1.560–67.
3. Hera's persecution of Herakles. 15.20–25: Zeus reminds Hera that in his anger because Hera persecuted Herakles, he bound her, and the other gods could not set her free; Zeus pitched off Olympus any god he caught trying to help her. 8.362–69: Athena recalls that she gratified Zeus by helping Herakles (*by implication*, when Hera was persecuting him). 1.589–91: Hephaistos recalls that Zeus pitched him from Olympus once when he tried to help Hera (*by implication*, when Zeus bound her for persecuting Herakles).
4. Zeus's plan. 15.59–77: Zeus tells Hera part of his plan and gives her a role in accomplishing it. 8.470–76: Unasked, Zeus tells Hera part of his plan, but excludes her from it. 1.540–67: Hera asks Zeus to reveal his plan, but he refuses.

After Poseidon has obeyed Zeus's order and left the battlefield, Zeus turns to Apollo and orders him to go *to* the battlefield to help Hektor and the Trojans (15.220–35). This reverses Zeus's command in book 8 (8.1–37) and puts Apollo in the role of performing as his father's surrogate.

1. 15.253–80: Apollo encourages Hektor with an exhortatory speech and by breathing *menos* into him. 8.170–83: Zeus encourages Hektor with a sign (thunder).
2. 15.281–305: The Greek Thoas concludes that Zeus favors Hektor, and calls for an orderly retreat. 8.137–56: Nestor concludes that Zeus favors the Trojans, and convinces Diomedes to retreat.
3. 15.306–27: Apollo frightens the Greeks with his aegis. 8.75–77, 133–36: Zeus frightens the Greeks with lightning.
4. 15.346–51: Hektor orders his men to charge, rebuking them for taking spoils. 8.184–97: Hektor orders his horses to charge, demanding they repay the nourishment given them by Andromache.
5. 15.355–66: Apollo breaks down the Greek trench, allowing the Trojans to cross. 8.343–49: Hektor is stopped at the Greek trench.
6. 15.367–78: The Greeks, especially Nestor, pray to Zeus for aid; Zeus sends a sign of thunder. 8.235–52: Agamemnon prays to Zeus; Zeus sends an eagle as a sign.
7. 15.390–404: Patroklos leaves Eurypylos to seek Achilles' help; he hopes the persuasion of a friend will move Achilles. 8.198–211: Hera urges Poseidon to help the Greeks; he refuses. 8.350–80: Hera urges Athena to join her in helping the Greeks; she agrees.

Figure 6.3 illustrates points 1–7.

In book 15, as in book 8, the Trojan charge is briefly held off by the archer Teukros.

1. 15.437–41: Ajax urges Teukros to fight because their comrade has been killed. 8.278–91: Agamemnon offers Teukros prizes when Teukros is already fighting.
2. 15.437–83: Teukros's *aristeia*; his bow breaks; unharmed, he continues to fight with heavy weaponry. 8.266–334: Teukros's *aristeia*; Hektor hits him with a rock and puts him out of the fighting.
3. 15.459–65: Zeus protects Hektor and breaks Teukros's bow. 8.309–13: Apollo protects Hektor and deflects Teukros's arrow.
4. 15.484–93: Hektor sees the hand of Zeus in Teukros's broken bow; he rallies his men. 8.169–79: Hektor sees the hand of Zeus in the thunderstrokes; he rallies his men.

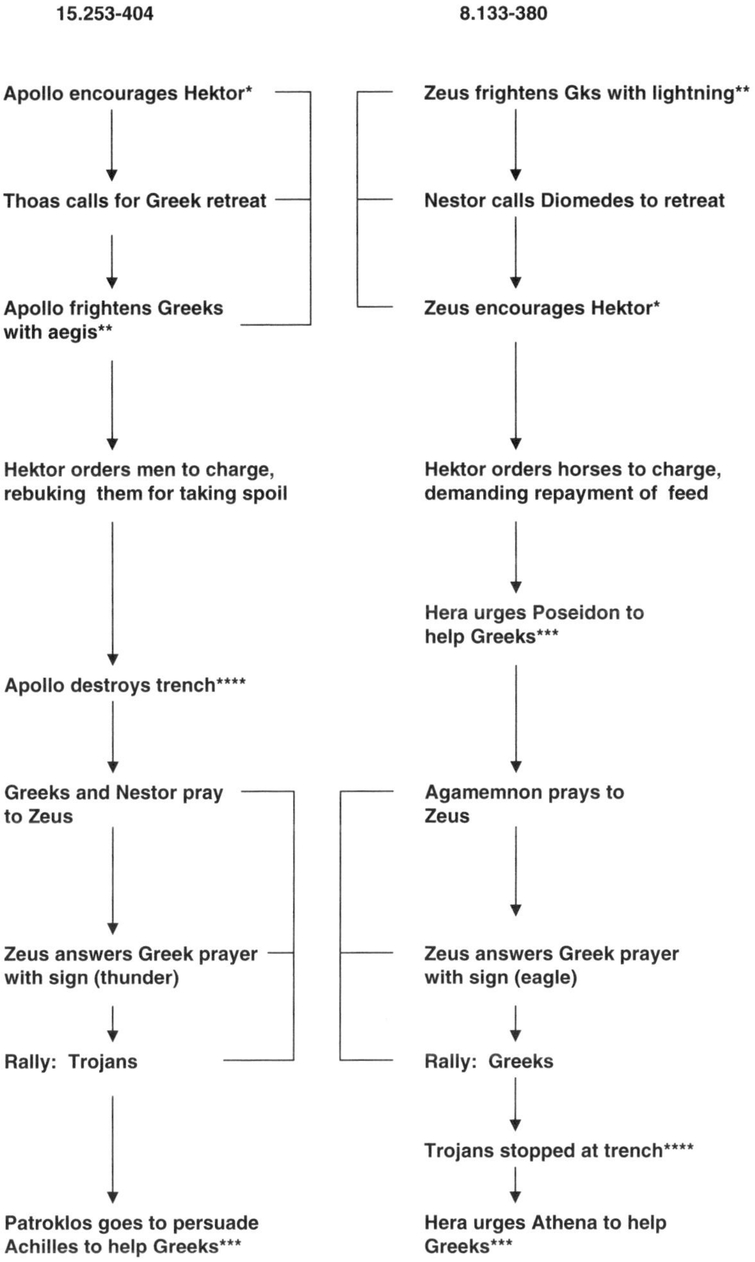

FIGURE 6.3. Zeus's support for the Trojans, points 1–7. Brackets indicate counterpart triplets. Elements marked with one or more asterisks are out-of-sequence counterparts to similarly marked elements.

Figure 6.4 (p. 168) illustrates points 1–4.

In book 15, a Greek rally follows Teukros's *aristeia*, while in book 8 the narration of the general Greek rally precedes Teukros's *aristeia*, and the rally ends when

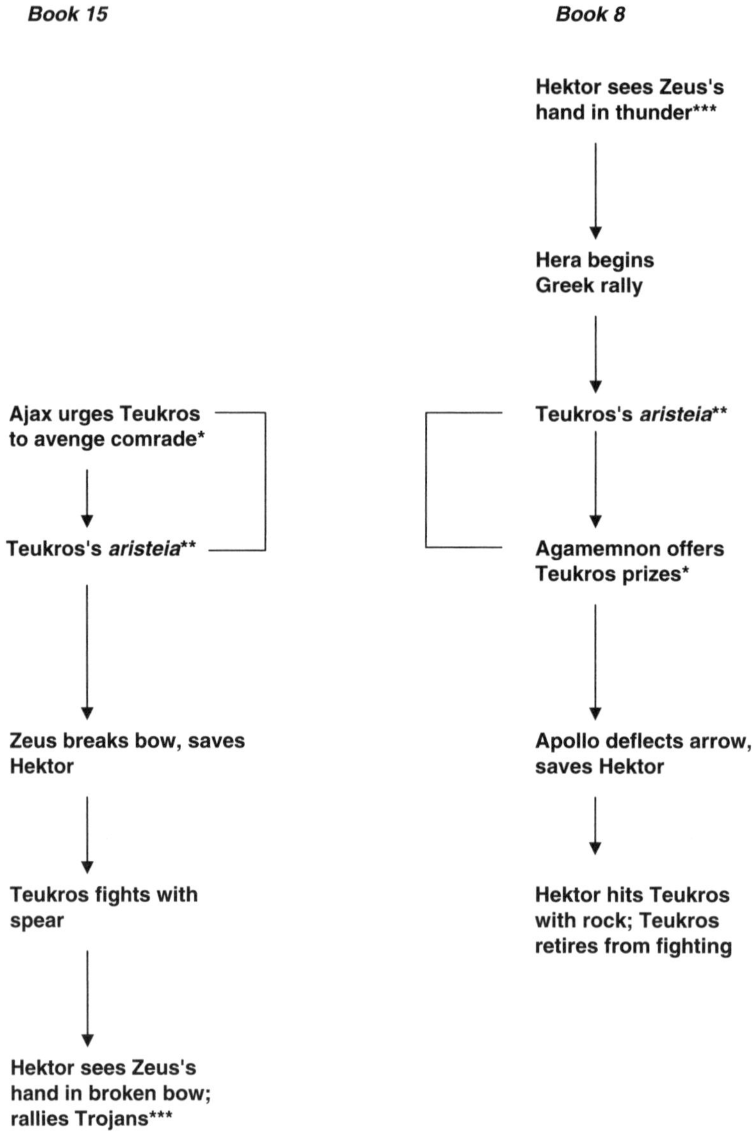

FIGURE 6.4. Teukros's *aristeiai*. Brackets indicate counterpart pairs. Elements marked with an asterisk are out-of-sequence counterparts.

Hektor hits Teukros with a rock and forces him to quit fighting. Apart from their variant positioning with respect to Teukros's *aristeiai*, the two rallies display a sequence of thematic analogies.

1. 15.486–99: Hektor sees an omen in the destruction of Teukros's bow; he calls the Trojans to attack the ships. 8.172–97: Hektor sees an omen in Zeus's thunder; he calls the Trojans to attack, hoping to reach the ships.

2. 15.500–513: Ajax rallies the Greeks. 8.217–35: Hera inspires Agamemnon to rally the Greeks.
3. 15.561–67: Ajax exhorts the Greeks to fight with cooperative discipline. 8.227–34: Agamemnon uses personal abuse and bribery to urge the Greeks on.
4. 15.568–91: Antilochos successfully uses the tactic of a swift foray and retreat to safety. 8.266–334: Teukros used the tactic of shooting arrows and retreating to shelter behind Ajax's shield.

In the final Action of book 15 and its Aftermath, Zeus watches as the moment approaches when Hektor will set a Greek ship afire, "accomplishing the prayer of Thetis." This sequence is analogous to the two Aftermath sequences that ended book 8.

1. 15.596–602: Zeus plans to repel the Trojans from the ships when Hektor has set one afire, accomplishing the prayer of Thetis. 8.473–74: Zeus tells Hera his plan to stop Hektor when Achilles rises up by the ships.
2. 15.699–725: Hektor commands fire to ignite the ships and end all chance of an Achaian escape. 8.507–16: Hektor calls for fires on the plain to keep the Achaians from escaping by night.
3. 15.719–25: Hektor proclaims that Zeus has granted the Trojans the power to burn the Greeks' ships. 8.526–41: Hektor prays that Zeus will allow the Trojans to drive the Greeks away in their ships.
4. 15.732–41: Ajax reminds the Greeks that they have no city behind them for defense. 8.517–22: Hektor gives orders for the young, the elderly, and the women to guard the city while the army is camped outside the walls.

THEMATIC TRANSFORMATION: INTERPRETATIONS

Interpretation of the trajectory of thematic transformations between books 8 and 15 might begin with two general observations. (1) Among the gods, Zeus's plan is still contested in book 15, but the manner and outcome have changed. In book 8 Zeus prohibited the gods from interfering in the battle, but Hera and Athena eventually opposed Zeus openly and had to be haled back to Olympus under threat of violence. In the aftermath, Hera conceded that she could not oppose Zeus, but affirmed that she would still help the Greeks by the means permitted to her, counsel. Zeus then revealed part of his plan to Hera, and told her that she could not change it whether she liked it or not (8.470–83). Between then and book 15, Athena has ceased to act in opposition to Zeus altogether, and Poseidon, who declined Hera's invitation to join her in open opposition, has helped the Greeks when Zeus's inattention allowed him to do so without being seen (Schäfer

1990: 87). In book 15 Zeus awakens to find that Hera has opposed him through subterfuge, but after Zeus threatens her, he maneuvers her into active cooperation with his plan. (2) Among the Greeks, Agamemnon, Achilles' replacement Diomedes, and Teukros, the backup hero of book 8, are wounded and off the battlefield in book 15. But the absent heroes are now replaced by backup tactics that rely upon disciplined group cooperation, instead of by more backup heroes.

The Plan of Zeus + the Plan of Hera: Divine Synairesis

Whereas Hera's acquiescence to Zeus at the end of book 8 affirmed both of them in their own objectives, the cooperation that develops between them in book 15 depends upon Hera substituting Zeus's objectives for her own, and vice versa. Hera's Decision to put Zeus unconscious with her lovemaking was a way for her to keep to her own goal and overcome Zeus's without replacing it (i.e., changing it), and when Zeus awakens he warns her that she will not succeed in using lovemaking as a instrument of hostility against him (15.32–33). Hera then replies by swearing an oath that she was not working with Poseidon and would even advise Poseidon to join her in cooperating with Zeus's leadership (15.45–46). The oath, which is itself a symbol of a relationship of trust and the possibility of enforcement *by Zeus* (she swears by Zeus's head), invokes symbols of the divine couple's intimate family relationship, their grandparents Earth and Sky, and their marriage-bed (as well as the river Styx) (15.36–40, with omissions):

> *ἴστω νῦν τόδε Γαῖα καὶ Οὐρανὸς . . .*
> [. . .]
> *σή θ' ἱερὴ κεφαλὴ καὶ νωίτερον λέχος αὐτῶν*
> *κουρίδιον κτλ.*
>
> May Earth and Sky be my witness . . . and your sacred head, and our own bed of marriage.

Thus the oath converts their lovemaking from the physical act by which Hera exercised her hostility to Zeus into the symbol of their cooperative relationship.

Hera's words, of course, are a substitute for the truth, inasmuch as they give Zeus a misleading impression of her sympathies. But Zeus, who a moment before had assured Hera that she could not deceive him with physical lovemaking, accepts her declaration at face value and enlists her cooperation (15.49–54):

> *εἰ μὲν δὴ σύ γ' ἔπειτα, βοῶπις πότνια Ἥρη,*
> *ἶσον ἐμοὶ φρονέουσα μετ' ἀθανάτοισι καθίζοις,*
> *τῶ κε Ποσειδάων γε, καὶ εἰ μάλα βούλεται ἄλλῃ,*
> *αἶψα μεταστρέψειε νόον μετὰ σὸν καὶ ἐμὸν κῆρ.*
> *ἀλλ' εἰ δή ῥ' ἐτεόν γε καὶ ἀτρεκέως ἀγορεύεις,*
> *ἔρχεο κτλ.*

> Well then, ox-eyed Lady Hera,
> if you should take your seat among the immortals and make plans
> alongside mine,
> then no matter what Poseidon wants,
> he'd immediately change his mind to conform to yours and mine.
> Well then, if what you're saying really is the truth,
> go . . .

Zeus is not gullible (Schäfer 1990: 95), but he prudently sees more advantage in holding Hera to the future cooperation implied by her oath than in punishing her for the past opposition it falsely disavows. Either way, Zeus advances his cause by accepting Hera's fiction of loyalty. In doing so, however, Zeus does not merely overcome Hera's plan with his own; he replaces part of his plan with Hera's, since after all it was Hera's idea—however insincerely proposed—to persuade Poseidon to cooperate. More important, however, Zeus implicitly accepts the symbolism of marriage by which Hera swears, and in this way he accepts a definition of his relationship to Hera as one in which they cooperate and he cannot always do as he wishes and dismiss her objections. After this point in the *Iliad* Zeus no longer commands and threatens Hera; in fact, when Sarpedon is about to die, Zeus actually consults her in his indecision about what he should do—and he follows her advice (16.431–61).

Immediately after Hera swears that she will urge Poseidon to follow Zeus, Zeus gives her a chance to prove her loyalty by assigning her to take his message to Iris and Apollo. In book 8 it was Hera who had to obey the message Zeus sent her through Iris (8.397–431), but now in book 15 Hera herself has become Zeus's obedient messenger: except that while Iris was restricted to repeating *Zeus's* precise instructions, Hera by cooperating makes *her own fiction* of loyalty into fact. After telling Hera what she is to do, Zeus continues without pause and explains what will happen through the work of Apollo in which she is about to cooperate (15.59–77). This explanation represents a significant cooperative concession by Zeus to Hera, since in book 1 Hera sought information about Zeus's plan and was refused (1.540–50), while in book 8 she was told a little, and that only as a threatening illustration of her powerlessness (8.470–83). Now Zeus actually gives Hera something she wants.[4] Zeus acknowledges that his plan fulfills the promise he made to Thetis (15.74–77), which he did not mention in book 8 and did not acknowledge in book 1 even when Hera asked about it directly (Schäfer 1990: 96).What Zeus reveals in book 15 also includes many details not mentioned in the brief threat of book 8. Whereas in book 8 Zeus merely told Hera when Hektor would be stopped from the fighting (*οὐ . . . πρὶν πολέμου ἀποπαύσεται . . . Ἕκτωρ, / πρὶν ὄρθαι . . . Πηλείωνα*, 8.473–74), now in book 15 Zeus tells her that Hektor will be killed (*κτενεῖ Ἕκτορα . . . Ἀχιλλεύς*, 15.68), the fighting will then take place away from the Greek ships, and the

4. Erbse 1986: 201 notes that Hera's opposition loses its point after Zeus reveals his plan to her in book 15.

Greeks will capture Troy through the designs of Athena, Hera's collaborator (*Ἀχαιοὶ / Ἴλιον . . . ἕλοιεν Ἀθηναίης διὰ βουλάς*, 15.70–71). Zeus is now assuring Hera that by cooperating with him she will help to bring about the very things she most wants, so there is no longer any need for her to oppose him. Moreover, while Zeus now tells Hera explicitly that one of her beloved Greeks will be killed (Patroklos), he adds that Patroklos will first kill Zeus's own son (*υἱὸν ἐμὸν Σαρπηδόνα*, 15.67), so that Zeus himself will share in the pain of the battle along with the other gods (Schäfer 1990: 96). This is very significant, because scarcely a moment before Zeus reminded Hera of how he punished her for tormenting his son Herakles, whom Zeus eventually saved (*τὸν . . . ἐγὼν . . . ῥυσάμην*) despite her efforts (15.25–30). Zeus would not let Hera destroy Herakles, but he spontaneously plans the death of Sarpedon.

Zeus's account of his plan in book 15 connects synaptically to his threatening account in book 8, since both cover the same planned events. Yet the second account, by virtue of its enhanced fullness, illustrates quite directly how later passages in the epic progressively display potentialities that were latent earlier. Zeus's plan is a work-in-progress that cannot be nullified, but can still be supplemented and possibly even transformed (Lynn-George 1988: 37–41; Morrison 1992; Stanley 1993: 162 and following). Moreover, Zeus's planning is a method-in-progress that increasingly accepts plans not originally his own (the plan of Athena to capture Troy, 15.71: Zeus does not state whether he already knows Athena's plan or will delegate her to make one) or anticipates the potential plans of others (dooming Sarpedon, and thus deflecting complaints that the other gods lose children and favorites but Zeus does not).

These concessions notwithstanding, Hera returns to Olympus angry, as she did in book 8. But whereas in book 8 she explicitly urged Athena to join her in opposing Zeus (8.352–53), in book 15 she rouses Ares to oppose Zeus by ironic implication alone, revealing to Ares that his son has been killed (15.110–12), and relying upon Ares to make up his own mind what to do about it. Thus even in opposing Zeus Hera must adopt tactics that are more cooperative with her potential allies and hence subject her will to replacement by another's. When Ares rises to go to the battlefield, it is Athena, formerly Zeus's opponent, who spontaneously—that is, uncommanded by Zeus—forces him to sit down. Athena's will replaces Zeus's and saves him the trouble of sending a messenger to stop Ares himself.

Mediated Negotiation: Zeus, Poseidon, and Iris

The message Zeus sends to Poseidon through Iris[5] is more cooperative than the one he sent to Hera and Athena in book 8. Zeus tells Iris that only if Poseidon disobeys is she to suggest that Zeus might resort to force (*εἰ δέ μοι οὐκ ἐπέεσσ' ἐπιπείσεται . . . κτλ.*, 15.162–65). In bringing Zeus's message Iris reminds Poseidon that Zeus's strength is greater than his, but she admits that the fight would be "strength against strength" (*ἐναντίβιον*, 15.179). When Poseidon at first refuses to

5. See Stanley 1993: 162.

cooperate, Iris, instead of repeating the threat or returning to Zeus without Poseidon's agreement, adds her own appeal to Zeus's message: she tells Poseidon that the minds of the excellent are flexible (στρεπταὶ ... φρένες ἐσθλῶν, 15.203) and that the Erinyes always follow the elder (πρεσβυτέροισιν Ἐρινύες αἰὲν ἕπονται, 15.204). The first point characterizes yielding as the choice of those who cannot (or cannot easily) be compelled to submit; thus Iris implies that Poseidon's cooperation would affirm his strength, not his weakness. Her second point implies that the physical conflict of the brothers can be displaced onto a third party, the Erinyes, who act in accordance with an impersonal principle—they always follow the elder (15.204). Birth order, it must be said, is not normally subject to arbitrary determination at all, and the claim that Zeus's priority confers superiority applies a baldly synaptic criterion (even supposing that it requires the elective mediation of the Erinyes). But the matter may not be quite so simple, because according to Hesiod's *Theogony* most of Kronos's children were born twice, first when they emerged from Rhea's womb and later when Kronos regurgitated them, apparently in reverse order, since the stone Kronos swallowed last reemerged first (*Theog.* 497). Therefore all of Kronos's children had two different positions in birth-order, first in the natural sequence and then a substitute position in the super-natural sequence. Do references in the *Iliad* to Zeus's prior birth simply allude to a story in disagreement with the *Theogony* in which there was only one sequence, the natural sequence, and Rhea bore Zeus before Poseidon? Alternatively, they might allude to the dual birth-sequences implied by the *Theogony*, in which Zeus, the latest born naturally to Rhea, *became* the first because he was not ingested by Kronos and so preceded his siblings' rebirths. In the latter case, Zeus's claim of priority would presume the *replacement* of the natural birth-order by a second order that arose from planning rather than nature.[6]

In any case, Poseidon recognizes that Iris's advice does not simply repeat Zeus's command but replaces it, and he praises her excellent fabrication (ἐσθλὸν καὶ τὸ τέτυκται, 15.207). Iris's counsel, according to Poseidon, conforms to a standard, external to the particular situation, that he accepts (κατὰ μοῖραν, 15.206; αἴσιμα, 15.207). Poseidon decides to yield (ὑποείξω, 15.211), but only on the explicit condition, expressed as a counterthreat (ἀπειλήσω, 15.212), that Zeus cannot exercise his will apart from Poseidon, Athena, Hera, Hermes, and Hephaistos and spare Troy (αἴ κεν ἄνευ ἐμέθεν κτλ., 15.213–17). Thus Poseidon agrees to cooperate with Zeus, but only with the understanding that Zeus too will cooperate with the other gods.

Replacing Divinities

The second half of Hera's mission called for her to summon Apollo, leading directly to Zeus's reintervention in the battle of Greeks and Trojans down below. In calling upon Apollo to lead the Trojans across the battlefield right to the site of the Greek ships, Zeus prepares to expand enormously the role of a character whose

6. The *Homeric Hymn to Aphrodite* makes this presumption in designating Hestia as Kronos's first and last born (πρώτην τέκετο Κρόνος ... / αὖτις δ' ὁπλοτάτην, *Hymn Hom. Ven.* 22–23); see Janko 1992:182–83.

sole action in book 8 was that of saving Hektor's life by deflecting the arrow of Teukros (8.311). In book 15, Zeus chooses Apollo to act as his surrogate: this gesture further highlights the development of substitution in book 15, especially since Zeus himself plans to take over again after Apollo has brought the Trojans to the Greek ships (*κεῖθεν δ' αὐτὸς ἐγὼ φράσομαι ἔργον τε ἔπος τε κτλ.*, 15.234–35). As Zeus's surrogate Apollo comes into the very midst of mortals, speaking to Hektor directly and breathing strength into him (15.243–61); Zeus himself never does anything like this in the *Iliad*. Yet while Apollo is closer to mortals than Zeus, his closeness is manifested by symbols even more arbitrary than those Zeus uses from a distance. In book 8, Zeus causes Nestor and Diomedes to retreat by hurling a lightning bolt directly in front of their chariot (8.133–58); this is as much an exercise of Zeus's will as a sign of it. In book 15, Apollo frightens the Greeks into flight by waving his aegis and making a great cry (15.320–27); and when Hektor, with Apollo's aid, charges the Greeks, Thoas *infers* from Hektor's presence that Zeus is against the Greeks and they should make a retreat (*οὐ γὰρ ἄτερ γε/Ζηνὸς . . . πρόμος ἵσταται κτλ.*, 15.292–99).

Zeus himself sends signs in book 15, but these are more arbitrary than his own signs in book 8. Then he responded to Agamemnon's prayer by sending an eagle, which dropped a fawn next to the very altar where the Greeks made sacrifices to him; they correctly interpreted this as a sign of Zeus's favor, and began a rally (8.247–52). In book 15, Zeus responds to Nestor's prayer by making a stroke of thunder (15.377–78), but the meaning of this gesture is not clearly related to Nestor's prayer, and the Trojans take the thunder as a sign of encouragement to *themselves* and continue their rally (15.367–89). Most important, Zeus converts the firing of the Greek ships from a material fact that concretely effects Trojan victory into the symbol of his fulfillment of his promise to Thetis—a doubly arbitrary choice, since Thetis's request said nothing about burning the Greek ships, and the symbol of imminent Trojan defeat is fashioned from the most material Trojan success.

Even Apollo's use of physical force in book 15 advances the replacement of material by symbol: he annihilates the material strength of the Greek fortifications (which had stopped the Trojan advance in book 8) *as if they were the make-believe constructions* (*ἀθύρματα*) *of a child* (15.361–64).

Replacing Heroes

Among the Greek fighters, the absence of Achilles, Agamemnon, Diomedes, and Odysseus elicits substitution in the form of cooperative tactics. The role of leader falls to Ajax, and he fulfills it as much by exhorting the others to cooperative action as by his personal strength. Whereas when Hektor threatened the ships in book 8 Agamemnon shamed the Greeks for not delivering on their boast to make easy work of the Trojans (*φάμεν εἶναι ἄριστοι κτλ.*, 8. 228–35), Ajax in a similar situation shames them for not defending their only means of *return* to their ancestral homes (15.502–13). The *aristeia* of Teukros in book 15 begins with Ajax encouraging his idle half-brother (out of action since sustaining a wound in book 8), while in book 8 Teukros was already fighting quite successfully when Agamemnon came beside him to offer superfluous material incentives. Ajax's encouragement, moreover, is not material, but a reminder of Teukros's personal relationship to a fallen comrade. "See, dear Teukros, our true companion, the son of Mastor, is killed, who came to us from Kythera and in our household was one we honored as we honored our beloved parents" (15.437–39). In book 8 Teukros fought by retreating to the shelter of Ajax's shield (8.267–72); in book 15 Antilochos makes lethal sallies against the Trojans, and quickly runs back to the protection of the mass of Greek fighters (*ἔθνος ἑταίρων*, 15.591).

BOOK 15 (Z_2) AND BOOK 9 (A_2): AERIAL SURVEYS

Like the A and Z books in the first cycle, books 9 (A_2) and 15 (Z_2) have a synaptic relationship, in that both concern the decision of Achilles to make the Greeks suffer. In book 9 Achilles reaffirms and elaborates his decision, and in book 15 Zeus reaffirms and elaborates his decision to fulfill his promise to Thetis.

In book 15 (Z_2) the Problem/Decision stage narrates how Zeus discovers Hera and Poseidon obstructing his plan, and how he peacefully and definitively ends their opposition. In book 9 (A_2) the Problem/Decision stage narrates how Agamemnon recognizes that Achilles' withdrawal has effectively obstructed his plan to conquer Troy, and how he tries unsuccessfully to end Achilles' opposition. A number of themes recur in these episodes of conflict and attempted resolution.

1. *Accusations of treachery*. 15.15–33: Zeus says that Hera has tried to overcome him by treachery, but that she cannot deceive him. 9.307–429: Achilles says that Agamemnon has cheated him, but cannot do it again.
2. *The accused party proclaims innocence, under oath*. 15.34–46: Hera swears an oath that she didn't order Poseidon to oppose Zeus (*ἴστω . . . / . . . Στυγὸς ὕδωρ, ὅς τε μέγιστος/ὅρκος . . . κτλ.*). 9.132–34: Agamemnon promises to affirm under sworn oath that he didn't sleep with Briseis (*ἐπὶ δὲ μέγαν ὅρκον ὀμοῦμαι*).
3. *The accuser gives conditions under which he will cease hostility*. 15.53–77: Zeus tells Hera that he will cease his anger against the Greeks only when he fulfills his promise to Achilles and Thetis (*τὸ πρὶν δ' οὔτ' ἄρ' ἐγὼ παύω χόλον . . . /[. . .]/ πρίν γε τὸ Πηλεΐδαο τελευτηθῆναι ἐέλδωρ κτλ.*). 9.650–55: Achilles tells Agamemnon's delegates that he will fight the Trojans only when Hektor reaches the ships of the Myrmidons (*οὐ γὰρ πρὶν πολέμοιο μεδήσομαι . . . /πρίν γ' υἱὸν Πριάμοιο . . . /Μυρμιδόνων ἐπί . . . νῆας ἱκέσθαι κτλ.*).
4. *The accuser's messenger reports that the accuser is unyielding*. 15.78–112: Hera returns to Olympus with the news that Zeus will have his own way. 9.669–92: Odysseus and Ajax return to the Achaians with the news that Achilles is unrelenting.

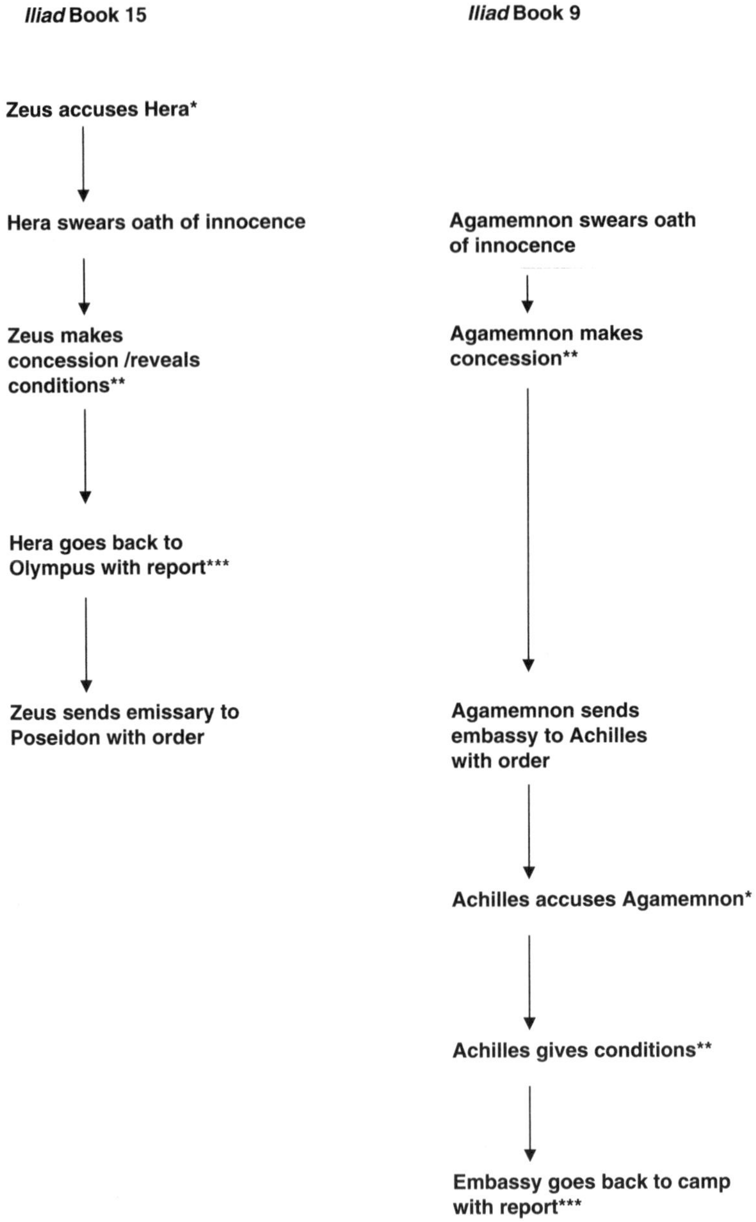

FIGURE 6.5. Conflict and attempted resolution in books 9 and 15. Elements marked with one or more asterisks are out-of-sequence counterparts to similarly marked elements.

Figure 6.5 schematizes these analogies.

Zeus's embassy to Poseidon and Agamemnon's embassy to Achilles also display many thematic analogies:[7]

7. Some noted by Stanley 1993: 166.

1. 15.157–67: Zeus sends Iris to Poseidon with a message that he should leave the battlefield. 9.115–81: Agamemnon sends delegates to Achilles with an offer of gifts and a demand that he return to the battle.
2. 15.162–67: Zeus's message warns Poseidon that he is older and stronger than Poseidon (*μή μ'. . . ταλάσσῃ / μεῖναι, ἐπεί ἑο φημὶ βίῃ πολὺ φέρτερος εἶναι/καὶ γενεῇ πρότερος κτλ.*). 9.161–62: Agamemnon's message reminds Achilles that Agamemnon is older and more kingly than Achilles (*καί μοι ὑποστήτω, ὅσσον βασιλεύτερός εἰμι/ἠδ' ὅσσον γενεῇ προγενέστερος εὔχομαι εἶναι*).
3. 15.185–99: Poseidon complains that Zeus is unfair, and rejects his command. 9.308–429: Achilles complains that Agamemnon is unfair, and rejects his offer.
4. 15.200–204: Iris appeals to Poseidon to change his mind and cooperate; she reminds him that the Erinyes always side with the elder. 9.432–605: Phoinix appeals to Achilles to change his mind and cooperate; he tells Achilles that the Prayers punish those who reject them.[8]
5. 15.205–17: Poseidon agrees to cooperate with Zeus immediately, but he stipulates that he will renew his anger if Zeus fails to fulfill certain conditions. 9.644–55: Achilles refuses to cooperate with Agamemnon, but he states that he will fight Hektor when Hektor fulfills certain conditions.

Figure 6.6 illustrates themes 1–5.

The disorderly scene on Olympus when Hera returns (15.84–142) recycles and transforms themes found in Phoinix's speech in the embassy: both Hera and Phoinix's mother are wives dishonored by their unfaithful husbands.

1. 15.113–18: Hera goads her son Ares into disobeying his father Zeus by revealing that Ares' son Askalaphos has been killed. 9.450–57: Phoinix's mother persuades her son to disobey his father by sleeping with his father's concubine; Phoinix's father punishes his son by making him incapable of having a son of his own (i.e., Ares loses a son, while Phoinix loses any possibility of a son).
2. 15.121–41: Athena, Ares' half-sister, forcibly prevents him from leaving their home on Olympus.[9] 9.458–61: Some immortal restrains Phoinix from killing his father. 9.462–73: Phoinix's relatives forcibly prevent him from leaving his father's house.

The battle narrative of book 15 recycles many themes from the embassy, although of course no battle occurred there.

8. Analogy between the mediation of Iris and that of Phoinix noted by Schäfer 1990: 102 n. 268.

9. Erbse 1986: 140 and Schäfer 1990: 98 note the analogy between Athena's restraint of Ares in book 15 and her restraint of Achilles in book 1. This analogy is redundantly cued by the cyclic design, since book 15 is a Z column book and book 1 is an A column book.

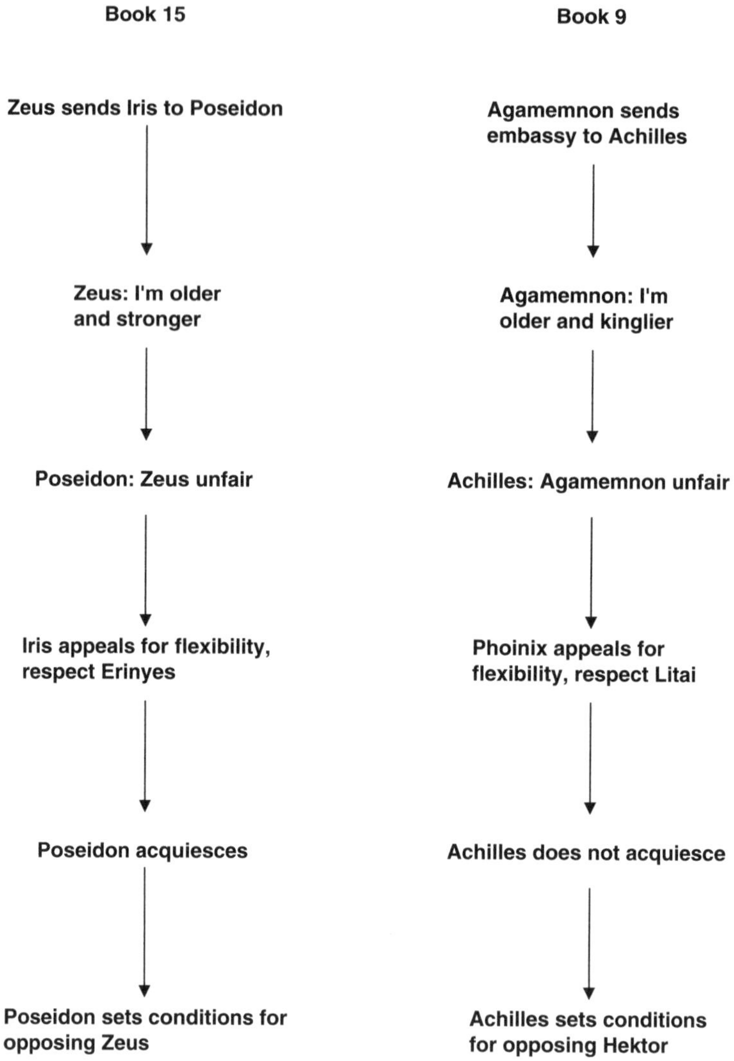

FIGURE 6.6. Zeus's embassy to Poseidon in book 15, Agamemnon's embassy to Achilles in book 9.

1. 15.239–62: Apollo revives Hektor, breathing strength into him (ἔμπνευσε μένος, 15.262); Hektor has been breathing out his life (φίλον ἄιον ἦτορ, 15.252) and thinking he will die. 9.400–409: Achilles says that when a man's life crosses his teeth it cannot be retrieved (ἀνδρὸς δὲ ψυχὴ . . . οὔτε λειστὴ . . . κτλ., 9.408–9).
2. 15.253–366: Apollo goes before the Trojans with his aegis and emboldens them (θάρσει νῦν·, 15.254–55). 9.419–20: Achilles tells the embassy that Zeus has held his hand over the city of Troy and emboldened its people (τεθαρσήκασι δὲ λαοί).

3. 15.352–66: Apollo destroys the Greek fortifications. 9.348–52: Achilles says that the Greek fortifications cannot hold back Hektor.
4. 15.395–404: The Trojans sweep over the rampart; Patroklos hears them and goes to entreat Achilles; he hopes that as a friend he can influence Achilles (ἀγαθὴ δὲ παραίφασίς ἐστιν ἑταίρου, 15.404). 9.432–95: Phoinix begins his appeal to Achilles by reminding him of their relationship. 9.573–99: In Phoinix's parable, Meleager's friends and family members appeal to him to defend them when they hear the sound of the Kouretes assaulting the gates and towers of the Aitolian city.
5. 15.429–41: Hektor kills Ajax's henchman Lykophron, who has come to Ajax's home under banishment of blood-guilt (παρ' αὐτῷ / ναῖ', ἐπεὶ ἄνδρα κατέκτα Κυθήροισι κτλ., 15.431–32). Ajax exhorts Teukros to fight their friend's killers. 9.624–42: Ajax compares Achilles to someone who forced a murderer into exile by refusing blood-money. He calls on Achilles to fight beside the Greeks out of respect for their friendship.
6. 15.484–99: Hektor exhorts the Trojans to fight to the death to defend their homeland, families, and family property. 15.661–66: Nestor urges the Greeks to remember their families and property, and maintain discipline for their sake. 9.393–420: Achilles says that he will return to his homeland and family, where he will live a long life without glory. He urges the Greeks to return to theirs. 9.573–99: In Phoinix's parable, Meleager's friends and family members plead for him to fight in their defense.
7. 15.610–14: Zeus gives Hektor glory, because he will have a short life (τίμα καὶ κύδαινε. μινυνθάδιος γὰρ ἔμελλεν/ἔσσεσθ'· 15.612–13). 9.410–13: Achilles says he has the option of a short life with fame or a long life without it.
8. 15.704–25: Hektor reaches the ship of Protesilaos, and calls for fire (οἴσετε πῦρ κτλ.). 9.649–55: Achilles says he will fight only when Hektor sets the ships afire (κατά τε σμῦξαι πυρὶ νῆας).

Many of these thematic analogies concern the roles of Achilles and Agamemnon in book 9 and of Zeus, Hera, and Poseidon in book 15. Agamemnon needs to send the embassy to Achilles because he feels that he is a victim, but his terms and rhetoric assume commanding authority, like Zeus's; themes of Agamemnon's offer therefore recur in book 15 in Hera's defensive oath (15.36–40), Zeus's threatening message to Poseidon (15.158–67), and Zeus's concessions to Hera (15.49–77). Achilles' replies to the embassy adopt a commanding tone whose themes recur in Zeus's rebuke of Hera (15.14–33); but Achilles also speaks as Agamemnon's victim, in tones heard again when Poseidon replies to Iris (15.184–99, 204–17).

THEMATIC TRANSFORMATION: INTERPRETATIONS

Negotiating with Symbols

Comparison of the mortal negotiations of book 9 to their divine counterparts of book 15 shows that the divinities always make exchanges through symbols of relatively greater arbitrariness than those the mortals use. In book 9, Agamemnon promises to swear an oath of innocence, which would arbitrarily link his statement to a symbol of authority; but he does not actually swear one (9.132–34). Hera does swear (15.34–46). Both Agamemnon's unsworn statement and Hera's sworn statement concern sexuality, but in very different ways. Agamemnon intends to affirm that he did not have sexual intercourse with Briseis (*μιγῆναι*, 9.133), although he affirms that sexual intercourse was a right among humans, male and female (*θέμις ἀνθρώπων . . . ἀνδρῶν ἠδὲ γυναικῶν*, 9.134). The right Agamemnon mentions concerns only the biological suitability of the opposite sexes, not an affective relationship the partners might hold either to one another or to anybody else; sexual intercourse of man and woman is for Agamemnon nothing other than a physical conjunction of bodies in accordance with nature, and the *θέμις* that governs this conjunction is merely an acknowledgment of biological nature itself. Agamemnon's sole concession to some possible degree of symbolism in sexual relations is to choose, without explicit reason, to *abstain* from intercourse, and this abstention is supposed to add some implicit symbolic value to the person of Briseis that Agamemnon offers to return. In book 15 Hera too stands under suspicion of a sexual crime, that of using lovemaking against her partner for the unloving purpose of obstructing his plan. To use lovemaking thus would implicitly reduce if not eliminate the symbolism of the sexual act as a relationship between the partners. But Hera neither denies that the physical act occurred (she hardly could, since Zeus was there) nor claims, as she might, that she was innocent of trickery because the sexual act was just a thing that goddesses have a right to do with gods, and therefore neutral with respect to her affective relationship to Zeus. Instead she affirms that she does have an affective relationship with Zeus, that she remains loyal to this relationship and did not obstruct his plan, and that a symbol of both the relationship itself and her declaration of loyalty to it is the very bed in which she and Zeus have physical intimacy. Or rather, the bed that *symbolizes* their intimacy, since earlier in the day the divine couple made love *al fresco* on an *extemporaneous* bed atop Mount Ida (14.346–51).

Zeus's threats of physical compulsion are also examples of symbolism, though at first glance they might seem the exact opposite. Granted, Zeus's threats have all the effect of disarming his opponents: Hera knows she cannot overpower Zeus physically unless she has the physical assistance of Poseidon, who in book 8 declined to give it ("I wouldn't want the rest of us to do battle with Zeus, since he is much stronger," 8.210–11). Nevertheless, Zeus's manner of threatening shows that his threats are actually symbolic deterrents rather than serious warnings; he tells Iris that he is sending her against Hera and Athena in order to *avoid* fighting them himself, which would not be "nice" (καλὰ, 8.400), and even in reminding Hera of his physical superiority he says he "doesn't know" whether he'll use it against her again (οὐ μὰν οἶδ' εἰ . . . , 15.16). Zeus even admits to Apollo that he is glad he didn't have to use force against Poseidon (ἐμοὶ πολὺ κέρδιον ἠδέ οἱ αὐτῷ . . . ἐπεὶ οὔ κεν ἀνιδρωτί γε τελέσθη, "it's better for me and him . . . since it wouldn't have been done without sweat," 15.226–28). In contrast, the threats Agamemnon and Achilles make against one another are intended quite seriously and are symbolic only to the extent that they exceed the heroes' power to execute them. Agamemnon cannot take Briseis from Achilles by himself, but he fully intends to take her, and sends his heralds to do it for him; Achilles cannot make the Trojans prevail against the Greeks all by himself, but he fully expects Zeus to make it happen for him.

Poseidon's reply to Iris and Achilles' to Agamemnon also illustrate in detail the greater development of symbolism among the divinities as compared to the mortals. Both Poseidon and Achilles complain that they are the victims of a violated apportionment. Poseidon says that he, Zeus, and Hades each received equal portions of the world (15.185–95; also note ἰσόμορον καὶ ὁμῇ πεπρωμένον αἴσῃ, 15.209), while Achilles says that all mortals have an equal portion of death (ἴση μοῖρα κτλ., 9.318–20) but that Agamemnon unequally distributed the booty for which Achilles risked his life (διὰ παῦρα δασάσκετο, πολλὰ δ' ἔχεσκεν, 9.333) and then unequally singled out Achilles' share for expropriation (ἐμεῦ δ' ἀπὸ μούνου, 9.335). The apportionment of death, however, is not a real apportionment, since death is not something like property that exists apart from owners until somebody divides it up and distributes it; the store of death is *necessarily* equal to the number of mortals because death is materially inseparable from each mortal body itself. Moreover, the booty Achilles refers to is also material, as he emphasizes by his enumeration of how many cities he has sacked (δώδεκα . . . ἕνδεκα, "twelve . . . eleven," 9.328–29) and his measurement of the unequal distribution (παῦρα . . . πολλὰ, "few . . . many," 9.333). Achilles confers symbolism primarily upon the *distribution* and only secondarily on the booty itself (when he likens Briseis to a wife, 9.336–43).

The negotiations between Zeus and Poseidon are more symbolic. When Zeus sends Iris to Poseidon, he tells the messenger to mention his greater strength and age (βίῃ . . . γενεῇ, 15.165–66) only if Poseidon refuses to obey him (15.162), and with this eventuality in mind he explains that Poseidon's "heart" (ἦτορ, 15.166) claims to be equal to Zeus (ἶσον ἐμοὶ φάσθαι, 15.167). Iris, however, relays Zeus's entire message very literally, and before Poseidon has a chance to reply to the first part of the message, she repeats the second and tactlessly reminds Poseidon of his inferiority (15.178–83). But although Poseidon does claim equality with Zeus, he does not really rise to the provocation, because he does not base his claim upon an equal endowment of strength, age, immortality, or anything else that could be said to inhere in a god's ἦτορ. Poseidon says that he and Zeus have the same status (ὁμότιμον, 15.186) because they were brothers born of the same parents (15.187–88) and each received a random allotment (παλλομένων, 15.191) of the world as an office and/or symbol of office (τιμῆς, 15.189). These allotments were of different regions (sky, sea, and underworld), hence commensurable only as symbols of dominion, not quantities of similar material (e.g. square miles of territory). Moreover earth and Olympus remained common to all (ξυνὴ πάντων, 15.193) and thus, like the brothers' shared parentage, symbolic of a relationship among them. Poseidon acknowledges that Zeus is physically superior (κρατερός περ ἐὼν, 15.195), but he insists nevertheless that in his relations with Poseidon, Zeus should respect the symbolic equality of his share (μενέτω τριτάτῃ ἐνὶ μοίρῃ, 15.195). Poseidon dismisses Zeus's threats of force, not because he is physically powerful enough to resist them, but because they are inappropriate to the brothers' relationship; he tells Iris the threats would be more appropriate (βέλτερον, 15.197) if directed by Zeus against his children, because of his relationship to them (οὓς τέκεν αὐτός, 15.198).

When Achilles rejects Agamemnon's offer in book 9, his friend Phoinix appeals to him to be flexible like the gods, and to respect the Prayers (9.496–514). This appeal deploys symbolic displacement, but ultimately it exhorts Achilles to accept the gifts Agamemnon has offered, which are material and not symbolic of a friendly affective relationship (and thus not like the "gentle prayers" with which Phoinix said mortals change the minds of gods, 9.499) (Bassett 1938: 196; Wilson 2002: 100). Ajax later calls upon Achilles to respect his own roof as a symbol of his friendship with the delegates (9.640–42), but he too does not understand that Agamemnon's offer lacks the symbolism he is invoking. Ajax expects Achilles to be satisfied by the quantity of women the embassy offers ("seven really fine ones," 9.638), as if his friend were offended by a material loss of female bodies; and in contrasting Achilles' unyielding anger with the complaisant flexibility of a man who accepts blood-money from a relative's killer (9.632–36), Ajax illustrates at best a limited cessation of hostility (the surviving relative "checks his anger," 9.635, the offender "remains in the district," 9.634), not a bond of friendship,[10] and not even the active cooperation Agamemnon seeks from Achilles.

After Poseidon rejects Zeus's command, Iris, like Phoinix, appeals to Poseidon for flexibility, but she does not offer Poseidon anything material at all. Instead she adopts Poseidon's own standards, implying that his uncompromising response conflicts with his family relationship to Zeus, because the Erinyes, a neutral third party charged with enforcing such relationships, "follow the elder" as a matter of principle ("always," 15.204). Poseidon accepts Iris's perspective, though he declares explicitly that it is not his own (he is still angry, 15.208–11), and not Zeus's either, but Iris's (the "messenger knows what's right," 15.207). But Poseidon acknowledges that Iris has spoken "according to allotment" (κατὰ μοῖραν . . . αἴσιμα, 15.206–7), that is, that her idea corresponds to a standard he recognizes and accepts. And well he might, since his whole claim to equality with Zeus is based upon exactly such an allotment, and since Iris's appeal also

10. *Pace* Wilson 2002: 105.

implicitly acknowledges that Poseidon and Zeus bear a relationship to one another that is subject to external mediation by the Erinyes. Thus Poseidon's acquiescence to Zeus's command does not imply his subjugation, and Poseidon can and does stipulate his own terms of compliance in advance without waiting for Zeus to accept them.

Achilles' replies to Phoinix and Ajax adopt a less arbitrary symbolism. Achilles tells Phoinix that he needs no honor from the Greeks, because he already has been honored "by the allotment of Zeus" (*τετιμῆσθαι Διὸς αἴσῃ*, 9.608), that is, by an allotment that was Zeus's to bestow and to which Zeus was not himself subject. Achilles then tells Ajax that his appeal to friendship is "in accord with my feeling" (*μοι κατὰ θυμὸν*, 9.645; compare Poseidon's expression *κατὰ μοῖραν*, 15.206). Unlike Poseidon Achilles does not recognize a symbolic standard external to personal feelings—or at least none that Agamemnon also recognizes, so that it could mediate between them. Thus Achilles' sense of offense leaves him with no relationship to Agamemnon or the other Greeks that can motivate him to protect them. His condition for returning to fight Hektor is only that he will defend the Myrmidons and his own encampment (*ἀμφὶ . . . τῇ ἐμῇ κλισίῃ κτλ.*, 9.654), because they are the only people and property with whom he has a communal relationship.

Replacing a Life

The trajectory of increasingly arbitrary symbolism is also visible in comparable situations involving only mortal characters. In book 9 Achilles says that a man's life is physically irreplaceable and therefore not commensurable with material objects that can replace one another (9.401–9). The context, however, implies "over the speaker's head" that life can be transmitted from one person to another within the synairetic ("chosen together") entity of a community. Book 15 further elaborates the symbolism of communal life in a number of passages already briefly mentioned. In one, Ajax calls on his half-brother Teukros as "brother" (*κασίγνητον*, 15.436) when Hektor kills their attendant Lykophron (15.429–41). This man was received into Ajax's household as a guest, since he was guilty of killing a man in his own land of Kythera (15.431–32). Ajax reminds Teukros of the relationship the three of them shared, in which Lykophron was their "trusted comrade" (*πιστὸς ἑταῖρος*, 15.437) whom they honored as much as their own parents (*ἶσα φίλοισιν τοκεῦσιν*, 15.439), in other words, the synairetic ("chosen together") bond of trust was as strong among them as the physical bond of birth. And this bond may persist beyond death, since it is precisely when Lykophron has died that his relationship to Ajax and Teukros gives them reason to fight.

Not long afterward, Hektor calls upon the charging Trojans and their allies to accept death if it should come, because death in defense of the ancestral land is "not unfitting" (*οὔ . . . ἀεικὲς*, 15.496), and the dead man's wife, children, and communal property will be safe if the Greeks are driven away (15.497–99). Hektor's terminology of fitness at first seems to imply a standard of fair compensation for lost life, but what he then describes is not compensation but continuance; the family and homeland survive. Therefore while the warrior's death is uncompensated, it is not unfitting either (οὔ . . . ἀεικὲς, 15.496), because it needs no compensation.

In the final example, Nestor exhorts the Greeks to "remember [their] children, wives, property and parents, whether living or dead . . . even though they are not present" (15.661–67). The community Nestor evokes explicitly spans generations dead and living, and its relevance to the fighters' valor is also highly synairetic ("chosen together"), since unlike the Trojans the Greeks are not defending their own communities, and that is why their relatives are not present to witness their valor. This community exists in the minds of the fighters.

A trajectory of increasing arbitrariness is also observable between Achilles' description of his choice of two destinies (9.410–16) and Zeus's decision to honor Hektor (15.610–14). Achilles says that his mother has told him that he "carried divided destinies toward the end of death" (διχθαδίας κῆρας φερέμεν θανάτοιο τέλοσδε, 9.411). The destinies Achilles describes are split apart from one another, but each one, qua destiny, represents in itself the inseparability of a condition and its consequent, so that the choice of fulfilling one condition by remaining at Troy necessarily entailed the choice of lost return and immortal fame, while choosing to fulfill the condition of returning home necessarily entailed the choice of lost fame and long life. The linkage between Hektor's honor and his short life is much more arbitrary; Hektor receives honor because Zeus *gives* it to him (Ζεύς, ὅς μιν . . . τίμα καὶ κύδαινε, 15.611–12), Zeus gives it for the reason that Hektor's life is to be short (μινυνθάδιος γὰρ ἔμελλεν / ἔσσεσθ', 15.612–13), Hektor's life is to be short because Athena is already setting his doom in motion (15.613–14), and Hektor's doom was ordained by Zeus in his plan as a prelude to the destruction of Troy (15.68–71). All of these circumstances were Zeus's choices, and any of them might have been different had Zeus chosen to make them so.

In fact, Zeus's reason for glorifying Hektor is so arbitrary that the narrator gives two explanations for it in the same passage: Zeus *feels like* glorifying Hektor (οἱ θυμὸς ἐβούλετο κῦδος ὀρέξαι, 15.596) so that Hektor can set fire to the Greek ships, and Zeus in this way can fulfill Thetis's prayer (Θέτιδος δ' ἐξαίσιον ἀρὴν / πᾶσαν ἐπικρήνειε' 15.598–99). But Thetis did not ask for the burning of the Greek ships (compare 1.503–10), and Zeus himself chooses this event to represent the point at which his promise is fulfilled; apparently it is Zeus's spontaneous adaptation of Achilles' statement to the embassy (9.650–55) that he would not fight Hektor until the Greek ships were burning. Hektor's imminent death can scarcely explain Zeus's glorification of him, since many fighters are about to die, but Zeus explicitly glorifies Hektor *alone* of all the men on the battlefield (μιν πλεόνεσσι μετ' ἀνδράσι μοῦνον ἐόντα/τίμα καὶ κύδαινε, 15.611–12). Nothing seems to entail Hektor's glorification or obligate Zeus to confer it: he glorifies Hektor as a kind of whim, favor, or act of grace.

This favor to Hektor is also more symbolic than the fame (κλέος) Achilles mentions to the embassy in book 9. The basic meaning of κλέος is "renown," without specification of renown for what, and therefore κλέος does not in itself signify an actual relationship between the renowned person and those who hear about him. Achilles does add a suggestion of further symbolization to his *κλέος* by the attribution *ἐσθλόν* ("excellent fame" 9.415), but it is only a suggestion, since Achilles does not explain what makes this fame excellent. But Achilles does qualify his *κλέος* according to material rather than symbolic properties by saying that it will either be "unwithering" (*ἄφθιτον*, 9.413) or will perish (*ὤλετο*, 9.415). What Zeus gives Hektor in book 15, however, is not *κλέος*; Zeus "honors and glorifies" Hektor (*τίμα καὶ κύδαινε*, 15.612), he "extends glory to him" (*κῦδος ὀρέξαι*, 15.596). These terms all denote symbols of regard within a community and not merely unqualified renown.

7

Homeric Sublimity

Iliad Book 24

Chapters 4 through 6 have examined pairs of thematically analogous books of the *Iliad* whose relationship is cued by their analogous positions in the epic's postulated three-cycle design. As the investigation proceeded further, the number of cued relationships grew, so that, for example, thematic aspects of book 15 (Z_2) could usefully be compared to aspects of both the A and Z books in both the first and second cycles (books 1, 8, and 9). This degree of complexity has a definite aesthetic and interpretive appeal, but I will also be the first to admit that schematizing and interpreting so much complexity makes for a thicker analysis than even a dedicated philhomerist (like myself) can comfortably digest. Accordingly, in chapter 6 I arbitrarily kept the analysis restricted to pairs of books, only occasionally adding observations about a third.

In the third cycle the complexity grows greater and the task of comprehension more challenging, while simplification seems less expedient and satisfying, for cycle III represents the climax toward which the action and its themes have been heading; we expect to be overwhelmed, and we are. And, as if the narrated action were not overwhelming enough, the poem's system of cuing attention to its thematic depth lures the thoughtful reader into deeper waters than he or she can manage. At any point in the third cycle the sheer volume of cued thematic analogies, as well as their intrinsic significance, "boggles the mind." This is an aspect of Homer's characteristic evocation of dimension beyond measurement, the quality Longinus and his intellectual descendants called "sublimity."[1] The finale of the *Iliad* arrives at the head of a long train of memories, some of which, like the allusion to the Judgment of Paris at 24.27–30, reach back well beyond the temporal frame of the narrative. The past of memory is not left behind but carried along, and a reader's archived impressions of the *Iliad* accompany the reading and offer themselves to retrospection as the story revisits earlier stages in its cyclic course. At any given moment, the narrative surface veils an immense depth of suggestion that, like Hermes when he escorts Priam across the battlefield, is present and elusive at once.

1. See Longinus 9.4, apparently referring to book 4.442: *τὸ ἐπ' οὐρανὸν ἀπὸ γῆς διάστημα· καὶ τοῦτ' ἂν εἴποι τις οὐ μᾶλλον τῆς Ἔριδος ἢ Ὁμήρου μέτρον* "the distance between sky and earth. And one might say that this was the measure of Homer as much as that of Strife."

As the culmination of the epic's monumental design, book 24 (Z_3) cues a denser network of thematic analogies than any other single position in the three-cycle path: analogies to the Z books in the preceding cycles (books 8 and 15), to the A book in the third cycle (book 16), and through A_3 to the A books in the preceding two cycles (books 1 and 9). These positions, the beginnings and ends of cycles, are the most emphatic of the design, and they narrate the most critical junctures of the epic action, the decisions of Achilles and Zeus. Moreover, since book 24 also brings the Trojan royal family together with the Achaians and the Olympians as nowhere else in the epic, it evokes thematic analogies with the books of the C and X columns (3, 6, 11, 18, and 22), where the Trojans were highlighted. Thus, attention to the thematic network of book 24 leads the memory back through almost half the books of the epic, extending to the very beginning.[2]

This chapter selects only a sample of important strands for analysis. As before, "aerial surveys" are followed by interpretive discussions that address the theme of choice as it continues its transformations.

THEMATIC ANALOGY: AERIAL SURVEYS

The overarching plot trajectories of the Z column books (8, 15, 24) all present Zeus fulfilling a plan by helping Trojans cross the battlefield to the Greek ships. In book 8, Zeus uses signs to help Hektor and the Trojans chase the Greeks across the battlefield back to their ships (8.75–77 and following , 8.133–36 and following, 8.169–71 and following). In book 15, Zeus sends Apollo to help Hektor and the Trojans chase the Greeks across the battlefield back to their ships (15.229–32). Now in book 24, Zeus sends Iris, Hermes, and an eagle to help Priam cross the battlefield to the Greek ships and bring back the corpse of Hektor.

Someone Else's Suffering

Within cycle III, the Problem stage of the final segment (Z_3, book 24) and the Problem stage of the initial segment (A_3, book 16) both present the problem of a helpless victim suffering incessant torment: in book 24, the dead Hektor abused by Achilles; in book 16 the Greek army routed by the Trojans. In each case the victim's plight elicits the pity of a third party, Apollo (with other Olympians) in book 24 (ἐλεαίρων, 24.19), Patroklos in book 16. Each then appeals to a fourth party (Hera-Athena-Poseidon in book 24; Achilles in book 16) who could end the abuse but instead has maliciously tolerated it. A second version of this trajectory, which might be called a *torment/appeal configuration*, occurs again later in A_3 (book 16), when Sarpedon is about to be killed: his father Zeus pities him (ἐλέησε, 16.431), and Zeus consults Hera about whether he should save his son (16.432–38). It also occurs in Z_3 (book 24), when Priam appeals to Achilles

2. Many scholars have discussed resonances between book 1 and book 24; for an extensive bibliography see Heiden 2000a: 34 n. 1.

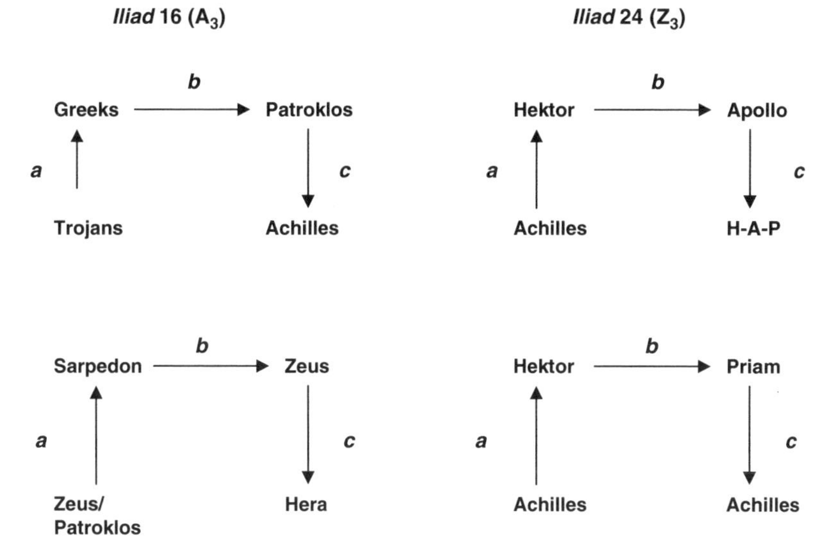

FIGURE 7.1. Torment/Appeal Configurations in *Iliad* Cycle III. a = p torments q; b = q elicits pity from third-party r; c = r seeks help from fourth-party s.

to return the corpse of Hektor. These torment/appeal configurations in cycle III are summarized in figure 7.1.

The torment/appeal configuration also appears in the A and Z column segments of cycles I and II. In A_1 (book 1) Agamemnon holds Chryseis in bondage and Chryses appeals to the Greeks and then to Apollo; later Thetis appeals to Zeus on behalf of Achilles. In A_2 (book 9) the embassy appeals to bystander Achilles on behalf of the Greek host, and in the embedded story of Meleager,

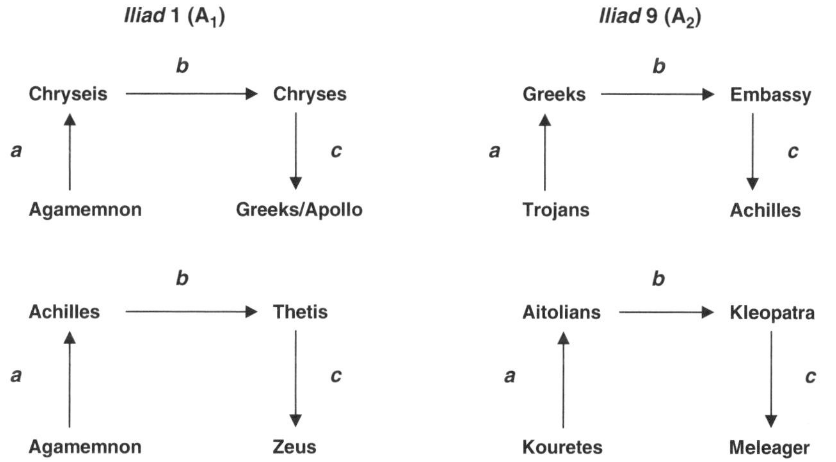

FIGURE 7.2. Torment/Appeal Configurations in *Iliad* Cycles I and II (Column A). a = p torments q; b = q elicits pity from third-party r; c = r seeks help from fourth-party s.

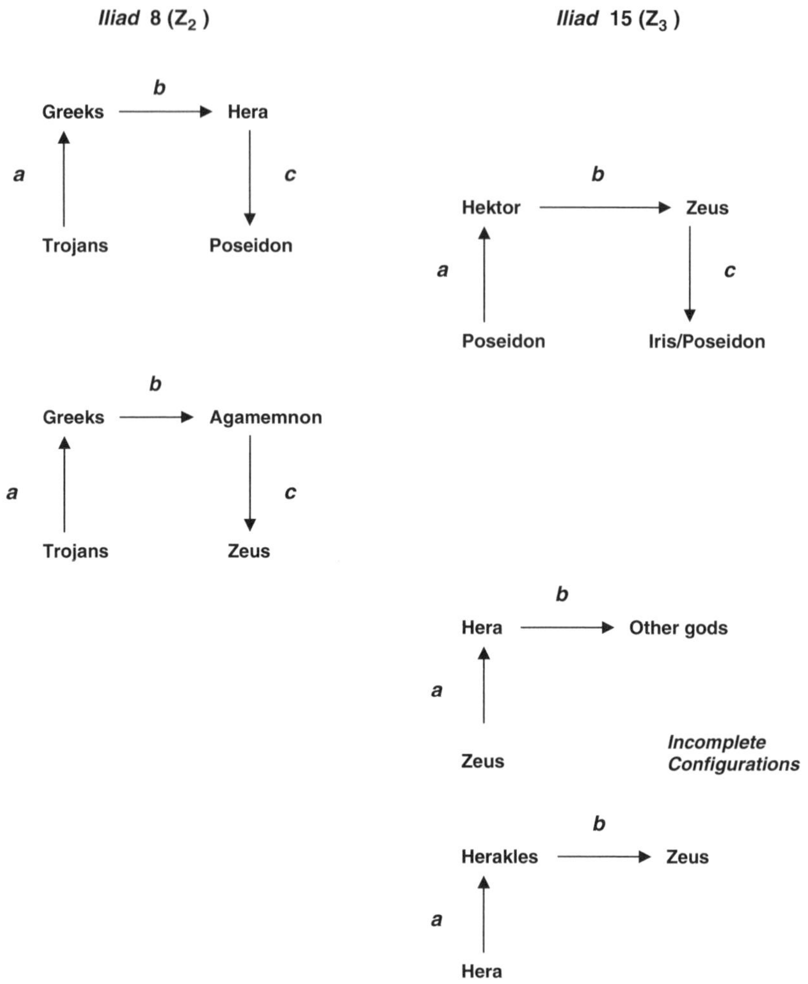

FIGURE 7.3. Torment/Appeal Configurations in *Iliad* Cycles I and II (Column Z).
a = p torments q; b = q elicits pity from third-party r; c = r seeks help from fourth-party s.

Kleopatra appeals to Meleager on behalf of the Aitolians.[3] The torment/appeal configurations in the A column segments of cycles I and II are summarized in figure 7.2.

The torment/appeal configuration occurs in Z_1 (book 8) when Hera appeals to Poseidon to join her in helping the Greeks, and when Agamemnon prays to Zeus. A version occurs in Z_2 (book 15) when Zeus, moved partly (and explicitly) by sympathy for Hektor (15.9–12), interrupts the Trojan rout by ordering Poseidon off the battlefield and Apollo onto it. Partial versions also occur in Zeus's allusions to his past punishment of Hera (15.18–24) and her past torment

3. See Burkert 1955: 101–102, and Richardson 1993: 280–81. On motifs common to the embassy (book 9) and Patroklos's appeal (book 16) see Stanley 1993: 166–67. Also see Rabel 1997: 154–59 for discussion of comparable themes in books 1, 9, and 16.

of Herakles (15.24–30). In these instances the sympathy of a third party is engaged, but rescue is undertaken (or attempted) by the third party directly without an appeal for extra help; hence the configurations are incomplete. Figure 7.3 (p. 190) summarizes these torment/appeal configurations in the Z column segments of cycles I and II.

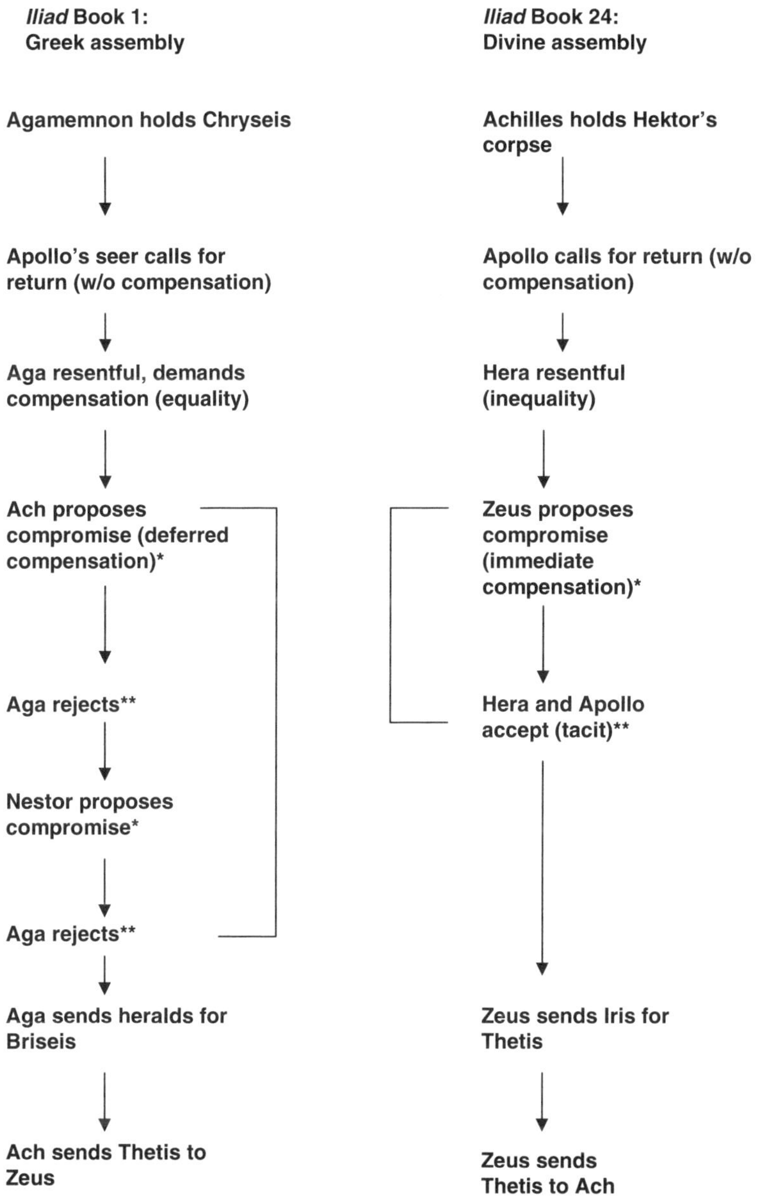

FIGURE 7.4. Greek assembly in book 1 and Olympian assembly in book 24. Brackets indicate counterpart sequences. Elements marked with one or more asterisks are counterparts to similarly marked elements.

Putting Heads Together

The divine assembly of *Iliad* 24 (24.23–76) culminates a series of critical deliberations that include the Greek assembly of book 1, the divine assemblies of book 8 (8.1–40, 8.442–84), the Greek assembly, council, and embassy of book 9, and, in book 15, Zeus's negotiation with Hera (15.4–77), the subsequent divine assembly where Hera brings Zeus's message to Iris and Apollo (15.78–148), and Zeus's negotiation with Poseidon, conducted through Iris (15.168–217). The extensive thematic approximations between the Greek assembly in book 1 and the Olympian assembly in book 24 are illustrated in figure 7.4.

Miraculous Missions

Yet another major sequence of thematic transformations culminates in book 24 in Hermes' role as Priam's escort in the miraculous return of Hektor's corpse for burial. Within cycle III an analogous situation arises in A_3 (book 16), when Apollo miraculously rescues Sarpedon's corpse from the battlefield so that Sleep and Death can return it to Lykia for burial (16.666–83). In fact, Zeus's decision to send Apollo for Sarpedon is also preceded by a decision-conference between Zeus and Hera (16.431–61) that bears comparison to the Apollo-Hera-Zeus decision-conference in book 24. Other miraculous returns occur in Z_2 (book 15), when Apollo, on Zeus's instruction, revives the nearly dead Hektor and spurs him into battle (15.239–62),[4] and in A_1 (book 1) when Apollo arranges for the return of Chryseis to her father.

These broad thematic analogies extend into many details. The theme of royal messengers in the A and Z segments of cycles I and II receives bravura development in book 24 as Iris summons Thetis to Zeus, who sends her to Achilles, and Zeus then sends Iris and Hermes to Priam. Careful examination of these analogies indicates a development whose approximate trajectory may be mapped by observing the sequential and thematic coordinates of each relevant passage. The analysis will take as samples three thematic strands in the divine conference scene in book 24: (1) Apollo's articulation of Achilles' abuse and his care for Achilles' victim; (2) Hera's uncooperative response to Apollo; and (3) Zeus's mediation of the opposing positions.

APOLLO'S ADVOCACY AND ITS ANTECEDENTS: SURVEY AND INTERPRETATION

The antecedents of Apollo's advocacy of Achilles' victim in book 24 include the following: book 1, Chryses' plea for his daughter's release (1.17–21) and his prayer to Apollo (1.35–52), and Kalchas's explanation of Apollo's anger (1.93–100);[5] book 8, Agamemnon's prayer to Zeus to save the Greeks from utter destruction (8.236–44); book 9, the appeals of Phoinix and Ajax in the embassy scene; book 15, Zeus's diatribe against Hera for helping Poseidon torment the Trojans (15.9–33); book

4. Erbse 1986: 183 n. 14 observes that at 24.20–21 Apollo protects Hektor's corpse with the aegis Zeus gave him in book 15 (15.229); its purpose, one might add, is to frighten the Greeks so that Hektor can safely advance against them.

5. On Apollo's roles in books 1 and 24, see Erbse 1986: 184 and Rabel 1997: 197–98.

16, Patroklos's plea to Achilles to help the Greeks (16.20–45), and Zeus's appeal to Hera for advice about whether to save Sarpedon (16.431–38).

Prayer of Chryses (Book 1); Speech of Apollo (Book 24)

The two passages at the extreme sequential coordinates are the prayer of Chryses in book 1 and the speech of Apollo in book 24. Analysis shows that they also lie far apart on the thematic trajectory from relative synapsis to relative synairesis.

1. In book 1 Chryses prays to Apollo on behalf of his daughter: the advocate and the victim therefore have a synaptic relationship. In book 24 Apollo, who is not related to Hektor and has received no prayers on his behalf, spontaneously protects Hektor's corpse and becomes his advocate before the other gods. The same god who in book 1 was the distant object of Chryses' prayer in book 24 replaces the victim's father as the advocate. Apollo is moved by pity for the victim (ἐλεαίρων, 24.19), not kinship. He makes a choice.

2. Chryses at first appeals to the Greeks for the physical return of his daughter (παῖδα δ' ἐμοὶ λύσαιτε, 1.20); when Agamemnon rebuffs him, he prays to Apollo to cause the Greeks physical suffering to compensate him for his tears (1.42). This second appeal involves substitution, but of a relatively nonarbitrary kind (one type of physical suffering for another). In book 24 Apollo protects Hektor's corpse physically with his aegis (περὶ δ' αἰγίδι πάντα κάλυπτε, 24.20). His advocacy, however, concerns enabling Hektor's family and community (λαοῖσι, 24.37) to give the hero his rites of burial (24.37–38), that is, symbolic-synairetic tokens of their relationship.

3. In book 1 Chryses reminds Apollo of *his own* past sacrifices to Apollo (1.39–41). In book 24, Apollo reminds the other gods of *Hektor's* former sacrifices to them (24.33–34).

4. Chryses asks Apollo to make the Greeks pay for his tears with his arrows (σοῖσι βέλεσσιν, 1.37–42). In book 24 Apollo pities and protects Hektor, but he does not seek punishment for Achilles.

5. When Apollo hears Chryses' prayer in book 1, he becomes angry at the Greeks (τοῦ δ' ἔκλυε . . . χωόμενος, 1.43–44). In book 24, Apollo says that the victim ("earth," 24.54) can make no appeal (it is κωφὴν, "speechless," 24.54), but the persecutor should fear divine anger (μὴ . . . νεμεσσηθέωμεν, 24.53) for this very reason. The anger Apollo threatens is potential rather than actual, that is, it is a choice Apollo contemplates. It is also somewhat impersonal, the anger of "we gods" (ἡμεῖς, 24.53) and not Apollo's alone, and in this way too it represents a choice that is open to the other gods, rather than a reaction to a particular privileged appeal.[6]

6. In book 1, Apollo's punishment of the Greeks indirectly leads to the return of Chryseis, when Apollo's seer reveals to the Greeks that the god wants her returned to her father (1.98). Despite the seer's specification that Chryseis is to

6. Taplin 1992: 262 notes the implication that " 'dumb' nature needs the gods to stand up for her"; i.e., justice does not occur automatically and naturally. Therefore, it must supervene on nature, and in this sense it must be *supernatural*.

be returned without compensation (*ἀπριάτην ἀνάποινον*, 1.99), Agamemnon takes compensation from Achilles, essentially by stealing it. In book 24, Apollo and other gods advocate having Hermes steal (*κλέψαι*, 24.24) Hektor's corpse from Achilles (i.e., take it without compensation), but no stealing takes place. Eventually (24.75–76) Zeus proposes that Achilles receive symbolic compensation (gifts) in exchange for Hektor's corpse.

7. In book 1 Apollo responds as soon as Chryses prays to him (*εὐχόμενος . . . τοῦ δ' ἔκλυε . . . βῆ δὲ κατ' Οὐλύμποιο κτλ.*, 1.43–44), and he continues killing Greeks without apparent respite until Chryseis is returned, a period of about ten days (1.52–54). In book 24 Apollo protects the corpse of Hektor while Achilles abuses it (24.19), but he defers further action until he speaks out in protest when the abuse has continued for twelve days (*ὅτε . . . δυωδεκάτη γένετ' ἠώς*, 24.31).

8. In book 1 Chryses appeals to Apollo with a brief and simple prayer, and Apollo responds instantly, decisively, and wordlessly (only his arrows and bow make sound, 1.46–49). In book 24, after tolerating Achilles' atrocious conduct for twelve days, Apollo addresses the gods with a long and complex speech (*ἀθανάτοισι μετηύδα κτλ.*, 24.32–54). Nothing happens to facilitate the burial until the matter has been deliberated in words: movement from problem to action occurs nonautomatically through the creation of imaginary, potential scenarios among which choices are made.

9. Apollo's speech in book 24 also demonstrates synairesis in its rhetorical operation (24.33–35):

> "*σχέτλιοί ἐστε, θεοί, δηλήμονες· οὔ νύ ποθ' ὑμῖν*
> *Ἕκτωρ μηρί' ἔκηε βοῶν αἰγῶν τε τελείων;*
> *τὸν νῦν οὐκ ἔτλητε νέκυν περ ἐόντα σαῶσαι . . .*"
>
> You are hard, gods, and destructive. Didn't Hektor honor you
> with burnt thighpieces of perfect cattle and goats?
> And now you can't stand to save him,
> although he is only a corpse

Apollo begins tactfully by choosing a substitute addressee—all the gods—in place of the real addressees, Hera, Poseidon, and Athena, who are the only gods actually obstructing Hermes from stealing Hektor's corpse (MacLeod 1982: 87). Apollo appeals for the gods' cooperation in terms of their dispositions (calling them *σχέτλιοι* and *δηλήμονες*), thus electively widening the scope of discussion beyond the particular case at hand. Apollo expects the gods to be fair to Hektor, but not in compensation for anything Hektor is doing for them at present or will do in the future, since Hektor is dead and can do nothing. Instead he expects them to be moved by their memory of the symbols of devotion Hektor gave them in the past and will give no longer. Thus Apollo calls on the gods to exercise choice on Hektor's behalf.

Apollo also criticizes the gods for favoring Achilles, who he says does not deserve their favor (24.39). Apollo does not imply that Achilles is unworthy of divine favor because he has done the gods any personal offense. His criticism concerns Achilles' character, so that like his criticism of the hero's divine supporters, it replaces the particular case with a synairesis that includes many actions and potential actions implicitly deemed similar. Apollo says Achilles' mind is not within limits and his intention cannot be bent (*ᾧ οὔτ' ἄρ φρένες εἰσὶν ἐναίσιμοι οὔτε νόημα/γναμπτὸν κτλ.*, 24. 40–41); his thoughts are not appropriate to a human, they are wild, like those of a lion. Lions cannot refuse to be savage, since savagery is their means of sustenance and survival (*ἵνα δαῖτα λάβῃσιν*, 24.43). For Achilles to rage like a lion marks him as sharing the lion's inability to choose whether to continue raging or stop. Achilles has destroyed pity (*ἔλεον . . . ἀπώλεσεν*, 24.44) and has no shame (*αἰδώς*, 24.44), which are considerations that affect the choices normal humans can make about their feelings and conduct. Apollo gives an example of an ordinary man (*τις*, 24.46) who eventually gives up lamenting "because the apportioners put an enduring heart in humans" (24.49). This means that the normal human heart is capable of withstanding compulsion and electively changing its feelings even in the face of unchanging circumstances.

Plea of Patroklos (Book 16); Speech of Apollo (Book 24)

The comparable situations in book 16 (A_3), the plea of Patroklos to Achilles and Zeus's consultation with Hera, lie between the extremes on the thematic trajectory as well as the sequential, and thematically closer to book 24 than to book 1.

1. Patroklos's speech had more ethical synairesis than the plea of Chryses in book 1, but still much less than Apollo's in book 24. Patroklos is neither kin to the suffering Achaians nor an immortal who looks on them from high above; their grief is not his personally, but he elects to feel it anyway. Neither Patroklos nor Apollo appeals to the party directly responsible for the suffering—the Trojans who are routing the Greeks (book 16), Achilles who is abusing Hektor's corpse (book 24)—but Achilles, the fourth-party bystander to whom Patroklos appeals, did actually plan the suffering the Trojans carried out, while Hera, Athena, and Poseidon did not plan the abuse of Hektor's corpse and only support it passively, by blocking Hermes from rescuing the corpse. Apollo's addressees are therefore connected to the abuse more tenuously than Patroklos's addressee, Achilles.

2. Patroklos reproaches Achilles for his anger (*χόλος*, 16.30), lack of compassion (*νηλεές*, 24.33), and unyielding mind (*νόος . . . ἀπηνής*, 35), but he points to no shared human endowment that might guide Achilles to a different manner of thought (16.33–35):

> *νηλεές, οὐκ ἄρα σοί γε πατὴρ ἦν ἱππότα Πηλεύς,*
> *οὐδὲ Θέτις μήτηρ· γλαυκὴ δέ σε τίκτε θάλασσα*
> *πέτραι τ' ἠλίβατοι, ὅτι τοι νόος ἐστὶν ἀπηνής.*

> Pitiless man, then the horseman Peleus was not your father after all,
> nor was Thetis your mother; it was the grey sea that bore you,
> and the steep cliffs, because your mind is unyielding.

Patroklos's idea that the parents of such an unyielding man must have been a cliff and the sea, not Peleus and Thetis, implies, like Apollo's simile of the lion (24.41–44),[7] that Achilles' character is not human, but unlike Apollo's simile it does not imply that Achilles' character *should* be human; on the contrary, it imagines Achilles as an undesirable special case, unchoosing by necessity of birth. And the inanimate sea and cliff are even more unchoosing than a lion, which Apollo says *yields* to its savagery (*εἴξας*, 24.43), implying that the lion does possess a portion, albeit an ineffectual one, of the capacity to refuse savagery.

3. Patroklos proposed deceiving the Trojans himself (16.41–42), while Apollo advocates sending a replacement, Hermes, to snatch Hektor's corpse from Achilles (24.24).

4. Patroklos also implies that Achilles should be motivated by a desire for personal advantage (*ὀνήσεται*, 16.31), and he allows that Achilles might be avoiding the battle to protect himself, because he fears something his mother told him (*θεοπροπίην ἀλεείνεις*, 16.36). Patroklos does not suggest that if this is the case Achilles should sacrifice himself to save the Greeks. On the contrary, he suggests that if Achilles is at risk on the battlefield he should let Patroklos take his place. Admittedly, this entails a significant synairetic substitution (Patroklos for Achilles), and so does Patroklos's suggestion that Achilles should act for advantage, since the imagined advantage would not accrue to Achilles himself, but rather to some unspecified future person (*ἄλλος . . . ὀψίγονός περ*, 16.31). Yet in book 24 Apollo's reminiscence of Hektor's dedications (24.33–34) is even more arbitrarily synairetic, since Hektor's dedications did the gods no actual benefit and can only matter after his death if the gods choose to remember them.

Zeus Consults Hera (Book 16); Speech of Apollo (Book 24)

When Apollo's speech in book 24 is set beside Zeus's speech to Hera in book 16 before the fight between Sarpedon and Patroklos, the transformations consistently indicate a greater degree of synairesis in the later passage. Here is Zeus's speech (16.431–38):

> *τοὺς δὲ ἰδὼν ἐλέησε Κρόνου πάις ἀγκυλομήτεω,*
> *Ἥρην δὲ προσέειπε κασιγνήτην ἄλοχόν τε·*
> *"ὤ μοι ἐγών, ὅ τέ μοι Σαρπηδόνα, φίλτατον ἀνδρῶν,*
> *μοῖρ' ὑπὸ Πατρόκλοιο Μενοιτιάδαο δαμῆναι.*
> *διχθὰ δέ μοι κραδίη μέμονε φρεσὶν ὁρμαίνοντι,*
> *ἤ μιν ζωὸν ἐόντα μάχης ἄπο δακρυοέσσης*

7. Richardson 1993: 281 also compares the two similes briefly.

θείω ἀναρπάξας Λυκίης ἐν πίονι δήμῳ,
ἦ ἤδη ὑπὸ χερσὶ Μενοιτιάδαο δαμάσσω."

When he caught sight of them the son of crooked-planning Kronos felt pity,
and he addressed Hera, his sister and wife:
"Ah me, that it is allotted that Sarpedon, the dearest of men to me,
be killed by Patroklos the son of Menoitios.
My heart thinks in two ways as I deliberate in my mind
whether I should snatch him while still alive from the tearful battle
and put him in the rich district of Lykia,
or kill him now with the hands of the son of Menoitios."

1. In book 16, Zeus feels pity for Sarpedon and Patroklos when they are about to meet in battle (*τοὺς δὲ ἰδὼν ἐλέησε*, 16.431). One combatant is his own son, the other a mortal who bears no relation to him, and both are alive but soon to die. In book 24, Apollo feels pity for a mortal who is no relation to him at all and whose life cannot even be saved, because it is lost already (*φῶτ' ἐλεαίρων/καὶ τεθνηότα περ*, 24.19–20).

2. Zeus seeks the personal advice of Hera, who is both his sister and his wife, as the narrator emphasizes in the speech introduction (*κασιγνήτην ἄλοχόν τε*, 16.432). Therefore Zeus bears two kinds of relationship to Hera, one of kinship and one of election. In book 24 Apollo addresses Hera, Athena, and Poseidon, but tactfully mentions none of them by name (*θεοί κτλ.*, 24.33). He seeks neither their advice nor their personal support, but instead articulates impersonal criteria he thinks should guide their choice.

3. In his dialogue with Hera about Sarpedon, Zeus does not reproach anybody for doing wrong. His concern is only to decide between two inclinations that are both his own, whether *he* should snatch Sarpedon away or whether *he* should kill him (*δαμάσσω*, 16.438, "should I kill him?") through Patroklos, as Zeus himself has already decreed will happen (15.67).[8] In consulting Hera, Zeus does not imply that his decision should be guided by an impersonal ethical criterion, or even by a standard of possibility: presumably either option is possible for Zeus, or he wouldn't need to ask.[9] It appears that Zeus consults Hera to find out how she would react personally if he saved Sarpedon. In book 24, in contrast, Apollo asks the obstructor gods to choose according to impersonal criteria that he and the other gods have chosen, not just to give their personal assent to the plan for Hermes to steal Hektor's corpse.

8. Stanley 1993: 173 correctly notes that Sarpedon's death arises from the "divine compromise enunciated in Book 15."

9. *Pace* Erbse 1986: 288 and Janko 1992: 375, among others. The translation of *μοῖρα* as "fate" carries an implication of impersonal necessity that narrative context and etymology do not support. If Zeus cannot possibly save Sarpedon, then his conversation with Hera makes no sense. But it makes perfect sense if *μοῖρα* means "apportionment," and this translation is not open to objection; see Schein 1984: 62–64. Also see Dietrich 1965: 11.

Zeus Berates Hera (Book 15); Apollo Berates Gods (Book 24)

Another comparable passage, a little earlier in the temporal sequence, is Zeus's complaint to Hera at the beginning of book 15 (15.12–17):

> *τὸν δὲ ἰδὼν ἐλέησε πατὴρ ἀνδρῶν τε θεῶν τε,*
> *δεινὰ δ' ὑπόδρα ἰδὼν Ἥρην πρὸς μῦθον ἔειπεν·*
> *"ἦ μάλα δὴ κακότεχνος, ἀμήχανε, σὸς δόλος, Ἥρη,*
> *Ἕκτορα δῖον ἔπαυσε μάχης, ἐφόβησε δὲ λαούς.*
> *οὐ μὰν οἶδ' εἰ αὖτε κακορραφίης ἀλεγεινῆς*
> *πρώτη ἐπαύρηαι καί σε πληγῇσιν ἱμάσσω...."*
>
> When he caught sight of [Hektor] the father of gods and men felt pity.
> Scowling angrily he addressed a speech to Hera:
> "So, Hera—I can't do anything with you—it was your deception, devised to do ill,
> that put shining Hektor out of the battle, and terrified his troops.
> I wouldn't be surprised if once again you are the first to reap
> the pain you have devised, and I put the lash to you."

The following differences between this complaint and Apollo's at the beginning of book 24 all indicate a relatively more arbitrary synairesis in the later passage.

1. In book 15 Zeus is the initial advocate on Hektor's behalf, as well as the authority who decides what to do, while in book 24 Apollo, who lacks the power to rescue Hektor's corpse himself, speaks on the dead man's behalf, and another party, Zeus, decides what to do.

2. In book 15 Zeus accuses Hera by name and speaks directly to her, while in book 24 Apollo tactfully avoids mentioning the gods he accuses.

3. In book 15 Zeus accuses Hera of planning the suffering of Hektor (*σὸς δόλος, Ἥρη,/Ἕκτορα ... ἔπαυσε μάχης κτλ.*, 15.14–15), while in book 24 Apollo accuses the gods of tolerating Achilles' abuse of Hektor's corpse (*τὸν νῦν οὐκ ἔτλητε ... σαῶσαι*, 24.35) but not of planning it.

4. In book 15, Zeus accuses Hera of a *particular* act of personal disobedience to him, that is, helping the Greeks when Zeus has prohibited intervention on either side. In book 24, Apollo accuses Achilles of particular actions, but he characterizes these as indicating a certain *disposition* (*φρένες κτλ.*, 24.40–52), which is blameworthy because it is like the normal disposition of a lion (*λέων δ' ὣς ἄγρια οἶδεν κτλ.*, 24.41–43) and unlike the normal disposition of humans (*ἄνδρας, τις, ἀνθρώποισιν*, 24.45–49).

5. In book 15, Zeus threatens Hera with a specific physical punishment, a whipping he would administer himself (15.17). In book 24, Apollo does not threaten either Achilles or his divine supporters at all, although he suggests that Achilles *might* incur anger from the gods collectively (*μὴ ... νεμεσσηθέωμέν οἱ ἡμεῖς*, 24.53). Apollo does not say how this anger might be expressed.

6. In book 15, Zeus reminds Hera of the punishments he once inflicted on her (15.18–24), implying that they should have deterred her from disobeying him again. In book 24, Apollo reminds all the gods (including Hera) that Hektor offered them sacrifices, implying that they should have earned him divine protection from Achilles' abuse (24.33–35). Both passages involve synairesis, inasmuch as the addressees, in making decisions, are supposed to take account of remembered (as opposed to current) events. But the degree of synairesis in the earlier passage is relatively small—Hera is to remember that Zeus physically restrained her from doing as she wished, and could do so again—while in the later it is relatively great, since the remembered event was (1) symbolic in character, and (2) could never be repeated.

7. In book 15, Zeus reminds Hera that he himself once subjected her to physical torture and would not allow the gods to set her free (15.18–24). In this scene of the recalled past, Zeus's role as tormentor approximates Achilles' role in book 24, Hera's role as victim approximates that of Hektor's corpse, and the gods who tried to release her approximate the gods who in book 24 want Hermes to steal Hektor's corpse from Achilles (see figs. 7.1 and 7.3). Thus while in book 24 Apollo opposes Hera by distancing himself from the cruelty Achilles practices even as Apollo speaks, Zeus in book 15 associates himself with a similar cruelty of *his own*, but practiced and concluded some time in the *past*.

HERA'S UNCOOPERATIVE REPLY TO APOLLO AND ITS ANTECEDENTS: SURVEY AND INTERPRETATION

The antecedents of Hera's reply to Apollo in book 24 include the following: book 1 (A_1), Agamemnon's replies to Chryses (1.24–32) and Kalchas (1.101–20); book 8 (Z_1), Athena's reply to Zeus in the Olympian assembly (8.30–37), and Hera's reply to Zeus after she returns to Olympus (8.461–68); book 9 (A_2), Achilles' replies to Phoinix and Ajax in the embassy scene (9.606–19, 643–55); book 15 (Z_2), Hera's semicooperative reply to Zeus's accusations of conspiring with Poseidon (15.34–46) and her denunciation of Zeus when she returns to Olympus (15.92–112); book 16 (A_3), Achilles' taunting of Patroklos when he comes to plead for the Achaians (16.5–19) and Hera's refusal to grant Zeus permission to save Sarpedon from death (16.439–57).

Agamemnon (1), Hera (15), Achilles (16), Hera (16), Hera (24)

Examination of the first and last items of the series (book 1, Agamemnon to Chryses and Kalchas; book 24, Hera to Apollo) and intermediate items in books 15 and 16 reveals transformations that follow a thematic trajectory from relatively little synairesis to relatively much.

1. When Agamemnon replies to Chryses' appeal, he says that he wishes to keep Chryseis for himself (ἡμετέρῳ ἐνὶ οἴκῳ κτλ., 1.30). When he replies to Kalchas, he denounces the seer for never saying anything useful to Agamemnon himself (μοι, 1.106). Egoism also appears in Hera's denunciation of Zeus in book

15, but in a more attenuated form. Hera blames Zeus for planning *by himself* (*ἀφήμενος*, 15.106), though not *for his own benefit* (15.105–7): the selfishness she complains about is of a moderate kind. As an example of the pain Zeus's inconsiderate planning has caused the other Olympians, Hera mentions a divinity (Ares) whose son (Askalaphos) has just recently been killed in the battle (15.110–12). Hera assumes that Ares feels a fair degree of egoism, since caring for one's offspring is rather like caring for oneself. But Hera herself acknowledges no egoism in denouncing Zeus's autocratic conduct, since *she* has no children on the battlefield at Troy. Ares, however, is Hera's son, and Askalaphos is therefore her grandson. Kinship is apparently part of Hera's deliberation, but she displaces it in her discourse, speaking about her son and grandson *as if* they were not kin.[10]

2. In book 16, when Hera objects to Zeus's thought of saving Sarpedon, none of her reasons involve benefit to herself: she tells Zeus that saving Sarpedon would violate the hero's allotment as a mortal (*ἄνδρα θνητὸν ἐόντα, πάλαι πεπρωμένον αἴσῃ κτλ.*, 16.441–42) and that it would arouse resentment on the part of other gods who have children on the battlefield themselves and would want to save them (16.446–49). As in her goading of Ares in book 15, Hera is sensitive to the attachment of divine parents to their children, but since none of her own children are at stake, her sensitivity manifests a degree of imaginative choice and not just necessity of kinship. However, while in book 15 Hera counts on Ares to feel a parent's grief and (one infers) anger at the loss of Askalaphos, in book 16 she calls on Zeus to *accept* the loss of Sarpedon, implying that even the ties of kinship represent an option Zeus can weigh against other options, such as his desire to avoid the resentment of the other Olympians.

3. Earlier in book 16, when Patroklos approaches Achilles to plead for the Achaians, but before he can say anything, Achilles ridicules his comrade's tears by suggesting that they should have a more worthy object than the Achaians, namely Patroklos's own father, or Achilles' father (16.13–16):

> *ἦέ τιν' ἀγγελίην Φθίης ἒξ ἔκλυες οἶος*
> *ζώειν μὰν ἔτι φασὶ Μενοίτιον, Ἄκτορος υἱόν,*
> *ζώει δ' Αἰακίδης Πηλεὺς μετὰ Μυρμιδόνεσσι,*
> *τῶν κε μάλ' ἀμφοτέρων ἀκαχοίμεθα τεθνηώτων.*
>
> Have you alone heard some report from Phthia?
> They do say that Menoitios the son of Aktor is still alive,
> and Peleus the son of Aiakos is living among the Myrmidons:
> we'd grieve indeed if both of them were dead.

In these lines Achilles applies a criterion of loyalty to kin, and he implies that the Achaians are unworthy of Patroklos's sympathy because they do not satisfy this

10. Erbse 1986: 140 notes that when Athena stops Ares (15.121–42), her express reasons concern the welfare of all the gods (15.136–37) and not her own purposes, as in earlier passages.

criterion. But Achilles goes on to say something else: the Greeks are perishing because of their transgressions (*ὑπερβασίης ἕνεκα σφῆς*, 16.18). This implies a different criterion, one not personal to Achilles, either with respect to his relationships or his feelings: the Greeks are suffering because what they did crossed a certain line, not because of who they are or how anybody personally feels about them.[11]

After Patroklos makes his plea, Achilles' answer develops the theme of transgression even further. Patroklos assumes that Achilles' refusal to help the Greeks is a personal matter; either Achilles is cruel (*νηλεές*, 16.33) and has no feeling of personal sympathy for the Greeks such as Patroklos himself has, or Achilles is protecting his own safety by avoiding some danger to himself that his mother has warned him about (*θεοπροπίην ἀλεείνεις*, 16.36). As noted earlier, Patroklos does not suggest that Achilles should sacrifice himself to save the Greeks; if Achilles is at risk, Patroklos wants to go in his place (*εἰ . . . θεοπροπίην ἀλεείνεις* / [. . .]/*ἀλλ' ἐμέ περ πρόες*, 16.36–38). Achilles, however, denies that his abstention from the battle is personal in either of the two senses Patroklos has mentioned. Self-preservation was out of the question: "What a thing to say!" (*οἷον ἔειπες*, 16.49). Achilles explains that he is angry because an impersonal criterion has been violated: he says that he feels anger "whenever a man wishes to rob his equal and take back his reward, because he [sc. the perpetrator] has more power" (*ὁππότε δὴ τὸν ὁμοῖον ἀνὴρ ἐθέλῃσιν ἀμέρσαι / καὶ γέρας ἂψ ἀφελέσθαι, ὅ τε κράτει προβεβήκῃ*, 16.53–54). In other words, Achilles does not claim the personal and relatively *compulsory* anger of a victim but the *chosen* anger of a victim's advocate. This refinement is less obvious than it might be, because it so happens that in the case at hand, the victim and the advocate are the same character: Achilles.[12]

11. When Achilles swears by the scepter in the assembly (1.233–44), he implies that Agamemnon has violated a rule of conduct given by Zeus, for the scepter was typically borne by the judges entrusted with enforcing those rules (*δικασπόλοι, οἵ τε θέμιστας/πρὸς Διὸς εἰρύαται*, 1.238–39). Also note the generality of the victim implied by the phrase *κατὰ στρατὸν* (1.229), the indefinite pronoun *ὅς τις* (1.230), and the epithet *δημοβόρος* ("public glutton," "fat cat," 1.231).

12. Achilles' generous and principled explanation of his motive at 16.53–54 is quite consistent with his characterization throughout the *Iliad*. He acts as a public advocate in the assembly in book 1, when he defends Kalchas's right to speak against the threat of Agamemnon (1.85–91), then later in the same scene when he replies to Agamemnon's demand for compensation for Chryseis—Agamemnon has not mentioned Achilles or anybody in particular as the donor—by declaring that *the Achaians* have no compensation available for him (1.123–24); on Achilles as protector of the people in the assembly, also see Haubold 2000: 79. Achilles also speaks as an advocate in book 9 when he tells the embassy to report back his refusal "publicly, so that the other Achaians may be resentful, if he [Agamemnon] should henceforth get the idea of tricking any one of the Danaans" (*ἀμφαδόν, ὄφρα καὶ ἄλλοι ἐπισκύζωνται Ἀχαιοί, / εἴ τινά που Δαναῶν ἔτι ἔλπεται ἐξαπατήσειν*, 9.370–71). Achilles also recommends a means to save the Achaians: he tells them to go home, as he plans to do himself (9.417–18). Even in wishing suffering on the Greeks, Achilles thinks about what they deserve: he wants Zeus to let the Trojans kill them "so that they all get the benefit of their king" (*ἵνα πάντες ἐπαύρωνται βασιλῆος*, 1.410—Thetis passed the request on to Zeus a little differently) and he tells Patroklos they are perishing "because of their own wrongdoing" (*ὑπερβασίης ἕνεκα σφῆς*, 16.18). As Achilles shows when he casts down the scepter in the assembly (1.245–46), he feels that Agamemnon's offense against him entails public transgression against decrees of Zeus that are upheld by official representatives of the "sons of the Achaians" (*υἷες Ἀχαιῶν. . .δικασπόλοι κτλ.*, 1.237–38). Thus I cannot agree with Haubold's statement that "by the time we arrive in book 9 [Achilles] can abuse the *laoi* in a more brutal way than his rival [i.e. Agamemnon] ever does" (Haubold 2000: 80). Achilles' conduct toward the Achaians is certainly insensitive and tragically unwise, but it is distinctly principled, not brutal or exploitative as Agamemnon's is.

4. In book 24, where Hera rebuffs Apollo's argument that the gods should save Hektor's corpse from Achilles, her position also does not benefit her personally (24.55–60):

> *τὸν δὲ χολωσαμένη προσέφη λευκώλενος Ἥρη . . .*
> *"εἴη κεν καὶ τοῦτο τεὸν ἔπος, ἀργυρότοξε,*
> *εἰ δὴ ὁμὴν Ἀχιλῆι καὶ Ἕκτορι θήσετε τιμήν.*
> *Ἕκτωρ μὲν θνητός τε γυναῖκά τε θήσατο μαζόν·*
> *αὐτὰρ Ἀχιλλεύς ἐστι θεᾶς γόνος, ἣν ἐγὼ αὐτὴ*
> *θρέψα τε καὶ ἀτίτηλα καὶ ἀνδρὶ πόρον παράκοιτιν . . ."*
>
> In anger white-armed Hera addressed [Apollo]:
> "This speech of yours might be valid, Silver-bow,
> but only if you attribute the same status to Achilles and Hektor.
> Hektor is mortal, and he nursed on the breast of a woman;
> while Achilles is the offspring of a goddess, whom I myself
> nursed and reared and bestowed on her husband as his mate . . ."

Like her goading of Ares in book 15 and her scolding of Zeus in book 16, Hera's words here imply sympathy with a divinity who has a mortal son (Thetis, mother of Achilles). In book 16, however, Hera implies that *any* mortal (*ἄνδρα θνητὸν ἐόντα*, 16.441), even one whose father is Zeus, should be the same as another with respect to death, and that Zeus should accept this necessity of nature as other gods have and do nothing to save Sarpedon's life. In book 24 Hera argues that two mortals should be different, but not with respect to death. Achilles and Hektor should be distinguished with respect to honor (*τιμήν*, 24.57). Mortality is something mortals have by nature, but honor must be given, and Hera objects to Apollo's choice to *give* the same honor to both the heroes: *εἰ δὴ ὁμὴν . . . θήσετε τιμήν* (24.57). Hera objects to Apollo's equal apportionment of honor because the heroes were of unequal parentage. Yet whatever the differences between Thetis and Hekabe, Achilles' half-immortal descent did not actually make him any less mortal than Hektor. Hera's distinction between Achilles and Hektor is therefore based upon a synairetic choice to *assign* Achilles status *by association* with the immortality of his mother Thetis, immortality that Thetis herself was unable to convey to her son. In other words, Hera accords Achilles honorary membership in the race of immortals. Hera's loyalty to Achilles does have a certain personal basis, since Hera raised Thetis (but did not bear her). Thus Hera and Thetis have a certain synaptic relationship, but one even more tenuous than immortal Thetis's biological relationship to her mortal son Achilles.[13]

13. The relationship between Hera and Thetis would be even more tenuous if it were an *ad hoc* invention, as Braswell 1971: 23–24 suggested. Davies 1989: 34 suggests that Hera was repaying Thetis for refusing Zeus's sexual advances (the story attested in *Kypria* fr.2). With this story in the background, one can easily imagine why Hera would tactfully invent another pretext for favoring Thetis.

The possibility that the respect due to an immortal could be electively transferred to a mortal is adumbrated in the very first scene of the *Iliad*, when Chryses comes before the Achaians bearing the staff of Apollo and its sacred wreaths (1.14–15). Agamemnon threatens Chryses with violence and specifically states that the objects sacred to Apollo will do the old man no good (1.28). In effect, Agamemnon denies Chryses' pretense that the respect due to the immortal Apollo could be extended to a mortal like himself: Agamemnon blocks the synairesis that connects Apollo to his sacred things and his priest. In book 16, Hera objects to Zeus saving his son Sarpedon because Sarpedon is mortal (ἄνδρα θνητὸν ἐόντα, 16.441), and he cannot be treated like an immortal. Nevertheless she acknowledges that Zeus can display favor to his son in a way that is appropriate to his mortality, by granting Sarpedon the symbolic favor of burial (γέρας . . . θανόντων, 16.457). In book 24, Hera accords Achilles more-than-mortal honor by association with his immortal mother (θεᾶς γόνος, 24.59). As already pointed out, Hera links Achilles and Thetis synairetically, since Thetis could not transmit her immortality to Achilles. Achilles only has a relationship to immortality because Hera chooses to say he does. She could have made (i.e., fabricated) an argument for extending the privileges of immortality to Hektor too, if she had chosen to.[14]

Deliberations: From Domination to Dialogue

The developing scope of choice in the deliberation scenes is also revealed in the regulation of disagreement.

1. In book 1, Agamemnon threatens Chryses and prohibits him from speaking in his presence (1.31). Kalchas is so afraid of saying anything that might displease Agamemnon that he refuses to open his mouth until Achilles guarantees his safety (1.83). In these scenes Agamemnon restricts and almost forecloses the possibility of deliberating the merit of viewpoints he opposes.
2. In book 15, when Zeus accuses Hera of conspiring with Poseidon to disobey him, he allows her to reply. Hera denies that Poseidon acted at her behest (μὴ δι' ἐμὴν ἰότητα, 15.41) and explains that he obeyed his own heart (αὐτὸν θυμὸς ἐποτρύνει, 15.43); but she declares that she will advise Poseidon to follow Zeus's leadership (κείνῳ ἐγὼ παραμυθησαίμην, 15.45). Thus while Hera avoids opposing Zeus's position openly, her pretense of obedience gives mediated expression to Poseidon's opposing viewpoint. Moreover by offering to advise Poseidon, Hera implies that Poseidon can choose whether or not to cooperate with Zeus, and that her cooperation is also a matter of choice that she can extend by choosing to advise Poseidon.
3. In book 16, Hera sharply disagrees with Zeus's wish to save Sarpedon, and she dismisses the idea as if it were not a feasible option: "What a

14. See the suggestion of Braswell 1971.

thing to say!" (*ποῖον τὸν μῦθον ἔειπες*, 16.440). Still, she acknowledges that Zeus can do as he wishes (*ἔρδ'*, 16.443): he has a choice.

4. In book 24, Hera concedes to Apollo that under certain conditions, which she hastens to add do not apply, his position could be correct: *εἴη κεν καὶ τοῦτο … εἰ κτλ.* (24.56); she therefore frames their disagreement as a choice between two alternatives either of which she explicitly acknowledges as possible.

ZEUS'S MEDIATION IN BOOK 24 AND ITS ANTECEDENTS: SURVEY AND INTERPRETATION

Antecedents of Zeus's mediation in book 24 include the following: book 1, Achilles' proposal in the assembly that Agamemnon accept deferred compensation for Chryseis (1.121–29), Nestor's proposal to resolve the conflict between Achilles and Agamemnon (1.275–84), and Hephaistos's temporary resolution of the conflict between Zeus and Hera (1.531–611); book 8, Zeus's conciliatory response to Athena at the divine assembly (8.38–40), and his disclosure of his plan to Hera (8.469–83); book 9, Nestor's proposal that Agamemnon offer Achilles gifts of friendship, and Agamemnon's offer (9.114–61); book 15, Zeus's acceptance of Hera's oath of loyalty (15.47–58); book 16, Achilles' agreement to let Patroklos wear his armor in battle (16.46–100) and Zeus's acceptance of Hera's suggestion to let Sarpedon die but facilitate his burial in his homeland (16.458–61).

Zeus's dispute with Hera follows a trajectory from book 1 (A_1) to book 8 (Z_1) to book 15 (Z_2) to book 16 (A_3) to book 24 (Z_3). Zeus at first completely refuses to share his planning with Hera. Then in book 8 he reveals a little of his plan, but only in order to humiliate her by displaying how powerless she is. In book 15, when Hera disingenuously swears that she has cooperated with Zeus and will encourage Poseidon to do the same, Zeus spontaneously reveals to her a plan that she can tolerate, however grudgingly, because it guarantees three things: that Troy will fall; that Zeus will involve other gods in his planning (since Troy will fall through the plan of Athena); and even that Zeus, like other gods, will endure the loss of a mortal child, a promise that addresses a grievance Hera has not expressly articulated in the *Iliad*.[15] In book 16 Zeus actually seeks Hera's advice in his moment of indecision, and though her advice does not accord with his predilection, he follows it. In book 24 he mediates the dispute between Apollo and Hera: he hears both arguments before speaking himself, gives neither advocate everything that was asked for, and openly commands a third alternative that each accepts as a substitute.

Dispute Resolutions in Books 1, 15, and 16

Analysis of the dispute resolutions of book 1 shows that synairetic substitution plays little role. In books 15 and 16 its role increases progressively.

15. See Schäfer 1990: 96; Stanley 1993: 162.

1. In book 1, Achilles offers Agamemnon a promise of compensation for Chryseis after Troy is sacked (1.127–29), but Agamemnon rejects the offer and insists on replacing Chryseis immediately with an equivalent (ἀντάξιον, 1.136) and, it turns out, physically similar substitute (another young girl captive). Achilles' proposal itself is synairetic only to a limited extent, since it would substitute compensation at a later time and in a greater quantity ("three and four times," 1.128), but not explicitly a different kind of material.

2. Nestor's proposal, which achieves no more success than Achilles', is perhaps even less synairetic, since it appeals to Agamemnon to refrain from taking Briseis (μήτε σὺ τόνδ'... ἀποαίρεο κούρην, /ἀλλ' ἔα, 1.275–76) but offers him no substitute at all, while appealing to Achilles to respect Agamemnon's authority on the basis of his strength as the ruler of more than Achilles (πλεόνεσσιν ἀνάσσει, 1.281), and appealing to Agamemnon to respect Achilles' strength as defender of the Achaians in battle (μέγα ... ἕρκος, 1.283–84). There was a small degree of synairesis here, in that the strength of each is evaluated in relationship to a certain group that is external to the immediate disagreement.

3. In the third dispute resolution of book 1, Hephaistos warns Hera to respect Zeus's physical mastery over her, but he adds that Zeus holds the same physical mastery over the other gods (1.580–81), and he offers himself as an example of someone Zeus physically tossed from Olympus (1.590–94). Thus he deflects Hera's feelings away from anger at Zeus and toward sympathy for her abused son. Of course this does not overcome Hera's frustration, it resolves the conflict between Zeus and Hera only temporarily, and it is minimally synairetic, since the party toward whom it directs Hera's sympathy is her own biological kin. Nevertheless it indicates a certain possibility of substitution that is developed later.

4. In book 15, Zeus accepts Hera's professed submission to his will and gives her a chance to prove her sincerity by assigning her the task of summoning Iris and Apollo (15.53–55); he expects her open support of his leadership to bring Poseidon around as well (15.49–52). Zeus makes peace with Hera on the explicit condition that his plan replace hers. But the actual substitution goes further, since Zeus then reveals to her a plan that incorporates some of her wishes, so that to a certain extent Zeus has accepted Hera's plan in replacement of his own.

5. In book 16, after Hera dismisses Zeus's trial proposal that he save Sarpedon from death at Patroklos's hands, she makes a counterproposal, suggesting that Zeus content himself with enabling Sarpedon to be buried in Lykia (16.453–57). The essence of this proposal is for Zeus to give Sarpedon a synairetic substitute for his life, and to adopt Hera's idea as a substitute for his own. Zeus assents, and adds a further synairetic gift for his son, according him honor (τιμῶν, 16.460) by pouring droplets of blood onto the earth, an apparent prefiguration of the honor paid to dead heroes at their cult sites (Lateiner 2002: 55).[16]

16. Burkert 1955: 83 minimized Sarpedon's burial in Lykia as "ein kleiner Liebesdienst" that Zeus performs for his son. Yet Zeus does no small favor for Priam at the end of the *Iliad* when he facilitates the burial of Hektor. Zeus would have liked to do more for Sarpedon, but what he did was not insignificant, especially when seen as part of a thematic trajectory.

Dispute Resolution in Book 24

In book 24, Zeus begins his reply to Hera by completely accepting her argument that Achilles and Hektor do not deserve equal honor and immediately assuring her that they will not receive it (24.65–66). Zeus submits to Hera's will, or rather to her articulation of her will. But he also acknowledges the validity of Apollo's argument that the gods should remember the gifts Hektor has given them (24. 66–70). He proposes helping Hektor and stopping Achilles, but not in the way Apollo advocates and Hera obstructs (24.71–76):

> *ἀλλ' ἤτοι κλέψαι μὲν ἐάσομεν—οὐδέ πῃ ἔστι—*
> *λάθρῃ Ἀχιλλῆος θρασὺν Ἕκτορα· ἦ γάρ οἱ αἰεὶ*
> *μήτηρ παρμέμβλωκεν ὁμῶς νύκτας τε καὶ ἦμαρ.*
> *ἀλλ' εἴ τις καλέσειε θεῶν Θέτιν ἆσσον ἐμεῖο,*
> *ὄφρα τί οἱ εἴπω πυκινὸν ἔπος, ὥς κεν Ἀχιλλεὺς*
> *δώρων ἐκ Πριάμοιο λάχῃ ἀπό θ' Ἕκτορα λύσῃ.*
>
> But I say, let's drop the idea of stealing brave Hektor from Achilles
> without his knowledge—there's no way to do it. For look,
> his mother is constantly beside him, night and day alike.
> But suppose one of the gods should summon Thetis into my presence—
> so that I might have a word with her, so that Achilles
> accept gifts from Priam and ransom Hektor.

Achilles, who promised the dead Patroklos that he would honor him approximately *in kind* by taking Trojan lives and abusing the killer's own dead body (23.19–23, 23.180–84), is now to be satisfied with gifts, the same symbolic honors that won Hektor the gods' love (*οὔ τι φίλων ἡμάρτανε δώρων*, 24.68).[17] Moreover, Hermes is not to steal the corpse from Achilles, but instead Achilles' own mother will take Zeus's message to her son and persuade him to give up the corpse voluntarily in an exchange with Priam. Apollo and Hera both accept this proposal as a substitute for their former positions.

Interestingly, while Apollo and Hera argued their positions in terms of impersonal criteria, Zeus's satisfactory alternative does not articulate alternative impersonal criteria that might compel Apollo, Hera, and the other gods to accept it as a substitute. For example, in refusing to allow Hermes to steal Hektor's corpse, Zeus does not claim that stealing it would be wrong, but instead that it would simply be impossible because of Thetis's constant presence beside Achilles: this is something of an open fib, since in the immediately following scene Iris seeks Thetis in the cave of Nereus and finds her there.[18] Zeus does not even justify permitting the burial of Hektor on the

17. Burkert 1955: 84, commenting on 22.169–72, astutely remarked that Zeus remembered Hektor's sacrifices as expressions of their "relatedness": "Akte . . . in denen ihre Zusammengehörigkeit zum Ausdruck kommt."

18. Aristarchus and Richardson 1993: 284 both circumvent the passage's challenge, the former by athetizing 24.71–73, the latter by explaining that "the exaggeration is quite natural."

grounds that burial is the appropriate reward of all the dead, although Hera herself made this very argument to Zeus in the case of Sarpedon (16.457) and could be expected to respect it here. Zeus also tacitly refrains from endorsing Apollo's critique of Achilles' savage character.

Zeus's avoidance of impersonal criteria might seem like a step backward from synairesis, but more likely it steps forward to an exercise of synairesis even more arbitrary than that which creates impersonal criteria. The reason Zeus prohibits the stealing of Hektor's corpse cannot be that it would be impossible, as he untruthfully says, or that it would be categorically wrong, which he could easily have said had he wished to. The essence of what Zeus says about the theft of Hektor's corpse is that Thetis stands physically in the way. What this implies, albeit falsely, is that Thetis's power replaces Achilles', and that it surpasses Hermes'. Zeus's disingenuous explanation has the effect of paying a compliment to Thetis, indicating the respect that he and the other gods who follow his counsel have for her;[19] in fact, because the situation Zeus has described is clearly *untrue*—Thetis could not prevent the theft of the corpse, and she is not even beside Achilles as Zeus claims—Zeus's characterization is all the more clearly complimentary to Thetis: for when Zeus insists that the gods treat Thetis as virtually an equal, he makes a voluntary choice. He explains as much to Thetis herself when Iris summons her to him (24.109–11):

κλέψαι δ' ὀτρύνουσιν ἐύσκοπον Ἀργειφόντην.
αὐτὰρ ἐγὼ τόδε κῦδος Ἀχιλλῆι προτιάπτω,
αἰδῶ καὶ φιλότητα τεὴν μετόπισθε φυλάσσων.

They have been urging far-seeing Argeiphontes to snatch the corpse.
But I have been according this to Achilles as an honor,
in hope of maintaining your respect and friendship.

In this way, Zeus's solution confers on Achilles—through Thetis—the unequal honor Hera demands for him. A solution that forbade the theft of the corpse as a matter of obedience to an impersonal criterion would not have had the same significance.

Zeus's solution also does not imply that the gods should merely *allow* Hektor burial as compensation for his offerings—as Apollo said they should (*τὸν ... οὐκ ἔτλητε ... σαῶσαι*, 24.35). Rather Zeus says that because of Hektor's gifts, the gods (collectively: *θεοῖσιν*, 24.67) felt great affection for him (he was *φίλτατος* to them, 24.67), and that Zeus himself specifically was among those who loved him (*ἐμοί γε*, 24.68). Zeus explains that he *wants* to help Hektor, because he loves him. Here is another elective substitution: Hektor gave the gods *gifts* they loved (*φίλων ... δώρων*, 24.68); the gods respond with *love* for Hektor.

19. Comparable observation by Edwards 1987: 305.

This, and Zeus's tacit demurral from Apollo's denunciation of Achilles' unchoosing character, show that Zeus knows—and knows from experience—something about character that Apollo does not. Apollo can distinguish bad character from good, but he does not know how to transform bad character into good. He advocated stealing Hektor's corpse from Achilles because he had no hope that Achilles' character might be changed so that he would surrender the corpse voluntarily (οὔτε νόημα γναμπτόν κτλ., 24.40–41). But Zeus explains to Thetis that Priam's gifts should "warm Achilles' heart" (τά κε θυμὸν ἰήνῃ, 24.119). Zeus knows that stubborn characters can be transformed, and well he might, because he has undergone this transformation himself and learned how respectful choices liberate the power of choice in others: having tried to repress Hera and other opponents with violence and threats of violence, he has developed a relationship of trust with the other Olympians that brings him their counsel as well as their cooperation. Zeus's solution to the problem of Hektor's corpse also facilitates the transformation in Achilles that Apollo deemed impossible.[20]

In an analysis of the sublime, it is impossible to say everything and foolish even to try. My basic point in this exploration of the Olympian deliberations in *Iliad* 24 has been that the system of thematic analogies in the three-cycle design can produce the effect of a translucent screen whose surface both conceals and reveals immeasurable depth. The depth in *Iliad* 24 lies in the remembering consciousness of the reader and the significance that can be found there. Recollection guided by the three-cycle design discovers a thematic development through the course of the *Iliad* in which symbolic substitutions open an ever wider potential for creative problem solving, and Zeus makes ever more use of it, effecting increasing cooperation among the gods and greater divine care for mortals.

In book 24 the scene of Zeus sending Hermes to escort Priam across the battlefield culminates a series of scenes in which gods assist mortals to perform dangerous journeys:

Book 1 (A_1): Apollo facilitates the return of Chryseis to her father, and then provides a fair wind so the Achaians can return in their ships.
Book 8 (Z_1): Zeus uses signs to assist Hektor and the Trojans across the battlefield, but their success ends at the Achaian trench.
Book 15 (Z_2): Zeus sends Apollo to help Hektor across the battlefield, Apollo destroys the Achaian trench, and Zeus pushes Hektor forward with his "big hand."
Book 16 (A_3): Zeus dispatches Apollo to rescue the corpse of Sarpedon so that Sleep and Death can bring it home for burial.
Book 24 (Z_3): Zeus dispatches Hermes to escort Priam across the battlefield.

20. Stanley 1993: 237 notes that Achilles' pity for Priam refutes the charge of Apollo. Taplin 1992: 263 felicitously suggests that Zeus's solution involves a redefinition of κῦδος. By taking an existing word and transforming its meaning, Zeus would of course display once again the very capacity for transformative choice that fabricates symbols and refabricates them as needed.

In each case Zeus becomes more involved in helping mortals, and helps them more tangibly and in ever more trying circumstances, through the use of surrogates. At first Apollo acts without Zeus, and acts as the "worker from afar," descending from Olympus but even so not coming near either Chryses or the Achaian ships (ἀπάνευθε νεῶν, 1.48). In book 8 Zeus bans all the gods from the battlefield and helps the Trojans, and also the Greeks, from far off and high above (ἐν κορυφῇσι κτλ., 8.51), whence he sends thunderstrokes as signals. Apollo, however, without Zeus's explicit permission, saves Hektor's life when he deflects Teukros's arrow onto a substitute victim (8.311). In book 15 Zeus sends Apollo right down to Hektor (ἀγχοῦ δ' ἱστάμενος ... ἑκάεργος κτλ., 15.243), so Apollo is not working from afar, but when Zeus takes over from Apollo he figuratively reaches down with his hand to help Hektor (15.695) without actually coming down into his presence as Apollo did. In book 16 Apollo has to touch Sarpedon's corpse physically and wash the impurities from it (16.667–70, 677–81) before handing it to the messengers Sleep and Death, who transport it back to Lykia for burial. In book 24 Zeus sends a different son as his surrogate, Hermes, who is not a "worker from afar" but precisely the god who "accompanies a man" (ἀνδρὶ ἑταιρίσσαι, 24.335) because he likes to (φίλτατον, 24.334), and who hears the prayers of any mortal he wishes to help (ᾧ κ' ἐθέλῃσθα, 24.335), which seems to mean that Zeus licenses Hermes to act on his own authority.

In book 15 Zeus's emissary Apollo identifies himself to Hektor by name (15.256) and goes in front of the Trojan horses (προπάροιθε κιὼν, 15.260), but Hermes appears to Priam in the disguise of an ordinary mortal youth (24.397), and he escorts the king all the way to the Achaian camp (24.440–42), miraculously puts the guards to sleep (24.444–46), and unbars Achilles' mighty door (24.457), before he reveals his divinity in plain words (24.460–64):

> *ὦ γέρον, ἤτοι ἐγὼ θεὸς ἄμβροτος εἰλήλουθα,*
> *Ἑρμείας· σοὶ γάρ με πατὴρ ἅμα πομπὸν ὄπασσεν.*
> *ἀλλ' ἤτοι μὲν ἐγὼ πάλιν εἴσομαι, οὐδ' Ἀχιλῆος*
> *ὀφθαλμοὺς εἴσειμι· νεμεσσητὸν δέ κεν εἴη*
> *ἀθάνατον θεὸν ὧδε βροτοὺς ἀγαπαζέμεν ἄντην*

> Old sir, I who have come before you am really a god immortal,
> Hermes; for my father sent me to be your escort.
> But I will return, and not go
> before Achilles' eyes; it would cause resentment
> for mortals to greet an immortal god face to face like this.

Homer's description of this epiphany is understated in the poet's familiar manner, which seems only the more understated now that we have observed the thematic analogies that surround every passage of the *Iliad* and those in book 24 most of all. But it is now also possible to appreciate how effectively Homer's manner conveys epiphany in every understated line of the epic. For an experience of epiphany reveals only what was there all along and seemed ordinary, to a viewer somehow become capable of seeing that the ordinary thing was already marvelous and always has been. Epiphany transforms the viewer, and most of all the way he views himself, his own capacity for perception and sympathy. In the scene following Hermes' epiphany, Priam appeals to Achilles, who in listening to the appeal turns away from the man bent before him and into himself, toward his memories of Patroklos and Peleus. These lead him beyond passive obedience to Zeus's command, and even beyond gratitude for Priam's respectful gifts, to a degree of insightful empathy with his humble victim. Achilles' experience, which is unique in the *Iliad*, clearly lies outside the hero's ordinary capacities, but it still comes within his reach when Zeus assists him toward it. What Achilles himself must contribute is attentive listening, searching thought, creative imagination, and a capacity for empathy. Priam kneels before Achilles as a weak old man, potentially only the next of the hero's already numberless victims; but what Achilles sees in Priam—and what Homer sees—is more than any poet could put into words. Homer's reader must look within, as Achilles did.[21] The design of the *Iliad* stimulates and facilitates this reflection by weaving each concrete moment of narrative into a vast, expanding web of memories and possibilities, which penetrate the susceptible mind and excite a meditative search of indeterminable limit.

21. I have discussed the encounter of Achilles and Priam at greater length in Heiden 1998b.

Conclusion

The Fabricated Cosmos and the Poetry of the Future

The preceding chapters have attempted to gauge the convergence of the *Iliad* with a hypothetical repertoire of adaptable reading practices. Initial trials found that a cognitive function seeking orientation to an overarching story trajectory in the *Iliad* would encounter (1) a distinct trajectory centered on Zeus's agency that organizes all the events in the epic, (2) a handful of distinct segments that coherently narrate all the chief crises of that trajectory, and (3) a transmitted arrangement of those segments that does all the work of supplying a clear system of orientation to them and to the trajectory, except without explicit paratextual cues. Noting that this "three movement design" appeared to reflect an authorial plan, the study provisionally accepted the arrangement's guidance and posited it as a basis for further experimental simulations that might uncover more orientational indications. The study then configured the three movements in parallel alignment and investigated whether similarity of positioning correlated with similarity of content. The investigation found substantial correlation. The same arrangement that cues attention to the analogous crises of the "orienting" books also cues attention to archsystemic themes in each marked segment in the *Iliad* that by thematic analogy relate each marked segment to every other marked segment of analogous position in the design. The study then examined a selection of specimen segment-groups to see whether their alignment in the design coincided with even more detailed thematic analogies. The intensive probe explored only ten of the twenty-four marked segments, but among those ten it discovered many important and subtle thematic developments.

This basis allows us to conclude, of course provisionally but with considerable confidence and without needing to prejudge what similarly intensive analysis of the other marked segments may show, that the presentation of material in the *Iliad* does converge with a specific three-cycle shape, indeed converges with it so closely that adoption of the shape by a reader yields abundant orientation to edifying and thought-provoking content, content that in many cases scholars have never before noticed or analyzed. Since the three-cycle arrangement does not conform to the shape of narrated events in the story (which do not describe, for example, a three-circuit voyage), the arrangement is imposed upon the narrative. And since the imposed shape serves the function of orientation so productively and efficiently, it is reasonable to infer that its orientational function is purposeful. From the standpoint of a reader of the *Iliad*, there is much to gain and nothing to lose in accepting the three-cycle arrangement as authorial work for the benefit of collaborative readers. What others have said before may now be reiterated with even better reason: the *Iliad* gives a very strong impression of being a designed artifact, and indeed an artifact designed for *reading*—that is, for cognitive functions associated with reading, although not necessarily for reading in the format of a physical book.

The cognitive functions the *Iliad* accommodates include the reader's fabricative work of bringing together promising passages and themes for exploration and interpretation. While this work of fabrication came into view as a technique of the reading process, it also converges with the themes of the *Iliad*, where problem-situations stir the characters to transform what circumstances give them in ever more imaginative and productively fictive ways. The superhuman, supernatural power of the Olympians that the *Iliad* evokes is ultimately the power of their imaginations, the same kind of power that imagined them. The thematization of fabrication permits the reader to regard the cyclic design of the *Iliad* as a symbol of design and not just a mechanism of orientation. The epic suggests *design* as a theme in many passages, but especially in book 18, where Thetis visits the home of Hephaistos to obtain a new suit of armor for her son Achilles. A meditation on fabrication and design could select no better point of departure.

HEPHAISTOS: GOD AT WORK

Hephaistos, the Olympians' master of design and fabrication, was something of a fabrication himself. He was born unnaturally, of a mother but without a father (Hes. *Theog.* 927–28; *Hymn. Hom. Ap.* 317); rejected by his mother Hera because of his natural deformity of lameness at birth (*Hymn. Hom. Ap.* 316–20; *Il.* 18.396–97);[1] and raised by the Nereids Eurynome and Thetis, substitute parents who "took him to their bosom" (or "lap": *ὑπεδέξατο κόλπῳ*, 18.398). In the sanctuary of their undersea cave he acquired the skill for which he was famous (Di Donato 1996: 233 n. 27), spending nine years (the number could suggest a period of artificial re-gestation) fabricating decorative objects (*δαίδαλα*, 18.400), "bent pins, spiral bracelets, artificial buds, and beads" (18.401).[2] Hephaistos himself vividly recalls his sojourn for Homer's readers (18.394–405).

The shield Hephaistos makes for Thetis is the most elaborate fabrication[3] described during the scene in his workshop, but hardly the only one.[4] Before Thetis even makes her request the narrator describes the house Hephaistos has built for himself (*δόμον . . . χάλκεον, ὅν ῥ' αὐτὸς ποιήσατο*, 18.369–71), the in-

1. Marg 1991: 220–21 and Hubbard 1992: 26 suggest that Hephaistos's craftsmanship compensated for this physical deficiency.

2. On Hephaistos's *daidala* and the Cretan craftsman Daidalos, see Hubbard 1992: 33.

3. Hubbard 1992: 17 stresses the shield's "artifacticity."

4. Becker 1995: 51–77 discusses the focus on the artificer in many descriptions of fabricated objects in the *Iliad*.

progress tripods in his forge (18.372–79; they still lack artificial "ears," i.e. handles: *οὔατα . . . δαιδάλεα*, 18.378); the elaborate chair and footstool Charis offers to Thetis (*θρόνου ἀργυροήλου/καλοῦ δαιδαλέου κτλ.*, 18.389–90); and the maidservants made out of gold but *like* living girls (*χρύσειαι, ζωῇσι νεήνισιν εἰοικυῖαι κτλ.*, 18.417–20) (Létoublon 1999: 217).[5] One might also add Charis's veil (*λιπαροκρήδεμνος*, 18.382), Thetis's robe (*τανύπεπλε*, 18.385), Thetis's coiffure (*καλλιπλοκάμῳ*, 18.407) (Hubbard 1992: 33), Hephaistos's tools (*ὅπλα*, 18.412), and their silver toolbox (*λάρνακ' ἐς ἀργυρέην*, 18.413). The narrator frames the description of Achilles' shield itself as a description of Hephaistos's work as fabricator,[6] starting from the smith-god's approach to the forge and his preparation of tools and materials (18.468–77) and proceeding on through his construction of the shield body itself (18.478–82), his crafting of the images on its surface (18.483, 490, 541, etc.), his construction of the breastplate, helmet, and greaves (18.609–13), and finally his hand delivery of the finished product (18.614–15).

Fabrication is always something other than nature (Aristotle *Metaph.* 1032a), but its relationship to nature may be understood in various ways.[7] To some theorists of art the dependence of fabrication upon nature as a model has seemed fundamental, inevitable, and wholly desirable.[8] Hephaistos's work as fabricator was not of that type: on the contrary, it assertively subjugated nature to the divine craftsman's imagination and transformed it into an object that replaced nature.[9] Hephaistos left nothing as found, imitated nothing as seen: in the fabrication of the shield, everything came into being by choice: *ὅπως Ἥφαιστός τ' ἐθέλοι . . .* ("[the bellows blew] however Hephaistos wished," 18.473). The narrator gives no reason why Hephaistos makes the shield first instead of the helmet, or why he makes the rim in three layers (18.480) and the rest of the shield in five (18.481). The narrator gives no explanation of the shield's unique design, which is superfluous to Thetis's request. Hephaistos makes the armor as he chooses to make it, with his mind (*ἰδυίῃσι πραπίδεσσιν*, 18.482). The narrator likewise describes the making as he chooses to describe it; and the poet composed the scene as he chose to compose it.

The description of the design begins by stating that Hephaistos fashioned "the land, the sky, and the sea, the weariless sun and the waxing moon, and all the signs that wreathe the sky, the Pleiades and Hyades and the strength of Orion, and the Bear, which they also call the Wagon" (18.483–87). Hephaistos did not get land, sky, and sea onto one human-sized shield—nor did the poet get them

5. Becker 1995: 81 suggests that Hephaistos's lifelike servants illustrate how his art erases the distinction between representation and life. I cannot agree, because the robots are not representations of natural servants, but replacements for them.

6. Emphasized by Lessing, who drew upon Servius's comment *ad Aen.* 8.625; see Lessing 1984: 95 and 215–16.

7. See Dipert 1993 for a careful conceptual analysis of artifacts and art works.

8. Aristotle *Protrepticus* B 13 (Dühring 52–53). For a history of such approaches see Abrams 1953: 6–14, 263–71 *et passim*.

9. Aubriot 1999: 46 astutely contrasts Hephaistos's creation of the world as artifact with the natural birth narrated in Hesiod's *Theogony*. Bouvier 2003: 99 observes that in the *Iliad* "souvent le verbe *poiein* indique la transformation d' un objet naturel en object fabriqué."

into one hexameter verse—by observing and representing their nature.[10] To state only the obvious, land, sea, and sky are just too big to fit on a shield, so Hephaistos had to make them much smaller, smaller than the shield and probably even smaller than the other scenes *on* the shield depicting human activities.[11] On the real planet Earth these human activities occupy only a small part of the real land, but the shield's images of that small part were apparently larger than its image of *all* the land, sea, and sky combined. The relative scale of the parts of the description is likewise far from natural. (Earth, sky, etc. + river Ocean at end = 9 lines total, while human activities = 117 lines total!) The scale of these images (and/or their description) is determined entirely by the artist (and the poet) and not by any physical relationships their real-world counterparts bear to each other. Moreover, in nature sea is contiguous to land, but the description puts the sky between them: *ἐν μὲν γαῖαν ἔτεξ', ἐν δ' οὐρανόν, ἐν δὲ θάλασσαν* (18.483). In nature's sky the weariless sun and the waxing moon are not usually visible at the same time, but they are simultaneously visible on the shield. Nor are all the constellations visible at once in nature, a fact the narrator stresses by mentioning that the Bear is the only constellation that never sinks below the horizon (18.489).[12] But they are all visible on the shield, because Hephaistos chooses to make them so.

From the Bear in the heavens Hephaistos moves to the two cities on earth (18.489–90):

> *οἴη δ' ἄμμορός ἐστι λοετρῶν 'Ωκεανοῖο.*
> *ἐν δὲ δύω ποίησε πόλεις μερόπων ἀνθρώπων*

> she alone is exempt from bathing in Ocean.
> And on the shield he made two cities of speaking humans

This transition would be shockingly arbitrary were the narrator describing anything but an act of fabrication, where the artist's wish is the norm: the words "and he made" can smooth the most jarring transition. The narrator mentions Hephaistos making two cities, although he could not have made both at the same time: here, as elsewhere, the poet's fabrication of the description adds another layer of synairesis over and above Hephaistos's fabrication of the

10. *Pace* Hubbard 1992: 34–35, who sees this part of the shield as "natural and elemental" and explains Hephaistos's arrangement as reflecting Homer's view of nature. Also contrast Becker 1995: 103, who likens the representation of the sun on the shield to our perception of the real sun. Even Schadewaldt 1991: 187 and Aubriot 1999 treat the world depicted on the shield as natural and/or in harmony with nature. All these critics recognize the artifice in the shield, but somehow they resist contrasting it with nature.

11. Edwards 1991: 211 proposes that 18.483 provides a summary of the content of the whole shield decoration and not description of one distinct illustration. Even if this is correct (and it is impossible to know for sure) it would not substantially affect the artificiality of the object described, since the sky would still occupy a separate sector of the design (18.484–89) consistent with the rest neither in scale nor relative position.

12. Aubriot 1999: 52 n. 171 observes that when Orion and the Bear are simultaneously visible, they are actually quite far apart in the sky; see the diagram of the December night sky in Lorimer 1951: 87. Aubriot 1999: 47 n. 147 notes that the reversal of a river's course was the *adynaton* par excellence. The circular course of the Ocean on the shield therefore marks it as counter-natural.

shield.[13] But the mere juxtaposition of these two cities—whether only in the description or on the shield as well—is equally arbitrary, and the narrative transition from the city at peace to the city at war equally abrupt (Di Donato 1996: 239),[14] because on earth two such cities could not actually be contiguous.[15] The people in the city at peace are not even aware of the battle around the other: these cities are neighbors on the shield only because Hephaistos saw fit to place them so. The transition from the city at war to the scene of plowing is just as abrupt: "and they were dragging each others' corpses. And he put in a soft fallow field . . . " (18.540–41) (Di Donato 1996: 242). No search of the world would discover the place where Hephaistos might have seen plowing like this in the immediate neighborhood of a raging battle. Again and again, the description of the scenes on the shield foregrounds the chosen, counter-natural course of Hephaistos's imagination as he fabricates the figures.[16] The imagination of the narrator as he describes the scene, and the poet's as he composes it, are only slightly less obvious.

The narrator's descriptions of movement on the shield, and of the human figures' thoughts and intentions, illustrate as well that the narration does not confine itself to empirically visible features, and that Hephaistos designed the shield for just such collaborative fabrication by an imaginative observer. The illusion of motion is one of several imaginative supplementations. The narrator denominates the stars on the shield as *τείρεα*, "signs" (18.485), that is, constellations. He gives some of their names, and mentions that one, the Bear, is also known by another name, the Wagon (*Ἄρκτον θ', ἣν καὶ Ἄμαξαν ἐπίκλησιν καλέουσιν*, 18.487). How, one might ask, could the same thing be both a bear and a wagon? The answer to this riddle was nothing more—and nothing less—than that somebody said so: if stars could be a *bear*, there was no reason they should not also be a *wagon*. Grouping stars together into "signs" and giving them names was already an audaciously creative act. The stars are natural, but the "signs" were fabrications. And these fabricated signs signified weather phenomena: the constellations, by providing information about the coming weather, enabled mortals to maintain a safe and even prosperous habitation *within* a natural environment that the *Iliad* usually evokes as violent and destructive.[17] Hephaistos's work appropriated nature as material for a fabrication that replaces it.[18]

13. See Aubriot 1999: 13 n. 15.

14. Byre 1992: 40–41 notes that the quasi-narrative scenes of the trial, the battle, and the attack by lions each imply a "plot" that is interrupted in mid-course.

15. Even the juxtaposition of the scenes of weddings and trial *within* the city at peace is rather unrealistic.

16. On the lack of verisimilitude, also see the comments of Di Donato 1996: 234 and Aubriot 1997: 29.

17. See Redfield 1975: 188. Also see Schadewaldt 1991: 186 on the constellations on the shield as signs that guide mortals, and Edwards 1991: 211 on farming and navigation. The similes that illuminate the battle scenes of the *Iliad* often depict nature as destructive; see Bouvier 1986.

18. Aubriot 1999: 27–28 notes the unnatural effects of color attributed to Hephaistos's work (the plowed field appears dark, although it is made of gold: *ἡ δὲ μελαίνετ' ὄπισθεν . . . χρυσείη περ ἐοῦσα*, 18.548–49). This is marvelous (*θαῦμα*, 18.549) because it transforms the natural appearance of the gold. Also see Becker 1995: 128.

The shield also includes fabrication in its own subject matter. Actually all but one of the human activities represented on the shield bring nature beneath the command of choice, the one exception being the battle, in which the battlefield is dominated by personifications that render human choice impossible (ἐν δ' Ἔρις, ἐν δὲ Κυδοιμὸς ὁμίλεον, ἐν δ' ὀλοὴ Κήρ, 18.535).[19] In the scene of the dancing-floor, however, everything is fabrication—the dancing-floor itself, the dancing, the fine garments, the wreaths, the ornamental swords, the music and song, and the acrobatics.[20] The description itself is also the most artistic on the shield. The narrator uses the verb ποίκιλλε ("he made a decoration," 18.590) for Hephaistos's work, where elsewhere he uses ἔτευξ'("he constructed," 18.483), ποίησε ("he made," 18.490, 573, 587), and ἐτίθει ("he put," 18.541, 550, 561). Of the four verbs, ποίκιλλε is the only one that specifically refers to some sort of planned design.[21] The narrator's description of the dancing-floor itself consists entirely of a simile: the floor is *like* the one that Daidalos made in Knossos (χορὸν . . . / τῷ ἴκελον οἷόν ποτ'. . . /Δαίδαλος ἤσκησεν, 18.590–92). Daidalos's dancing-floor is not on the shield, but the narrator, performing an act of pure synairesis, elects to mention it anyway. Another simile occurs a few lines later, when the narrator compares the revolving dancers to a potter's turning wheel (οἱ . . . θρέξασκον . . . ὡς ὅτε τις . . . κεραμεὺς κτλ., 18.599–601).[22]

Hephaistos's fabrication takes materials out of their natural relationships and puts them into new ones. Most obviously, it takes diverse metals mined from the earth—bronze, tin, gold, and silver—and puts them into functional relationship as a suit of armor.[23] Each piece of the suit has a design; concerning the shield, the narrator indicates that it consists of a determinate number of folds (i.e., layers)—three at the edge (τρίπλακα, 18.480) and five in the body of the shield (πέντε . . . πτύχες, 18.481)—and has a continuous border decorated with an image of the river Ocean (18.607–8), which also suggests that the shield is circular. Speculation about the configuration of the scenes on the shield has usually assumed that they are arranged in circular bands, a common archaic design for decorated objects like bowls.[24] But except for its reference to the

19. In fact, the battle began when the ambushers from the city attacked the herdsmen and caused an uproar (18.530–31), apparently interrupting the deliberations of the besiegers (18.510–12); see Edwards 1991: 220.

20. Hubbard 1992: 33 sees the chorus as "an emblem for Art in its purest form." Aubriot 1999: 39–52 provides an excellent analysis of the whole scene. Also see Aubriot 1997: 32 on art as substitute for nature in the chorus scene.

21. And this passage is its only occurrence in Homer; see the comments of Hubbard 1992: 33; Becker 1995: 144; and Aubriot 1999: 39. On the narrator's various words for making, see Sheppard 1966: 7–8 and Gärtner 1976: 51.

22. The simile of Daidalos's dancing-floor is only the third simile in the shield description and the first that goes beyond saying that the depiction was lifelike (the other two are 18.539 and 18.548). On similes on the shield see further Marg 1991: 215; Hubbard 1992: 33–34; and Aubriot 1999: 43–44. Hubbard 1992: 33 and Aubriot 1999: 40–44 stress the role of artisans in the similes of the choral scene. Aubriot 1997: 35 n. 39 notes that the simile of the dancers-as-pottery is the only one in Homer in which both elements compared are works of art. As she points out (Aubriot 1997: 32), Homeric similes usually compare an aspect of the story action to a phenomenon in nature.

23. See Hubbard 1992: 27. Aubriot 1999: 48 n. 153, extending the sense of artificiality in the use of metals, proposes an allegorical interpretation of the metals used and their effect.

24. On the bands on the shield, see Schadewaldt 1991: 179–82; Edwards 1987: 279; and Taplin 1991: 234–44. Agamemnon's shield (11.33) has ten bronze "circles" around it. Edwards 1991: 203–6 gives illustrations of shields and dishes designed in bands.

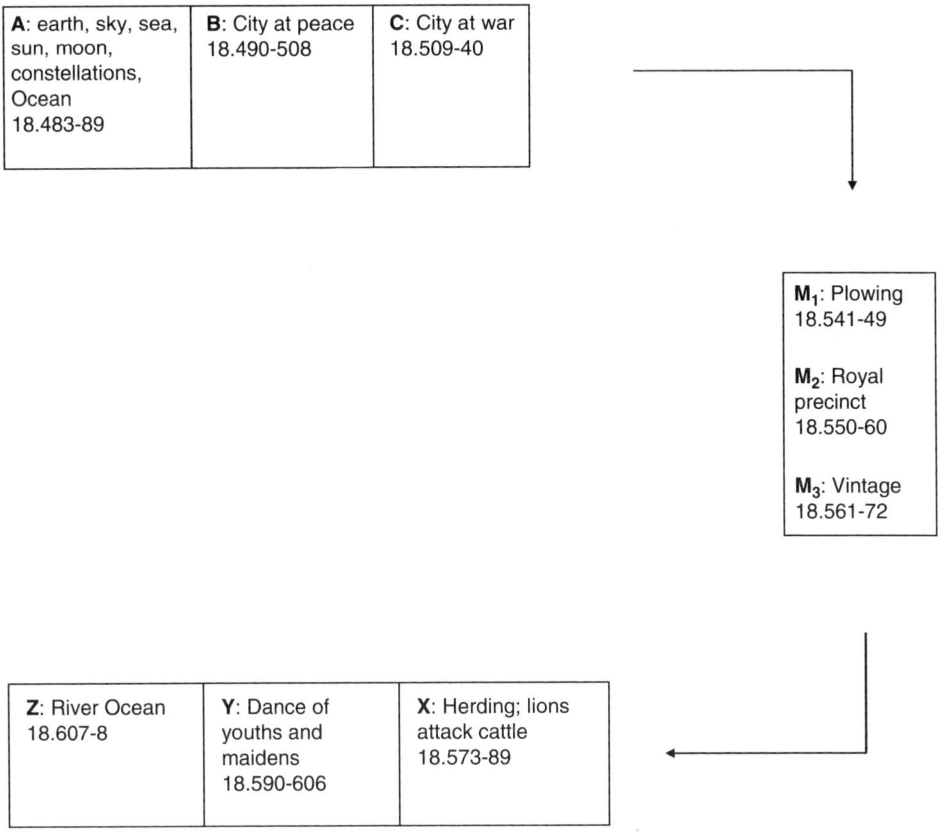

FIGURE 8.1. The design of the shield-description.

stream of Ocean surrounding the shield's border, the Homeric description is vague about the relationships of the images to one another and to the shield that serves as their support (Sheppard 1966: 6; Rabel 1997: 172; Aubriot 1999: 13 n. 15). Probably Homer assumed that his "readers" would visualize the scenes on the shield as illustrated bands; thus readers would *put* the scenes into a familiar design and attribute the design to Hephaistos.[25]

Homer, Poet at Work: The Design of the Description

But whatever Hephaistos's design may be supposed to have been, the narrator's description itself has its own design, one that could not simply reflect the putative design on the shield. The scenes in the description are arranged in a single closed band (the first section, 18.483–89, ends with reference to Ocean, and the last section, 18.607–8, describes Ocean surrounding the rim), but the shield itself must be imagined to have more than one band (the river Ocean

25. See Gärtner 1976: 49 and Di Donato 1996: 234.

around the rim + whatever else is on the shield).[26] The narrator has redesigned Hephaistos's design (see fig. 8.1).[27]

This single-band description follows a cyclic course just like a single cycle of the *Iliad*. It is articulated in three sequences that trace a path out, a turn, and a path back, each element consisting of three segments.[28] The path out comprises the tableau of the earth seen amid the surrounding heavens (segment A in fig. 8.1), the city at peace (segment B), and the city at war (segment C). The middle segment (M) comprises the three agricultural scenes of plowing, harvesting, and vintage. The path back begins with the pasturage (segment X), and it also contains the ritual dance of the youths and maidens (Y) and the river Ocean that surrounds the land on earth (Z). The M segment is clearly identified by the georgic subject matter that is common to all three scenes but absent elsewhere on the shield. Moreover, the narrator introduces each georgic scene by the same formula, ἐν δ' ἐτίθει, which first occurs immediately after the city at war; while the narrator switches to the opening formula ἐν δ' + accusative direct object + ποίησε in the two-part pastoral segment that immediately follows the georgic sequence (18.573, 18.587).[29] This change signals both the end of the georgic sequence and a reversal of direction, since the same formula also began the description of the two cities that preceded the georgic sequence (ἐν δὲ δύω ποίησε πόλεις κτλ., 18.490; ἐν δ' ἀγέλην ποίησε κτλ., 18.573).

The scenes that follow the georgic sequence do indeed follow a thematic trajectory that corresponds to the trajectory of the scenes preceding the georgic sequence, but in reverse order. As a number of scholars have observed, heavens-surrounding-earth (A) is thematically analogous to Ocean surrounding land (Z),[30] the city at peace (B) thematically analogous to the ritual dance (Y),[31] and the city at war thematically analogous to the pasturage scene (X) in which the domesticated cattle are attacked by lions.[32] Gärtner (1976: 52–53) in particular noted that the earlier scenes of human life (i.e., the outward path) follow a thematic course from joy to terror, while the last scenes (i.e., the path back)

26. See Létoublon 1983: 21.

27. "Zwei Anordnugsprinzipien überlagern sich sehr kunstvoll": Gärtner 1976: 55. Also see Rabel 1997: 173–75 on the narrator's design.

28. This analysis substantially follows that of Stanley 1993: 9–13 (diagram p. 10), except that Stanley does not configure the pattern as a cyclic path. Stanley's important forerunners were Sheppard 1966: 7; Myres 1930: 517–23; Redfield 1975: 187–88; and Gärtner 1976: 51–55. For a different analysis of the shield description, see Cavallero 2003: 190–91.

29. On the formulas as cues to articulation, see Sheppard 1966: 8; Gärtner 1976: 51; Di Donato 1996: 242–43 and 250; and Aubriot 1997: 28–29. Gärtner 1976: 51 also suggests that the initial spondees in lines 18.540 (end of city at war) and 18.572 (end of georgic scenes) cue closure of sequences.

30. On the scenes of uninhabited environment as a frame, see Sheppard 1966: 5 and Rabel 1997: 175.

31. On the analogy of the scene of dancing to the city at peace, see Bassett 1938: 98; Schadewaldt 1991: 192; Taplin 1991: 241; and Cavallero 2003: 192. Aubriot 1997: 33 suggests that the poet in the choral scene (18.604–5) corresponds to Arktos in the constellation scene (18.487–89). Aubriot 1999: 45 notes the relationship between astronomical movement and the circular dance on the shield. The Pleiades, the Hyades, and the Bear were associated with ritual choruses; see Lonsdale 1993: 171–95 and Calame 1997a: 23, 29.

32. On the analogy between the lions and the city at war, see Sheppard 1966: 8 and Aubriot 1999: 17 n. 26. Aubriot 1999: 33 makes very intriguing observations connecting the cottages that conclude the description of pasturage (18.587–89) with the concluding tableau of the city at war.

proceed from terror to joy. Gärtner also noted that the georgic scenes (M in fig. 8.1) evoke joy without terror, which reinforces their distinction from the sequences that precede and follow.[33]

The reversal of direction is also cued by the subject matter of the shield, for the scene of plowing that begins the middle segment literally describes a course that proceeds out to a turn, and then back: this is the route of the field laborers, who plow the field in three cyclic furrows (18.541–47):[34]

ἐν δ' ἐτίθει νειὸν μαλακήν, πίειραν ἄρουραν,
εὐρεῖαν τρίπολον· πολλοὶ δ' ἀροτῆρες ἐν αὐτῇ
ζεύγεα δινεύοντες ἐλάστρεον ἔνθα καὶ ἔνθα.
οἱ δ' ὁπότε στρέψαντες ἱκοίατο τέλσον ἀρούρης,
τοῖσι δ' ἔπειτ' ἐν χερσὶ δέπας μελιηδέος οἴνου
δόσκεν ἀνὴρ ἐπιών· τοὶ δὲ στρέψασκον ἀν' ὄγμους,
ἱέμενοι νειοῖο βαθείης τέλσον ἱκέσθαι.

He made upon it a soft field of fallow, fertile farmland,
wide and plowed in three furrows. And on it were many plowmen
who wheeled their teams at the turn and drove them this way or that.
And some, when they had come around and reached the limit of the field,
a man would come up and hand them a cup of honey-sweet wine;
meanwhile others were still going around along the furrows
eager to reach the limit of the deep cropland.

Some of the terms in this description (*δινεύοντες, στρέψαντες, ἱέμενοι*) also occur in narrations of races (as in *Iliad* book 23).

The relationships between segments in the cyclic shield-description, like those within the Iliadic macrocycles, are synairetic rather than synaptic; i.e., they do not depict events that occur in close proximity or immediate sequence, but they do evoke analogous themes. The thematic relationship of the C-Y pair is particularly interesting, because the conceptual analogy between them concerns the resemblance between warriors and lions, which many similes in the *Iliad* develop explicitly; but here the poet leaves the analogy to the reader's imagination.[35] In this case if no other the poetic design indicates a thematic relationship that the poet himself verifiably thought about and expected his readers to ponder.

Under the Sign of Encirclement

Many cycles and/or enclosures are also represented *on* the shield. I have already mentioned the cyclic course of the plowmen. The constellations are imagined as

33. Gärtner 1976: 52–53. He also notes other interesting details not discussed here.

34. On the meaning "three furrows" for *τρίπολον* see Hainsworth in Heubeck, West, and Hainsworth 1988: 267 and Di Donato 1996: 244–45.

35. The lions are linked to the similes by Beye 1972: 144; Taplin 1991: 240; and Aubriot 1999: 17 n. 26.

encircling the sky (ἐστεφάνωται, 18.485) and moving across it in a cyclic course (in and out of the "baths of Ocean"), except for the Bear, which rotates in the same spot (αὐτοῦ στρέφεται, 18.487) (Aubriot 1999: 46 n. 137).[36] The river Ocean flows around the shield's perimeter (ἄντυγα πὰρ πυμάτην, 18.608). Unmarried boys and girls perform a circular dance (18.599–601);[37] the girls wear wreaths (στεφάνας, 18.597), the boys knives hung from belts (τελαμώνων, 18.598). In the scene of the trial the shield depicts the elders seated "in a sacred circle" (ἱερῷ ἐνὶ κύκλῳ, 18.504).[38]

Many of the shield's fabricated circles and cycles serve in rituals.[39] Of course these are not the only ritual cycles and bands that appear in the *Iliad*; the epic abounds in them.[40] The funeral games devoted to Patroklos include a chariot race around a cyclic course, whose turning-post is the subject of Nestor's long discourse to his son Antilochos about the science of winning with slower horses (23.322–45). At the funeral of Patroklos, the Myrmidons parade their horses around the corpse three times (τρὶς περὶ νεκρὸν, 23.13), and later Achilles drags the corpse of Hektor three times around Patroklos's grave-marker (τρὶς . . . περὶ σῆμα, 24.16). The bones of Patroklos are placed in a double fold of fat (δίπλακι δημῷ, 23.243, δίπλακα δημόν, 23.253), a type of encirclement like that of a shroud in which the bodies of the dead were placed for burial; in fact, in the *Iliad* the remains of the cremated dead are also surrounded in cloth (Patroklos: ἑανῷ λιτὶ κάλυψαν, 23.254; Hektor: πέπλοισι καλύψαντες, 24.796). Women mourners cover their heads in a veil (κάλυμμα, 24.93), an object conceptualized as surrounding the head and not merely concealing it from view. Garments veiling and/or encircling the head were worn on other ceremonial occasions as well; Andromache wears a headdress, the shining "bonds" (δέσματα, 22.468) symbolic of her marriage, which

36. On the name Ἑλίκη for the constellation Great Bear see Le Boeuffle 1977: 84.

37. Cavallero 2003: 193–94 associates the dance on the shield with the "necklace dance" (ὅρμος) discussed by Lucian *De Salt*. 12–13. Although the narrator does not describe the dancing area as circular, he does compare it to the χορὸς fashioned by Daidalos. Aubriot 1999: 40–41 n. 108 points out that Daidalos is associated with circular dances in Pl. *Euth*. 15b, and that circular platforms, possibly used for dancing, have been found at Knossos. Lyric choruses were routinely circular; see Calame 1997a: 34–36. For discussion of circles in Greek dance and ritual see Lonsdale 1993: 92.

38. On circles in the litigation scene see Yoshida 1964: 14; Di Donato 1996: 238; Scully 2003: 42; and Nagy 2003: 86. Many more circles and cycles have been noted on the shield: the georgic scenes + the pasturage scenes represent the cycle of the year from spring to winter (Taplin 1991: 238–40; also Di Donato 1996: 242); Di Donato also points out (246) that the georgic scenes represent the agricultural cycle from sowing to reaping. On the potter's wheel see Stanley 1993: 13 and Aubriot 1997: 32. The dance may be a version of the crane-dance Theseus established to mime the winding path of the Cretan labyrinth (Leaf 1900 vol. 2: 609–10; Stanley 1993: 11 and 310 n. 34; Calame 1997a: 53; Rabel 1997: 177; and Aubriot 1997: 33). The myth of Theseus and the labyrinth alludes to a tripartite initiation ritual (Calame 1997a: 126); and the three stages of an initiation ritual constitute a cycle.

39. On rituals on the shield see especially Aubriot 1999: 21 n. 35 and 40–52. On the ritual association between the triple plowing (τρίπολον, 18.542) and the culture hero Triptolemos, see Di Donato 1996: 244. According to the T scholium *ad* 18.483, some texts of the *Iliad* included a line after 18.551 that identified the harvested grain as "the fruit of Eleusinian Demeter who gives fine gifts" (καρπὸν Ἐλευσινίης Δημήτερος ἀγλαοδώρου). The critic Agallis of Corcyra cited this line to support her view that the two cities on the shield were Athens and Eleusis (Edwards 1991: 223). Di Donato 1996: 246–47 notes the sacrifice in the royal precinct; he also acknowledges the ritual associations of the term *temenos* but denies (citing Hainsworth *ad Od*. 6.293) that they are relevant to the precinct on the shield. On the king's scepter see Yoshida 1964: 14–15. Cavallero 2003: 193 n. 21 notes that the μάχαιρα (18.597) was used for making sacrifices.

40. On cycles in the *Iliad*, and words such as δινεύω and στρέφω, see Aubriot 1999: 50 n. 163.

include a plaited wreath (πλεκτὴν ἀναδέσμην, 22.469) and a veil (κρήδεμνον, 22.470) that Aphrodite bestowed on her when she married Hektor. Achilles calls the walls encircling Troy the city's "holy veils" (ἱερὰ κρήδεμνα, 16.100).[41]

Cycles, circles, and encirclements are used in rituals because they can make an object sacred, separating it from the profane environment and in this way rendering it acceptable to the divine. Thus circular or encircled objects were especially suitable for dedications. When the Greeks return Chryseis to her father and prepare to sacrifice to Apollo, they arrange the victims "around the altar in a continuous line" (ἑξείης ... περὶ βωμόν, 1.447–48), that is, in a closed circle. When performing a sacrifice, the participants stand all around the victim (βοῦν ... περιστήσαντο, 2.410). The sacred thigh-bones dedicated to the deity are thoroughly wrapped (κατά ... ἐκάλυψαν, 1.460) in fat, forming a double fold (δίπτυχα, 1.461). Homer even describes the smoke of the fat rising to the heavens in the form of a spiral (ἑλισσομένη, 1.317). The priest of Apollo comes before the Greeks bearing the sacred staff of Apollo, which is wound in wreaths (στέμματα, 1.14–15).

Gifts offered to the Homeric gods were separated from the profane environment because the gods shunned the natural. Immortals are supernatural, and the supernatural is to the natural as choice is to necessity: to choose is to escape necessity and thus to master nature. The gods of Homer make choices: the narrator shows them doing so, and the mortal characters show their belief in divine choice whenever they pray, for by prayer they hope to move the gods to choose in their favor. The gods in turn are presumed willing to listen to those who have won their affection by presenting pleasing gifts. And the gifts that please the gods are those that mortals *choose* to give them; the gods have no needs, so whatever mortals might dedicate, "it's the thought that counts"—the choice to please the gods at one's own cost, despite the utterly negligible value to the gods of anything a mortal might offer. Thus when mortals sacrificed they made every effort to present objects that displayed choice. These objects had to be special: separated from other objects of their type, not used for mundane purposes, and highly worked-over. Dedications had to be fabrications, and the more skill and effort that went into them, the more likely the gods would appreciate the devotion they were meant to display.

The circles and cycles that enclosed and wrapped dedications therefore marked them as counter-natural fabrications, and by this very gesture recommended them to the pleasure of the supernaturals. But fabricated cycles had another significance that also enhanced their suitability for dedications: they reenacted the gods' choice of enclosing and protecting regions and communities under their care. Mortals built homes, cities, and fortifications in partnership with the gods. Therefore the fabrication of enclosed dedications emulated and gratefully acknowledged the gods' own grander enclosures. Sometimes called microcosms, these enclosed dedications might better be called *paracosms*, since

41. On Troy's wall and the city's sanctity see Scully 1990: 16–40.

they were not point-for-point scale models of macrocosms (as microcosms, strictly speaking, would be) but novel fabrications that shared the *concept* of design with other fabrications, but without the same materials or details. It takes imaginative work to join two paracosms, just as it does to fashion diverse materials into one.

The grandest of the gods' fabrications was the great cosmos itself, the vastness of nature's unchosen materials shaped by divine choice into a safe domestic habitation, a home.[42] The design of this cosmos was cyclic. The year was a cycle of months, and longer spans of time were measured in cycles of years; thus Odysseus acknowledges to the impatient Greek fighters that the "ninth year has come around" while they have been at Troy (2.295–96). The sun moves across the sky in a cyclic path every day, and the occurrence of events during the day could be identified according to their relationship to the sun's position in this path. On the second day of battle, the fighting was even between the two sides as long as the sun was rising ("the sacred day was increasing," 8.66); but when the sun stood in the middle of the sky (*μέσσον οὐρανὸν*, 8.68), Zeus set the portions of the Greeks and Trojans upon the scales. The regular cyclic course of the sun corresponds to certain regular cycles of human behavior, such as the return of the woodcutter from his work in the mountains (11.84–91), against which the narrator situates the wildly irregular variations of the battle (Austin 1975: 100–102). Human life, of course, also moves in a cycle, which is why Hektor can pray that his infant son will gladden his mother's heart when he becomes a warrior, that is, when his life cycle reaches the same stage Hektor's has reached when he makes the prayer.

Hephaistos's Thoughtful Gift: Masterpiece, Cosmos, and Vice Versa

So it was not a far stretch to conceive of dedicated objects and performances as paracosms, symbols of design given to the greatest of designers. The shield fabricated by Hephaistos is a paracosmic object.[43] The first line narrating the designs on the shield packs in more description than all the rest put together: "On it he fashioned the land, the sky, and the sea" (18.483). Hephaistos's design, which explicitly includes all regions of the mythical cosmos except the underworld, recalls the division of the world among the three sons of Kronos and Rhea, mentioned by Poseidon (15.189–93): "Everything was distributed in three parts, and each received a share; when the lots were shaken, it was I who got the grey sea to inhabit forever, while Hades got the foggy darkness, and Zeus got the wide sky, both clear and cloudy; but the land and high Olympus are still common to all of us."[44] By omitting Hades Hephaistos does not make the shield less of a paracosm, but more, because in this way it is more *fabricated*, and the charac-

42. "Every construction or fabrication has the cosmogony as paradigmatic model": Eliade 1959: 45.

43. Many have observed that the shield is a kind of microcosm of the universe; see Heraclitus *Homeric Allegories* 43.1 (*τῆς κοσμικῆς περιόδου . . . εἰκόνα*); Lessing 1984: 216; Bassett 1938: 96–98; Schadewaldt 1991: 173, 183, 185; Marg 1991: 208; Redfield 1975: 187; Gärtner 1976: 49; Taplin 1991: 244 and following; Hardie 1985; and Aubriot 1999: 44.

44. On the explicit arbitrariness of this division, see the discussion in chapter 6.

teristic of a cosmos is its design, not its comprehensiveness. After stating that Hephaistos represented land, sea, and sky on the shield, the narrator also specifies that he depicted the sun, the moon, and all the constellations (18.484–85), meaning not only the whole expanse of sky but the whole expanse of cyclic time in which the sky changes—day, night, and the entire astronomical year. This passage concludes with a reference to the river Ocean, which encloses the entire sublunary region, and whose image also encloses the shield itself, as the narrator states at the end of the whole description (18.607–8).

Within this frame, the shield presents scenes from human life that, while they exclude certain important features (no seafaring, trade, or slavery),[45] represent a vast but organized potential within its selected terms. The shield represents all the inhabited land in three parts: the cities, the cultivated land outside them, and the pasturage that abuts the wild nature beyond human habitation (Redfield 1975: 190). The scope of city life is represented by two paradigmatic conditions, peace and war, represented on the shield by two different cities.[46] The scope of rural life is represented by the farming work of three seasons (plowing, reaping, and vintage) and possibly winter as a fourth. In the city at war, both sexes and all age groups are represented: when the adult males go out to fight, the city wall is defended by the wives, children, and old men (18.514–15).

Hephaistos's shield would have made a splendid dedication. Victorious warriors often dedicated armor to the gods who had answered their prayers for success (e.g., Odysseus and Diomedes dedicate the arms of Dolon to Athena, *Il.* 10.570–71). Dedicating Hephaistos's shield to its maker would render grateful acknowledgment of his beneficence. But Hephaistos's shield, even discounting its divine origin, is neither an ordinary shield nor an ordinary gift, because it is not primarily intended for use in battle (it explicitly cannot protect the life of Achilles, 18.463–65),[47] or intended to be the possession of one particular recipient (18.466–67):

> *. . . οἱ τεύχεα καλὰ παρέσσεται, οἷά τις αὖτε*
> *ἀνθρώπων πολέων θαυμάσσεται, ὅς κεν ἴδηται*

> he will have equipment so beautiful that afterwards any one
> of many humans who beholds it will wonder.

The actual recipient of Hephaistos's *design* is not to be the individual Achilles, who will possess the armor during his brief remaining span of life, but a multitude of

45. On omissions from the shield, see Schadewaldt 1991: 191; Taplin 1991: 245; and Aubriot 1999: 21 n. 35. Gärtner 1976: 54 suggests that the field workers might be slaves.

46. Schadewaldt 1991: 186 emphasizes polarity as the ordering principle of the shield.

47. On the impracticality of the shield as defensive armament, see Aubriot 1999: 49–50. Its design was not altogether practical even in terms of ornamentation, since Hephaistos placed a layer of gold inside where it could not be seen (see 20.268–72); Edwards 1991: 202 observes the anomaly but opts for interpretation and emendation to correct it.

anonymous mortals who will gaze on it with wonder. These mortals could be anybody, anywhere, at any time, because the design on the shield can be transmitted in speech.[48] In fact, the specific marvels the narrator describes can only be transmitted in the speech of the *Iliad*. The shield Homer describes in the *Iliad* is no less marvelous than any physical shield Hephaistos might have designed, but it does not inspire admiration for Hephaistos's workmanship, since to the reader of the *Iliad* the workmanship remains invisible. For the reader of the *Iliad*, the wonder lies in the poetic description itself.[49]

Hephaistos designed the shield as an object of contemplation rather than use, and those who contemplate it are not its possessors. The gift of the shield, therefore, is the opportunity to contemplate it from a place of detachment. The shield is free of ownership, and its beholders are free to contemplate it without seeking to own it: Hephaistos said that many would *wonder* at it, not that they would desire it. Hephaistos imagined his gift circulating in a condition without necessity. This liberation from necessity is implicit in the shield's artistic fabrication and the poet's description, as we have seen. It is also implicit in the shield's subject matter and the very circumstances in which it comes to be made.[50] When Achilles learns that Patroklos is dead, he does not actually need a new suit of armor, since he could easily borrow someone else's, just as Patroklos borrowed his.[51] The poet had only to say so, and no reader would have detected any implausibility in relation to what preceded. On the contrary, when Thetis comes to Achilles he is badly needed to assist the rescue of Patroklos's corpse, and eager to rejoin the fighting immediately. All the emotional and practical elements of the situation call for him to rush into battle with minimal preparation. But the poet gives Thetis a different idea. This is plausible, because Thetis is not moved by the same concerns as her son. Thetis has not even been part of the story since book 1; since then she has remained in her undersea dwelling, surrounded by her supernatural sisters, physically remote from the battle, and uninterested in it except as it affects the welfare of her son. Since she does not share her son's eagerness to kill Hektor and immediately bring death upon himself, the poet could cast her as a *deus ex machina* who diverts the narrative from Achilles' immediate goal toward one that he could not have imagined himself.[52]

48. On the recipient of the design as the indeterminate audience of the poem see Marg 1991: 223; Becker 1995: 150; and Di Donato 1996: 234.

49. On the shield as poetry see Marg 1991: 200 and following; Reinhardt 1961: 410–11; Becker 1995: 140; and Bouvier 2003: 100–2. Hubbard 1992: 28–29 observes that the shield descriptions correspond to the poetic genres of didactic, heroic, georgic, and bucolic. Also see Di Donato 1996: 248. Probably the genres of epithalamium, *komos*, and elegy could be added to the list.

50. On the tenuous relationship between the description of the shield and the action of the *Iliad* see Schadewaldt 1991: 195–96; Owen 1947: 188; and Marg 1991: 201. Di Donato 1996: 252 emphasizes the shield's generic anomalousness in the heroic narrative.

51. This possibility must have occurred to ancient readers, since the scholia provide reasons Achilles could not have borrowed armor; see Edwards 1991: 169. Hubbard 1992: 20 and Di Donato 1996: 231 insist on the shield's necessity. But Achilles actually saves the corpse of Patroklos, and causes many Trojan fatalities, *without* armor. Note also that in the *Odyssey* Odysseus slays 108 suitors without special armor.

52. Owen 1947: 187 notes the effect of diversion.

Thetis's ascent to Hephaistos's Olympian home transfers the narrative to a site even more remote from the Trojan War than the undersea cavern of the Nereids. Hephaistos and Charis have no interest in the war. They are busy with other things. When Thetis arrives her hosts have no idea why she might have come ("Why have you come?" asks Charis. "In the past you haven't been here much"; ditto Hephaistos: 18.385–86, 18.424–25). The warriors at Troy are correspondingly indifferent to Hephaistos: they never pray to him. Prior to book 18 Hephaistos has scarcely been mentioned in the *Iliad*. Hephaistos's complete detachment permits the narrator a leisurely description of his home and work, and one might say even invites it. Permits it, because in Hephaistos's home there is no business necessary to the story to demand attention from the narrator and reader; invites it, because the leisurely description mimes Hephaistos's detachment and challenges readers to share it for a duration of 247 lines in which nothing happens to satisfy their anxiety about Achilles' imminent return to combat. In shaping this counterintuitive scene the poet chose as arbitrarily as Zeus did when he lost interest in the battle and turned his eyes toward the far away Thrakians, Mysians, Hippomolgi, and Abii, "most just of men" (13.1–6).

Gods were free to choose whether to be interested in the Trojan War or not, and apparently so was Homer, since at the most emotional juncture of the story he chose to remove the narrative to the most remote point imaginable. This put the reader's interest to a stern test, for all the emotional involvements that have sustained it so far are diminished or completely absent in Hephaistos's home. No mortal characters are present, either Greek or Trojan; nothing is said or done that advances the plans of the mortals or affects their fortunes; nobody is angry or vengeful. The indifference of Hephaistos and Charis to the Trojan War and the story of the *Iliad* shows how unlike Homer's readers they are. But Homer's scene invites the reader to develop a new interest: an interest in detachment itself.[53]

Hephaistos's detachment teaches no lesson in indolence. On the contrary, when Hephaistos leaves his forge to greet Thetis, Homer's description insists that the blessedness of this divinity somehow coexists with work that is physically demanding (18.412–15):

> . . . ὅπλα τε πάντα
> λάρνακ᾽ ἐς ἀργυρέην συλλέξατο, τοῖς ἐπονεῖτο·
> σπόγγῳ δ᾽ ἀμφὶ πρόσωπα καὶ ἄμφω χεῖρ᾽ ἀπομόργνυ
> αὐχένα τε στιβαρὸν καὶ στήθεα λαχνήεντα . . .

> and into a silver box
> he gathered all the tools he was working with,
> and with a sponge he wiped off his face and arms,
> his muscular neck and hairy chest

53. On the implication of affective detachment, see Schadewaldt 1991: 192–93; Reinhardt 1961: 405–9; and Aubriot 1999: 39 *et passim*.

The description could almost be that of a slave. But Hephaistos labors—unrelieved by his robots and other machines, which are labor-enhancing rather than labor-saving devices—without external compulsion. Hephaistos's detachment is therefore somehow qualified, for he would not work hard—or at all—if he were simply indifferent to everything. Hephaistos is detached from necessity. Far from obviating purposeful activity, this detachment excites Hephaistos to fulfill purposes of his own design and choosing. Free *from* the cares of natural existence, he is free *to* care about Thetis and her mortal son. Synaptic detachment permits synairetic engagement.

Hephaistos's design for the shield manifests engaged detachment.[54] One might have expected that a decorated shield for the short-lived Achilles would—besides defending his life, which this shield cannot do—illustrate the hero's exploits and perpetuate their memory. But Hephaistos does not design the shield as a monument to Achilles personally. Those who wonder at the shield do not wonder at the *kleos* of Achilles, or any warrior's *kleos*, since nobody on the shield is identified by proper name except divinities.[55] The detachment of the shield from the Trojan War is matched by the detachment of the represented scenes from one another; as I have pointed out, the scenes on the shield do not coexist in the same imaginary space: the siege and the plowing are not imagined as contiguous, but apart, despite their proximity on the shield. The narrator's description shares this detachment, for it never lingers long in one place, but rapidly shifts attention from one scene to another, and finally draws attention outside the images altogether to the shield as an object and to the rest of the suit of armor: "And when he had constructed this huge and heavy shield, he constructed a corselet that shone brighter than gleaming fire, and he constructed a helmet, heavy, and fitted to the temples . . ." (18. 609–11).

But because the scenes on the shield are narratively detached from one another, from the story of the *Iliad*, and from the onlooking reader, they offer little resistance to contemplative refabrication. The city at peace and the city at war are not particular cities connected to one another by a chain of circumstances, but representative types that may be construed to comment upon one another, if the viewer chooses to consider them that way. The reader/viewer of the shield is likewise invited to bring the scenes on the shield together with scenes in the narrative and derive some meaning from the comparison.[56] The path is eased by the fact that the narrator has frequently chosen (in similes) to compare events in

54. Especially in comparison to other poetic shields; Schadewaldt 1991: 183–85 and 194–95 compares the pseudo-Hesiodic *Aspis*, Agamemnon's shield in *Il.* 11, and the shield of Achilles described in Euripides' *Elektra* (457); likewise Taplin 1991: 228–29. Also see Edwards 1987: 278; Aubriot 1997: 27; and Aubriot 1999: 54.

55. On the lack of proper names on the shield and its implications see Marg 1991: 210–11; Di Donato 1996: 241; Aubriot 1997: 30; and Aubriot 1999: 16, 19, 21, and 41.

56. Many critics have compared the scenes on the shield to scenes in the narrative; see Marg 1991: 206; Andersen 1976; Taplin 1991: 236–37, 245; Scully 1990: 32; Byre 1992: 42; Hubbard 1992: 29–34; Aubriot 1997: 30–32; Hammer 2002: 110–12; and Nagy 2003: 81–84. Aubriot 1999 is the definitive treatment to date.

the narrative to scenes outside it but similar to those on the shield.[57]

Hephaistos's gift to mortals, the shield that excites wonder, is a "gift that keeps on giving," because what it gives is an opportunity for broader, more creative deliberation than the exigencies of daily life usually allow. The onlooker is drawn away from needs that press on him or her personally, and instead takes pleasure seeing human life as an outsider, exempt from immediate desire and harm, but involved enough to take an interest.[58] The elevated perspective of the shield discloses a vast range of possibilities, and nothing appears inevitable or compelling, because the figures are so small and literally malleable. The onlooker who has been absorbed in violent conflict beholds it on the shield without the stakes of personal involvement, and as one human activity among many that are more pleasant. The images display the capacity of building a shelter against nature by choice; the onlooker-reader exercises choice in directing attention from one part of the shield to another, in making comparisons between the scenes, and in drawing comparisons between his or her own predicaments and those represented on the shield.

EPIC AS PARACOSM

Most of what has just been said about the shield of Achilles could also be said of the *Iliad* itself. After all, the shield is part of the *Iliad*, its description a passage of poetry and not a real object. The shield that represents the universe in paracosm is also a paracosm of the epic, a refabrication of its themes minus its characters and plot.[59] The shield refabricates the Trojan War into the shield's city at war, and refabricates the narrator's similes into the peacetime activities of courtship, marriage, agriculture, and dispute resolution. The shield even appropriates the image of the poet himself into the scenes of the vintage (18.569–71) and the dancing youths (18.605–6).[60] And as already pointed out, the cyclic design of the shield description is a paracosm of a cycle of the *Iliad*, and each cycle is a paracosm of the three-cycle design of the *Iliad* as a whole. This analogical convergence between the shield and the whole *Iliad* is itself a kind of synairesis.

The *Iliad* too is a paracosm that invites contemplation of a vast but organized body of myth, much as the tiny shield contains the vast universe that contains it in turn.[61] The *Iliad* both availed itself of, and projected itself into, an already existing

57. On the shield and similes in the narrative see Bassett 1938: 95–96; Redfield 1975: 186–89; Taplin 1991: 238–39; Edwards 1987: 278; Pigeaud 1988: 59; and Hubbard 1992: 32–34. On similes as contrast with the narrative see especially Porter 1972 and Aubriot 1999: 22.

58. Marg 1991: 214 astutely notes the important presence of spectators *on* the shield.

59. Aubriot 1999 is the most comprehensive and thoughtful discussion of the shield as a kind of microcosm of the whole *Iliad*. Important earlier discussions include Schadewaldt 1991: 193 and following; Andersen 1976 *et passim*; and Taplin 1991: 245. Aubriot occasionally indicates that the shield is not just a reflection of the *Iliad* but a refabrication, e.g. Aubriot 1999: 12 ("une autre alchimie"), 18 ("décalage"), 53 ("remodèle").

60. These verses were not transmitted in the vulgate, but are known from Athenaeus, who mentions that Aristarchus deleted them. Many scholars accept them as authentic. For recent discussion see Cavallero 2003: 197–201.

61. Heubeck 1991; Whitman 1958: 269–70; Kullmann 1960; Schein 1984: 19–30; Latacz 2000a: 155–57; Rousseau 2001; and Létoublon 2003: 31–33. Dowden 1996, Burgess 2001 and Finkelberg 2002 emphasize allusion to relatively fixed versions of the Epic Cycle; also see Lang 1995.

treasury of divine and heroic myth. But scholars have increasingly recognized that this treasury was already shaped as a coherent story within whose comprehensive trajectory shorter stories were situated; in fact, the shorter stories may only have developed as elaborations of the grander one. The *Iliad* presupposes some knowledge of this compendious mythic tale, and in making allusion to many of its events it produces the impression of incorporating it whole. The link most evident to the modern reader is the epic's evocation of the Trojan War before and after the narrated action. Within its span of fifty-three narrated days the *Iliad* concentrates allusions to events that began the war (the Judgment of Paris; 24.27–30), those that ended it (the fall of Troy), some that followed the end (the destruction of the Greek fortifications, the Greeks' returns home , the escape of Aineias with the surviving Trojan remnant), and many in between, including the abduction of Helen, the recruitment of the Greek forces and their gathering at Aulis, the Greek landing at Troy, the beginning of the siege, a mutiny of the Greeks, the coming of the Trojans' allies, Achilles' combat with Memnon, the death of Achilles himself, and the contest between Odysseus and Ajax in which Achilles' armor was the prize.[62] But the *Iliad* also makes allusion to the two Argive expeditions against Thebes,[63] an earlier expedition against Troy led by Herakles (5.640–51), and a "plan of Zeus" whose multiple goals included ending the "age of heroes" and whose means included the Theban and Trojan wars.[64] And the *Iliad* also alludes to characters and events that preceded and followed the "age of heroes." It mentions the Titans, the division of realms among Zeus, Poseidon, and Hades (15.187–93), and violent contestation of Zeus's authority by Hera, Poseidon, and Athena.[65] And it offers forward glimpses beyond the "age of heroes" to improve-

62. And many other episodes known from the Cyclic epics. These episodes may include Thetis's warning to Achilles not to be the first ashore when the Greeks landed at Troy (Apollod. *Epit.* 3.29 and following; recall the allusions to a warning from Thetis at *Il.* 11.794–95 and 16.36–37), Antilochos's rescue of Nestor from Memnon (known from Proclus's summary of the *Aithiopis*; see *Il.* 8.130 and following), Thetis's warning to Achilles that he would meet his own death soon after he killed Memnon (Proclus's summary of the *Aithiopis*; Davies 1989: 53 compares *Il.* 18.94 and following), the death of Memnon and his translation to a blessed afterlife (Proclus on *Aithiopis*; compare the miraculous rescue of Sarpedon's corpse, *Il.*16.666–83), Achilles' killing of Thersites for taunting him (Proclus on *Aithiopis*), the rescue of Achilles' corpse by Ajax and Odysseus (Proclus on *Aithiopis*; see the rescue of Patroklos's corpse by Ajax and Menelaos in *Iliad* 17), games that honored Achilles at his funeral (Apollod. *Epit.* 5.5, possibly from *Aithiopis* according to Davies 1989: 57, who compares the games for Patroklos), the judgment that Odysseus rather than Ajax would be honored with Achilles' arms (Proclus on *Little Iliad*; compare the wrestling contest of Odysseus and Ajax at *Il.* 23.700–739), the theft of the Palladion by Odysseus and Diomedes (Proclus on *Little Iliad*; compare their exploit together in *Iliad* 10; on the relationship between the *Doloneia* and the Palladion see Dowden 1996: 56), the Achaians' breach of Troy via the Trojan horse (Proclus on *Little Iliad* and *Iliupersis*, with the comments of Davies 1989: 66; compare Zeus's statement at *Il.* 15.71 that Troy will fall via the plans of Athena, and the prominence of Epeios, the Trojan horse's builder, at 23.670–71), the murder of Astyanax by Neoptolemos (*Little Iliad* fr. 20, *Iliupersis* fr. 3; compare the foreboding of Andromache at *Il.* 24.734–35), and the murder of Priam by Neoptolemos (Pausanias on *Little Iliad*; compare Priam's supplication of Neoptolemos's father Achilles in *Iliad* 24). Also see the list in Burgess 2001.

63. Allusions to the expedition of the "Seven against Thebes," in which Tydeus participated, occur at *Il.* 4.376–400, 5.799–808, 6.222–24, and 10.285–90; allusion to the expedition of the "Epigoni," in which his son Diomedes participated, occurs at *Il.* 4.404–10.

64. See especially Clay 1999 and Rousseau 2001; also Scodel 1982a.

65. Marriage of Peleus and Thetis at 18.432–34 and 24.59–63; plot against Zeus and Thetis's assistance at 1.397–406; Hera's persecution of Herakles at 8.362–69, 15.18–31, and 19.95–133; Hera's ejection of Hephaistos at 18.395–405.

ments in the lot of mortals (afterlife, Hermes as helper, Eleusinian mysteries, hero cult, and civic institutions).[66]

Like the narrator-viewer of Achilles' shield, Homer's reader refabricates the *Iliad* and sees more than really is there. In the proverbial wisdom of Homeric poetry, the ability to see past, present, and future is intelligence, while the lack of this ability is stupidity. Kalchas, the best of seers, "knew present, past and future" (ὃς ᾔδη τά τ' ἐόντα τά τ' ἐσσόμενα πρό τ' ἐόντα, 1.70); among the Trojans, wise Poulydamas "alone saw ahead and behind" (οἶος ὅρα πρόσσω καὶ ὀπίσσω, 18.250); Menelaos warns Euphorbos that "a fool understands a thing after it has been done" (ῥεχθὲν δέ τε νήπιος ἔγνω, 17.32). The *Iliad* embodies this common wisdom in its story, where—to mention only one prominent example—the tragic fate of Hektor takes special poignancy from the hero's inability to see that the good fortune of the present may not extend into the future: as Hektor confidently dons the armor worn by his recent victim Patroklos, Zeus looks on from above and exclaims, "Ah poor man, death is not at all in your mind, although it is very near you" (17.201–2). As we have seen, the cyclic design of the *Iliad* also prompts the epic's reader to look backward and forward; and while the apparently closed cyclic shape might be suspected of imposing itself as a horizon upon the reader's search, it actually resists the expectation of closure by suggesting an indefinite continuation of additional and different paracosms: because the cycles are multiple, each succession of one upon another serves to emphasize that formal completion is merely provisional, and even the last cycle, like those before it, ends with anticipation of more to come.

A reader who did not look behind and ahead would certainly miss a lot in the *Iliad*, and might even find its story unintelligible, at least in places. Like the shield, the narrative elicits attention, admiration, and imaginative supplementation. While the shield invites its viewer to supply temporal extension where the object itself has none, the narrative, which already possesses an extended temporal dimension, invites the reader to extend its trajectory even further. At every point in the *Iliad*, including its last word and the silence that follows, the narrative poses the question of where events might lead. Indeed, as the scenes on the shield and the narrator's similes show, the temporal trajectory of the *Iliad* extends beyond myth entirely into the time of the reading, without indication that it terminates even there, or would terminate anywhere. Thus, although its events are set in the distant past, and its reading at any particular moment occurs in the immediate present, the guiding orientation of the *Iliad* faces forward into the future.[67]

66. On Hermes see *Il.* 24.334–35; hero cult at 16.459–61 (with Lateiner 2002); civic institutions at 16.385–92 and 18.18.497–508. On the afterlife and the Eleusinian Mysteries see note 71 here. On allusions to events after the "age of heroes" also see Kullmann 1960: 5–11 and Burgess 2001: 209 n. 1. As many scholars have noted, the similes evoke the time of the audience and include it within the epic; see e.g. Bassett 1938: 166–67.

67. Di Donato 1996; Nagy 2003: 72–87; and Scholten 2004 make this point very well with respect to the shield of Achilles.

Zeus's Major Projects

In this regard the *Iliad* is like any other narrative, because for a story to be told the teller must have in mind some goal of affecting an addressee. All stories, even those whose surface rhetoric narrates only the past, look pragmatically toward the future. The *Iliad*, however, belongs to a special subclass of stories that imply the reader's inclusion within a tale of truly "epic proportions" whose supernatural characters make choices that design a cosmic trajectory. In chapter 1 we saw that Zeus is the agent whose choices most affect the action narrated inside the temporal frame of *Iliad*. But Zeus's plan to fulfill his promise to Thetis is not the only Plan of Zeus that affects the action of the *Iliad*. Jenny Strauss Clay has observed that Homer inserted the story of the *Iliad* into a transcendent mythic action shaped by its own Plan of Zeus. In fact Clay identifies three Plans of Zeus whose trajectories combine to effect the action narrated in the *Iliad*: (1) his plan to fulfill the promise he made to Thetis in *Iliad* book 1; (2) his plan to destroy Troy; and (3) his plan to reduce the weight of humanity on Earth and end the age of the heroes (Clay 1999).[68]

Zeus's plan to curb the abuses of the heroes entailed separating gods from mortals. But it did not entail leaving mortals destitute forever, for Zeus assigned a number of delegates—including Hekate, Hestia, Apollo, Hermes, Persephone, Herakles, and the Muses—to help mortals. These Zeus-appointed helpers did not just give mortals things they could use without the gods (as Prometheus did when, as Hesiod tells it in the *Theogony*, he tried to ameliorate the mortal state by tricking Zeus at Mekone and later stealing fire from him); instead they engaged mortals in cooperation with the Olympians and with one another. By teaching mortals justice and piety, the Olympians and their gifts promised to transform human existence from a merely physical weight that oppresses goddess Earth to a chosen condition of friendship with fellow mortals and benevolent divinities.[69] In the *Iliad* allusions to Zeus's improvements in mortal existence include reference to Hermes as the helper of mortals (24.334–35) and to Zeus's anger when cities pass crooked rulings (16.384–93). More subtle are the allusions to the oracles given by Apollo from his holy seat at Pytho (9.404–5)[70] and to a blessed afterlife made possible for mortals by the Eleusinian mysteries.[71] The similes of the *Iliad* and the images on the shield of

68. Also see Davies 1989: 35; Murnaghan 1997; Rousseau 2001; Marks 2002:13–19; and Aubriot 2003: 137.

69. Clay 1989 is the most extensive elaboration of Zeus's plan to ameliorate mortal existence. Murnaghan 1997 takes a much dimmer view. Thalmann 1984: 78–112 is in between; but his discussion of the *Hymn to Demeter* strangely says nothing about the establishment of the Mysteries.

70. Of course during the narrative of the *Iliad* Apollo furnishes divine insight to the seers Kalchas and Helenos. Apollo's oracular responses are explicitly mentioned at *Od*. 8.79–81, so there can be no doubt that the reference to Pytho at *Il*. 9.404–5 would be read as implying the oracle.

71. A line that appeared in some manuscripts after 18.551 mentions Eleusinian Demeter and her gifts (*καρπὸν Ἐλευσινίης Δημήτερος ἀγλαοδώρου*). Even without this line the scene of plowing on the shield of Achilles evokes a blessed afterlife in the "three furrows" (*τρίπολον* 18.542), which suggest Triptolemos (one of the kings to whom Demeter revealed the Mysteries, *Hom. Hymn. Dem*. 473–77), and in the refreshing drink that awaits the laborer at the end of each swath (*Il*. 18.544–46). Aubriot 1999: 35–38 tentatively suggests that the scene of the uninhabited sheepfold (18.587–89) alludes to the Isles of the Blessed mentioned by Hesiod at *Op*. 167–73. Aubriot 1999: 42 also

Achilles also suggest general improvement in human life after the end of the Trojan War, for like the *Works and Days* they evoke the era of the reader as one in which war has a reduced role, and mortals, while they often struggle against a hostile environment, also cooperate in work, celebration, and justice (Edwards 1991: 36).

In Zeus's evolving postheroic and post-Promethean dispensation, one of the Olympians' chief gifts to mortals was the poetry that the Muses, Zeus's daughters, could inspire. The *Iliad* sometimes states that a consequence of events is a song that preserves their memory: Helen declares (6.357–58) that this was Zeus's goal in planning a terrible fate for her and Paris.

> *οἷσιν ἐπὶ Ζεὺς θῆκε κακὸν μόρον, ὡς καὶ ὀπίσσω*
> *ἀνθρώποισι πελώμεθ' ἀοίδιμοι ἐσσομένοισι.*
>
> Zeus imposed a bad allotment on [us], so that even later
> we should be subjects of song for men to come.

Stories, in turn, can affect mortals' lives by giving them pleasure (such as the pleasure Achilles derives from the *κλέα ἀνδρῶν* he sings in his encampment, 9.189) and by teaching them lessons (such as those Diomedes learns from the impiety of Lykourgos, 6.130–42; or those offered by Phoinix in his story about Meleager, 9.524–605) (Nagy 1979: 238 n. 4).[72] Any events that can be turned into story are potentially part of a trajectory leading to the *telling* of a story and the further effects of the storytelling. The events of the Trojan War therefore also belong to a trajectory that leads to their telling in myth, to the creation of the *Iliad* itself, to its performances among mortals, and to the effect of these performances.[73]

Performing the Cosmic Gift

In this mythic trajectory the gift of poetry marks a programmatic shift away from thought directed at particular existing problem situations, and toward thought about paradigmatic strategies adaptable to whatever problems the future may bring. Synairetic substitution is the most indispensable element in this shift, since epic poetry substitutes for whatever it narrates, and in doing so it exposes precisely how problems are solved: by transforming them from necessities into

observes that the scene of dancing could point to death and rebirth through its association with the labyrinth. Hephaistos's story of his expulsion from Olympus and his pleasant underground sojourn with the Nereids indicated a path of suffering and relief like that of a mortal (Aubriot 2003: 145). Priam's journey in *Iliad* 24 has suggested a *katabasis* to many scholars (Whitman 1958: 217; Nagler 1974: 184; Nethercut 1976; and Stanley 1993: 237–40). On the relevance of the Mysteries to this episode, see Heiden 1997: 228–31 and Heiden 1998b: 7–8. Turcan 2003: 7–21 suggests that the transcendence of the mortal condition in mysteries extended the communion of divine and mortal implied by all ancient Greek festivals.

72. On choruses in Greek education, see Calame 1997a: 207–63.

73. See Nagy 1979: 29, who in making a similar point links the *kleos* of the *Iliad* more exclusively to Achilles than I would. Also see Thalmann 1984: 134–56 on the "self-reflectiveness" of hexameter poetry. Nagy 2003: 86–87 suggests that the litigation scene on the shield of Achilles implies the performance of the *Iliad* in a polis.

playful fabrications.[74] When threatened by necessity a person must trust the automatic responses of organic instinct, but within a fabricated enclosure one can playfully deliberate, imagine, choose, test one's choices, and even revise them. It is because this safety is protected by the gods within the fabricated sanctuary of ritual time and space that poetry, teaching, and communal planning take place within it.[75]

The events of the *Iliad* therefore point forward to the performance and reading of the *Iliad* itself. A casual glance at the epic might suggest that this occurs because such great events as those performed at Troy would automatically leave a glorious report on the lips of men. But the *Iliad* denies that this is the reason whenever the narrator invokes the Muses to give him the story, as he does immediately before naming the Greek contingents who gathered at Aulis for the expedition to Troy and numbering their ships (2.484–92):

> *ἔσπετε νῦν μοι, Μοῦσαι Ὀλύμπια δώματ᾽ ἔχουσαι—,*
> *ὑμεῖς γὰρ θεαί ἐστε, πάρεστέ τε, ἴστέ τε πάντα,*
> *ἡμεῖς δὲ κλέος οἶον ἀκούομεν οὐδέ τι ἴδμεν—*
> *οἵ τινες ἡγεμόνες Δαναῶν καὶ κοίρανοι ἦσαν·*
> *πληθὺν δ᾽ οὐκ ἂν ἐγὼ μυθήσομαι οὐδ᾽ ὀνομήνω,*
> *οὐδ᾽ εἴ μοι δέκα μὲν γλῶσσαι, δέκα δὲ στόματ᾽ εἶεν,*
> *φωνὴ δ᾽ ἄρρηκτος, χάλκεον δέ μοι ἦτορ ἐνείη,*
> *εἰ μὴ Ὀλυμπιάδες Μοῦσαι, Διὸς αἰγιόχοιο*
> *θυγατέρες, μνησαίαθ᾽ ὅσοι ὑπὸ Ἴλιον ἦλθον.*

> Now tell me, Muses whose homes are on Olympus—
> for you are goddesses, you are at hand, and you know everything,
> while we only hear report, and know nothing—
> who were the leaders and chiefs of the Danaans?
> As for the multitude, I will not put them in speech or name their names,
> not even if I should have ten tongues and ten mouths,
> a tireless voice, and a heart[76] of brass within me,
> unless the Olympian choir, the Muses, daughters of aigis-bearing Zeus,
> should recount how many went up to Ilium.

This passage and others like it affirm that without the gods the story could not be told and would have disappeared, like the great Greek wall that Zeus, Poseidon, and Apollo obliterated (*ἀμαλδύνας*, 12.32) without leaving a trace—except in the epic poetry furnished by the Muses. The story, in other words, is not synaptically

74. Inspiration from Huizinga 1955.

75. Motte 2003: 113–31 brilliantly observes that the practice of philosophy was nurtured (if not indeed born) in the *θεωρία* (*theoria*, watching, contemplation) of the divine festivals. Reucher 1983: 478–79 has very thoughtful comments about festival, divinity, art and society in relation to the gods of the *Iliad*.

76. I here present the usual translation of *ἦτορ* in this passage. I have reservations, but they are not relevant to this discussion. For an alternative translation, see Heiden 2008b: 5–7.

linked to precedent events that it narrates, and the actual occurrence of any such events was incidental to their survival in memory and appearance in the poem. It is a fabrication, like all stories, including those fabricated from facts. The *Iliad*, an artifact just as blatantly fabricated as the shield of Achilles, is just as persuasive and just as meaningful. Thematically, the events of the *Iliad* form a trajectory in which the Olympians display increasing care for the problems of life on Earth, and improvise solutions that deploy synairetic substitution with increasing imagination and with increasing satisfaction to the various parties involved. This trajectory implies continuation beyond the frame of the narrative, and when the theme of synairetic substitution is thus extended, it leads eventually to the divine gift of fabrications, such as the shield and the epic, with which mortals can study and practice the wisdom of fabrication in deliberating problems.

This gift, like any gift, implied another in return, and such a gift could be a song in praise of the benevolent deity.[77] After the Greeks return Chryseis to her father and perform their sacrifices to Apollo, they propitiate the god by celebrating him in song and dance all day (1.472–74). Apollo enjoys it, and the next day he sends the Greeks a favorable wind to accompany them on their way home. In the case of the *Iliad* the reciprocal dedication was the performance of the *Iliad* itself at festivals such as the Panathenaia.[78] Savor pleasing to the gods rose from earth to heaven in a visible spiral: *κνίση δ' οὐρανὸν ἶκεν ἑλισσομένη περὶ καπνῷ* (1.317). Performances of the *Iliad* would have reached the gods the same way. A dedication of cyclic design, the *Iliad* was truly a "crown of song," like the epinician odes—also of cyclic design—to which Pindar gave that explicit designation.[79]

Of course, all the terms of this analysis are fabrications themselves: the themes, their perceived trajectory, and the gods of myth and ritual, are all conceptions of the imagination. But none of them were less worthy of awe because minds created them. The image of the gods may have been fabricated, but the power of fabrication itself was mysterious, unlimited, and beyond the range of "nature" (in the sense of physical necessity).

The marvelous gift of the *Iliad* was occasion for thanksgiving and celebration, but not for complacency. Zeus's plan was not genuinely teleological, for its aim was not a permanent state but a possibility, a hope. The *Iliad* offered no actual solutions to any actual problems. For those a Greek person or a Greek community needed wisdom, and the readers who turned to the *Iliad* for wisdom found—if they had any wisdom to begin with—that the gift of the Muses pointed them

77. On performance of the *Hymn to Demeter* as an offering, see Calame 1997b and Heiden 1997: 232–33.

78. Nagy 2002: 98 suggests that the performances of the Homeric epics at the Panathenaia were metaphorical "weavings" analogous to the peplos that was dedicated to Athena. On festival performances of Homer as symbolic enactments of "institutional progress," see Haubold 2000: 188–96. I would add that synoicism is a kind of *synairesis*, and that the polis is a beneficial fabrication. Turcan 2003: 9, noting the etymology of ἑορτή in the unattested ἕορ ("sister"), observes that festivals forge a community among the participants, and between them and the gods.

79. On this metaphor see Steiner 1986. On the cosmic significance of circular choruses, see Aubriot 1999: 42, 44–45.

inward and told them to approach life's unending dilemmas with humility, compassion, open eyes and ears, hard thought, and hopeful imagination. The *Iliad* revealed that even the blessed gods confronted problems, and the opportunity of contemplating Homer's masterpiece gave mortals, not exemption from work, but a turn at working as Olympians might. A fabricated object, the outcome of choices made with insight and care, Homer's *Iliad* still invites the searching deliberation of readers, and still rewards it.

Works Cited

The following abbreviations are used:

ABSA	*Annual of the British School in Athens*
AJP	*American Journal of Philology*
BAGB	*Bulletin de l'Association Guillaume Budé*
C&M	*Classica et Mediaevalia*
CA	*Classical Antiquity*
CJ	*Classical Journal*
CP	*Classical Philology*
CQ	*Classical Quarterly*
CR	*Classical Review*
G&R	*Greece and Rome*
GRBS	*Greek, Roman, and Byzantine Studies*
HSCP	*Harvard Studies in Classical Philology*
ICS	*Illinois Classical Studies*
JHS	*Journal of Hellenic Studies*
MD	*Materiali e Discussioni per l'Analisi dei Testi Classici*
PCPhS	*Proceedings of the Cambridge Philological Society*
REG	*Revue des Études Grecques*
SCI	*Scripta Classica Israelica*
SO	*Symbolae Osloenses*
TAPA	*Transactions of the American Philological Association*
ZPE	*Zeitschrift für Papyrologie und Epigraphik*

Abrams, M. H. 1953. *The Mirror and the Lamp: Romantic Theory and the Critical Tradition*. Oxford.

Adkins, A. W. H. 1960. *Merit and Responsibility*. Oxford.

Alden, M. 2000. *Homer beside Himself: Para-narratives in the Iliad*. Oxford.

Andersen, Ø. 1976. "Some Thoughts on the Shield of Achilles." *SO* 51: 5–18.

———. 1987. "Myth, Paradigm, and 'Spatial Form' in the *Iliad*." In Bremer, de Jong, and Kalff 1987: 1–13.

Aubriot, D. 1985. "Remarques sur le chant IX de *l'Iliade*." *BAGB*: 257–79.

———. 1997. "Le Bouclier d'Achille ou les oeuvres d'art en miroir." In Chefdor 1997: 25–35.

———. 1999. "*Imago Iliadis:* Le Bouclier d'Achille et la poésie de *l'Iliade*." *Kernos* 12: 9–56.

———. 2003. "Autour des représentations artistiques chez Homère." *Gaia* 7: 135–46.

Austin, N. 1975. *Archery at the Dark of the Moon: Poetic Problems in Homer's Odyssey*. Berkeley.

Barker, E. 2004. "Achilles' Last Stand: Institutionalizing Dissent in Homer's *Iliad*." *PCPhS* 50: 92–120.

Bassett, S. E. 1922. "The Three Threads of the Plot of the *Iliad*." *TAPA* 53: 52–62.

———. 1938. *The Poetry of Homer*. Berkeley.

Becker, A. S. 1995. *The Shield of Achilles and the Poetics of Ekphrasis*. Lanham, Md.

Ben-Porat, Z. 1992. "Poetics of the Homeric Simile and the Theory of (Poetic) Simile." *Poetics Today* 13: 737–69.

Beye, C. R. 1972. *The Iliad, the Odyssey, and the Epic Tradition*. Gloucester, Mass.

Blickman, D. R. 1987. "The Role of the Plague in the *Iliad*." *CA* 6: 1–10.

Bouvier, D. 1986. "La tempête de la guerre." *Métis* 1: 246–57.

———. 2002. *Le Sceptre et la Lyre*. Grenoble.

———. 2003. "Quand le poète était encore un charpentier . . . Aux origines du concept de *poésie*." In Heidmann 2003: 85–105.

Braswell, B. K. 1971. "Mythological Innovation in the *Iliad*." *CQ* 21: 16–26.

Bremer, J. M. 1987. "The So-Called *'Götterapparat'* in *Iliad* XX–XXI." In Bremer, de Jong, and Kalff 1987: 31–46.

Bremer, J. M., I. J. F. de Jong, and J. Kalff, eds. 1987. *Homer: Beyond Oral Poetry*. Amsterdam.

Brenk, F. E. 1986. "Dear Child: The Speech of Phoinix and the Tragedy of Achilleus in the Ninth Book of the *Iliad*." *Eranos* 84: 77–86.

Broccia, G. 1967. *La Forma Poetica dell' Iliad e la Genesi dell' Epos Omerico*. Messina, Italy.

Brooks, P. 1984. *Reading for the Plot*. New York.

Burgess, J. 2001. *The Tradition of the Trojan War in Homer and the Epic Cycle*. Baltimore.

Burkert, W. 1955. *Zum altgriechischen Mitleidsbegriff*. Ph.D. diss. Friedrich-Alexander University at Erlangen. Munich.

Byre, C. 1992. "Narration, Description, and Theme in the Shield of Achilles." *CJ* 88: 33–42.

Calame, C. 1997a. *Choruses of Young Women in Ancient Greece*. Trans. D. Collins and J. Orion. Lanham, Md.

———. 1997b. "*L'Hyme homérique à Déméter* comme offrande." *Kernos* 10: 111–33.

Cavallero, P. 2003. "La danse du bouclier d'Achille (*Iliade* 18: 590–606): Questions textuelles." *Gaia* 7: 189–203.

Chefdor, M., ed. 1997. *De la palette à l'écritoire*. Vol. 1. Nantes.

Clark, M. 2001. "The Concept of Plot and the Plot of the *Iliad*." *Phoenix* 55: 1–8.

Clausing, A. 1913. *Kritik und Exegese der homerischen Gleichnisse im Altertum*. Ph.D. diss., University of Freiburg. Parchim, Germany.

Clay, J. S. 1989. *The Politics of Olympus: Form and Meaning in the Major Homeric Hymns*. Princeton.

———. 1999. "The Whip and Will of Zeus." *Literary Imagination* 1: 40–60.

———. 2002. "Dying Is Hard to Do." *Colby Quarterly* 38: 7–16.

———. 2003. *Hesiod's Cosmos*. Cambridge.

Collins, D. 2002. "Reading the Birds: *Oiônomanteia* in Early Epic." *Colby Quarterly* 38: 17–41.

Danek, G. 1988. *Studien zur Dolonie*. Wiener Studien Supplementary vol. 12. Vienna.

Danto, A. 1981. *The Transfiguration of the Commonplace*. Cambridge.

Davies, M. 1989. *The Greek Epic Cycle*. London.

Davison, J. A. 1965. "Thucydides, Homer, and the 'Achaean Wall.' " *GRBS* 6: 5–28.

de Jong, I. J. F. 1985. "*Iliad* I.366–392: A Mirror Story." *Arethusa* 18: 5–22.

———. 1987. *Narrators and Focalizers: The Presentation of the Story in the Iliad*. Amsterdam.

———. 1996. "Sunsets and Sunrises in Homer and Apollonius of Rhodes: Book-Divisions and Beyond." *Dialogos* 3: 20–35.

Di Benedetto, V. 1998. *Nel Laboratorio di Omero*. Turin.
Di Donato, R. 1996. "Omero: Forme della narrazione e forme della realtà. Lo scudo di Achille." In Settis 1996: 227–53.
Dietrich, B. C. 1965. *Death, Fate and the Gods*. London.
Dipert, R. R. 1993. *Artifacts, Art Works, and Agency*. Philadelphia.
Dowden, K. 1996. "Homer's Sense of Text." *JHS* 116: 47–61.
Ebbott, M. 2003. *Imagining Illegitimacy in Classical Greek Literature*. Lanham, Md.
Edwards, M. W. 1980. "Convention and Individuality in *Iliad* 1." *HSCP* 84: 1–28.
———. 1987. *Homer, the Poet of the Iliad*. Baltimore.
———. 1991. *The Iliad: A Commentary*. Vol. 5: Books 17–20. Cambridge.
———. 2002. *Sound, Sense, and Rhythm*. Princeton.
Eliade, M. 1959. *The Sacred and the Profane*. Trans. W. R. Trask. New York.
Emmott, C. 1997. *Narrative Comprehension: A Discourse Perspective*. Oxford.
Erbse, H. 1986. *Untersuchungen zur Funktion der Götter im homerischen Epos*. Berlin.
———. 1994. "Zur Orthographie Homers." *Glotta* 72: 82–97.
Fenik, B. C., ed. 1978a. *Homer: Tradition and Invention*. Cincinnati Classical Studies 2. Leiden.
———. 1978b. "Stylization and Variety: Four Monologues in the *Iliad*." In Fenik 1978a: 68–90.
Finkelberg, M. 2002. "The Sources of *Iliad* 7." *Colby Quarterly* 38: 151–61.
Fish, S. 1980. *Is There a Text in This Class? The Authority of Interpretive Communities*. Cambridge, Mass.
Foley, H. P. 1978. " 'Reverse Similes' and Sex Roles in the *Odyssey*." *Arethusa* 11: 7–26.
Foley, J. M. 1999. *Homer's Traditional Art*. University Park, Pa.
Fowler, D. P. 1989. "First Thoughts on Closure: Problems and Prospects." *MD* 22: 75–122.
Gärtner, H. A. 1976. "Beobachtungen zum Schild des Achilleus." In H. Görgemanns and E. A. Schmidt, eds., *Studien zum antiken Epos*. Beiträge zur klassischen Philologie 72. Meisenheim am Glan, 46–65.
Gill, C. 1996. *Personality in Greek Epic, Tragedy, and Philosophy: The Self in Dialogue*. Oxford.
Goold, G. P. 1960. "Homer and the Alphabet." *TAPA* 91: 272–91.
———. 1977. "The Nature of Homeric Composition." *ICS* 2: 1–34.
Griffin, J., ed. 1995. *Homer: Iliad IX*. Oxford.
Hainsworth, B. 1993. *The Iliad: A Commentary*. Vol. 3: Books 9–12. Cambridge.
Hammer, D. 2002. *The Iliad as Politics: The Performance of Political Thought*. Norman, Okla.
Hardie, P. 1985. "*Imago Mundi*: Cosmological and Ideological Aspects of the Shield of Achilles." *JHS* 105: 11–31.
Harries, B. 1993. "'Strange Meeting': Diomedes and Glaucus in *Iliad* 6." *G&R* 40: 133–46.
Haubold, J. 2000. *Homer's People: Epic Poetry and Social Formation*. Cambridge.
Heiden, B. 1991. "Shifting Contexts in the *Iliad*." *Eranos* 89: 1–12.
———. 1996. "The Three Movements of the *Iliad*." *GRBS* 37: 5–22.
———. 1997. "The Ordeals of Homeric Song." *Arethusa* 32: 221–40.
———. 1998a. "The Placement of 'Book Divisions' in the *Iliad*." *JHS* 118: 68–81.
———. 1998b. "The Simile of the Fugitive Homicide, *Iliad* 24.480–84: Analogy, Foiling, and Allusion." *AJP* 119: 1–10.
———. 2000a. "Major Systems of Thematic Resonance in the *Iliad*." *SO* 75: 34–55.
———. 2000b. "Narrative Discontinuity and Segment Marking at *Iliad* 3/4, 7/8, and 10/11, and *Odyssey* 4/5, 17/18, and 23/24." *C&M* 51: 5–16.
———. 2000c. "The Placement of 'Book Divisions' in the *Odyssey*." *CP* 95: 247–59.

Heiden, B. 2002a. "Hidden Thoughts, Open Speech: Some Reflections on Discourse Analysis in Recent Homeric Studies." In F. Montanari, ed., *Omero Tremila Anni Dopo*. Rome, 431–44.

———. 2002b. "Structures of Progression in the Plot of the *Iliad*." *Arethusa* 35: 237–54.

———. 2003a. "Cyclic Design and Thematic Resonance in *Iliad* Books 3 and 6." *Gaia* 7: 159–81.

———. 2003b. Review of *Homer beside Himself: Para-narratives in the Iliad*, by M. Alden. *CW* 96: 334–35.

———. 2004. Review of *Essays on Homeric Epic*, ed. H. M. Roisman and J. Roisman. [*Colby Quarterly* 38 (nos. 1–2) (2002)]. *CR* 54: 281–82.

———. 2008a. "Common People and Leaders in *Iliad* 2: The Invocation of the Muses and the Catalogue of Ships." *TAPA* 138: 127–54.

———. 2008b. "Two Notes on the Invocation of the Muses at *Iliad* 2.484–93." *SCI* 27: 1–7.

Heidmann, U., ed. 2003. *Poétiques comprés des mythes: En hommage à Claude Calame*. Études de Lettres. Lausanne.

Heitsch, E. 2001 [1967]. "Der Zorn des Paris." In *Gesammelte Schriften I*. Beiträge zur Altertumskunde. 152. Munich, 178–209.

Hellwig, B. 1964. *Raum und Zeit im homerischen Epos*. Hildesheim.

Heubeck, A. 1958. "Zur inneren Form der Ilias." *Gymnasium* 65: 37–47.

———. 1984 [1943]. "Das Meleagros-Paradeigma in der *Ilias* (I 529–599)." In *Kleine Schriften*. Erlangen, 128–35.

———. 1991 [1950]. "Studien zur Struktur der *Ilias* (Retardation-Motivübertragung)." In J. Latacz, ed., *Homer: Die Dichtung und ihre Deutung*.Wege der Forschung. 634. Darmstadt, 450–74.

———. 1992. *A Commentary on Homer's Odyssey*. Vol. 3. Oxford.

Heubeck, A., S. West, and J. B. Hainsworth. 1988. *A Commentary on Homer's Odyssey*. Vol. 1. Oxford.

Hölscher, U. 1939. *Untersuchungen zur Form der Odyssee: Szenenwechsel und gleichzeitige Handlungen*. Hermes Einzelschriften. 6. Berlin.

Howald, E. 1946. *Der Dichter der Ilias*. Zurich.

Hubbard, T. K. 1992. "Nature and Art in the Shield of Achilles." *Arion*, 3rd ser., 2: 16–41.

Huizinga, J. 1955. *Homo Ludens*. Boston.

Iser, W. 1978. *The Act of Reading: A Theory of Aesthetic Response*. Baltimore.

Janko, R. 1992. *The Iliad: A Commentary*. Vol. 4: Books 13–16. Cambridge.

Jensen, M. S., et al. "SO Debate: Dividing Homer." *SO* 74: 5–91.

Kakridis, J. 1949. *Homeric Researches*. Lund.

Kirk, G. S. 1978. "The Formal Duels in Books 3 and 7 of the *Iliad*." In Fenik 1978a: 18–40.

———. 1985. *The Iliad: A Commentary*. Vol. 1: Books 1–4. Cambridge.

———. 1990. *The Iliad: A Commentary*. Vol. 2: Books 5–8. Cambridge.

Kullmann, W. 1960. *Die Quellen der Ilias (Troischer Sagenkreis)*. Hermes Einzelschriften. 14. Wiesbaden.

Lang, M. 1995. "War Story into Wrath Story." In Jane P. Carter and Sarah P. Morris, eds., *The Ages of Homer: A Tribute to Emily Townsend Vermeule*. Austin, 149–62.

Latacz, J., ed. 1991a. "Die Erforschung der Ilias-Struktur." In J. Latacz, ed., *Zweihundert Jahre Homer-Forschung*. Stuttgart, 381–414.

———. 1991b. *Homer. Die Dichtung und ihre Deutung*. Wege der Forschung. 634. Darmstadt.

——— , ed. 2000a. *Homers Ilias. Gesamtkommentar. Prolegomena*. Munich.

——— , ed. 2000b. *Homers Ilias. Gesamtkommentar*. Vol. 1: 1. Gesang. Fascicle 2: *Kommentar*. Munich.

Lateiner, D. 2002. "Pouring Bloody Drops (*Iliad* 16.459): The Grief of Zeus." *Colby Quarterly* 38: 42–61.
Lattimore, R., trans. 1951. *The Iliad of Homer*. Chicago.
Leaf, W., ed. 1900. *The Iliad*. 2nd ed. 2 vols. London.
Le Boeuffle, A. 1977. *Les noms latins d'astres et de constellations*. Paris.
Lessing, G. E. 1984. *Laocoön*. Trans. E. A. McCormick. Baltimore.
Létoublon, F. 1983. "Le miroir et la boucle." *Poétique* 53: 19–36.
———. 1999. "L'indescriptible bouclier." In J. N. Kazazis and A. Rengakos, eds., *Euphrosyne: Studies in Ancient Epic and Its Legacy in Honor of Dimitris N. Maronitis*. Stuttgart, 211–20.
———. 2003. "Ilion battue des vents, Troie aux larges rues: La représentation de Troie dans *l'Iliade*." In *La Naissance de la Ville dans l'Antiquité*. Paris, 27–44.
Lohmann, D. 1970. *Die Komposition der Reden in der Ilias*. Berlin.
Lonsdale, S. 1993. *Dance and Ritual Play in Greek Religion*. Baltimore.
Lord, A. B. 1960. *The Singer of Tales*. Cambridge, Mass.
Lorimer, H. L. 1951. "Stars and Constellations in Homer and Hesiod." *ABSA* 46: 86–101.
Louden, B. 1993. "Pivotal Contrafactuals in Homeric Epic." *CA* 12: 181–98.
———. 2006. *The Iliad: Structure, Myth, and Meaning*. Baltimore.
Lowe, N. J. 2000. *The Classical Plot and the Invention of Western Narrative*. Cambridge.
Lynn-George, M. 1988. *Epos: Word, Narrative, and the Iliad*. Atlantic Highlands, N.J.
Mackie, C. J. 2002. "Homeric Phthia." *Colby Quarterly* 38: 163–73.
Mackie, H. 1996. *Talking Trojan: Speech and Community in the Iliad*. Lanham, Md.
MacLeod, C. W., ed. 1982. *Homer: Iliad Book XXIV*. Cambridge.
Marg, W. 1991 [1957]. "Homer über die Dichtung. Der Schild des Achilleus." In Latacz 1991b: 200–226.
Marks, J. 2002. "The Junction between the *Kypria* and the *Iliad*." *Phoenix* 56: 1–24.
Marrou, H. I. 1956. *A History of Education in Antiquity*. Trans. G. Lamb. New York.
Martin, R. P. 1989. *The Language of Heroes*. Ithaca, N.Y.
Miller, G. A. 1956. "The Magical Number Seven Plus or Minus Two: Some Limits on Our Capacity for Processing Information." *Psychological Review* 63: 81–93.
Morrison, J. 1992. *Homeric Misdirection: False Predictions in the Iliad*. Ann Arbor, Mich.
Motte, A. 2003. "Fêtes chez les hommes, fêtes chez les dieux: Signification religieuse de la fête dans la Grèce antique." In A. Motte and C.-M. Ternes, eds., *Dieux, fêtes, sacré dans la Grèce et la Rome antiques*. Turnhout, Belgium, 113–31.
Mueller, M. 1984. *The Iliad*. London.
Murnaghan, S. 1997. "Equal Honor and Future Glory: The Plan of Zeus in the *Iliad*." In D. H. Roberts, F. M. Dunn, and D. Fowler, eds., *Classical Closure: Reading the End in Greek and Latin Literature*. Princeton, 23–42.
Myres, J. L. 1930. *Who Were the Greeks?* Berkeley.
Nagler, M. 1974. *Spontaneity and Tradition*. Berkeley.
Nagy, G. 1979. *The Best of the Achaeans*. Baltimore.
———. 2002. *Plato's Rhapsody and Homer's Music*. Washington, D.C.
———. 2003. *Homeric Responses*. Austin.
Nethercut, W. R. 1976. "The Epic Journey of Achilles." *Ramus* 5: 1–17.
Nicolai, W. 1973. *Kleine und grosse Darstellungseinheiten in der Ilias*. Heidelberg.
Nimis, S. 1999. "Ring-Composition and Linearity in Homer." In E. A. Mackey, ed., *Signs of Orality*. Leiden, 65–78.
Nünlist, R. 2006. "A Neglected *Testimonium* on the Homeric Book-Division." *ZPE* 157: 47–49.
Onians, R. B. 1951. *The Origins of European Thought*. Cambridge.

Owen, E. T. 1947. *The Story of the Iliad*. London.
Parry, A. 1956. "The Language of Achilles." *TAPA* 87: 1–7.
———, ed. 1971. *The Making of Homeric Verse*: The Collected Papers of Milman Parry. Oxford.
Pavel, T. 1985. *The Poetics of Plot*. Minneapolis.
Peppmüller, R. 1876. *Kommentar des vierundzwanzigsten Buches der Ilias*. Berlin.
Phelan, J. 1989. *Reading People, Reading Plots: Character, Progression, and the Interpretation of Narrative*. Chicago.
Pigeaud, J. 1988. "Le Bouclier d'Achille (Homère, *Iliade* XVIII, 478–608)." *REG* 101: 54–63.
Porter, D. 1972. "Violent Juxtaposition in the Similes of the *Iliad*." *CJ* 68: 11–21.
Pucci, P. 1987. *Odysseus Polutropos: Intertextual Readings in the Odyssey and the Iliad*. Ithaca, N.Y.
Rabel, R. 1997. *Plot and Point of View in the Iliad*. Ann Arbor, Mich.
Redfield, J. 1975. *Nature and Culture in the Iliad*. Chicago.
Reichel, M. 1994. *Fernbeziehungen in der Ilias*. Tübingen.
Reinhardt, K. 1961. *Die Ilias und ihr Dichter*. Göttingen.
Reucher, T. 1983. *Die situative Weltsicht Homers*. Darmstadt.
Richardson, N. J. 1993. *The Iliad: A Commentary*. Vol. 6: Books 21–24. Cambridge.
Richardson, S. 1990. *The Homeric Narrator*. Nashville, Tenn.
Riedinger, J.-C. 1976. "Remarques sur la TIMH chez Homère." *REG* 89: 244–64.
Rosner, J. 1976. "The Speech of Phoinix: *Iliad* 9.434–605." *Phoenix* 30: 314–27.
Rousseau, P. 1990. "Le deuxième Atride: Le type épique de Ménélas dans l'Iliade." *Mélanges Pierre Lévêque* 5: 325–54.
———. 2001. "L'intrigue de Zeus." *Europe* 79 (May): 120–58.
Rubin, D. 1995. *Memory in Oral Traditions*. Oxford.
Russo, J. 1968. "Homer against His Tradition." *Arion* 7: 275–95.
Schadewaldt, W. 1944. *Von Homers Welt und Werk*. Leipzig.
———. 1966. *Iliasstudien*. 3rd ed. Berlin.
———. 1975. *Der Aufbau der Ilias*. Frankfurt.
———. 1991 [1938]. "Der Schild des Achilleus." In Latacz 1991b: 173–99.
Schäfer, M. 1990. *Der Götterstreit in der Ilias*. Beiträge zur Altertumskunde. 15. Stuttgart.
Schein, S. 1984. *The Mortal Hero*. Berkeley.
Scholten, H. 2004. "Die Schildbeschreibung Homers als Spiegel der frühgriechischen Staatswerdung." *Gymnasium* 111: 335–57.
Scodel, R. 1982a. "The Achaean Wall and the Myth of Destruction." *HSCP* 86: 33–50.
———. 1982b. "The Autobiography of Phoenix: *Il*. 9.444–95." *AJP* 103: 128–36.
———. 1992. "The Wits of Glaucus." *TAPA* 122: 73–84.
———. 2002. *Listening to Homer: Tradition, Narrative, and Audience*. Ann Arbor, Mich.
Scott, W. C. 1974. *The Oral Nature of the Homeric Simile*. Mnemosyne. Supp. 28. Leiden.
Scully, S. 1990. *Homer and the Sacred City*. Ithaca, N.Y.
———. 2003. "Reading the Shield of Achilles: Terror, Anger, Delight." *HSCP* 101: 29–47.
Segal, C. P. 1971. *The Theme of the Mutilation of the Corpse in the Iliad*. Mnemosyne. Supp. 17. Leiden.
Settis, S., ed. 1996. *I Greci: Storia Cultura Arte Società*. Vol. 2. *Una storia greca*. Pt. 1. *Formazione*. Turin.
Sheppard, J. T. 1966 [1922]. *The Pattern of the Iliad*. New York.
Slatkin, L. M. 1991. *The Power of Thetis: Allusion and Interpretation in the Iliad*. Berkeley.
Stanley, K. 1993. *The Shield of Homer: Narrative Structure in the Iliad*. Princeton.

Steiner, D. 1986. *The Crown of Song: Metaphor in Pindar*. London.
Steinrück, M. 1997a. *Kranz und Wirbel: Ringkomposition in den Büchern 6–8 der Odyssee*. Spudasmata. 64. Hildesheim.
———. 1997b. "Structure annulaire et le xxe siècle." *Chronozones: Bulletin des Sciences de l'Antiquité de l'Université de Lausanne* 3: 60–73.
Stevick, P. 1970. *The Chapter in Fiction: Theories of Narrative Division*. Syracuse, N.Y.
Taplin, O. 1991 [1980]. "The Shield of Achilles within the *Iliad*." In Latacz 1991b: 227–53.
———. 1992. *Homeric Soundings: The Shaping of the Iliad*. Oxford.
Tatum, J. 1993. "Into the Midpoint of Things: Aristotle, Bartlett, and the Meaning and the Memory of a Poet." In R. Rosen and J. Farrell, eds., *Nomodeiktes: Greek Studies in Honour of Martin Ostwald*. Ann Arbor, Mich., 491–504.
Thalmann, W. G. 1984. *Conventions of Form and Thought in Early Greek Epic Poetry*. Baltimore.
Thornton, A. 1984. *Homer's Iliad: Its Composition and the Motif of Supplication*. Hypomnemata. 81. Göttingen.
Turcan, R. 2003. "La fête dans les rituels initiatiques." In A. Motte and C.-M. Ternes, eds., *Dieux, fêtes, sacré dans la Grèce et la Rome antiques*. Turnhout, Belgium, 7–21.
Turner, M. 1996. *The Literary Mind*. Oxford.
van Groningen, B. A. 1958. *La Composition Littéraire Archaïque Grecque*. Verhandelingen der Koninklijke Nederlandse Akademie van Wetenschappen, Afd. Letterkunde. Vol. 65. No. 2. Amsterdam.
Van Wees, H. 1992. *Status Warriors: War, Violence and Society in Homer and History*. Amsterdam.
Wade-Gery, H. T. 1952. *The Poet of the Iliad*. Cambridge.
West, M. L., ed. 1966. *Hesiod: Theogony*. Oxford.
West, S., ed. 1967. *The Ptolemaic Papyri of Homer*. Papyrologica Coloniensia. Vol. 3. Cologne.
———. 1988. *A Commentary on Homer's Odyssey*. Vol. 1. Oxford.
Whitman, C. 1958. *Homer and the Heroic Tradition*. Cambridge, Mass.
Willcock, M. M. 1964. "Mythological Paradeigma in the *Iliad*." *CQ* 14: 141–54.
———., ed. 1978. *The Iliad of Homer*. 2 vols. London.
Wilson, D. 2002. *Ransom, Revenge, and Heroic Identity in the Iliad*. Cambridge.
Wolf, F. A. 1985. *Prolegomena to Homer*. Translation, introduction, and notes by A. Grafton, G. W. Most, and J. E. G. Zetzel. Princeton.
Wyatt, W. 1989–90. "Homeric Transitions." *Archaeognosia* 6: 11–24.
Yoshida, A. 1964. "La Structure de l'Illustration du Bouclier d'Achille." *Revue Belge de Philologie et d'Histoire* 42: 5–15.

Index of Passages

General Index